W9-CQC-865

HANDBOOKS

SAN DIEGO

ERICKA CHICKOWSKI

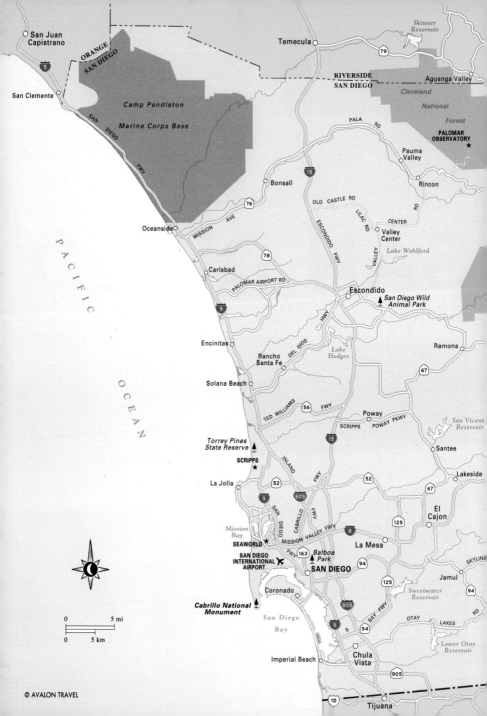

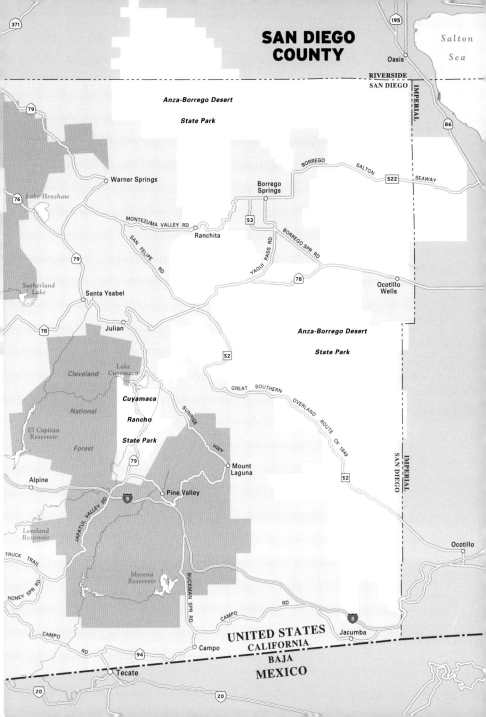

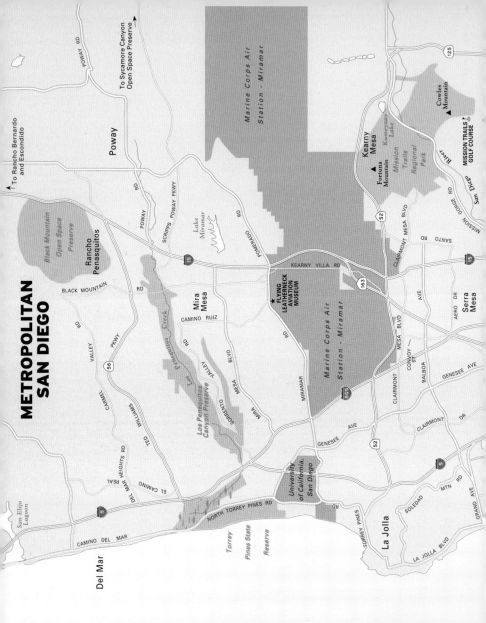

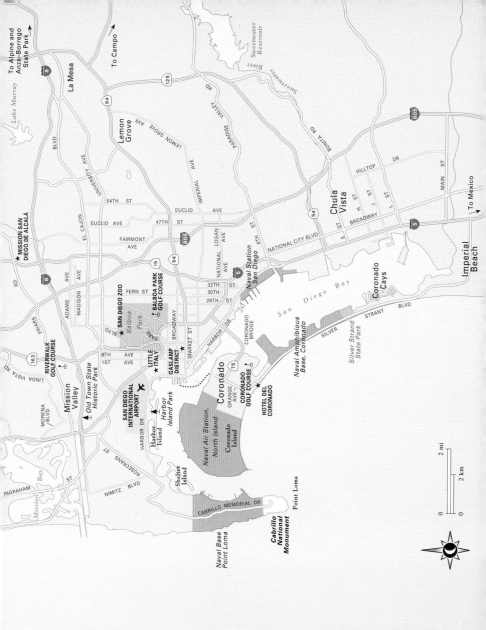

© AVALON TRAVEL

DISCOVER SAN DIEGO

San Diego is less a place and more a state of mind. Something about the constant sunshine, the sandy beaches, and the friendly people makes for a laid-back atmosphere that is as inescapable as a wave's pull to shore.

Located in the southwestern corner of the United States, the sprawling city is part of an even more expansive county of the same name. Topping out at 4,255 square miles, San Diego County is a rambling maze of geographical diversity. The sun rises over the vast Anza-Borrego Desert, the largest state park in the contiguous United States. It traces over the peaks and valleys of the San Marcos and Laguna Mountain Ranges and sets on the 70 miles of shoreline on the San Diego coast. All of this is sandwiched between the bustle of Orange County and Los Angeles to the north and the slow siestas of Baja Mexico to the south.

The region is certainly one of many personalities. It is at once a sleepy navy enclave and a bustling nightspot. It is a sanctuary for

waves breaking, La Jolla

the arts and a surfing mecca. Locals wear flip-flops to the opera, but won't hesitate to spend a mint to get their hair done flawlessly. Rather than creating a cognitive dissonance, these contrasts only serve to accentuate the area's colorful uniqueness.

The region's claim to fame is its temperate weather, and nothing makes it stand out so well as the bodies of water that sparkle under all of that sunshine. At every turn, there are enough bays and beaches to give even the biggest water enthusiast her fill with places to sail, fish, swim, and more.

San Diego's waterways are also home base to the largest fleet of naval ships in the world, including the carrier *Midway*, a 20th-century stalwart now open as a museum. It is not uncommon to hear the roar of jets over county airspace or have a door held open for you by a serviceperson in uniform. As the navy's Pacific Fleet headquarters, the region is home to thousands of sailors and marines stationed at ten different bases across the county.

cypress trees and roses, Escondido

With such a large military population and lots of year-round sunshine, it only follows that San Diego has a thriving recreational sports scene. The region is the birthplace of the modern triathlon – in 1974 the first-ever triathlon was held as a run-bike-swim event on Mission Bay. But visitors don't have to be endurance athletes to take a spin along the county's curvy mountain roads or to dip into choice swimming holes like La Jolla Cove.

Even in winter golfers can stroll some of the most pristine links in the nation, and the county's extensive system of backcountry trails are ideal for hiking, horseback riding, and mountain biking. Summertime visitors have the opportunity to join hundreds of runners in the area's signature race, the Rock and Roll Marathon, an event that entertains participants with live music along the race course.

There are dozens of sports and pastimes to partake in, but none of them is quite as definitively San Diego as surfing. To say San Diegans like to surf would be shortchanging the impact that the sport has on the region. Surfing isn't just a sport in San Diego, it is a way of life, permeating the culture all the way into the vernacular.

flamingos at SeaWorld

You're as likely to hear a buttoned-down boardroom exec use the word "dude" as a tow-headed beachgoer in board shorts.

But don't let the easygoing nature of the residents fool you. The always-casual atmosphere belies the deep intellectual, philosophical, and religious roots, roots that reach as far back as the 16th century.

In 1542 – 65 years before English colonists settled Jamestown on the continent's other coast – Juan Rodriguez Cabrillo sailed into San Diego Bay. A Portuguese sailor hired by Spain, Cabrillo was first in a long line of Spanish adventurers to reach San Diego.

Among them was Father Junípero Serra, who in 1769 founded California's first mission. The spiritual foundation he laid was solid – today the Mission San Diego de Alcalá is still an active parish as well as a visitor attraction.

Serra also helped establish an appreciation for learning and culture that persists today. San Diego is home to dozens of first-rate museums, and its performing arts scene is known nationally as an experimental proving ground for productions before they hit Broadway.

Located in the heart of San Diego, Balboa Park epitomizes the

Anza-Borrego Desert State Park

region's love affair with the arts. At more than 1,200 acres, the park itself is a work of art. Many of the buildings are over 90 years old, built with elaborate Spanish Colonial flourishes for the Panama-California Exposition, and today house over 17 of the city's finest museums. These institutions hold collections that range from very beautiful to extremely quirky – they're home to everything from miniature railroad models to masterpieces by El Greco. In addition to hosting hundreds of species of flora, Balboa Park is also prime residence to gorillas, pandas, and other assorted animals that make up the world-famous San Diego Zoo.

In a way, the park is a microcosm of what the region offers its visitors. On any given day, athletes sweat it out on the ball fields and courts of the park, debonair museumgoers nod their heads thoughtfully at works of art, and small children come face-to-face with hippos and polar bears.

If there is one lesson to learn from the locals it is that San Diego is meant to be enjoyed leisurely. The majority of the area's residents are transplants, visitors that never quite got around to leaving. So don't pack lightly, because you might find so much to do in San Diego that you become one of them.

Coronado Beach at dusk

ranunculus, Carlsbad Flower Fields   Museum of Art, Balboa Park   moon and palm, Kensington

Contents

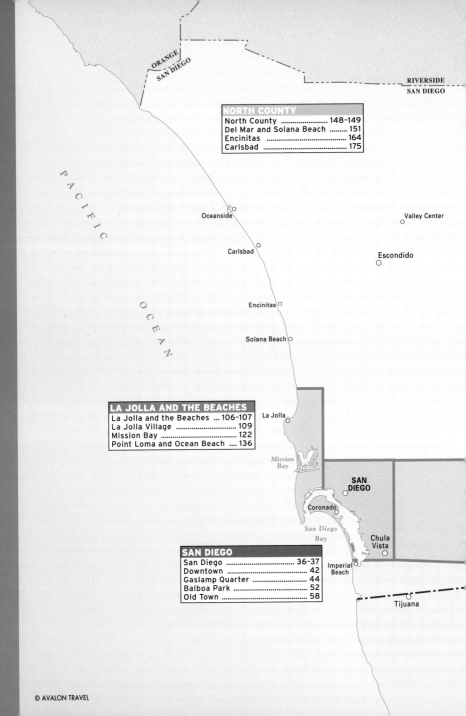

ORANGE
SAN DIEGO

RIVERSIDE
SAN DIEGO

PACIFIC

Oceanside

Valley Center

Carlsbad

Escondido

OCEAN

Encinitas

Solana Beach

La Jolla

Mission
Bay

**SAN
DIEGO**

Coronado

San Diego
Bay

Chula
Vista

Imperial
Beach

Tijuana

© AVALON TRAVEL

MAP CONTENTS

Salton Sea

RIVERSIDE

SAN DIEGO

IMPERIAL

Anza–Borrego

Desert State Park

Borrego
Springs

Julian

Anza–Borrego

Desert State Park

Cuyamaca
Rancho
State Park

IMPERIAL
SAN DIEGO

Mt Laguna

UNITED STATES
CALIFORNIA

BAJA
MEXICO

Tecate

0   10 mi
0   10 km

The Lay of the Land

SAN DIEGO

Situated on a large bay protected from the Pacific, San Diego is the biggest city in the county of the same name. This geographical and cultural center is a sprawling patchwork of neighborhoods, with its downtown core creeping up to the waterfront that looks west across **San Diego Bay** to the tip of **Coronado Island.** A misnamed isthmus, Coronado is a long barrier that makes the J-shaped bay a possibility. On the east edge is **Hillcrest** and the pride of the city, **Balboa Park.** Keep going north and you'll hit the historic first neighborhood of the city, **Old Town.** Even farther north is **Mission Valley,** home of California's first religious outpost, Mission San Diego de Alcalá. Beyond the valley are the remote reaches of North City, including Marine Air Station Miramar and numerous open space preserves such as Mission Trails Regional Park.

LA JOLLA AND THE BEACHES

The central core of the city of San Diego is augmented by its beach neighborhoods to the northeast. Southernmost is **Point Loma,** named for the peninsula that bounds the other side of San Diego Bay's inlet. Sprawling north along the ocean side of the peninsula is the warm-hued **Sunset Cliffs Natural Park.** Next comes the hippie town of **Ocean Beach,** and just over the jetties is **Mission Beach,** a thin strip of a neighborhood that is corralled by the ocean to the west and by the aquatic wonderland of Mission Bay Park to the east. Keep moving up the coast and you'll come across **Pacific Beach,** which is the city's hottest party scene outside of the Gaslamp. One neighborhood up is the jewel of San Diego, La Jolla. Known for its craggy coves and sandy beaches, this is a pocket of luxury that holds the finest dining, lodging, and art galleries along the city shoreline.

NORTH COUNTY

Mostly populated along the coast and the major freeway corridors of I-5 and I-15, North County is best known for its **idyllic beach towns.** Southernmost is **Del Mar,** known as the place where the "turf meets the surf" at the **Del Mar Racetrack.** Next comes **Encinitas,** which is known for some of the **best surfing breaks** in all of California, including Swami's, Cardiff reef, and Pipes. Carlsbad has a five-mile-long stretch of uninterrupted sand along **Carlsbad State Beach.**

The military town of Oceanside boasts the longest fishing structure in the west, **Oceanside Pier,** and is just south of Camp Pendleton, which stretches the rest of the way north to the county line. Inland, **Escondido** is a cultural hub and the home of the California Center for the Arts. It is also a departure point into San Diego's backcountry.

JULIAN AND ANZA-BORREGO

San Diego's backcountry is a rugged and ecologically diverse span of shaded riparian glades, rocky chaparral-covered mountains, and baked desert landscapes. San Diego–area mountain ranges bisect the county from north to south, starting with the Border Ranges, then moving up to the **Laguna and Cuyamaca Mountains,** followed hopscotch style by the **Volcan, San Ysidro, and Santa Rosa Mountain Ranges.** Nestled in these peaks lies the quiet hamlet of Julian, the Sierra-like peak of **Palomar Mountain,** and the hidden healing waters of Warner Springs. All of the mountainous slopes drop east into the expansive Anza-Borrego Desert, home of the largest park owned by the state, **Anza-Borrego Desert State Park.** Explorers here are rewarded with badland vistas, cactus-lined trails, and palm-filled oases. Sitting on the desert's western edge is the small town of **Borrego Springs.**

GATEWAY TO BAJA

South of San Diego city limits is where the march down Mexico Way begins. The waterfront territory south of the Coronado Bay Bridge is frequently referred to as **South Bay.** This is where the lazy little town of **Imperial Beach** sits along the ocean. It also harbors important estuarine habitats in the Sweetwater Marsh National Wildlife Refuge and the Tijuana River Estuary. Only about a half-hour drive from downtown, **Tijuana** is the busiest border town in the world. It is crammed into the corner formed by the international border and the Pacific Ocean, a hodgepodge of shopping, clubs, and restaurants. Just 20 miles south of that lies the partying beach town of **Rosarito.** Another 50 miles and you hit **Ensenada,** which holds one of the most famous marine blowholes in North America, **La Bufadora.** Notable **surf spots** nearby such as Todos Santos make this a road trip–worthy destination in the eyes of wave riders.

Planning Your Trip

Most people know San Diego as a city, the southwesternmost metropolis in the United States, the home of a famous zoo, SeaWorld, and a few nearby beaches, and worthy of a weekend getaway or a side trip from Los Angeles.

While these folks are technically right, they're sadly missing out on the big picture. San Diego in its entirety is a county, and a large one at that, and it's within a jumping bean's hop from the Mexican border.

So, sure, it is possible to come here for the weekend and visit all the old standards. Those who stay downtown or near the city beaches are within easy striking distance to the sand, SeaWorld, Balboa Park, the San Diego Zoo, and the Embarcadero. Most are able to get to the majority of the biggies in just a few days.

But visitors who linger will be able to top the normal touristy stops with desert Jeep trips, mountain hiking, and parties in Mexico. They'll have time to pick and choose between surf spots or wait out a flat spell until the swells kick in. And they'll be able to better savor the neighborhoods within the city and spend some time roaming its historic sites.

All of this takes time of course, especially considering the geographical sprawl. Driving straight down from the northernmost boundary of San Diego County all the way south to Ensenada in Mexico will take you at least two and a half hours without stopping once. From the ocean to the eastern edge of the Anza-Borrego Desert it's at least an hour and a half. It will take a little foresight and planning to prioritize your interests and then triangulate that with geographical realities. I've tried to help the process along by suggesting in the following pages a few itineraries based on specific interests.

WHEN TO GO

San Diego is blessed with some of the most temperate weather in the country. The old joke is that there are two major seasons here, spring and summer.

But really there is a little more nuance to the climate than that. San Diego County actually rests within numerous microclimates that can result in drastically different weather conditions from one zone to the other. Some days it can be foggy along the coast and pleasantly sunny just a few miles inland. The desert can be baking hot while it snows in the mountains. These are extreme examples, of course, but they go to show that it pays to be aware of the seasons in all of the microclimates when you're planning to explore the county.

Early springtime is actually one of the most universally pleasant times in the county. Delicate flowers are blooming along the coast and the weather is often warm enough for shorts, especially if you're from someplace like Wisconsin. The water is still a little chilly, but it isn't something that a wetsuit can't cure. The mountains are cool, but not too cold to camp out. And even in the heat of midday sun, it is still cool enough in the desert to keep hiking along. This is also when the desert starts to explode into riotous colors, as the normally-drab succulents and ocotillo begin to bloom.

If you check airline tickets and hotel rates and are wondering why they dip a little bit lower in May and June let me fill you in. These two months are known for **"May Gray" and "June Gloom."** Along the coastal areas the marine layer rolls in thick during these months and some days it never has the chance to completely burn off. It is definitely not something that will wreck a vacation. There are a lot of nice days where the fog does go away and this is not a problem at all in the inland areas. But it is something to be aware of if you were really counting on consistently sunny days during your trip.

July through August is the high season. The beaches are rockin', bars are open late, and the crowds are absolutely everywhere. If you don't have school vacations to worry about, try coming in September while the weather is still warm and the crowds have thinned.

In the late fall and winter the weather dips down between the low 60s and the high 50s. The locals dust off their jackets, but many cold-weather snowbirds find it heavenly. So do the surfers, who consider winter the best time to stake out local breaks. Winter usually brings the biggest swells and nicest waves. It also occasionally blows in some rain showers. If you are the surfing type, be aware that San Diego waterways almost always become too polluted to safely enter after a dousing. The general rule of thumb is to wait 72 hours after the last rain.

Del Mar sunset

WHAT TO TAKE

This is a no-brainer, but your vacation preferences will dictate your packing choices. San Diego is generally a very casual town—we residents like to consider it "beach-ready." The usual uniform is a T-shirt, board shorts, and flip-flops for guys, tank top, beach sarong, and flip-flops for gals. Basically, if guys tuck a polo shirt into a pair of belted shorts or girls put on a flouncy sun dress, they're considered dressed up.

There are exceptions to these standards, of course. If you plan on going club-hopping in the Gaslamp, be sure to bring a set of dress clothes. Same goes for the fancy restaurants downtown, in La Jolla or in North County.

No matter what time of year, be sure to bring a light jacket. Add a sweater to that in the winter. The chill kicking off the coast at night tends to surprise first-time visitors. Don't skip the sunscreen in the winter, either. Even under cloud cover the sun is known to burn the unprepared.

If you plan to go to Mexico, be sure to pack a passport. New regulations from Homeland Security now require international travelers to present this form of ID when crossing back into the States. A Spanish-English dictionary also might help, but isn't completely necessary. Most of the service workers in the border cities are bilingual.

Finally, don't forget to pack a pair of comfortable and worn-in sneakers. The majority of this county's best sites require a ton of walking. A blister early in the trip can really chafe your plans.

Explore San Diego

BEST OF SAN DIEGO

With so much to offer, the San Diego region can be a daunting place to visit from the vacation planner's perspective. But it is possible to condense many of the top sights, shopping trips, hiking excursions, and dining experiences down into a single week-long trip. The following itinerary offers a sample of the very best the region has to offer.

Day 1

Open your trip with a jaunt over to **Coronado Island.** Ditch your car in the city and take the ferry from the Embarcadero. Shop your way down **Orange Avenue** and stop for a bite and some people-watching at Tent City. Then mosey next door to the Coronado Historical Association to buy a ticket for a tour of **Hotel del Coronado.** If there's time before dinner, you can rent a bike at Holland's Bicycles and ride up to **Silver Strand State Park.** Dine at Peohe's for dinner and check out the city lights reflected off San Diego Bay.

Day 2

Wake up early to hit up the city's most famous site of all, the **San Diego Zoo.** Be sure to get the pandas out of the way first—there's a line to get into that special enclosure. If you need to prioritize, some favorite exhibits are Monkey Trails and Forest Tales, Cat Canyon, and Gorilla Tropics. Take lunch in Balboa Park at El Prado and you won't even have to move the car. Once you're rested and full, visit the **Balboa Park Visitors Center** and rent the self-guided audio tour featuring some of the best sights and stories this massive park has to offer. After freshening up a bit and changing into nicer threads, zip over to the **Gaslamp Quarter** for dinner at Trattoria La Strada or Monsoon. From there you're in a great position to find any number of clubs to dance the night away.

Day 3

Hop on the Blue Line trolley in downtown San Diego and ride it south all the way to the border at San Ysidro for a day trip to Tijuana. Walk across the border and meander down to **Avenida Revolución** to haggle with the vendors there or take a cab to the **Tijuana Cultural Center** to check out its museums and catch a showing at the OmniMax movie theater there. You can get lunch on the go from a taco stand, but be sure to leave room for dinner. Head over to the restaurant district for a fine meal at Cheripan or La Diferencia. Finally, dance away your gastronomical excesses in the Zona Río at clubs such as Baby Rock and Como Que No.

Day 4

After the previous day's activities you deserve a break. Sleep in as long as you like and head over to Kono's in **Pacific Beach** for grub. They serve breakfast all afternoon here. Now you're ready to while the time away on the beach. Grab a towel and a book and do nothing at all. Or **rent a boogie board** (and maybe a wetsuit) from one of the shops here to catch a few waves. When you're feeling peckish, take a break to dash across Mission Boulevard for a taste of a San Diego classic, the fish taco, at Taco Surf. Once the sun goes down unwind with the locals at Cass Street Bar and Grill for beer or Café 976 for coffee and tea.

Day 5

Trade in your bathing suit for your hiking

Warner Springs Ranch with a wintry dusting of snow

boots with an excursion out into the county's mountains. From the city center, zip up I-15 and then take Highway 76 out to **Palomar Mountain State Park.** You can either hike or drive up the mountain to the famous Palomar Observatory, home of the famed Hale telescope. Once the tour is complete, you've got a choice to make: Either rough it in a tent at the nearby Doane Valley Campground and explore more local trails or trek another 40 minutes northeast via Highway 76 and 78 to **Warner Springs Ranch.** This resort offers a nice comfy bed, and if there's still daylight to burn, the option to cap the day's activities with a round of golf or a horseback ride under the shadows of Hotsprings Mountain. If you go to the ranch, be sure to relax in the spring-fed hot pool there, which is open past dark for a relaxing end to a busy day.

Day 6

Today you'll continue to take in the mountainous countryside by winding along more of the region's scenic byways. You'll be heading back toward the coast, but this time it will be via Highways 78 and 79. Take 78 all the way west

to the county's northernmost city, **Oceanside.** Spend the afternoon casting a line off of the Oceanside Pier and maybe checking out memorabilia at the California Surf Museum. In the evening you should head farther south along Coast Highway to stay someplace close enough to allow you to spend your final day within city limits. But before you hit the road, consider a casual dinner at 101 Café. First opened in 1928, this diner is an Oceanside landmark.

Day 7

Your last day is back in the city, this time up in the **La Jolla** neighborhood. You'll want to start your day here by dropping in on the **Birch Aquarium at Scripps.** This colorful home of sea life is a public interpretation of the scientific research conducted by the hometown Scripps Institution of Oceanography. Now get out there and conduct a little field research of your own! Head to **La Jolla Cove** and take a guided snorkel tour of the aquatic sanctuary, **San Diego-La Jolla Underwater Park.** You'll see bright orange garibaldi, spindly lobster and giant sea bass in the protected waters here.

A WEEKEND IN THE SUN

Sure, it can take weeks to really make a dent in the San Diego region. But not all of us have the luxury of time to take off into the countryside. Fortunately some of the very best San Diego sights are concentrated close to the city. In just a long weekend visitors can sample the sights, soak up the relaxing atmosphere, and work on an even tan to flaunt in front of envying coworkers back home.

Day 1

Start your San Diego adventure by taking a walk by the waterfront along the **Embarcadero**. Get a good perspective of the city by checking it out by water—hop aboard a **San Diego Bay harbor cruise** from either San Diego Harbor Excursions or Hornblower Cruises, both of which send off boats from the Embarcadero throughout the day. Once you get back, traipse up to **Little Italy** to browse the shops in the **Kettner Art and Design District** and check out the eclectic neighborhood. Whet your whistle at San Diego's longest established bar, **The Waterfront Bar and Grill,** along the way. Finish everything off with a meal at one of Little Italy's trattorias, such as Mimmo's or Zagarella's.

Day 2

Today you'll spend the day in "the jewel" of San Diego, **La Jolla.** Start with a trip to the La Jolla branch of the **Museum of Contemporary Art San Diego.** Then stroll along Girard Avenue to browse the shops and art galleries. For a simple lunch with a view, pop into Goldfish Point Café overlooking La Jolla Cove. It is just a two-minute walk from there over to the Cave Store, where you will get a chance to descend the steep steps down to one of La Jolla's magnificent sea caves. If you still have time, sneak in a walk down to **Children's Pool** and check out the seals lolling on the beach. Once you're back in your car, consider driving up to Del Mar for dinner. For something more casual, try Americana right in downtown Del Mar. For

seals at Children's Pool in La Jolla

Sicilian Festival, Little Italy

a fine meal, drop into Papachino's over by the racetrack.

Day 3

This morning you'll tromp over the docks at **Quivira Basin** in **Mission Bay Park** and pick out your ride over at Seaforth Boat Rentals. Be it by motorboat, sailboat, or personal watercraft, you're going to ply the calm water of Mission Bay on your own. Bring your lunch and pack a fishing pole if you like, or maybe some water skis, and take off for a couple of hours. Once you get your feet back on solid land, drive to nearby Ocean Beach and mosey down **Newport Avenue Antique Row** for some relaxing window shopping until your tummy grumbles. Once you're ready, head over to Thee Bungalow for an early dinner.

Mission Bay

FAMILY HARMONY

Planning and executing a family vacation is a lot like lion taming or snake charming. Do it right and you'll entertain and amaze. Do it wrong and you'll be hurtin'. Fortunately, San Diego affords the trip planner with a whole arsenal of tools to gain the adoration and admiration of spouse and children. There are tons of kid-friendly sights and destinations in the city and around the county to keep the brood content for days.

Day 1

Delight the kids with the antics of Shamu and company at **SeaWorld.** This all-day affair will amuse with a variety of water- and land-based shows, animal exhibits, and a few amusement park–type rides. If your stamina is high, try to stick around for the nightly fireworks extravaganza that shoots and flashes over Mission Bay.

Day 2

Pack a lunch, plenty of sunscreen, and an umbrella to make it a day of sun and sandcastles at **Mission Beach.** Take a break from splashing in the ocean by pitter-pattering over the boardwalk blacktop to **Belmont Park,** positioned right on the beach at South Mission. The kids will love clambering onto the carnival rides here. Older kids will especially dig the exciting Giant Dipper wooden roller coaster. Enjoy an early dinner at the informal Saska's Steak and Seafood before walking a couple blocks inland to catch a Mission Bay cruise aboard the paddlewheelin' *Bahia Belle.*

Giant Dipper, Mission Beach Boardwalk

Day 3

It's road-trip time. Pack up the brood early and head southeast from downtown 45 miles on Highway 94 to the **San Diego Railroad Museum** in Campo. During the morning hours check out the collection of more than 80 old steam and diesel engines, cabooses, passenger cars, and more at the facility. Ideally this will be a Saturday; that way the kids can step aboard the Golden State from the restored Campo Depot and experience what it feels like riding the rails for themselves.

Upon your return, refuel at the Campo Diner and recommence your wanderings. This time head northwest, first via Buckman Springs Road, then backtracking west along I-8 a few miles until you can go north on Highway 79. Driving straight through it is less than an hour to Julian from Campo on this route. But take your time along 79 and enjoy the scenery along the way. This curvy mountain road heads straight through the heart of **Cuyamaca Rancho State Park** and right by the scenic **Lake Cuyamaca.** Stretch your legs with a little nature hike along the **West Side Trail,** a ramble of less than a mile that features a number of Indian grinding holes scattered trailside.

Day 4

Spend the day surveying the historical sights and friendly shops in **Julian.** Start with a tour through a real-life gold mine at **Eagle & High Peak Mines.** If the family's history quota still doesn't feel full, skip on over to the **Julian Pioneer Museum.** Ramble the streets and shops full of antiques, souvenirs, and scented candles. Don't forget to reward the kids for their good behavior with a genuine slice of heaven—a piece of **Julian apple pie** with a dollop of ice cream. Complete this leisurely day by sitting down in one of Julian's **horse-drawn carriages** and clip-clopping through parts of town that you may have missed.

Day 5

Time to hit the asphalt again. This time head due east along Highway 78 and then Palomar Airport Road to the world of clickety bricks at **Legoland** in Carlsbad. Marvel at the engineering of the scale cities in Miniland and join the kids with a few squeals on the gentle little roller coasters here. Then head into Carlsbad Village for a light supper and a final walk along the sand at **South Carlsbad State Beach.**

Ride the rails aboard the Golden State from the San Diego Railroad Museum.

ON A MISSION

Yes, San Diegans' favorite salutation just might be "dude." Many people here do consider flip-flops with rhinestones appropriate for a formal dinner. And tattoo art is a serious medium of expression here. But coexisting with the ethos of informality is a rich tapestry of history, art, and culture that rivals some of the very best scenes in the entire country. This tour takes you through some of the most interesting museums, art galleries, and architectural districts that the region has to offer. Best of all, you can bet your surfboard that no one is ever going to put on airs while you're visiting.

Day 1

San Diego's first European settlers were the soldiers and priests of Spain. Learn about these pioneers by first strolling the grounds and visiting the small museum at **Mission San Diego de Alcalá,** California's first. Then head over to **Presidio Park,** the site of the city's first

Yuma Building, Gaslamp Quarter

European settlement and fortification. Take a tour through **Junípero Serra Museum** to learn about the Native Americans who proceeded the Spaniards and the period of first settlement, as well as the shift to Mexican and American rule. Sitting at the foot of Presidio Hill is your next stop, **Old Town State Historic Park.** Celebrate the Californio heritage with dinner at Old Town Mexican Café, which is within easy walking distance from the park.

Day 2

On your second day make a trip to the **Gaslamp Quarter,** with one of the finest collections of restored Victorian-era commercial buildings on the West Coast. Feast your eyes on beauties like the **Louis Bank of Commerce** and the **Yuma Building** as you walk through this historic area.

North of the Gaslamp, Little Italy is a burgeoning haven for the arts. Perhaps the

Presidio Park is the site of San Diego's first European settlement.

only district within a district in the city, the **Kettner Art and Design District** here is home to art studios, galleries, and high-end furniture stores. Walk here to shop and browse for a while, stopping for lunch at one of the neighborhood trattorias. Then double back along Kettner and stop for a visit to the beautifully renovated Santa Fe Depot complex, which contains the fresh and innovative collection of the downtown branch of the **Museum of Contemporary Art San Diego.**

Day 3

Drive up to **Cabrillo National Monument** to get a bird's-eye view of sheltered San Diego Bay and gain an understanding of why it has fostered a naval and maritime history that dates back to the 16th century. The highlight of the monument is the **Old Point Loma Lighthouse.** This 1850s-era building is dressed in period furniture and open for a look. Head back downtown to continue your tour of the city's waterlogged history by taking a walk down the **Embarcadero.**

Ambitious museumgoers might be able to tackle both, but I'd suggest choosing between the two major floating attractions here. First there's the **Maritime Museum of San Diego,** which has an impressive collection of restored vessels. Military buffs may prefer the **USS *Midway* Museum,** a retired and restored aircraft carrier. Up on deck there is a remarkable array of military aircraft to explore.

No matter which you choose, finish off the day at **Seaport Village** with a seafood meal at either San Diego Pier Café or Harbor House.

Day 4

Art and history abound at **Balboa Park.** Get a head start and arrive just before museum doors open at 10 A.M. so that you don't miss any of the great stuff inside. Start by walking through the **Timken Museum of Art,** then stroll next door to the **San Diego Museum of Art.** Between the two of them you'll find masterpieces by El Greco, Rembrandt, and Eastman Johnson. Skip the ice cream cart and try a bento box at the Tea Pavilion at the Japanese Friendship Garden. From there it is just a quick jaunt to the **Museum of Photographic Arts.** If you

San Diego's past is steeped in maritime history.

still have time before closing, check out the artifacts in the folk-art collection at the **San Diego Natural History Museum.** Take a break from the park by driving just a couple of minutes away to Gulf Coast Grill. Once rested, return back to Balboa for an evening performance at **Old Globe Theatre.**

Day 5

Head north of the city along the historic byway **Coast Highway 101,** and drive back in time to when this was the only route to San Diego from Los Angeles. Stop in Solana Beach's **Cedros Design District** to window-shop the boutiques and galleries. Then it is back into the car and up to Encinitas for a history lesson about tribes native to this area at the **San Dieguito Heritage Museum.** While you are in the neighborhood, pick through the folksy collection of bohemian shops before continuing up Coast Highway to Carlsbad. Bring your pavement pounding to a close with disrobing at **Alt Karlsbad Spa** to rest in the healing mineral waters that built this town into a spa destination way back in the 1880s. Once you're thoroughly relaxed, step into the subdued and classy atmosphere of West Steak Seafood and Spirits and enjoy

a prime cut of beef complemented by a fine glass of wine.

Day 6

Take it easy today. Drive inland to Vista and roam the grounds at the **Antique Gas and Steam Engine Museum.** If the timing's right shoot for a demonstration day, when volunteers are on-site stoking the fires at the blacksmith shop, laboring in the fields at the working farm, and running the engines of dozens of old tractors, trucks, and more.

Day 7

Head along Highway 78 toward Escondido and into the San Pasqual Valley. Stop off at the **San Pasqual Battlefield** and pick up some perspective about a Mexican-American battle that still has historians quibbling over the victor. While in the valley, stop in at scenic **Orfila Vineyards and Winery** for a tour. Then head back to Escondido for an afternoon in the **Escondido Art District.** Don't forget to visit the collection of contemporary art at the **California Center for the Arts** before heading back down to San Diego. The airport is about 45 minutes from this final stop in the tour, so an evening flight is within easy reach.

SURF 'N' TURF

You don't have to throw away your worldly possessions, drive a VW bus, or even grow out your hair to take an authentic surf trip down the San Diego coast. Nope, all you need is a little equipment and a lot of time to take an unhurried tour of the region's best outdoor adventures both on and off the water. You don't even need a ton of money—just rely on the campgrounds, hostels, motels, and cheap eats along the way. This trip works best with a surfboard and a mountain bike at hand for each of the travelers in your group. Your best bet is to do this tour in fall through spring. That's when the swell comes in and the desert's cool. Because Mother Ocean is a fickle girl, I've provided alternative activities for days when the surf's not up.

North County

Get yourself into a relaxed frame of mind by kicking the trip off with a serene day and night at **San Onofre State Park.** Spend the daylight hours paddling out to the long-board-friendly break at Old Man's, or make the trek up to Lower Trestles if that storied left is firing. Should you be skunked by glassy conditions, hop on your bike for an easy spin along an abandoned stretch of **Old Highway 101** that runs south of the park for a little over three miles. Once nighttime rolls around, chill around a fire at your campsite and make friends with some of the San Diego locals who come here to get away from the grind.

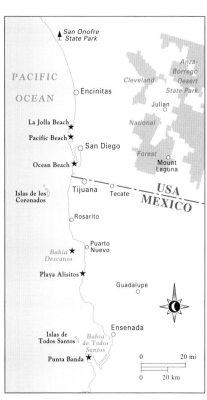

Depending on the conditions, a dawn patrol session at Old Man's or Trestles may be in order to finish off your time up at San O. Then head south down to **Encinitas.** Stuff yourself silly with a cheap and tasty breakfast at Pipes Cafe and keep your ears open at this surfer-friendly spot to hear where the waves might be best around here. Do a little reconnaissance along the coast while you digest to pick out a location for your afternoon session. The first obvious place to look is **Swami's,** less than five minutes away along Coast Highway. If there's no luck there, follow the highway south to Pipes and Suckouts farther south. If the water's flat, consider making the best of the situation by pulling out the skateboard and ripping up the vert ramps at the Encinitas YMCA. Or backtrack north a couple of minutes to the **Agua Hedionda Lagoon** for some wakeboarding. Pitch your tent again, this night at **San Elijo State Beach.**

La Jolla and Pacific Beach

Head along Coastal Highway 101 to **Torrey Pines State Reserve.** From the visitors lot atop the park's sandstone cliffs it is about a mile down a nature trail to one of the county's very best beach breaks, **Black's Beach.** Here surfers coexist with a healthy contingent of nudists who use this out-of-the-way spot as a place to sunbathe in the buff. If the waves aren't cooperating and you'd like to stay active, zip east along Highway 52 from La Jolla out to Mission Trails Park and hike to the top of **Cowles Mountain.** Otherwise, get a head start on your evening activities by continuing south into **Pacific Beach.** Set up shop at Mission Bay Motel and catch your first real shower in several days before hopping the bars along Mission Boulevard and Garnet Avenue.

Stumble out of bed and across the street to treat your hangover with a lazy breakfast at The Eggery. Walk off the belly-busting meal and the remaining cobwebs with an amble up the **Mission Beach Boardwalk.** Once you are ready to get wet again, head a few minutes north to **Tourmaline Surfing Park.** Even on a calm day this combination reef and point break is worth lugging out the longboard. Plus, between here and Crystal Pier is one of the best beach scenes in the city. For lunch or dinner try one of the flavorful and filling Mexican sandwiches at La Torta. Your stomach and your wallet will thank you.

Julian and Anza-Borrego

Dry off your quiver and clean the dust off your mountain bike for an adventure through San Diego's backcountry. You'll want to rise early, pack a lunch, and head east on I-8 until you reach Sunrise Highway. Take this serpentine road up through the **Laguna Mountains.** Your first stop along the way will be at **Big Laguna Meadow** for a scenic ten-mile ride along the trail here. You'll have the opportunity to lengthen it if you choose

Torrey Pines State Reserve

to climb the hills along the spur of **Noble Canyon Trail.**

Once you've exhausted yourself, hop back in the car and continue north until Julian. Hang a right on Highway 78 and follow the signs into the desert town of **Borrego Springs.** When you reach Borrego Springs, pull into the comfy developed Borrego Palm Canyon Campground and relax in the desert twilight.

Start your exploration of the desert with a hike up **Borrego Palm Canyon Trail** to an honest to goodness oasis. Once you've returned back to camp, walk over to the **Anza-Borrego State Park Visitors Center** and pore through its interpretive exhibits. Then the best way to get out there and actually see the park is to hop aboard one of the retrofitted troop transport trucks operated by California Overland. Once you get back into town, snag an affordable meal at the counter of Jilberto's and use this pit stop as an opportunity to hit the grocery store for any last-minute camping supplies

and water. Then head southwest on Highway S-22 up the curving Montezuma's Grade. You'll travel seven miles until you reach a dirt road that leads into Culp Valley. Here in **Anza-Borrego Desert State Park** you're allowed to set up camp any place you like, so pitch your tent anywhere between the boulders here.

If you have the time and climbing is your kind of thing, chalk up and try some bouldering. The granite-speckled Culp Valley is known as one of the best bouldering spots in the county.

Prepare for an epic day on the saddle in the desert landscape of **Grapevine Canyon** for an exhilarating ride for as many as 16 miles to Yaqui Well. Once you've gotten your fill of activity, make your way back into San Diego at your leisure and head to **Ocean Beach** for a little R&R. You can affordably snuggle into a real bed at the OB International Hostel, which is also conveniently located along Newport Avenue's stretch of bars and cheap eats.

A surfer checks out the waves.

The crowd hopes for a big one at La Bufadora in Ensenada.

Baja Coast

Get your passport and your gear together and head south of the border to wander the Baja coast. Once you cross over, head south along the **Tijuana-Ensenada Scenic Toll Road.** Exit just south of Rosarito onto the free road and roll along until you hit kilometer marker 38. Also called Theresa's, **K38** is one of the best-known breaks on the route to Ensenada, a right-handed point break that will make for a perfect late-morning session. When you work up a powerful hunger, jump into your car and head a couple minutes south down to Puerto Nuevo to nosh on an inexpensive lobster meal at Lobster House. Then go south until you reach **K58** and the camping spot perched above a cliff at **Playa Alisitos.** Surf till the sun goes down, eat dogs and s'mores by firelight, and smile because this is a place where worries wash away with the tide.

Eventually you'll want to make your way back to the toll road and continue south to **Ensenada,** which is less than thirty miles away. Make a beeline to the El Fenix taco stand downtown. You can gorge on the best fish taco spread on the coast for under five bucks. Practice your Spanish with the regulars at Hussong's Cantina while sipping a margarita. Bargain with a shop owner over a *luche libre* mask along Boulevard Lopez Mateos. Down a few cervezas at Papas and Beer. For a modest motel in the heart of the tourist district, try Posada El Rey Sol.

Wake early and continue your exploits at Punta Banda, only about a half hour southeast of Ensenada. Drive to **La Bufadora,** a thundering marine geyser set in the cliffs of this beautiful peninsula. In the village near the sea spout, rent gear and join a boat led by Dale's Dive Shop for an undersea exploration of the rocky depths off Punta Banda. If you aren't dive-certified, you can rent kayaks from Dale instead. Either way you'll be able to admire the craggy vistas along the shoreline here, a panoramic exclamation point to a thoroughly spectacular circuit through the region's finest outdoor adventures.

SAN DIEGO

It seems impossible, but San Diego is at once a small little beach town and a thriving metropolis. It's an urbane center of culture and a rowdy roost for partiers. It's a surf town, it's a mountain town, a golf course, and a skate park.

The truth is, this town is hard to completely get a handle on—it's a patchwork of more than 100 neighborhoods stitched together over hundreds of square miles, a mishmash of villages, barrios, and stomping grounds. It's up to newcomers to make it what they want it to be.

The birthplace of California, San Diego is a city of great historical significance to some. It is the site of the very first of the 21 California missions founded by Spanish Franciscan priests, Mission San Diego de Alcalá. It is home to remarkable adobe haciendas of the Mexican-California period. It has one of the most impressive concentrations of restored Victorian commercial buildings on the entire West Coast. And its location on the San Diego Bay has cultivated a rich and long-running maritime and naval history.

Home of Balboa Park, San Diego is a place of great culture and learning. The park is an amazing public treasure—the second-oldest city park in the United States, just behind Central Park, filled with beautiful and ornate Spanish Colonial Revival buildings that hold the city's best museums. Collections of art, history, and science are all here, surrounded by lush and fascinating gardens and the world-famous San Diego Zoo.

Cradled between mountains and ocean, San Diego is a town of amazing recreational opportunities. The city takes its open spaces seriously,

© ERICKA CHICKOWSKI

HIGHLIGHTS

◖ Gaslamp Quarter: The heart of the city's nightlife scene, this is also the birthplace of San Diego as a true metropolis. Its Victorian-era commercial buildings are some of the most beautifully restored in the West (page 43).

◖ USS *Midway* Museum: The longest-serving aircraft carrier in U.S. naval history, the *Midway* is now a floating museum. Its berthing spaces, decks, and bridge are all open for curious civilians and nostalgic vets (page 47).

◖ Maritime Museum of San Diego: This flotilla of historic ships celebrates San Diego's salty roots. Here visitors can duck into an ex-Soviet sub, walk the deck of tall sailing cutters, and sit on the benches of vintage wooden yachts (page 47).

◖ Silver Strand State Beach: Unfolding along the southern half of Coronado Island, this stretch of dunes and beaches is a natural and recreational getaway from city madness (page 49).

◖ Hotel del Coronado: The red cupolas and gables of this renowned Victorian seaside resort are an architectural masterpiece (page 49).

◖ Balboa Park: The pride of San Diego, this 1,200-acre park is home to dozens of museums, stunning Spanish Colonial Revival architecture, vibrant gardens, and the world's best-known zoo (page 51).

◖ San Diego Zoo: Both an institution of conservation and of fun, the rambling grounds of the zoo are home to a legendary collection of animals in a natural environment (page 52).

◖ Old Town State Historic Park: Before San Diego became a proper port city it was a simple inland pueblo at the foot of a Spanish presidio. This park relives that history with a mix of original and reconstructed structures (page 57).

◖ Mission San Diego de Alcalá: The simple curves of this whitewashed church is a living documentation of the city's ecclesiastical heritage (page 62).

◖ Mission Trails Regional Park: The largest urban park in the country, this mountainous open space is a sanctuary for hikers, bikers, bird-watchers, and climbers (page 63).

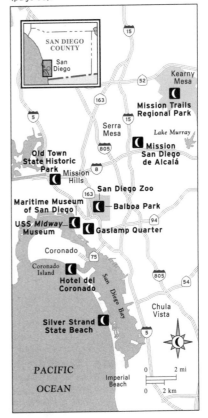

LOOK FOR ◖ TO FIND RECOMMENDED SIGHTS, ACTIVITIES, DINING, AND LODGING.

so within city limits there are literally hundreds of parks, preserves, and trails that are meant to be hiked and biked. Anglers frequently dip their lines in lakes or in the sparkling water of San Diego Bay. Boaters ply those same waters by motor and sail. Golfers swing their way along the fairways of the city's links. And picnickers have many opportunities to just lie around and enjoy the sunshine—a pastime that is so common on the public lawns here that it is practically a city sport.

As neighbor to Coronado Island, San Diego is also an easy departure point to this lazy seaside getaway. A municipality all its own, Coronado is a 10-minute drive or a half-hour ferry ride across the bay from San Diego. On the north end, its idyllic tree-lined village is a place to stroll leisurely through shops and restaurants. And just a few minutes south is a remote seven-mile sandy strand that is perfect for a family day at the beach.

HISTORY

The San Diego River watershed was home to the oldest known people of California, the San Dieguito Indians. Archeological evidence shows that these Paleo-Indians were around about 12,000 years ago, probably enjoying the same mild climate that has made "Sun Diego" so famous worldwide.

The San Dieguitos' ancestors greeted Spanish explorers in 1542, when Juan Rodrïguez Cabrillo landed briefly in San Diego, and again in 1602 at the landing of Sebastián Vizcaíno. It took the Spanish more than a century to return to what they called Alta California (Upper California), but they did return and San Diego was their first stop on the journey north.

When the soldiers and priests of Spain first settled San Diego, they initially chose a high perch over the San Diego River Valley to establish a military complex and a small mission to act as a center for both social and political activities. Known as Presidio Hill, this vantage point provided a defensive view of the surrounding Indian territory and acted as a symbol of dominance to the natives. Not too long after the Presidio was established, the

church moved the mission a few miles inland to be closer to running water and to distance itself from the sometimes brutal army. But the hill still remained an important political and military base until the Mexicans gained independence and left the Presidio to fall to pieces. During this period in the early 19th century settlers trickled into the area, settling in at the bottom of the hill to form a dusty pueblo, the first real neighborhood in San Diego.

However, as San Diego transitioned from Mexican to American rule, some citizens believed that the town would never grow into a true city if it remained at the foot of Presidio Hill. The location was more than three miles away from the bay and the distance between city center and the harbor would keep the city from establishing itself as a major shipping hub of the United States.

And so the idea of New Town San Diego was born, giving rise to what would eventually become today's downtown Gaslamp Quarter. Moving an entire city is no easy task, so it isn't surprising that the transition from Old Town to New came in fits and starts. Especially considering the fact that at the time the land by the bay was completely devoid of trees or fresh water.

The first civic leader to spearhead the move was William Heath Davis, who purchased land by the bay in the 1850s with the expectation of selling lots to families and business people nearby. While his zeal for the plan planted a seed that would eventually germinate decades later, he was unable to sell many lots. For years the area was derisively called Davis's Folly.

Alonzo Horton was the man who actually managed to make New Town a reality. Already a successful entrepreneur when he first stepped foot in San Diego in 1867, Horton already had experience marketing and developing towns out of thin air. As a young man Horton had founded a town in Wisconsin that he called Hortonville.

His westward migration brought him to the Mother Lode in San Francisco during the height of the Gold Rush, where he made a

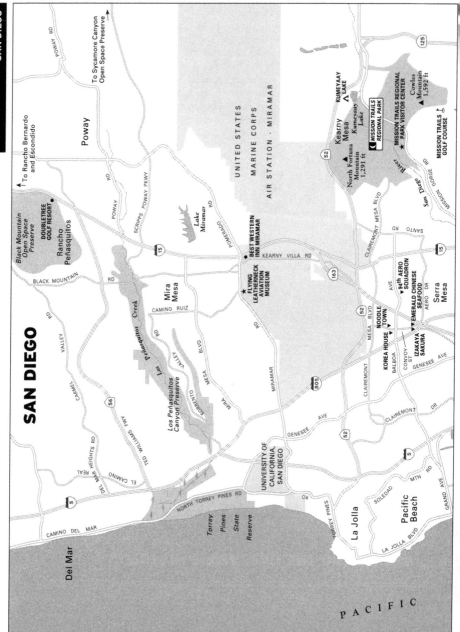

SAN DIEGO

Poway

To Sycamore Canyon
Open Space Preserve

To Rancho Bernardo
and Escondido

Black Mountain
Open Space
Preserve

DOUBLETREE
GOLF RESORT

Rancho Peñasquitos

BLACK MOUNTAIN RD

Lake
Miramar

Mira
Mesa

CAMINO RUIZ

Los Peñasquitos
Canyon Preserve

Los Peñasquitos Creek

UNITED STATES
MARINE CORPS
AIR STATION - MIRAMAR

Kearny
Mesa

North Fortuna
Mountain
1,291 ft

KUMEYAAY
LAKE

Kumeyaay
Lake

MISSION TRAILS REGIONAL
PARK VISITOR CENTER

Cowles
Mountain
1,592 ft

MISSION TRAILS
REGIONAL PARK

MISSION TRAILS
GOLF COURSE

San Diego River

SANTO RD

MISSION GORGE RD

KEARNY VILLA RD

BEST WESTERN
INN MIRAMAR

FLYING
LEATHERNECK
AVIATION
MUSEUM

94th AERO
SQUADRON

EMERALD CHINESE
SEAFOOD

IZAKAYA
SAKURA

NOODLE
TOWN

KOREA HOUSE

CLAIREMONT MESA BLVD

AERO DR

Serra
Mesa

BALBOA AVE

CONVOY ST

GENESEE AVE

CLAIREMONT DR

GENESEE AVE

CLAIREMONT

UNIVERSITY OF
CALIFORNIA,
SAN DIEGO

Torrey
Pines
State
Reserve

NORTH TORREY PINES RD

CAMINO DEL MAR

Del Mar

EL CAMINO REAL

DEL MAR HEIGHTS RD

TED WILLIAMS FWY

CARMEL VALLEY RD

SORRENTO VALLEY BLVD

MIRA MESA BLVD

MIRAMAR RD

POWAY RD

SCRIPPS POWAY PKWY

POWAY RD

POMERADO RD

La Jolla

SOLEDAD MTN RD

Pacific
Beach

LA JOLLA BLVD

GRAND AVE

PACIFIC

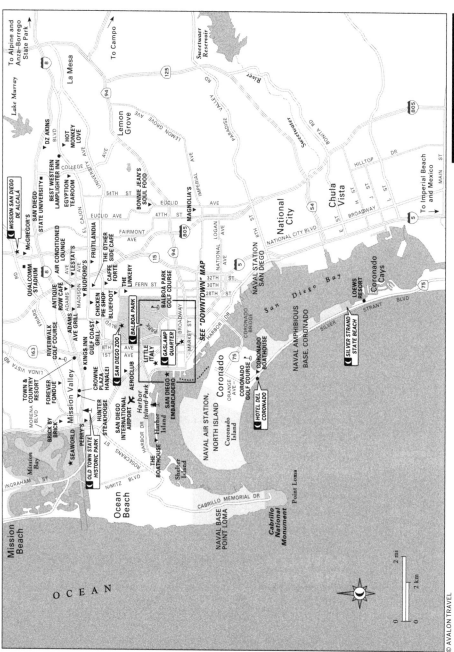

© AVALON TRAVEL

fortune selling ice to those seeking riches themselves in the streams of the gold fields.

In the 1860s Horton heard of the opportunities in San Diego and came down to check it out himself. When he arrived he found that the town had potential, but like Davis he believed that the key to building the pueblo into a proper city would be to establish the city center by the bay. In 1867 he bought up 960 acres next to Davis's land and began the process of promoting the area. He was tireless, sailing up to San Francisco to hawk the possibilities of San Diego and the lots on his new subdivision. He invested early earnings to build a new wharf, a hotel, and a library, and he gave away lots to congregations willing to build churches.

The only missing link was the municipal government. Stubborn Old Town residents still insisted that the future of San Diego was there, not over on crazy old Horton's waterfront property. Even though momentum was swinging in New Town's favor by 1870, Old Town still clung feverishly to the control it had over the county court system.

As long as it remained home to the county court and the county records, Old Town would stay relevant in city politics and business. And all of Old Town's staunch supporters knew it. Which is why when Horton donated building space in New Town to relocate the courthouse and records, Old Town locals fought the scheme tooth and nail.

The battle raged through legal channels until the California Supreme Court settled the matter in 1871. The court and its records were ordered to be moved from Old Town. This still didn't deter Old Town politicos. They refused to comply, going so far as to post a cannon and armed guards in front of the building that housed the court's records.

But Horton's contingent was persistent. One March night his allies, led by the county clerk, rolled in to Old Town on express wagons and forcibly removed the court's records. As they loaded up these documents and left a trail of dust as they rolled back down to the waterfront, San Diego's future was changed forever. From then on, it would be known as the city on the bay.

PLANNING YOUR TIME

So what *do* you want San Diego to be to you? Thinking about that before you arrive can help alleviate vacation frustration, because San Diego is a big town and no one likes to spend most of their vacation on the roads or freeways.

If its history you want, it might make sense to stay downtown and split your time between the core downtown area and Mission Valley. While downtown you can ramble through the streets of the **Gaslamp Quarter,** which are lined with scores of restored buildings from the late 19th century. From there it is an easy walk to the waterfront to visit the **USS *Midway* Museum** or the historic ships of the **Maritime Museum of San Diego.**

In Mission Valley, the historical highlight is obvious. This is the home of the **Mission San Diego de Alcalá,** California's first. Also adjacent to the valley is Presidio Hill, the site of the first Spanish fort and an impressive view of downtown. Sitting below the hill is Old Town State Historic Park, which gives an interesting perspective of early San Diego with its restored and original buildings from that era.

Art lovers could probably spend a whole week just exploring the nooks and crannies of **Balboa Park,** so they would do well to stay in a nearby Uptown or Midcity hotel. While at the park, a stop at the Timken Museum of Art, the San Diego Museum of Art, and the Mingei International Museum are all in order. A day at the park might even be extended by staying for a production at the Old Globe Theatre, which is on the premises.

The park is also a major draw for families, who come for at least a day to check out the pandas, gorillas, and more at the **San Diego Zoo.** Other kid-friendly options at Balboa include the Reuben H. Fleet Science Center, the San Diego Natural History Museum, and the San Diego Aerospace Museum.

Those looking to get away from it all without actually driving away from it all can take a ferry or drive over the Coronado Bay Bridge to Coronado Island to spend time shopping the quaint Orange Avenue or taking a walk along the beach at Silver Strand State Beach. Another active alternative is to make a trek out to the northern outposts of the city for a hike on Cowles Mountain at **Mission Trails Regional Park** or bike to the waterfalls in Los Peñasquitos Canyon Preserve.

ORIENTATION

San Diego wouldn't be a self-respecting Southern Californian city if it weren't guilty of a little urban sprawl. Geographically this town is massive, with a whopping 325 square miles bulging within its municipal borders.

Though the town is best known for its sandy beaches, the central core of San Diego is actually situated on the sheltered San Diego Bay, whose inlet from the Pacific Ocean is bounded on the north by Point Loma and on the south by Coronado Island.

Point Loma is actually the southernmost tip of the city's beach communities, which are in the northwestern part of the city. Because of their isolated geography and unique character, these communities have a whole chapter of their own. In order to explain the rest of the city's geography, I've broken it up into several regions.

Downtown

Just east of North Harbor Drive, between the airport down to the **Coronado Bay Bridge** are the downtown neighborhoods. In the northeast part of this district you'll find Little Italy, whose major attractions lie on **India Street** and **Kettner Boulevard.**

The central downtown core is south of Little Italy. This is the practical area of San Diego, where the courthouses and the county lockup are found. It is also home to the Santa Fe Depot, a major transportation hub and a beautiful building to boot. The station sits on the corner of Kettner and **Broadway,** the major east–west thoroughfare here.

Just a few blocks farther south is the city's entertainment nerve center, the **Gaslamp Quarter** and San Diego's East Village. East

Village tries as it might to distinguish itself from its neighbor, but most locals continue to expand their colloquial boundaries, often referring to East Village establishments as being "in the Gaslamp." Who am I to argue? I tend to do the same when describing area restaurants and bars.

Waterfront and Coronado Island

The bay curves like an upside-down J around the east side of Coronado Island, which runs parallel to the downtown core. Interestingly enough, Coronado is not actually an island. It's an isthmus, which joins back up with the mainland in the border beach town of Imperial Beach.

San Diego's major waterfront attractions lie directly across the bay from the northern part of Coronado Island. This is where the popular **Embarcadero** runs alongside **North Harbor Drive.**

Balboa Park, Uptown, and Midcity

North of the I-5 S-curve is a collection of neighborhoods loosely referred to as Uptown. These include **Bankers Hill,** which has its core north of **Laurel Avenue** and west of **5th Avenue,** and Mission Hills, which overlooks Old Town to the north and downtown to the west. Old Town is also referred to as being in Uptown, but for organizational purposes I've lumped it in with Mission Valley.

Balboa Park is also in the district, surrounded to the north by the other Uptown neighborhoods of **Hillcrest, North Park,** and **University Heights.**

East of the park lies Midcity, a rather unglamorous part of town that is dominated by **San Diego State University.** Neighborhoods that surround the school include **Normal Heights, Kensington,** and **College Heights.** Though there aren't many sights to see here, these neighborhoods do have a healthy nightlife and restaurant scene due to the students and freshly graduated young'uns who live in the area.

Mission Valley and Old Town

East of I-5 along the I-8 corridor, Mission Valley

runs all the way to I-15. Besides the freeways, the major roadways include **Hotel Circle North** and **Hotel Circle South,** which curiously enough have a lot of lodging options. Friars Road is another major arterial, running parallel to I-8 along the valley's northern rim.

Old Town is just south of Mission Valley, on the arrow point of land bounded by **Pacific Highway** and I-8. The neighborhood sits below **Presidio Hill.**

North City

North of Mission Valley, between I-5 and eastern city limits, is North City. This expansive stretch of land includes the residential neighborhoods of **Clairemont Mesa, Kearny Mesa,** and **Mira Mesa** on the south end. These neighborhoods are directly west of the city's recreational wonderland, **Mission Trails Regional Park.**

Go north from any of these points and you'll eventually encounter the massive **Marine Corps Air Station Miramar.** Just north of the base along I-15 is the exclusive Rancho Bernardo community. And beyond that is where things get fun. To the east of I-15 are **Los Peñasquitos Canyon Preserve** and **Black Mountain Open Space Park.** To the west, **San Pasqual-Clevenger Canyon Open Space Park.**

Sights

While there is plenty to see in most of San Diego's neighborhoods, much of the fun can be broken up by interest. On the waterfront get a keen feeling for the city's rich naval and maritime history. In Old Town and Mission Valley one can find much of the city's historical roots. Downtown is a grab bag of museums and architectural sights. Arts and culture organizations are concentrated in Balboa Park. And in the northern stretch of city limits one can find plenty of open space and natural beauty.

DOWNTOWN
Museums

Housed right in the heart of the 1915 Santa Fe Depot complex, the downtown branch of the **Museum of Contemporary Art San Diego** (MCASD, 1100 & 1001 Kettner Blvd., between Broadway and B St., 858/454-3541, www.mcasd.org, 11 A.M.–6 P.M. Sat.–Tues., 11 A.M.–9 P.M. Thurs.–Fri., $10 adults, $5 military and seniors, ages 25 and under free) offers a central location for art lovers looking to get their fix without driving out to Balboa Park or to the MCASD main branch in La Jolla. The museum's newly expanded facility was opened in 2007, featuring artistic touches from the renowned architect Richard Gluck-

man and several permanent pieces commissioned by the museum. As the second branch of the museum, MCASD Downtown shares with the La Jolla branch some 4,000 works of art and also features a rotating stock of international exhibitions.

Also located downtown is the **San Diego Firehouse Museum** (1572 Columbia St., 619/232-3473, www.thesdfirehousemuseum .org, Thurs.–Fri. 10 A.M.–2 P.M., Sat.–Sun. 10 A.M.–4 P.M., admission $3) in Little Italy, which gives a glimpse of San Diego's firefighting history from bucket brigades to modern fire engines. This little gem of a museum is housed in the former San Diego Fire Station No. 6 and features a host of old equipment and memorabilia, including pumps, hand-crank sirens, fire nozzles, and more.

The museum is run by the fire department, which encourages its firefighters to volunteer as docents in order to keep the history and lore of the department alive and well in the public eye.

Don't blink or you'll miss it, but as you travel between Little Italy and the Gaslamp you'll pass through Chinatown. Not much more than a few historic buildings, this area is home to the **San Diego Chinese Historical Museum**

(404 3rd Ave., 619/338-9888, www.sdchm .org, 10:30 A.M.–4 P.M. Tues.–Sat., noon–4 P.M. Sun., $2), which chronicles the Chinese American experience in San Diego and the rest of the West Coast and offers an interesting perspective on Chinese history, culture, and art.

I don't know but I've been told, those Devil Dogs are mighty bold. And San Diego's got them in spades. Not only is the county home to Camp Pendleton and Marine Corps Air Station Miramar, but it also plays host to the Marine Corps Recruit Depot, one of two Marine boot camps in the nation. Located right next to the airport, the MCRD is generally closed to the public at large so you probably won't be able to get in to watch the drill sergeants go all R. Lee Ermey on the recruits. But if you'd like to learn about the making of a marine, drop by the **Marine Corps Recruit Depot Command Museum** (Marine Corps Recruit Depot, 1600 Henderson Ave., Bldg. 26, www.mcrdmuseumhistoricalsociety.org, 8 A.M.–4 P.M. Mon.–Sat., free) on base. This patriotic museum pays tribute to the thousands of recruits who have thrown their covers up in the air following graduation from the grueling 13-week training program. Be prepared to show your driver's license and proof of insurance when driving onto base.

Little Italy

The Italian American tradition is strong in San Diego, where in the 1920s a large community of Italians established themselves and helped to build the region into a tuna fishing juggernaut.

They came primarily from Sicily and Genoa, building homes just north of downtown and close to the water for easy access to the docks and the city center. According to some old-timers, this was the kind of neighborhood you could walk past and just smell the cooking wafting through the windows.

It was this way for several decades until the community suffered multiple setbacks. In the 1940s, many Italians lost their jobs as the tuna industry shrank in response to the war and increasing mechanization of the fishing fleet.

And in the late 1950s, Little Italy itself was ravaged by the construction of I-5, which cut directly through the district.

As a result many Italian families moved out and the neighborhood became the type of area where fathers wouldn't want their daughters walking alone. However, there were still a few stubborn stalwarts who continued to operate their businesses through the bad times.

In the early 1990s they led the charge to revitalize the district. Small restaurant and retail store openings were followed up with civic projects and street beautifications. This paved the way to larger building redevelopments, including a number of high-profile condo towers.

Little Italy has completely remade itself, while maintaining the flair and culture of its original residents. The colorful new buildings reflect the area's Italian heritage and there are still plenty of buildings from the old guard that were lovingly restored by community members who take pride in the neighborhood's roots. The delicious smells now waft out of the restaurants that have opened up in and around these historic buildings, particularly on the main drag on India Street.

While you stroll along this street be sure to take a moment at **Piazza Basilone** on the corner of West Fir, which pays tribute to the naval and marine heroes from San Diego. The piazza is named after Gunnery Sergeant John Basilone, an Italian American marine who won both the Navy Cross and the Congressional Medal of Honor for his service during World War II.

North of India Street, on the corner of State and Date Streets, there is a tribute to Italian heroism on a whole other "battlefield"— the kitchen. Among its other features, **Amici Park** is dotted with table statues festooned with the traditional white-and-red-checkered tablecloth and engraved with Italian recipes donated by local community members. The park serves as a hub of activity for the district, with its playgrounds, bocci ball courts, and a small open-air amphitheater.

If the bocci courts aren't hopping, it might be because the athletic types are just a block away playing stickball. Running for over a

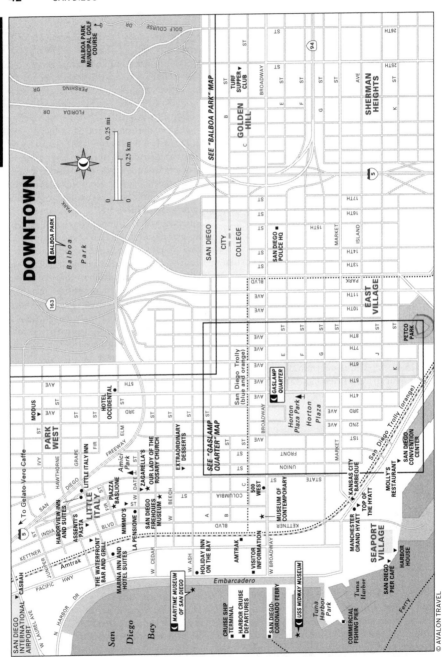

DOWNTOWN

San Diego Bay

Balboa Park

0.25 mi
0.25 km

BALBOA PARK MUNICIPAL GOLF COURSE

GOLF COURSE DR

FLORIDA DR

PERSHING DR

SEE "BALBOA PARK" MAP

GOLDEN HILL

TURF SUPPER CLUB

SHERMAN HEIGHTS

SAN DIEGO CITY COLLEGE

SAN DIEGO POLICE HQ

EAST VILLAGE

PETCO PARK

GASLAMP QUARTER

Horton Plaza Park
Horton Plaza

San Diego Trolley (blue and orange)

San Diego Trolley (orange)

SAN DIEGO CONVENTION CENTER

SEE "GASLAMP QUARTER" MAP

PARK WEST

HOTEL OCCIDENTAL

EXTRAORDINARY DESSERTS

OUR LADY OF THE ROSARY CHURCH

ZAGARELLA'S

LITTLE ITALY

Amici Park

LITTLE ITALY INN

PIAZZA BASILIONE

ASSENTI'S PASTA

MIMMO'S

To Gelato Vero Caffe

HABORVIEW INN AND SUITES

SAN DIEGO FIREHOUSES MUSEUM

LA PENSIONE

500 WEST

MUSEUM OF CONTEMPORARY

THE WATERFRONT BAR AND GRILL

MARINA INN AND HOTEL SUITES

HOLIDAY INN ON THE BAY

AMTRAK

VISITOR INFORMATION

KANSAS CITY BARBEQUE

MOLLY'S RESTAURANT

MANCHESTER GRAND HYATT

TOP OF THE HYATT

SEAPORT VILLAGE

HARBOR HOUSE

SAN DIEGO PIER CAFÉ

CASBAH

SAN DIEGO INTERNATIONAL AIRPORT

Embarcadero

MARITIME MUSEUM OF SAN DIEGO

CRUISE SHIP TERMINAL

HARBOR CRUISE DEPARTURES

SAN DIEGO-CORONADO FERRY

USS MIDWAY MUSEUM

Tuna Harbor Park

Tuna Harbor

COMMERCIAL FISHING PIER

Ferry

© AVALON TRAVEL

SAN DIEGO

decade, the **West Coast Stickball League** (www.westcoaststickball.com) was created by some kids at heart who fondly remembered their stickball sessions in the streets of another Little Italy, in New York City. The league usually stages matches on Columbia and State Streets; if you are lucky enough to pass by during a game you'll be entertained by the mix of competitive, sometimes overweight, middle-aged *paisans* huffing and puffing to vie with some of the younger participants.

Also in the neighborhood is **Our Lady of the Rosary Church** (1629 Columbia St., 619/233-7039, www.olrsd.org), which offers fine examples of art for those who favor religious depictions. This Italian National Parish was consecrated on November 15, 1925, to serve the thriving population that yearned for a church that reminded them of the old country. Particularly beautiful are the oil paintings on the ceiling and walls that were painted by Fausto Tasca, a Venetian artist living in Los Angeles at the time who was recruited by the church's founding priest to adorn the sanctu-ary. Also of note are the colorful stained-glass windows and the statues of Mary, St. Anne, and St. Joseph. Our Lady is an active Catholic parish today, so be aware that on Sundays you might have to wait for services to conclude before whipping out your camera.

Gaslamp Quarter

Like Little Italy, the Gaslamp Quarter has experienced a renaissance after spending many decades as a rats' nest of porno theaters, low-rent hotels, and boarded-up buildings.

Named for the gas lanterns that lit area streets during downtown's formative years, the Gaslamp Quarter is at the epicenter of downtown's ritzy club and lounge scene. Today the streets are lit with neon and if you walk them at night you'll hear the clink of glasses, the pounding bass, and the hoots and whistles emanating from the bars that blanket the district. On any given night throughout the year, smartly dressed couples and groups of singles on the prowl climb out of taxis and scurry into the throng of revelers that line up to gain access

© ERICKA CHICKOWSKI

The Gaslamp Quarter was the birthplace of modern San Diego's downtown.

SAN DIEGO

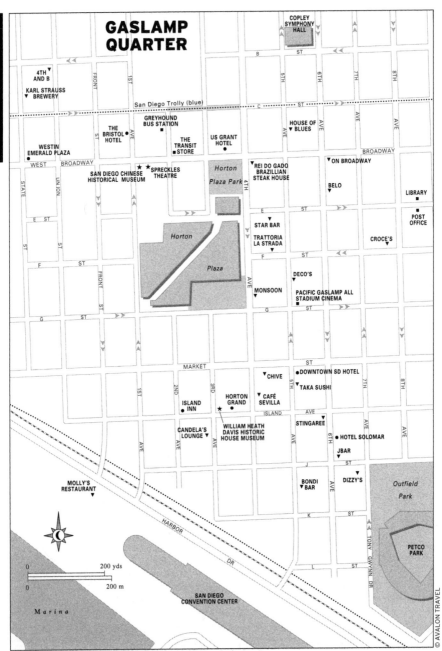

GASLAMP QUARTER

COPLEY SYMPHONY HALL

4TH AND B
KARL STRAUSS BREWERY

San Diego Trolly (blue)

GREYHOUND BUS STATION

THE BRISTOL HOTEL

THE TRANSIT STORE

US GRANT HOTEL

HOUSE OF BLUES

WESTIN EMERALD PLAZA

BROADWAY

ON BROADWAY

SAN DIEGO CHINESE HISTORICAL MUSEUM

SPRECKLES THEATRE

Horton Plaza Park

REI DO GADO BRAZILLIAN STEAK HOUSE

BELO

LIBRARY

POST OFFICE

Horton

STAR BAR

TRATTORIA LA STRADA

CROCE'S

Plaza

DECO'S

MONSOON

PACIFIC GASLAMP ALL STADIUM CINEMA

MARKET

CHIVE

DOWNTOWN SD HOTEL

TAKA SUSHI

ISLAND INN

HORTON GRAND

CAFÉ SEVILLA

CANDELA'S LOUNGE

WILLIAM HEATH DAVIS HISTORIC HOUSE MUSEUM

STINGAREE

HOTEL SOLOMAR

JBAR

MOLLY'S RESTAURANT

BONDI BAR

DIZZY'S

Outfield Park

PETCO PARK

0   200 yds

0   200 m

HARBOR

DR

Marina

SAN DIEGO CONVENTION CENTER

TONY GWYNN DR

© AVALON TRAVEL

WANDERING THE GASLAMP'S HISTORIC BUILDINGS

This is a favorite route of mine that passes dozens of fantastic examples of Victorian commercial architecture and points of historical interest in the Gaslamp Quarter.

Start on the south end at Island Street to take a gander at the oldest of the bunch, the **William Heath Davis Historic House** (410 Island Ave., 619/233 4692, www.gaslampquarter .org, 10 A.M.-6 P.M. Tues.-Sat., 9 A.M.-3 P.M. Sun., $5). This saltbox-style home was one of 14 prefabricated houses that were hauled all the way around Cape Horn from New England by William Heath Davis in 1850 in order to jumpstart the development of New Town San Diego. At the time, the bay-front property was completely devoid of trees (and fresh water for that matter), making it necessary to import "modern" wood houses for potential buyers.

Unfortunately, Davis's initiative wasn't matched by his promotional skills and it took seventeen years and the brash salesmanship of Alonzo Horton to make New Town a reality. The house on Island Street is the last remaining home imported by Davies and stands today as a symbol of the groundwork he laid to make today's downtown a possibility.

Kitty-corner to the Davis House is the **Horton Grand Hotel,** which is actually made up of two historic hotels that were moved to this spot in the 1980s to avoid demolition. Both constructed in 1886, they were two very different establishments. The Grand Horton was an elegant structure built as a replica of Innsbruck Inn in Vienna, Austria. The Brooklyn Hotel was casual, and eventually became known as the Kahle Saddlery Hotel for the saddle and harness shop that did business in the ground floor. They were painstakingly dismantled from what is now Horton Plaza and stored in a warehouse by the city until the opportunity arose to rebuild them together on their current lot.

Some of the most stunning structures are between the 600 and 800 blocks of 5th Avenue. First comes the **Yuma Building** (631 5th Ave.), an Italianate baroque beauty that was one of downtown's first brick structures when it was built in 1888. At that time it was used for legitimate business, but by 1901 its upstairs "offices" were transformed into dens of debauchery instead. When the police were pressured to crack down on prostitution in the area in 1912, the Yuma was the first building they raided.

Across the street from the Yuma on the corner of G and 5th stands **Old City Hall.** Built originally as a bank in 1874, this Florentine Italianate structure was purchased by the city in 1891 and housed City Hall until 1938. During the early years here, city leaders gave a wink and a nod to the illicit activities across the street at the Yuma and many more prostitution parlors, opium dens, and gambling halls that flanked city hall to comprise what was known widely as the Stingaree District.

Keep to the west side of 5th and cross G Street. About halfway down the block you'll stumble across the **Llewelyn Building** (722 5th Ave.), which is probably one of the best examples of commercial Victorian architecture in the Gaslamp.

Now, head up one more block and look across the street to see two of my absolute favorites side by side (you'll have a better vantage point to view the upper stories from a little distance). First comes the Romanesque Revival-style **Nesmith-Greely Building** (825 5th Ave.). Right next door is the intricate and ornate Victorian-style **Louis Bank of Commerce** (835 5th Ave.). The twin mansard roof towers of this baroque revival building are the most recognizable features in the entire Gaslamp. The ground floor of this building was rented by Wyatt Earp, who ran a saloon here in the years following the O.K. Corral incident.

into some of the highest-profile clubs south of Hollywood.

In spite of the partying, the area hasn't lost touch with its heritage and actually affords the quiet artsy type a lot to see during the day. Art galleries, boutiques, and fine restaurants are sprinkled in between the clubs. And of course, a relaxing afternoon drink can be had at many places without mortgaging your home to pay a cover.

The real show-stealer is the buildings that house all of these establishments. Within the nearly 17-block neighborhood there are over 90 buildings listed on the National Register of Historic Places.

There are dozens of historic buildings scattered throughout the Gaslamp. Keep a lookout for the bronze placards that are affixed to buildings at street level. They'll give you the lowdown on the date of construction and perhaps a tidbit or two on what makes that structure unique. And don't forget to point that camera upward—you just might capture a one-of-a-kind architectural flourish that can't be found anywhere else.

WATERFRONT AND CORONADO ISLAND
San Diego Embarcadero

San Diego has long lived and died by the sea, so it is no surprise that much of the city's hubbub still surrounds the waterfront. San Diego Bay, or the "Big Bay" as locals call it, is sheltered from open water by Coronado Island and Point Loma. The easily defendable inlet and calm waters created by these land masses make it an ideal harbor, one which San Diegans have taken advantage of for centuries.

The Big Bay's present still echoes its past. Naval steamers have been replaced by aircraft carriers. The tuna fleet has largely been replaced by sports fisherman. Lumbering cruise ships tower over the pleasure craft that still zip around the bay to this day.

With a dazzling view of the bay and Coronado Island, the Embarcadero is one of the perfect places to soak up the flavor of San Diego's maritime tradition. This bayfront path is dotted with parks, museums, shops, and restaurants. Along the way, the salty air is permeated with the scent of waffle cones and fried fish. Here the jingle of pedicab bells is occasionally interrupted by deep-bass cruise ship horns, giggling children, and the call of the seagulls.

Seaport Village

Dominating the waterfront on the south end is Seaport Village (849 W. Harbor Dr., #D, 619/235-4014, www.seaportvillage.com, 10 A.M.–9 P.M. daily), a 14-acre shopping and dining complex. With its cutesy shops filled with clever T-shirts, 101 varieties of hot sauces, and precious little kitten figurines, this place is the prototypical tourist trap. But it manages to rise above the whimsy through its sublime setting and scenic grounds. Plus, visitors hardly need to spend the whole day at the village.

But there is enough to see and do here to provide a good intergenerational afternoon or morning of fun. Mom and Dad can snap photos of the little ones on the circa-1895 carousel designed by Charles Looff; Gram and Gramps can browse through the shops' tchotchkes to their hearts' content; and teenagers can sullenly pretend they aren't with their parents while walking the waterfront and plunking quarters into the binoculars facing the bay.

With ample parking and several good restaurants, the village makes a good point of embarkation toward the rest of the Embarcadero. Parking isn't free, but if you pick up a souvenir or a bite to eat in the village you can get your ticket validated for some free time.

Embarcadero Marina Park

Really two parks in one, Embarcadero Marina Park juts out into the bay like two green pinkies embracing the south end of the Embarcadero.

The north and south parks border Seaport Village and the San Diego Convention Center. The two peninsulas feature a fishing pier, basketball courts, gazebos, and a concession stand that sells food and bait.

© PAUL CHICKOWSKI

USS *Midway* Museum along the Embarcadero

◖ USS *Midway* Museum

A few blocks north of Seaport Village is the USS *Midway* Museum (937 N. Harbor Dr., 619/544-9600, www.midway.org, 10 A.M.–5 P.M. daily, $15 adults, $10 seniors, students, and military, $8 youth 6–17, children 5 and under and active-duty military in uniform free), a floating monument that honors San Diego's naval tradition.

One of the longest-serving carriers in the nation's history, the *Midway* saw several generations of sailors serve our country aboard her decks during her 47 years. Commissioned during World War II, she was a major contributor during the Korean War and the Vietnam conflict and even served as the navy's flagship during the Gulf War.

This floating fortress has been lovingly restored by a crew of staff and volunteers who kept it from rusting into the ocean when it was mothballed in 1992. Visitors are invited over the gangplanks to explore dozens of sections that have been restored and are open for touring including engineering, the mess deck,

berthing spaces, the hangar and flight decks, and the island superstructure.

The audio tour is remarkably good (and this is coming from someone who usually hates wearing those goofy headphones). You'll not only hear commentary, but also sounds similar to what you would have heard back in the day in the areas you visit.

As an added bonus, there are over two dozen different aircraft featured on the flight deck. If you visit during the weekend or during summertime, be sure to spend some time listening to former pilots and crew members explain the complicated and dangerous tasks of landing and taking off from a postage stamp–size runway in the middle of an ocean. Most of these volunteers are still full of the spit and vinegar that made them flight-worthy, making these talks a lively highlight.

◖ Maritime Museum of San Diego

Those who have already found their sea legs aboard the *Midway* should wobble two blocks

The Maritime Museum of San Diego allows visitors to tour through seven historic ships, including this B-39 Russian submarine.

© PAUL CHICKOWSKI

north to the Maritime Museum of San Diego (1492 N. Harbor Dr., 619/234-9153, www .sdmaritime.com). Similar to the Midway, the Maritime Museum's exhibits float dockside. The museum owns a fleet of historic ships that include an ex-Soviet submarine, an 1898 steam ferry, and a 1904 luxury yacht.

The pride and joy of the museum is the *Star of India,* the world's oldest active ship. This full-rigged iron windjammer was built at Ramsey Shipyards in the Isle of Man in 1863. Another highlight is the HMS *Surprise,* a replica 24-gun frigate of Great Britain's Nelson-era Royal Navy. Russell Crowe fans may recognize her—she was the boat used in the hit movie *Master and Commander.*

In addition to exploring the museum's collection of ships, consider paying the extra fee for the Adventure Package, which buys you a three-hour sail aboard a replica of a mid-19th-century revenue cutter. The museum is open 9 A.M.–8 P.M. daily, until 9 P.M. Memorial Day–Labor Day. Admission is $12 for adults, $9 for seniors and active military, $8 kids 6–17, and kids under 5 are free.

Harbor Island

Away from the hustle of the Embarcadero, Harbor Island offers similar views of San Diego Bay with a lot less competition for legroom. The west side of the island is lined by the appropriately named **Harbor Island Park,** a shoreline park that offers lots of green stuff to throw down a blanket or a towel. It is also bisected by a nice flat sidewalk for strolling or rolling along the bay.

On the typical day this is a pretty quiet park compared to some others. However, it does get crowded when an event is on. For example, the Big Bay's Fourth of July fireworks are usually based on the island.

Though not actually on Harbor Island, **Spanish Landing Park** is also very close by. It runs on the mainland parallel to the island's northern half. This park commemorates the 1769 meeting in San Diego between the

SAN DIEGO

© ERICKA CHICKOWSKI

Hotel del Coronado

Serra-Portola overland expedition and Spanish ships making the simultaneous journey north from La Paz in order to settle the area.

Also parallel to the island, just on the southern half, is **Cancer Survivor's Park,** a bright piece of public green space designed to provide hope to those diagnosed with the disease. The park is decorated with optimistic artwork and sculptures and is a pleasant place for all.

This trio of parks is conveniently located right across the street from Lindbergh Field, where San Diego International Airport is located. Any one of them can be a great place to lounge in the sun while killing time before a flight.

(Silver Strand State Beach

Frequently rated as a Blue Wave Beach by the Clean Beaches Council, Silver Strand State Beach has seven miles of sugar-sand beaches and undulating sand dunes. The strand is at the base of the spit that makes up Coronado Island, stretching from Imperial Beach all the way up to Naval Air Station Coronado. Fans of wild and remote beaches would do well to cross

the Coronado Bridge or drive up from Imperial Beach in the winter to spend some time here. Though the beach is not far from downtown as the crow flies, its position on the island makes it a bit out of the way compared to other beaches in town. It rests on the narrowest part of the island and there are no restaurants or stores nearby. As a result, there is a good chance that you can have a whole stretch of beach to yourself on certain days during the off-season.

The beach parking lot is open to RV camping, so during the summer it may be crowded with out-of-towners and it is also a popular spot for residents from all over San Diego to spend a summer day. As a result, it is not going to be nearly as private as it is during the winter. However, the crowd is perhaps one of the most family-friendly among San Diego's beaches and the beach can still offer a relaxing day during peak season.

(Hotel del Coronado

The grand dame of San Diego architecture is Hotel del Coronado (1500 Orange Ave.,

Coronado, 619/435-6611, www.hoteldel.com), a stunning Victorian masterpiece whose red-hued turrets, gables, and cupolas have been drawing wealthy guests for more than 115 years.

Known simply as "The Del," this hotel has hosted every kind of rich and famous caller imaginable: statesmen and royalty, Hollywood starlets and country singers, railroad barons and technology magnates. Eight U.S. presidents have stayed here during their terms and several movies have been filmed on the property, including the 1958 Marilyn Monroe classic *Some Like it Hot*.

The list of accomplishments would make Elisha Babcock and H. L. Story proud. In 1885 the two Midwestern entrepreneurs bought up Coronado Island for $110,000 with the intention of building an ocean resort that would be "the talk of the Western world." Three years later their work came to fruition when the hotel opened its doors. Even today the Western world hasn't stopped talking about it.

Docents from the **Coronado Historical Association** lead one-hour tours (619/437-8788, www.coronadohistory.org, $15, children 6 and under free) through the hotel on Tuesdays at 10:30 A.M. and Fridays, Saturdays, and Sundays at 2 P.M. You'll learn about the architecture and the history of this San Diego landmark. The tour meets at the Coronado Museum of History and Art at 1100 Orange Avenue.

Other Coronado Sights

Coronado Bay Bridge is as integral to the San Diego waterfront view as the aircraft carriers and sailboats. The simple arching curves of this clean-lined beauty are meant to pay homage to the Spanish Revival architecture found locally. The design earned it the Most Beautiful Bridge Award of Merit from the American Institute of Steel Construction in 1970. Its high towers are made to accommodate tall naval ships passing through. Depending on how you feel about heights, a trip across can either be harrowing or breathtaking, but either way it is the easiest way to cross over to the island from downtown.

Coronado's shopping and recreational activity pivots around tree-lined **Orange Avenue,**

Orange Avenue in downtown Coronado

© ERICKA CHICKOWSKI

the main thoroughfare that seems to link every "here" to "there" on the island. And just as any journey is more important than the destination, the sum of Orange Avenue is more than its parts. So be sure to stay long enough to soak it all in: the shops, the restaurants, the museums, and the parks.

Glorietta Bay Park sits bayside just where Orange Avenue begins transitioning into Rte. 75. With fantastic views of the downtown skyline, grass galore, picnic tables, benches, and grills, this is a primo spot for a summertime barbecue. The park is also an excellent departure point to walk, jog, or ride along the Silver Strand bike path.

Farther along the highway near the Loews Resort there's another grassy bayside park called **Coronado Cays** that is ideal for picnicking and family relaxation. This six-acre park has playgrounds and ball fields and is adjacent to **Grand Caribe Park,** which features a nature path with native plants and outdoor art. Both can be a good place to cap off a day on the sands of Silver Strand, which is just across the highway.

The Gondola Company (4000 Coronado Bay Rd., Coronado, 619/429-6317, www.gondola company.com, 3 p.m.–midnight Mon.–Fri., 11 a.m.–midnight Sat.–Sun.) offers a bit of Venetian-style touring on its gondola boat rides through the tony Coronado Cays. Munch on the hors d'oeuvres or dessert plate served with the ride and imagine you're Robin Leach as you glide past some of the region's most exclusive estates. Rides cost $85 for two people and an additional $20 for each extra passenger, with a maximum of six per boat.

BALBOA PARK AND UPTOWN
Balboa Park

As early as 1789, Spain's King Carlos III ordered the present-day site of Balboa Park to be reserved for "pasturage or for recreational purposes" and the land has remained a recreational reserve ever since.

The jewel of San Diego, Balboa Park epitomizes the dual nature of San Diego. Athletes sweat it out on the ball fields and courts of the park, while nearby museumgoers nod their

© ERICKA CHICKOWSKI

Balboa Park's Spanish Revival architecture and lush greenery offer a picturesque backdrop for San Diego's best museums.

heads thoughtfully at works of art. At more than 1,200 acres, the park hosts more than 85 different cultural and recreational organizations, including the world-famous San Diego Zoo. The park also features hundreds of species of flora, many of them planted near the turn of the 20th century by the city's first official gardener, Kate O. Sessions.

The offerings can be a bit overwhelming, so it might make sense to make your first stop at the **Balboa Park Visitors Center** (1549 El Prado, 619/239-0512, www.balboapark.org, free). Tucked away into a building along El Prado, the visitors center is staffed by a number of knowledgeable volunteers who can point you to the best spots based on your needs for the day. They can also arm you with informative books and maps to enrich your stay.

The visitors center also sells the Passport to Balboa Park, a special pass that can be a great bargain for those who wish to fully experience the museums and attractions within the park.

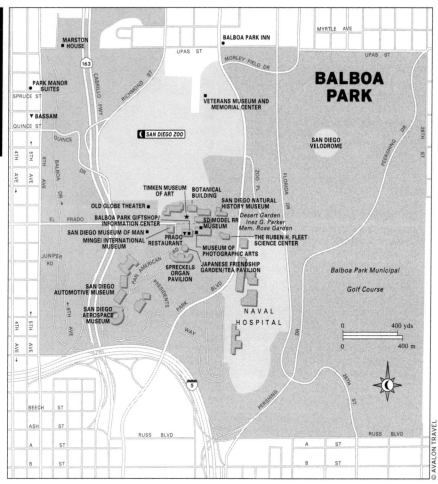

The deal offers admission to thirteen different museums at the park and is valid for seven days after purchase. The passport costs $35 for adults and $19 for kids. You can also add zoo admission to the mix, making it $59 for adults and $33 for children.

◖ San Diego Zoo

Arguably the most famous zoo in the world, the San Diego Zoo (2920 Zoo Dr., 619/234-3153, www.sandiegozoo.com, $33 adults, $22 children 3–11) has long been the standard-bearer for keeping animals in captivity. Zoo visitors come face to face with creatures great and small and will also learn about the efforts that zookeepers and researchers are making to save endangered species and their habitats.

The grounds are almost as impressive as the menagerie of animals, with a lush jungle of exotic plants serving as the setting for the roars of lions and screeches of monkeys. The property is extremely expansive compared to the typical city zoo. There are over 100 acres to explore, so be prepared with sturdy walking shoes and at least three or four hours of your time. Those with limited mobility will be happy to find that there are a number of options to quickly peruse the park, including a tour bus, a sky tram, and shuttle service for those in wheelchairs.

In the summer, one of the highlights of the park is Nighttime Zoo, when the zoo is open through 9 P.M. Visiting during evening hours allows animal lovers to catch a glimpse of nocturnal animals who might spend most daylight hours holed up in their caves. The facilities open at 9 A.M. year-round and from fall through spring they close at 5 P.M. each day.

Timken Museum of Art

The Timken Museum of Art (1500 El Prado, 619/239-5548, www.timken.com, 10 A.M.–4:30 P.M. Tues.–Sat., 1:30–4:30 P.M. Sun., closed Sept., free) is probably one of the best deals in the city for museumgoers. This intimate art gallery offers a collection of very well-known pieces free to the public. The trick is visiting while the museum is open, as hours are more limited than other museums in the park and it is closed annually during the month of September.

It is home to the Putnam Foundation Collection of artwork from European old masters, early American artists, and Russian iconographers. This collection is so well regarded that many museums around the world beg to borrow numerous pieces from Timken—but don't worry, this small museum rarely consents, so you'll likely get to see every piece when you visit. Included in the collection are masterpieces by Rembrandt, Rubens, Petrus Christus, Fragonard, Jacques-Louis David, Veronese, John Singleton Copley, and Eastman Johnson.

Two of my particular favorites are Rembrandt's "Saint Bartholomew" and "The Cranberry Harvest, Island of Nantucket" by Eastman Johnson.

The Timken has a very active docent program. Visit Tuesday through Friday between 10 A.M. and noon to ask for a docent to lead you on a half-hour to hour tour of the art here.

Docents are also available every second and third Saturday 11 A.M.–1 P.M.

San Diego Museum of Art

San Diego County's oldest and largest art institution is the San Diego Museum of Art (1450 El Prado, 619/232-7931, www.sdmart .org, 10 A.M.–6 P.M. Tues.–Sun., 10 A.M.–9 P.M. Thurs., closed Mon., $10 adults, $4 children), which features a collection that is particularly strong in representing the works of Spanish masters such as Murillo, Rivera, and El Greco. There are also many other examples from the French Impressionists, the Barbizon School, and French Academic painters. In addition, the collection of American art spans from the colonial period to early 20th century, with work by Durand, Cassatt, Inness, Eakins, Chase, and O'Keeffe all hanging from the gallery. Docent-led tours are held hourly between 10 A.M. and 2 P.M. Tuesdays through Thursdays.

San Diego Natural History Museum

One of the most esteemed institutes for cultivating archeological, geological, and biological discovery and learning in the county is the San Diego Natural History Museum (1788 El Prado, 619/232-3821, www.sdnhm .org, 10 A.M.–6:30 P.M. Mon.–Thurs., 10 A.M.–7:30 P.M. Fri., 9 A.M.–8:30 P.M. Sat.–Sun., $9). This institution is the leading local scientific research organization studying the geology and biology of San Diego County and Baja Norte and has amassed an amazing collection of specimens over a hundred years of field work. Selected samples are displayed in a variety of permanent and temporary exhibits throughout the year. Best known for attracting first-rate traveling exhibits, the museum has been on a push in recent years to do better justice to its permanent collections of fossils, rocks, and other natural curiosities. The most evident product of these labors is the impressive "Fossil Mysteries" exhibit on the second floor, highlighted by an enormous model of a Giant "Mega-Tooth" Shark hanging over the museum atrium.

SAN DIEGO

San Diego Air and Space Museum

While there are numerous museums around town that offer a peek into some pristine restored aircraft, none offer the same depth and breadth of aeronautical history as the San Diego Air and Space Museum (2001 Pan American Plaza, 619/234-8291, www.aero spacemuseum.org, $15). The museum takes you through the annals of human flight with hundreds of models, photos, and restored airplanes, from the Montgolfier brothers' hot-air-balloon ride in 1783 to today's space-exploring astronauts. The museum is open daily between 10 A.M. and 4:30 P.M. in the off season and 10 A.M. to 5:30 P.M. between Memorial Day and Labor Day.

Spreckels Organ Pavilion

Home to the world's largest outdoor instrument, Spreckels Organ Pavilion was gifted to San Diego by brothers John D. and Adolf Spreckels in preparation for the 1915 Panama-California Exposition. Built by the Austin Organ Company, this impressive musical behemoth is made up of more than 4,500 pipes. Protected from the elements by the ornate Italian Renaissance–style pavilion and surrounded by bench seating for 2,400 listeners, the organ is played regularly for park visitors. Free concerts are held every Sunday at 2 P.M. and on summer Mondays at 7:30 P.M. seats are filled for the annual International Organ Festival.

In addition, the stage hosts a Twilight in the Park Concert Series in the summer on Tuesday, Wednesday, and Thursday at 6:15 P.M. Visit the Balboa Park website (www.balboapark.org) for specifics.

Gardens

Balboa Park is replete with plantlife of all shapes, sizes, and colors. The flora here is so verdant it seems that the park has its own little ecological system, especially in contrast to the native scrubs that cling to surrounding hillsides and mesas. In addition to the abundance of decorative plants that surround the park's structures, there are over fifteen official gardens.

Balboa Park's gardens are unsurpassed.

© ERICKA CHICKOWSKI

Most famous among them is the collection of plants in the **Botanical Building** (10 A.M.–4 P.M. Fri.–Wed., free), which sits behind the park's renowned Lily Pond. If you've got a taste for ironic humor, step back and snap a shot of the throngs of photographers that line up on the weekends to capture the beauty of the pond and building—this is one of the most photographed landscapes in the entire park. It is no wonder; it really is a lovely spot.

Kids will love to watch the koi float lazily through the pond, couples can cuddle on the expansive lawn nearby, and garden lovers will enjoy a walk through the building, which is home to more than 2,100 permanent plants. Some of the highlights include an impressive orchid collection, numerous ferns and palms, and a really fun touch-and-smell herbal garden. My favorite scent is the chocolate basil.

Those in a more meditative mood can escape the crowds at the **Japanese Friendship Garden.** Sitting at the edge of a canyon by the Spreckels Organ Pavilion grounds, this garden charges a nominal $3 fee, which tends to keep traffic down a bit. The garden path is lined with bamboo, Japanese ornamentals, a koi pond, and bonsai. The centerpiece of the grounds is a serene Zen Garden. The garden is viewable from the exhibit house, which features a collection of Japanese art. The gardens also have a *shishi odoshi*, a traditional Japanese fountain made of bamboo tubes that pivot up and down as they fill up and empty themselves through the effects of water flow and gravity.

Located at the entrance, this can be a particular favorite for curious toddlers.

From the friendship garden, cross the organ pavilion grounds to find a living oasis right in the park. **Palm Canyon** contains more than 58 species of palm trees—nearly 500 trees in all. Many of them were the original Mexican fan palms planted by Kate Sessions in 1912.

There's a nice trail there that links up the canyon to a small cactus garden, but for a real

KATE O. SESSIONS: MOTHER OF BALBOA PARK

San Diego wasn't always as lush and flowerful as it is today. Very little except low scrubs and succulents grow naturally here. The city owes a great deal of gratitude for the greenery to Kate O. Sessions, an enterprising botanist that many consider the first lady of gardening in San Diego. Many of the trees and gardens she planted over 100 years ago still grow strong, providing shade and shelter today.

An independent and progressive woman, Sessions was a feminist ahead of her time. While studying for her science degree at University of California–Berkeley in 1881, she wrote an essay titled "The Natural Sciences as a Field for Woman's Labor." This was about a hundred years before Women's Studies was established at Berkeley.

She moved to San Diego a few years after graduation, part of the tidal wave of San Franciscans headed south due to Alonzo Horton's promotion of the area, and started her love affair with horticulture when she partnered with some friends in 1885 to buy the San Diego Nursery.

From there Sessions threw herself into the business of growing plants, owning a number of nurseries all over the city and corresponding with many horticulturalists around the state and the country through published articles and letters. Her studies helped her pinpoint flora that would work in this clime and she introduced many of the popular plants that remain in San Diego today: the bright red bougainvillea, fragrant star jasmine, bird of paradise, and numerous shady trees such as the Brazilian pepper tree, banyan, and Italian cypress.

In 1892, she brokered a deal with the city to become City Gardner. The city agreed to lease her land for a nursery within Balboa Park, then called "City Park," if she would plant 100 trees per year on park land and supply the city with 300 more to plant around town. Sessions more than lived up to her end of the bargain and she personally worked the soil to lay the groundwork for Balboa's amazing gardens

Together with Mary B. Coulston and George Marston (whose gorgeous Arts and Crafts home is a museum at the park today), Sessions formed the park improvement committee in order to take her stewardship one step farther. This civic work combined with her gardening has earned her the title "Mother of Balboa Park" in the annals of San Diego History. A statue in her honor can be found just in front of the Cabrillo Bridge at the Laurel Avenue entrance to the park.

Sessions was determined to help her legacy of a green San Diego to live on. After garnering the appointment to be supervisor of agriculture and landscaper for city schools in 1915, she went about educating the next generation of gardeners by teaching students about horticulture. Together with the children she helped develop gardens at schools throughout the city.

Sessions' work in the city and her involvement in the horticulture world at large made the scientific community take notice of her achievements. Just a year before her death in 1940 she was given the Frank N. Meyer Medal from the American Genetic Association, becoming the first woman recipient of the honor.

succulent treat, you'll have to venture over the pedestrian bridge that arches over Park Boulevard. There you'll be greeted by the sight of an amazing collection of desert flora. This two-and-a-half-acre park, **Desert Garden,** has over 1,300 succulents and cacti.

For a more traditional form of beauty, **Inez Grant Parker Memorial Rose Garden** is right next to Desert Garden. San Diego's weather is ideal for many varieties of roses, and this particular garden features over 200 variations. The groundskeepers keep excellent care of the plants and they've been honored by having the garden distinguished as an All America Rose Selection Display Garden. The roses bloom nearly all year, but the peak time to visit is in April and May. You don't even have to stop and smell the flowers then—the scent surrounds you as you crunch along the gravel paths.

Other Museums

The **Reuben H. Fleet Science Center** (1875 El Prado, 619/238-1233, www.rhfleet .org, 9:30 A.M.–5 P.M. Mon.–Thurs., 9:30 A.M.–9 P.M. Fri., 9:30 A.M.–8 P.M. Sat., 9:30 A.M.–6 P.M. Sun., $8 adults, $6.75 seniors and children 3–12) gives weary parents a break from yelling out "Don't touch that!" every five seconds. The hands-on science exhibits here encourage visitors to learn through interaction. One of the special favorites in the permanent exhibit is the Tornado, a mini wind funnel that visitors can put their hands through and experiment with to learn about the larger natural phenomenon.

Located right next to the visitors center along El Prado, the **Museum of Photographic Arts** (1649 El Prado, 619/238-7559, www .mopa.org, 10 A.M.–5 P.M. Tues.–Sun., until 9 P.M. Thurs., $6 adults, $4 students, seniors and military, free kids under 12) holds a diverse collection of 4,000 photographs that span the spectrum of photographic medium, including daguerreotypes, salt prints, Woodbury types, albumen prints, ambrotypes, and tintypes, through such contemporary processes as 20- by 24-inch Polaroid photographs and laser holograms. This permanent collection is

augmented by an always inspirational rotation of traveling exhibits.

A product of the Japanese words *min* (all people) and *gei* (art), *mingei* is a term used to describe "arts of the people." The **Mingei International Museum** (1439 El Prado, 619/239-0003, www.mingei.org, 10 A.M.– 4 P.M. Tues.–Sun., $6 adults, $4 seniors, $3 students, military, and children ages 6–17) features revolving exhibitions of folk arts and crafts that reflect the culture of people from around the world and throughout time.

Across El Prado from the Mingei is one of the architectural highlights of the park, the colorful and ornate **California Building.** Punctuated by the 200-foot California Tower and the dome decorated in blue and white floral tiling, the building has been described as historically impure because of its jumble of architectural references, with elements of Spanish Plateresque, baroque, rococo, and Mexican Ultrabaroque, or Churrigueresque, adorning every cornice and crevice of the building's facade. I say, "Churri-What?" Whatever the mishmash style is, the building is a masterpiece.

When the building opened in 1915 for the Panama-California Exposition it housed an exhibit called "The Story of Man." Today the tradition of anthropological exhibits within the building continues with the **San Diego Museum of Man** (1350 El Prado, 619/239-2001, www.museumofman.org, 10 A.M.–4:30 P.M. daily, $8 adults, $6 students, seniors, and military, $4 ages 6–17, free kids under 6).

The **San Diego Model Railroad Museum** (1649 El Prado, 619/696-0199, www.sdmodel railroadm.com, 11 A.M.–4 P.M. Tues.–Fri., 11 A.M.–5 P.M. Sat.–Sun., $6 adults, $5 seniors, $3 students, free children under 15) is a secret little treasure that offers a fascinating and comprehensive collection. There are very realistic train models in several scales, as well as miniature landscapes of San Diego County to run them on. It is a well-curated setup that is a pleasure even for museumgoers who have had absolutely zero experience with model trains.

Beware—drop a car buff inside the **San Diego Automotive Museum** (2080 Pan

SAN DIEGO

American Plaza, 619/231-2886, www.sdauto museum.com, 10 A.M.–5 P.M. daily, $8 adults, $6 seniors and military, $4 children 6–15, free under age 6) and they might disappear forever. This amazing collection of restored vehicles and memorabilia covers seemingly every trend in auto history, from Model T Speedsters to high-octane muscle cars.

Housed in the old chapel of the Naval Hospital on Inspiration Point, the **Veterans Museum and Memorial Center** (2115 Park Blvd., 619/239-2300, www.sdvmc.org, 9:30 A.M.– 3 P.M. Tues.–Sat.) pays tribute to men and women of all branches of the armed forces who served the United States in time of war. The setting is fitting considering how many in the military remember San Diego only by the hospital, which has continuously operated from its facilities next to Balboa Park for more than 80 years. The museum's collection dates from the Civil War through the present, with exhibits on World War I, World War II and Pearl Harbor, the Korea and Vietnam conflicts, Desert Storm, and women in the military. It also displays a number of very evocative military paintings by local artists and veterans.

If you make the trek to the northwest corner of the park you'll find a pristine example of the Arts and Crafts architectural movement that swept the city at the turn of the 20th century. The **Marston House** (3525 7th Ave., 619/298-3142, www.sandiegohistory .org, $5) is a Craftsman mansion built in 1905 for prominent San Diego civic leader George Marston and his wife, Anna. A progressive innovator, Marston was a founder and the first president of the San Diego Historical Society, an important supporter of Balboa Park development, and even could be called the city's first environmentalist politician. In 1917 he ran for mayor under the "Smokestacks vs. Geraniums" platform, rallying to balance industrial and environmental concerns. These ideals were probably what attracted him to the Arts and Crafts philosophy, which was a backlash against the lavish excesses of the gilded Victorian era. The architect Marston commissioned for this house was a young Irving Gill, who would go on to

become one of Southern California's most well-regarded modern architects. The house is run by the San Diego Historical Society and is only open through guided tours held Friday through Sunday at 10 A.M., 11 A.M., 1 P.M., 2 P.M., and 3 P.M.

Hillcrest

The epicenter of San Diego's gay and lesbian community, Hillcrest is cultured, urbane, and just a little bit cheeky. Set in the canyons and mesas northeast of Balboa Park, this vibrant neighborhood is a kaleidoscopic patchwork of cozy art-house theaters, naughty leather shops, elegant cafés, vintage bookstores, and swanky night spots. Side streets are a fun maze of canyon dead ends and meandering hillside lanes sprinkled with Victorian mansions and Craftsman cottages. The main drags here are **University Avenue** and **Washington Street,** around which most of the neighborhood's best independent restaurants and boutiques are clustered.

Hillcrest has long been an open-minded and welcoming community. Even though it is strongly identified with the gay and lesbian community, straight couples needn't worry that the proverbial record will screech to a halt when they walk arm-in-arm down the street. All are welcome and none are judged here.

MISSION VALLEY AND OLD TOWN
◖ Old Town State Historic Park
Before Alonzo Horton managed to swing development three miles west to his newly built wharf and adjacent tracts of land by San Diego Bay, the town wasn't much more than a dusty pueblo at the foot of Presidio Hill. Horton's movement to transplant the town from this area led to the creation of "New Town" San Diego, now downtown San Diego.

What was left behind is still called Old Town, an area whose history is commemorated by many reconstructed buildings and a few originals within Old Town San Diego State Historic Park (San Diego Ave. at Twiggs St., 619/220-5422, www.parks

SAN DIEGO

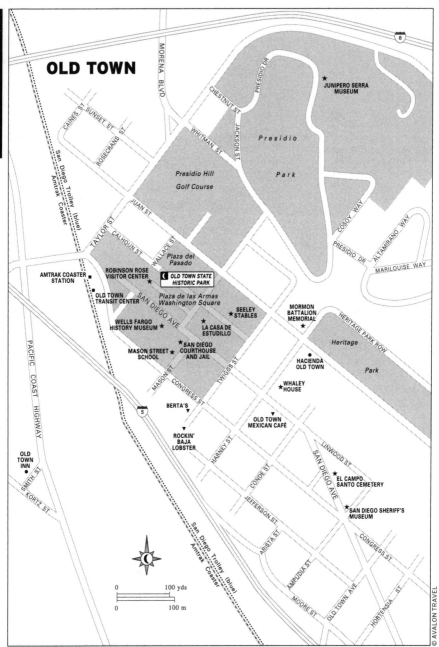

OLD TOWN

MORENA BLVD

CAINES ST
SUNSET ST
ROSECRANS ST

WHITMAN ST

CHESTNUT ST

JACKSON ST

PRESIDIO DR

★ JUNIPERO SERRA MUSEUM

Presidio

Park

San Diego Trolley (blue)
Amtrak Coaster

Presidio Hill

Golf Course

JUAN ST

TAYLOR ST

CALHOUN ST

WALLACE ST

Plaza del Pasado

COSOY WAY

PRESIDIO DR

ALTAMIRANO WAY

MARILOUISE WAY

AMTRAK COASTER STATION

ROBINSON ROSE VISITOR CENTER ★

■ OLD TOWN TRANSIT CENTER

■ OLD TOWN STATE HISTORIC PARK

SAN DIEGO AVE

Plaza de las Armas
Washington Square

★ SEELEY STABLES

MORMON BATTALION MEMORIAL ★

HERITAGE PARK ROW

WELLS FARGO HISTORY MUSEUM ★

★ LA CASA DE ESTUDILLO

Heritage

Park

MASON STREET SCHOOL ★

★ SAN DIEGO COURTHOUSE AND JAIL

TWIGGS ST

● HACIENDA OLD TOWN

MASON ST

CONGRESS ST

▼ WHALEY HOUSE

PACIFIC COAST HIGHWAY

I-5

BERTA'S ▼

LINWOOD ST

▼ ROCKIN' BAJA LOBSTER

HARNEY ST

▼ OLD TOWN MEXICAN CAFÉ

SAN DIEGO AVE

OLD TOWN INN ●

SMITH ST

KORTZ ST

CONDE ST

★ EL CAMPO SANTO CEMETERY

JEFFERSON ST

★ SAN DIEGO SHERIFF'S MUSEUM

CONGRESS ST

San Diego Trolley (blue)
Amtrak Coaster

ARISTA ST

AMPUDIA ST

OLD TOWN AVE

HORTENSIA ST

MOORE ST

0   100 yds

0   100 m

© AVALON TRAVEL

© ERICKA CHICKOWSKI

Casa de Estudillo in Old Town State Historic Park

.ca.gov, 10 A.M.–5 P.M. daily, free). The complex celebrates the town's Californio and early American heritage through museum displays and old-timey shops.

Most of the park's buildings are clustered around grassy Washington Square. To get your bearings and to bone up on the history of Old Town, stop by **Robinson-Rose House Visitor Center** at the northeast edge of the square. Directly across the square from the visitors center is **Casa de Estudillo,** a classic adobe hacienda. If you are short on time, or if you are in the company of children who get antsy after one too many historic sites, make a visit to Casa de Estudillo your highest priority. This building was rebuilt in 1910 and features rooms with period furnishings and an authentic garden to give visitors a feel for how Old Town's first Californio residents lived.

Other historic buildings that surround the square include the Colorado House, which is home to the fascinating **Wells Fargo Museum,** a replica of the first **San Diego Courthouse and Jail,** and the **Mason Street Schoolhouse,** a one-room shack that was built in 1865 as the area's first public school.

Be sure to cap off your tour of Old Town with a visit to the **Seely Stables Museum.** This is a reconstruction of an 1850 stage stop in the San Diego to Los Angeles Stage Line, run by Albert Seely until it was put out of business by the railroad in 1887. The museum sports a collection of antique carriages and other odds and ends related to stage travel.

The state park runs free guided tours of Old Town State Historic Park at 11 A.M. and 2 P.M. every day. The tour departs from the Robinson-Rose House Visitor Center and will give you a rich understanding of the cultural and historical background of San Diego's oldest community.

Presidio Park

Though the Spanish had discovered San Diego first in 1542 by way of Portuguese explorer Juan Cabrillo, and then by Sebastián Vizcaíno in 1602, its preoccupation with the settlement of mainland Mexico and Baja California kept it from establishing roots farther north for more than a century after that.

By 1769, though, Spanish leaders worried about the encroachment of Russian fur traders from Alaska down the west coast of the continent. Combined with the success of the English colonies on the east coast, these factors made them fear that they would lose possession of the west coast if they did not establish settlements quickly. That year the king ordered four expeditions up to San Diego in order to start the development of missions and settlements in Alta California.

Two expeditions were by sea, the other two by land. The most famous of the four was that of Gaspar de Portolá, who would eventually become the first governor of Alta California, and Father Junípero Serra, the priest responsible for establishing a system of missions that would form the backbone of Spanish colonies in Alta California. The pair led a party that journeyed through the desert and scrubland of Baja California from La Paz up to San Diego to become the first group to make it to the area.

Serra officially established San Diego's first mission by planting a cross atop Presidio Hill and saying Mass. Overlooking San Diego Bay, the hill would become the main military installation for early San Diego as well as the mission's first home.

Today the site is a public park that honors these first Spanish settlers. The 49-acre Presidio Park (2811 Jackson St., 619/692-4918) still has great views of the bay on clear days and plenty of grassy spots to sit and look out.

It is also home to the **Junípero Serra Museum** (2727 Presidio Dr., www.sandiego history.org, 619/297-3258, 10 A.M.–4:30 P.M. daily, $5), a historical museum run by the San Diego Historical Society that displays artifacts from Native American, Spanish, Mexican, and American periods through 1929. The museum is housed in a bright-white distinctive mission-style building that can be spotted from I-8 as you drive through Mission Valley.

In addition to cruising through the museum, park visitors can attend an outdoor tour of Presidio Park that is lead by park rangers every second Sunday of the month from 1 P.M. to 2 P.M. These tours meet in front of the Serra Museum and are free of charge.

Whaley House

The Whaley House (2476 San Diego Ave., 619/297-7511, www.whaleyhouse.org, 10 A.M.–5 P.M. Mon.–Tues., 10 A.M.–10 P.M. Thurs.–Sun.) is as well known to paranormal investigators as it is to historians. Named the Most Haunted House in America by the Travel Channel, this brick structure is as much a part of the fabric of Old Town as the state park itself.

It was built in 1857 by Thomas Whaley for his wife, Anna, and their young family. Whaley was one of the most prominent entrepreneurs and civic leaders of Old Town and he and his family lived in the house off and on through 1953. In that time the house also doubled as a granary, a city courthouse, and Old Town's first commercial theater and a polling place.

The site is said to be haunted by numerous spirits. Prior to the building's construction it was home to Old Town's gallows and the ghosts of some of the area's most notorious criminals are said to be living here. Even early on the Whaleys were frightened by mysterious heavy footsteps that they believed belonged to a criminal named "Yankee" Jim Robinson whom Thomas had seen hang at the plot years before he bought it.

The home itself saw more than its fair share of tragic deaths under its roof as well. Just a year after the house was built, young Thomas Jr. died at the age of 18 months. Years later, daughter Violet shot herself here in 1885 after a scandalous divorce. Anna, son Francis, and daughter Lillian also all died while living in the house.

The house is restored as it was in the late 1860s and has extended hours between June and September, during the first week in April, and the last two weeks of December, when it is open daily 10 A.M.–10 P.M. Cost of admission is $6 for adults, $5 for seniors age 55 and over, $4 for children ages 3–12, and free to toddlers under 3.

Campo Santo Cemetery

Steps away from the haunted house is another

SAN DIEGO HAUNTS

No historic city worth its weight in ectoplasm can make it through a few centuries of existence without accumulating its fair share of resident spooks and spirits. Never one to be left out of the hauntings, San Diego bills itself as the home of the "Most Haunted House in America" and enough other paranormal sites to keep both believers and skeptics arguing about their veracity until they become ghosts themselves.

WHALEY HOUSE

Dubbed as the "Most Haunted House in America" by the Travel Channel, this brick structure spooked the Whaley family way back in 1857 when they first moved in. They heard mysterious heavy footsteps upstairs, which they later believed to be an outlaw who was hanged on the property before they owned it – the land had served as the town gallows. Since that time a number of tragic deaths on the site have only added more ghostly stories to the Whaley House mystique over the years.

EL CAMPO SANTO

One of the earliest recorded graveyards in the city, El Campo Santo is believed to be haunted by the spirits of those whose graves were paved over by the adjacent San Diego Avenue. Just a block away from the Whaley House, this is many ghost investigators' second most favorite place to wave around tape recorders and EMF meters on moonless nights.

OLD POINT LOMA LIGHTHOUSE

Perched atop the Point Loma Peninsula at the Cabrillo National Monument, this lighthouse is the site of a controversial haunting – even steadfast paranormal believers quibble over the spirit that supposedly resides here. Skeptics say that the lighthouse was never the site of any kind of tragedy or trauma that would invite a haunting, but others are adamant about seeing the ghost of a forlorn sailor on the property.

HOTEL DEL CORONADO

Like any good old hotel, the Del has its share of hauntings. There are reports of cold spots,

Star of India, **the world's oldest active ship**

© JOANNE DIBONA/SAN DIEGO CVB

flickering lights, a general sense of dread, and even indentations in pillows – like someone's head is resting there – that won't go away even after fluffing. The hotel's best-known ghost is thought to be that of Kate Morgan, an Iowa girl who turned up dead here in 1892. Officially ruled a suicide, her body was found on the steps leading to the beach, a bullet wound in her head.

STAR OF INDIA

Sitting on the docks of the Embarcadero as a part of the Maritime Museum of San Diego, *Star of India* is the world's oldest active ship and her sometimes tragic history is studded with deaths on the high seas. For example, in 1868 her captain died while the ship was underway. Some visitors say they've smelled phantom scents and seen apparitions while aboard.

HORTON GRAND

Guests who have stayed in room 309 at Horton Grand have reported the bed shaking, unexplained opening and closing of armoire doors, and unearthly movement of objects. The paranormal activity is believed to be the work of Robert Whitaker. Legend has it that this cheating gambler of the mid-1800s was caught one night and his accuser followed him to his room at what was then the Kale Saddlery Hotel and shot him over the dispute. Guests in other rooms have reported hearing shuffling cards coming from inside room 309 when it was unoccupied.

Old Town site popular with area paranormal investigators. Campo Santo Cemetery (2410 San Diego Ave.) is San Diego's oldest existing cemetery and is the final resting place for both the prominent and the unknown among original Old Town citizens.

Pay your respects to Yankee Jim, who was buried here after hanging at the Whaley House lot, Antonio Garra, a Cupeño Indian who was actually executed at the cemetery for having led an insurrection over the taxation of local tribes, and numerous members of prominent Californio families such as the Machados, Estudillos, and Aguirres.

On your way in, look down at the sidewalk and street in front of the gate. There you'll see little brass dots scattered around. These are the only markers left to acknowledge the graves that were built over when a street-car line was built on the site of present-day San Diego Avenue and that continued to lay in anonymity until the 1980s. Rather than re-inter the bodies, city leaders chose to leave them here. The community has tried to make amends with these markers, which were placed after locating burial sites via ground-penetrating radar. Ghost hunters suspect that this token gesture of respect to the dead was not enough to quell the spirits who are rumored to lurk in the area. Legends live on of misty vapors, cold spots, and car troubles that have been reported by those unlucky enough to park above the graves that remain.

Other Old Town Museums

A few blocks north of the state park stands a museum that chronicles the 150-year history of the San Diego Sheriff's Department. The **San Diego Sheriff's Museum** (2384 San Diego Ave., 619/260-1850, www.sheriff museum.org, 10 A.M.–4 P.M. Tues.–Sat., free) is at the site of Old Town's first cobblestone jail, which was replaced early on by the iron cage behind the first courthouse after a high-profile escape. Now the Sheriff's Department runs the museum, harboring an assortment of guns, badges, communication equipment, a patrol car, helicopter, and other mementos of law enforcement history.

Also in the Old Town neighborhood is **Heritage Park** (2454 Heritage Park Row, 619/291-9784), a nearly eight-acre piece of land that features some of the city's finest examples of Victorian architecture. The county park was the product of preservation efforts by local public and private groups to save important historical buildings in the downtown area that were set to be demolished in the wake of development. Seven different houses and buildings were moved to this park, with architectural flourishes in the Stick Eastlake, Classic Revival, Queen Anne, and Italianate styles.

Another interesting side trip from the state park is to take a short walk over to the **Mormon Battalion Historic Site** (2510 Juan St., 619/298-3317, www.mormonbattalion .com), which honors 500 Mormon men who marched 2,000 miles from Iowa to San Diego in order to help fight in the Mexican-American War. This was the only religious unit to ever be formed by the U.S. military and was one of the longest marches in military history. By the time they arrived in San Diego the tide of war had turned in favor of the Americans, but this band of troops carried out a number of civic improvement projects in Southern California in the months after their arrival.

◖ Mission San Diego de Alcalá

California's very first mission, Mission San Diego de Alcalá (10818 San Diego Mission Rd., 619/283-7319, www.missionsandiego .com, 9 A.M.–4:45 P.M. daily, free), stands along the San Diego River basin in the heart of Mission Valley. The buildings were reconstructed in 1931, when the mission was but a whisper of its former self after years of disuse and neglect.

The exterior is white-washed adobe, accented by a distinctive five-bell *campañario* and a surrounding complex that includes gardens, a rectory, and a smaller chapel. Inside the main church are high wooden ceilings supported by timber beams decorated with delicate hand paintings. The ornate altar and many of the walls also have these hand-painted embellishments and are decorated with recessed reredos holding beautiful sculptures of holy figures.

Visitors are invited to walk the grounds any time and to visit the church interior when Mass is not being said. There is also a small museum and a gift shop on the property.

NORTH CITY
◖ Mission Trails Regional Park
At over 5,800 acres, Mission Trails Regional Park is one of the largest urban parks in the country and offers visitors a taste of what San Diego was like before the metropolitan areas were built up and out into the surrounding mountains.

Rocky crags and chaparral sprawl across the hills and valleys of Mission Trails and there are plenty of opportunities to explore by foot, bike, or horseback. Before heading out, learn a little about the nature and history of the park at the **visitors center** (One Fr. Junipero Serra Trail, 619/668-3281, www.mtrp.com).

If time is limited, the signature expedition in Mission Trails is a trek up **Cowles Mountain,** the highest peak within city limits at 1,591 feet. The way to the top is steep but the reward for bagging this peak is a panoramic view of the city that on a clear day will grant you vistas of Point Loma, downtown San Diego, and even Mexico to the south. Remember which trail you hiked up—there are two trails and if you don't take the same one back you are in for a boring walk through surrounding neighborhoods back to the car.

Flying Leathernecks Museum
Flying to give close support to grunts on the ground, the squadrons of the Marine Aircraft Wings have a long tradition of heroism that dates back to World War I. San Diego has a special link with these flying leathernecks as the home of the Marine Corps Air Bases Western Area headquarters at Marine Corps Air Station (MCAS) Miramar.

Those interested in the history of the aviators and the aircraft that built the marine flight program should definitely wander over to Miramar to take a look at the Flying Leathernecks Museum (T-4203, Anderson Ave., 877/359-8762, www.flyingleathernecks.org, 9 A.M.–3:30 P.M. Tues.–Sun., free). This is the only museum in the country dedicated to Marine Corps Aviation and it features a patriotic collection of memorabilia, uniforms, and documents highlighting the rise of the flying leatherneck. Be sure to check out the more than 20 restored helicopters, fighter planes, and jets on display, as well as the museum's unique exhibit on women in the marines.

Entertainment and Events

The velvet rope of San Diego extends mostly around the Gaslamp Quarter, but there are plenty of bars and cafés for all temperaments throughout the city. San Diego also has a thriving music scene (particularly punk). Notable bands to make their start in San Diego include Blink-182, Rocket from the Crypt, Pinback, Jason Mraz, and Jewel. Visitors can check out the next big thing at one of the city's many intimate venues.

NIGHTLIFE
Live Music
If you're the type of music fan who likes to brag about having seen such-and-such of a famous band back in the day, then the **Casbah** (2501 Kettner Blvd., 619/232-4355, www.casbah music.com) is your kind of place. This spot has been welcoming up-and-comers and cult favorites since Nirvana was cutting its teeth on the small-venue circuit. Grunge's flannel has been replaced by emo's skinny jeans, but Casbah remains as relevant now as it was nearly two decades ago.

Music purists hate it for the corporate influence, but **House of Blues** (1055 5th Ave., 619/299-2583, www.hob.com) really is one of the better venues in the city. The main hall has two stories in order to keep the drinkers happy and still invite the under-21 crowd. There's

FAMOUS SAN DIEGO BANDS

San Diegans love their music. Their loyalty – and eclectic tastes – has helped support a homegrown crop of performers who keep venues large and small thumping with a healthy mix of tunes.

The scene here is best known for its punk and ska influences – this is where Blink-182 got its start as a hard-edged punk band before toning it down for mainstream popularity, and where cult favorite Rocket from the Crypt kept true to those roots for fifteen years of sold-out shows until retirement in 2005. But San Diego is far from a one-trick pony. It is also where singer-songwriter Jewel made her big break – story goes that she was living in her van in the town's beach communities just to keep things going between coffeehouse shows.

When you are in town, check the *San Diego Reader* or *CityBeat* for upcoming shows from the following bands.

B-SIDE PLAYERS

Best described as Latin Reggae, the music of B-Side Players throbs with the thumping rhythm of percussion, horns, and throaty vocals belting a mix of English and Spanish lyrics. The crew can be seen at a range of small to large venues while on its own turf and are a particular favorite at local music festivals.

BUCK-OH-NINE

Now that Rocket from the Crypt has called it quits, Buck-Oh-Nine has taken over as the granddaddy of San Diego's punk scene. This band verges more toward the ska end of the spectrum, though. Shows put up a frenetic field of energy – be prepared with some closed-toe shoes and the resignation that your ears will ring the next morning.

A. J. CROCE

Son of folk legend Jim Croce, this eclectic musician has made a name for himself with his diverse mix of jazz, blues, and funk. He's opened for a number of headliners such as Dave Matthews, James Brown, and Carlos Santana on the worldwide circuit, but his most comfortable and welcoming shows are still held where he first soaked up the limelight – on the small stage at Croce's, his mom's venue in the Gaslamp Quarter.

LOUIS XIV

Think "Ziggy Stardust"-era David Bowie and you've got this band's MO in a nutshell. Its worship at the altar of '70s-era British glam rock eccentricity extends down all the way to the tight pants and heavy eyeliner. The group regularly plays arena shows around the country, but will pay tribute to its local roots by playing a few smaller venues while in town.

ANYA MARINA

Known simply as Anya to the thousands of listeners who tune in every afternoon to hear her spin tunes on the popular alternative station KBTZ (FM 94.9), Marina is a solid musician in her own right. Her girlish voice

also a side-stage room that features many of the city's emerging rockers. Both have the best sound quality in the city.

If your favorite band is coming to **4th and B** (345 B St., 619/299-2583), then by all means attend the show. But don't bother taking a gamble on an unknown band for the sake of this so-so venue. Also owned by House of Blues, this facility is the inferior cousin to the main HOB venue. The one major upside is that it brings in a pretty eclectic lineup of acts, from comedy to "Xtreme" cage fighting and every genre of music in between.

Located in a humble space within a former warehouse near the Gaslamp, **Dizzy's** (344 7th Ave., 858/270-7467, www.dizzysandiego.com) is focused on one thing and one thing only: the music. There is no bar or restaurant or fancy lighting. Just a stage, intimate seating, and a soft spot for jazz and blues.

Croce's Jazz Bar (802 5th Ave., 619/232-2891, www.croces.com) is another spot in the Gaslamp for those hoping to sit in on a good charms the socks off of her avid fans, who are partial to her smart lyrics and proficiency with a guitar pick.

JASON MRAZ

An East Coast native, Jason Mraz was adopted by San Diegans long before his honey-sweet voice, crackling acoustic guitar licks, and cheeky stage persona stormed into the mainstream music community. Mraz made his name playing coffee shops and tiny venues in town. Even touched by fame, he still thanks the region that helped vault him to stardom by frequently playing local festivals and smaller shows when he's back relaxing at his pad in North County.

PINBACK

This two-man indie rock band is still building nationwide appeal, but in its hometown Pinback is frequently greeted by sold-out crowds full of loyal followers. Its music is known for complex bass lines and captivating hooks. The group fleshes out its sound during live shows by adding a few extra bandmates.

SPRUNG MONKEY

This band flirted with serious national attention with a couple of memorable radio-friendly singles in the late '90s. Music-label bungles and promotional limbo held the group back from major exposure, but it still kept doing its own thing here in San Diego. Since then its influences have made a sharp turn toward more hard-core influences, with an equal measure of punk and metal working its way into its small-venue showings.

REEVE OLIVER

This trio is a San Diego darling on an ascending star that keeps rising by the minute. Self-described as indie rock, the band is now signed to a major label (Capitol). Its success is based in part on the tunes (a bit of Weezer meets Jimmy Eat World) and the band members' incredible work ethic. It seems like they play damned near every weekend at some venue or another around the county. If you get a chance, go. Their music plays well in front of a crowd.

ROOKIE CARD

A blend of funky new-wave country, alternative rock, and a little something you can't put your finger on, Rookie Card has been flummoxing band labelers since they busted onto the local scene in 2003. Whatever it is, it's good stuff and very much worth the cheap entrance to the typical small venues the band plays around town.

SWITCHFOOT

This alternative band has managed to make it big without alienating fans, with an accessible pop rhythm balanced with just enough of an edge to keep the music snobs from branding it a "sell-out." These days its shows are mostly at the arenas.

---

jam session. Located within the popular restaurant run by Ingrid, the widow of folk legend Jim Croce, this venue has been welcoming nightly acts since the 1980s. Traditional, contemporary, and Latin jazz are all part of the scene here, with a little blues thrown in for good measure. Shows usually start at 8:30 P.M. and run through 1:30 A.M.

With such a healthy contingent of hard-core skaters and surfers, this town has always been a hotbed of creativity for the punk, ska, and hardcore metal community. You can catch punk shows in all of the mainstream venues around town, but one particular underground favorite for these kinds of performances is **Brick by Brick** (1130 Buenos Ave., 619/275-5483, www.brickbybrick.com).

Rockabillies, goths, and punks, oh my! **Zombie Lounge** (3519 El Cajon Blvd., 619/284-3323, 8 P.M.–2 A.M. daily) has all of 'em, luring them in with a frenetic mix of shows. Once just a jukebox joint, this bar added live music into already cramped quarters, so expect to press the flesh a bit. If you've ever owned a can of pomade or have cut your bangs like Bettie Page then don't worry, you're in familiar company.

One of the largest live music venues in the county, **Cox Arena** (5500 Campanile Dr., 619/594-6947, www.cox-arena.com) is the place to go for big-name artists and music festivals. The arena is on campus at San Diego State University, so parking and traffic can be a real nightmare—try taking the trolley, which has a large station right on campus. SDSU also plays host to smaller acts on the more intimate stage in its **Open Air Theatre** (5500 Campanile Dr., 619/594-6947).

Gaslamp Quarter Clubs

Stingaree was the not-so-nice nickname city residents had for the district of bordellos located within the Gaslamp during the late 1800s. Today, the club **Stingaree** (454 6th Ave., 619/544-9500, www.stingsandiego.com, 9:30 P.M.–2 A.M. Fri. and Sat., 1–9 P.M. Sun.) has taken the same name to pay homage to the saucy ladies that first rouged their cheeks and flaunted their bodies on nearby streets. Far classier than the red-light district the building sat in so long ago, this place still offers the ghost of debauchery to modern clientele. Skirts are short, rouge still abounds, and booze flows freely. Ask how much a girl costs for the night, though, and risk a drink to the face. The club offers three levels of entertainment and dancing, but some of its most notable amenities are the rooftop cabanas, which can be rented for the evening along with bottle service—if you are willing to part with upwards of $350.

Right across the street from Stingaree within the Hotel Solamar is **Jbar** (616 J St., 619/531-8744, noon–2 A.M. daily), a trendy rooftop watering hole that attracts a similar set of hipsters who might be a little more intent on lounging than dancing for the evening. The bar is set by the poolside and lushly padded lounge chairs and patio tables are scattered about for those looking for a leisurely drink and an appetizer while the night is still young.

The parties aren't all on rooftops, either. The subterranean hot spot **Belo** (919 4th Ave.,

619/231-9200, www.belosandiego.com, 7 P.M.–4 A.M. Fri., 7 P.M.–2 A.M. Sat.) is a super-swank club with retro 1960s decorative accents that is a haven for fans of trance and house music. It regularly brings in big-name DJs such as Paul Oakenfold to spin for the night.

On Broadway (615 Broadway, 619/231-0011, www.obec.tv, 9 P.M.–2 A.M. Thurs.–Sat.) offers clubgoers a little less pretension and a lot of space to kick up their heels. The multiroom disco features a wide array of music and fickle clubgoers can spend hours hopping from room to room to find the right atmosphere to get down with their bad selves. The club is set within a former bank. Be sure to check out the huge vault door that acts as the centerpiece of the club's lower level. Like many clubs in the Gaslamp the major downside to this place is the cover charge—$20 or more on some nights—but you can often dodge the bullet by either arriving early or dropping some greenbacks at the very tasty sushi restaurant on premises.

Named for its architecture, **Deco's** (731 5th Ave., 619/696-3326, 9 P.M.–1:30 A.M. Thurs., 6 P.M.–1:30 A.M. Fri.–Sat.) was built to resemble the South Beach clubs in Miami. Though this place aspires to achieve the same upscale vibe as some of its Gaslamp neighbors, the crowd is more hip-hop than hipster. This may partially be due to the current and old-school rap that plays heavy in the rotation on all of the dance floors. However, this unpretentious club can be a thankful relief when your neighbors are putting on airs somewhere else.

Bring your dancing shoes, because at **Café Sevilla** (555 4th Ave., 619/233-5979, www.cafesevilla.com, 5–12 P.M. Sun.–Thurs., 5–1 A.M. Fri.–Sat.) you're probably gonna need 'em. The club is the best place in town to shake those hips to the beat of salsa and merengue, featuring live Latin bands at least three nights a week. If watching is your fetish, then consider coming out to the café's restaurant on Friday and Sunday nights, when it features a dinner show that includes a three-course Spanish meal and an authentic flamenco dance performance.

Bars

Aussie Aussie Aussie! Oi oi oi! The Australian owners of **Bondi Bar and Kitchen** (333 5th Ave., 619/342-0212, www.thebondi.com, 8 A.M.–2 A.M.) have poured their love of their homeland into this fresh and lively hangout in the Gaslamp. The selection of Australian beers on tap is unsurpassed in Southern California and the environs make it a great place to sit and enjoy these brews. The place is open and airy with two bars; between them are standard tables and chairs as well as giant nest-like pods set with circular benches and a table in the middle.

Candelas Lounge (416 3rd Ave., 619/702-4455, 5 P.M.–1:30 A.M. daily) offers classy ambience with its flickering lighting and thumping house techno. The place has DJs spinning many nights, but it avoids the typical sweaty-meat-market vibe that many Gaslamp clubs are guilty of cultivating. It is possible to find a cozy nook and just relax with a drink and friendly conversation with friends and good-looking people you hope will soon be friends.

A San Diego institution, **The Waterfront Bar and Grill** (2044 Kettner Blvd., 619/232-9656, 6 A.M.–2 A.M. daily) has offered no-frills sustenance and spirits since the 1930s, when the Italian Americans in the surrounding community would gather there to share stories from the sea. Now it is the longest continuously operating bar in the city. High-rises block the path to the waterfront these days, but you can still sit at the open windows along the sidewalk and smell the hint of salt water that blows with the breeze in here.

Like a well-appointed eagle's aerie atop one of San Diego's most distinctive waterfront towers, **Top of the Hyatt** (1 Market Pl., 619/232-1234, 3 P.M.–1:30 A.M. daily) offers unparalleled views of San Diego Bay, Coronado Island, Point Loma, the ocean, and, it seems, even Asia if you've had enough to drink. This swanky spot is an ideal destination to impress companions. Many a high-value business deal and wedding proposal have been made as the sun sets in time with the rhythm of the bar's tinkling piano.

It's a name, it's an advertisement, it's **Air**

Conditioned Lounge (4673 30th St., 619/501-9831, www.airconditionedbar.com, 4 P.M.–2 A.M. Mon.–Fri., 7 P.M.–2 A.M. Sat.–Sun.). Housed in a former warehouse in University Heights, this bar looks like a seedy, underground spot from the exterior but is actually pretty lush inside.

An everyman's local bar, **Bluefoot** (3404 30th St., 619/756-7891, 3 P.M.–2 A.M. daily) is a great place to mingle into the local scene and it really does offer a little something for every man (and woman too!). Stack your quarters along the pool table rails in the main room to challenge the bar's loyal regulars, hop on a stool and order one of the 20 different beers on draft, or get your groove on in the back room by the live DJ booth. Be sure to look up—Bluefoot hosts a monthly rotation of artists to work in their viewable studio in the loft above the bar.

Hillcrest Wine and Martini Bars

Many of the city's best wine bars are located in the chic Hillcrest neighborhood, including the perennial favorite, **Wine Lover** (3968 5th Ave., 619/294-9200, www.thewinelover.us, 4:30–10 P.M. Sun.–Mon., 4:30 P.M.–midnight Tues.–Sat.). Approaching the place you might wonder if you bumped your head and woke up in Paris. The vibrant garden patio is ringed with ornate wrought-iron railings and furniture to match. And brightly colored canopies over the entryway practically beg you to enter. Inside the ambience is extended with romantic overhead lighting and a beautifully underlit marble bar. The wine flights are the stars here, but in my mind they just barely beat out the selection of cheeses, meats, and olives.

Only a few doors down on the corner of 5th and University is another favorite with the oenophiles: **Crush** (530 University Ave., 619/291-1717, www.crushsd.com, 4 P.M.–midnight Sun.–Thurs., 2 P.M.–2 A.M. Fri.–Sat.). Less traditional than Wine Lover, Crush's main bar is backlit with neon aqua lighting, which bathes the room in a sexy blue undertone.

Those who prefer their glasses angular rather than curvy don't need to go far, either. **Martinis Above Fourth** (3940 4th Ave.,

619/400-4500, www.martinisabovefourth .com) is also very close to these Hillcrest wine bars. This hip cabaret can serve a classic martini with the best of 'em, but will oblige if you insist on a froofy specialty drink. The tinkling piano completes the swanky scene, making this a very enjoyable spot to unwind.

Holes-in-the-Wall

As far as holes-in-the-wall go, **Star Bar** (423 E St., 619/234-5575, 6 A.M.–2 A.M. daily) has divey ambience by the pint full. Just a stone's throw away from some of the hottest clubs in the glitzy Gaslamp district, Star Bar offers a different kind of glitter. Namely, that coming off of the tacky Christmas decorations and lights that adorn the bar all year long.

Let's see, a bar that is right next to the airport? Check. So close to the freeway that it's practically beneath it? Check. Has a decades-old neon sign that practically buzzes with stories of drinks long since drained? Check. **AeroClub** (3365 India St., 619/297-7211, 2 P.M.–2 A.M. daily) has all of the makings of a classic hole-in-the-wall, and a quick look inside confirms its authenticity as a "contagiously fun" dive, rather than an "afraid I might catch something" hole. Along the bar, tattooed elbows rub against Oxford-shirted ones, and old-timers mingle with just-turned-21 youngsters. The bar is the draw here, with a full selection of liquors and more than 20 beers on tap.

Pompadours and chops are de rigueur at **Tower Bar** (4757 University Ave., 619/284-0158, www.thetowerbar.com, 2 P.M.–2 A.M. Wed.–Sun., 7 P.M.–2 A.M. Mon.–Tues.), a dive-bar favorite among the hipsters who flock to its somewhat sketchy neighborhood to strut their stuff and pound Pabst Blue Ribbon from a tall can. The bar serves booze as well. Be sure to bring your tweezers—the drinks here are strong enough to put hair on your chest.

Brew Pubs

San Diego's biggest name in beer is Karl Strauss Brewery, which has produced its craft beer since the infancy of the microbrew craze in 1989. The lineup consists of seven core beers

and a number of seasonal specialties that can be found on tap at a number of bars around town and are usually stocked by the bottle at local liquor stores.

One of the best places to sip on a pint of Karl Strauss, though, is at **Karl Strauss Brewery and Grill** (1157 Columbia St., 619/234-2739, www.karlstrauss.com, 10 A.M.–11 P.M. Mon.–Thurs., 11 A.M.–midnight Fri., 11:30 A.M.–midnight Sat., 11:30 A.M.–10 P.M. Sun.), located at the business's first brewery location downtown. The restaurant serves everything you'd expect, like burgers, pizza, sandwiches, and steaks. Be aware that the kitchen shuts down an hour before closing on every night but Sunday.

A relatively young upstart in the San Diego brew scene is **Coronado Brewing Company** (170 Orange Ave., Coronado, 619/437-4452, 11 A.M.–2 A.M. daily), which runs a microbrewery restaurant in the middle of Coronado Island's village. All the usual pub grub is there, but the menu also has quite a few gourmet pastas, seafood, and salads thrown into the mix.

Late-Night Cafés

When the urge to hang out with friends into the wee hours of the morning is strong and the itch for boozing it up is inversely proportional to that urge, nothing hits the spot like a café open late.

The Other Side (4096 30th St., 619/521-0533, 6:30 A.M.–3 A.M. Mon.–Fri., 7 A.M.–3 A.M. Sat.–Sun.) is one of those midnight oil–type establishments, caffeinating the graveyard crew from its trendy North Park corner shop. On a warm night a big iced coffee here can really hit the spot.

Café Bassam (3088 5th Ave., 619/808-3714, 8 A.M.–1:30 A.M. daily) has a thing for leaves. The nocturnal prowl specializes in loose-leaf teas and fine cigars, and it encourages patrons to enjoy both very leisurely. Yes, you read that right. This establishment is one of the few holdouts in the state that still allows smoking indoors. The haze of fine tobacco smoke adds even more moody ambience to this masculine, Old World café. The social environment is warm and inviting, with the owner,

Bassam, taking the lead. He can often be seen in his trademark fedora sitting and chatting with customers into the wee hours.

If the sweet tooth strikes in the middle of the night, pass up that crusty piece of Denny's pie and hump over to **Lestat's** (3343 Adams Ave., 619/282-0437, 24 hours daily) in Normal Heights. This 24-hour café has some tasty desserts along with plenty of strong coffee to match. Right next door it runs Lestat's West, a small venue that caters to local bands, comedy acts, and open-mic sessions.

Quite possibly the most irreverently named coffeehouse on the planet, **Hot Monkey Love** (5960 El Cajon Blvd., 619/582-5908, 9 A.M.–midnight daily) packs enough cheeky spontaneity into its atmosphere to live up to curious expectations. The café is a hotbed of creativity, hosting some form of live performance, dance session, or artistic endeavor nearly every night of the week. The bohemian vibe cultivated here fits in with its College-area setting. Like the apartment of your college friends who followed their passions instead of a steady paycheck, the interior here is all about function over form. But that's ok, because this place really does what it loves to do.

PERFORMING ARTS
Theater and Comedy
Initially founded in 1935 in order to stage abridged Shakespearean productions for the California Pacific International Exposition, **Old Globe Theatre** (1363 Old Globe Way, 619/238-0043, www.oldglobe.org) is one of the best-regarded regional theater companies in the country. Though productions have branched out considerably since the 1930s, Old Globe is still well known for its interpretations of The Bard's work. The annual Summer Shakespeare Festival is a highlight in the season's schedule.

Today's Old Globe is actually a complex of three theaters: Old Globe Theatre, Cassius Carter Centre Stage, and Lowell Davies Festival Theatre. As a result, patrons can choose between a number of productions during the season.

Downtown, the **San Diego REP** (79 Horton Plaza, 619/544-1000, www.sandiegorep.com) stages contemporary productions at Lyceum Theatre within Horton Plaza.

Let **Broadway San Diego** (3666 4th Ave., 619/564-3000, www.broadwaysd.com) give you the ol' song and dance with its renditions of the most popular Broadway musicals. The company puts on shows at two venues downtown, the San Diego Civic Center (1100 3rd Ave.) and **Spreckels Theater** (121 Broadway Ave.). Named after the sugar magnate, Spreckels is also one of the top downtown venues for big-name comedy acts and a range of music sets.

Music and Dance
San Diego Symphony (750 B St., 619/235-0804, www.sandiegosymphony.com) plays a range of classical music at Copley Music Hall, a 1929 French rococo building that is one of the West Coast's premier classical music venues. The symphony plays over 100 performances per year, including some very accessible sets through its well-received Summer Pops series. This annual concert series is typically held away from Copley, at Embarcadero Marina Park.

The **San Diego Chamber Orchestra** (858/350-0290, ext. 7, www.sdco.org) primarily performs in venues scattered about North County, but on Friday nights they are often found playing at St. Paul's Cathedral downtown. The church has incredible acoustics and the setting is perfect to enjoy the classics.

Acclaimed as one of the top 10 opera companies in the United States by *Opera America,* **San Diego Opera** (1200 3rd Ave., 18th Floor, Civic Center Plaza, 619/533-7000, www.sdopera.com) usually undertakes about five productions per season. Its solid reputation and the long-term stability of its management staff helps it attract some of the most respected guest performers and conductors in the world. The opera is well known for its rich, opulent sets—the in-house studio is so well respected that it is often contracted by other major opera companies across the country to create their sets.

Watch the dancers with the **San Diego Ballet** (2650 Truxtun Rd., 619/294-7378, www.sandiegoballet.org) pirouette and plié their way across the stage during one of the troupe's performances. The intimate venue at the ballet's training and studio complex gives patrons a very close and personal connection to the movements of the dancers.

CINEMAS

Like most major metropolitan areas, San Diego is home to dozens of movie theaters of all sizes. In Mission Valley, close to the lodging of Hotel Circle, **Mission Valley AMC** (1640 Camino Del Rio N., 858/558-2262) offers the typical googolplex experience. This place has 20 screens packed with the latest blockbusters. Similarly, **Pacific Gaslamp All-Stadium** (701 5th Ave., 619/232-0400) screens Hollywood megaproductions at its downtown location. The tiered stadium seating ensures that you won't have to crane your neck around the eight-foot giant with a cowboy hat that may claim the seat in front of you.

If indie movies are more your thing, **Hillcrest Cinemas** (3965 5th Ave., 619/819-0236) plays one of the best selections of independent and foreign films in the city.

San Diego County is also home to a pair of drive-in theaters that have managed to elude the wrecking ball that has typically ravaged these dinosaurs of the cinematic age. One of them is just east of the city, the **Santee Drive-In Theatre** (10990 Woodside Ave. N., 619/448-7447). If you've never been to a drive-in, this one will likely fulfill all of your expectations. It has two huge screens and a snack shop in the middle. Sound is provided on the FM band of your radio, so the sound is as good as your stereo system. The cost of admission covers a whole night of entertainment, as it includes two movies for the price of one.

EVENTS

San Diegans are a social bunch, so it is no surprise that they look for any excuse they can to gather together for a little organized fun now and again.

Every February **San Diego Restaurant Week** makes a splash with penny-pinching gourmands. All week diners can visit some of the best restaurants in town for a three-course meal at an unbelievable price.

Also in February is **Little Italy Carnevale,** a joyful celebration of food and fun that culminates in an authentic Venetian masked costume ball.

In early May, **Fiesta Cinco de Mayo** in Old Town is the biggest party in town to celebrate the Mexican holiday. It is also the most family friendly, with food and craft booths set around Washington Square.

Streets are cordoned off in June for the **Rock and Roll Marathon,** which winds its way through downtown and Balboa Park. This unique running event features bands along the way and a concert for all (even non-athletes) to enjoy once the course has been shut down.

The **Fourth of July** is a very big deal in this patriotic town. During the day there is usually always something going on at the USS Midway Museum, and Old Town State Historic Park celebrates by dressing volunteers in period dress and celebrating the holiday 19th-century style. One of the best parades in town is over in Coronado, which swathes itself in bunting and has events that last from 10 A.M. through the grand finale of its big fireworks show over the water. The biggest San Diego Bay fireworks show comes from the San Diego side; the **Big Bay Firework Show** on Spanish Island is one of the best in the county.

The last weekend in July brings hordes of comics, sci-fi, and fantasy fans to the San Diego Convention Center for **Comic-Con.** This colorful convention packs the days with a full slate of speakers, but the real action is on the showroom floor, where hundreds of vendors convene to sell comic books, movies, toys, and more.

September is when the events season really heats up. Early in the month the **San Diego Film Festival** pits filmmakers against one another in a competition for viewer and critic popularity.

San Diego Street Scene is another September favorite. This musical event hosts dozens of nationally recognized bands on numerous open stages in the Gaslamp for a raucous party. The music tends to be pretty heavy, with a focus on punk, metal, and rap.

Adams Avenue Street Fair is a lighter music alternative that happens right around the same time as Street Scene. This Normal Heights event is Southern California's largest free music festival and it features over 80 acts that play blues, roots rock, Latin jazz, reggae, alt-country, and zydeco for a family-lovin' crowd.

Fleet Week caps off the fall with a series of events that honor those San Diegans who serve in the U.S. Navy, Marine Corps, and Coast Guard. The event's name is a bit of a misnomer—it actually lasts over a month with numerous parades, concerts, charity events, and air shows filling the schedule.

Things stay a bit quiet until the holiday season, when the city really pulls out all of the stops with some of the year's best events. In Balboa Park, buildings and walkways are bedecked in lights and a full-size nativity is set up around the Spreckels Organ Pavilion. The park welcomes visitors in early December for the annual **December Nights** celebration, which features an international food fair, music, and entertainment all beneath the glittering lights.

Those who can't get enough pretty lights should head across the water to Coronado Island, whose well-decorated Orange Avenue leads you to the best display of them all, at the Hotel del Coronado. **Christmas at Hotel del Coronado** has always been a production. The lighting ceremony in early December officially begins the holiday season for many locals as hotel staff flips the switch on more than 60,000 lights that illuminate this Victorian beauty's best architectural features. The hotel also erects an enormous Christmas tree on its lawn.

Another holiday treat is the **San Diego Harbor Parade of Lights.** Hundreds of boat owners decorated their watercraft for the big event, putt-putting along the bay for the benefit of the happy audience along the shore.

The **Big Bay Balloon Parade** usually starts the holiday season wrap-up. This downtown parade of large balloons usually falls a couple of days after Christmas.

Shopping

San Diego's shopping scene is enough to challenge even those with a black belt in shopping. In Mission Valley the malls extend for miles, making it a prime spot for shoppers that need to find something specific.

Downtown there are plenty of great boutiques and art galleries meant for meandering. That's also where you'll find the towering Horton Plaza, a giant center with hundreds of establishments to choose from.

If you run away at the mere mention of a mall, then continue your sprint to Hillcrest. This neighborhood is a sanctuary for shoppers who prefer to spend their cash at local and independent shops.

Along the waterfront is the place to go to get that special someone you left behind a little trinket. Same goes for Old Town, which has bath salts and candies by the bushel full.

And those with a love of the rustic and the rusted should venture north of Balboa Park to Normal Heights, which has a quiet little antique row that can make the time fly.

MISSION VALLEY MALLS

In some respects Mission Valley is just one long shopping mall with roads and a freeway running through it. With just about every big-box chain retailer setting up shop in the valley, you're guaranteed to find comfort in shopping the same places you're used to seeing at just about any city in the United States. With the big stores comes traffic, though, and a trip to shop anywhere in Mission Valley can quickly turn aggravating to those with little tolerance for sitting in backups, circling parking lots, and dodging space cadets walking out the stores' doors.

On the northwest end of the valley along

SAN DIEGO

Friar's road, **Fashion Valley** is one of the highest-end malls in all of Mission Valley. This open-air mall is anchored by Nordstrom, Saks Fifth Avenue, and Bloomingdales, among others. It also has a number of upscale chain eateries such as The Cheesecake Factory.

Running alongside I-8, **Westfield Mission Valley** is the most visible jumble of stores from the freeway. The mall has a movie theater and is anchored by Target, Macy's, Bed Bath & Beyond, and Sports Chalet. Across Mission Center Road is its West Annex, which features a large Borders, Old Navy, DSW, and an assortment of sit-down chain restaurants such as Gordon Biersch.

Hazard Center may be hazardous to your driving health—tucked away in the north end of the valley, this plaza is one of the valley's most difficult to navigate. Once you are there, though, it is pretty nice, boasting two coffee shops, a movie theater, and five restaurants, including the well-regarded Italian Prego Ristorante. It is also home to a handful of stores, including a small Barnes & Noble, Relax the Back, and Stuart Benjamin and Co. Jewelry Designs.

ART GALLERIES

Downtown some of the best art galleries are concentrated in Little Italy's **Kettner Art and Design District** (www.taddsd.com), centered around Kettner Boulevard. The multifaceted collections of art galleries here feature many mediums and styles. Some of the highlights in the district include **Perry L. Meyer Fine Art** (2400 Kettner Blvd., Ste. 251, 619/358-9512, www.plmeyerfineart.com, 11 A.M.–5 P.M. Tues.–Thurs., 11 A.M.–6 P.M. Fri.–Sat., or by appointment) with 18th century to contemporary paintings and drawings; **Scott White Contemporary Art** (2400 Kettner Blvd., Ste. 238, 619/501-5689, www.scottwhiteart.com, 9 A.M.–5 P.M. Tues.–Fri., 11 A.M.–5 P.M. Sat.) featuring contemporary and modern paintings, sculpture, and photography; and contemporary art and furniture at **David Zapf Gallery** (2400 Kettner Blvd. #104, 619/232-5004, noon–5 P.M. Thurs.–Sat.).

The Gaslamp also has a few gallery finds,

including the collection of work from emerging artists at **Michael J. Wolf Fine Arts** (363 5th Ave., 619/702-5388, noon–8 P.M. daily) and the assemblage of sculpture and jewelry at **Shorelines Gallery** (411 Market St., 619/231-6151, 10 A.M.–8 P.M. Sun.–Thurs., 10 A.M.–10 P.M. Fri. and Sat.). Another unique and captivating collection is inside the Gaslamp's **Ashby Galleries** (527 4th Ave., 619/235-6990), which features the captivating and ethereal work of Tim Cantor.

DOWNTOWN SHOPPING

Horton Plaza (324 Horton Plaza, 619/238-1596, 10 A.M.–9 P.M. Mon.–Fri., 10 A.M.–8 P.M. Sat., 11 A.M.–7 P.M. Sun.) is plopped down right in the thick of the activity of the Gaslamp Quarter. Like the bustling neighborhood, this mall's design is a jumble of frenetic energy. The labyrinthine mazes created by the stairs and ramps and elevators leading up and down the fractured multistory levels are the stuff of legends. Rumor has it whole families have been lost for days, subsisting only on Cinnabon and Hotdog on a Stick. The stores are pretty standard mall chains (Nordstrom,

Horton Plaza

© JOANNE DIBONA/SAN DIEGO CVB

Macy's, Gap), but what the selection lacks in creativity it makes up in quantity. There are nearly 200 shops in total. Also on premises is the Lyceum Theater, home to San Diego REP, and a couple dozen food-court restaurants.

For more unique shops just strike out in any direction from Horton Plaza. The Gaslamp side streets are a great place to pick up new designer threads. Ladies can check out the wardrobe options at places like **Le Bijou** (557 4th Ave., 619/232-1454) or **Jacques LeLong** (635 5th Ave., 619/234-2583, 10 A.M.–11 P.M. Sun.–Thurs., 10 A.M.–midnight Fri.–Sat.), maybe stopping by **Poz** (228 5th Ave., 619/234-5625, 1–6 P.M. daily) afterward to pick out a new pair of shoes and a purse to match all those clothes. And guys can unleash their inner metrosexual at the slick Italian shop **Boutique Voss** (946 5th Ave., 619/233-4830) or the ultra-designer "jeanery" **G Star** (946 5th Ave., 619/233-4830, www.g-star.com).

Little Italy is the best neighborhood for trendy knickknacks and furnishings to deck out home sweet home. It has a number of cutting-edge boutiques and studios that are a part of the Kettner Art and Design District. There you can find shabby-chic furnishings at **Dear Prudence** (1644 India St., 619/234-9595, 11 A.M.–5 P.M. Tues.–Sat.), vintage handblown glass at **Vetro** (1760 Kettner Blvd., 619/546-5120, www .vetrocollections.com, 10 A.M.–6 P.M. Tues.–Sat.), and sleek modern furniture and art at **ADORN** (2400 Kettner Blvd., Suite 105, 619/794-2729, www.adornsd.com, 10 A.M.–6 P.M. daily).

SEAPORT VILLAGE

Seaport Village (849 W. Harbor Dr., #D, 619/235-4014, www.seaportvillage.com, 10 A.M.–9 P.M. daily) tends to grow on you. Sure, this shopping center along the waterfront sometimes feels a little manufactured and the souvenirs here are on the pricey side. The thing is, it knows what it is and it does it well. Those expensive souvenirs are the best in town and the atmosphere is very fun on the weekends when the village invites musicians to play in the public spaces.

In addition to the T-shirt shops, camera stores, and trinket boutiques, there are also a few stores that break the souvenir-shop mold. For example,

the **Kite Store** sells a colorful selection of windsocks and kites for the experienced flyer and the beginner. **The Toy Cottage** offers an array of quality toys that are often one of a kind. And **Whitt/Kruss** has an amazing collection of sculptures, paintings, and fine art on display.

HILLCREST BOUTIQUES

Hillcrest takes the cake in the individuality department. That goes for shopping, too. This offbeat neighborhood is a refuge for the independent-minded shopper. Many of the boutiques and shops here are mom-and-pops (sometimes pop-and-pop, too) that are stocked to the gills with unique items.

Take **Wear It Again Sam** (3823 5th Ave., 619/299-0185, 11 A.M.–7 P.M. Mon.–Sat., 11 A.M.–6 P.M. Sun.), for instance. This used apparel store sells only vintage clothes from the 1940s, '50s, and '60s. We're talking cashmere sweaters, pinstripe suits, fedoras—the works. Shop here and you'll never worry about seeing your outfit on somebody else.

Another one-of-a-kind favorite is **Co-Habitat** (1433 University Ave., 619/688-1390, 11 A.M.–8 P.M. daily), which sells rich and colorful Indian and Southeast Asian furnishings.

Tag for Dogs and Cats (142 University Ave., Ste. D, 619/497-0180, 10 A.M.–8 P.M. daily) is a must visit for anyone who's ever considered buying their pets a massage. This ritzy pet store has plenty of items waiting to help you cross the line from "pet lover" to "one of *those* people." Don't worry, I'm as guilty as the rest of 'em.

OLD TOWN SHOPS

Many of the historic buildings in Old Town double as shops. There you can find an apothecary and bath-salts shop, a coffee house, a gem store, a tobacconist, a pottery shop, and a milliner. The park is also home to **Plaza del Pasado,** a Mexican-inspired *mercado* that has a book store, more pottery, and other souvenirs.

The space there was for decades the home of **Bazaar del Mundo** (4133 Taylor St., 619/296-3161, 10 A.M.–6 P.M. daily), a collection of authentic Latin American shops that was eventually booted out of the park when the state decided it wanted to go in a different direction with the space. It was well-loved by locals, who know to continue their knickknack shopping at the new location just a few blocks away on Taylor Street.

Don't forget to save a little cash for the other shops outside of the park. Some highlights east of the park include **Made in San Diego Chocolates** (3941 Mason St., #1, 619/299-9830) for sweets, **Ye Olde Soap Shoppe** (2497 San Diego Ave., 619/390-3525) for handmade soaps, and **Jarabe Tapatio** (2607 Congress St., 619/574-0039) for fine women's apparel. Another favorite is **Captain Fitch's Mercantile** (2627 San Diego Ave., 619/298 3944, 10 A.M.–9 P.M. daily), which sells books, cards, and sundries.

ANTIQUES IN NORMAL HEIGHTS

Antique Row in Normal Heights is a nice, neighborly lineup of mom-and-pops set in historic homes and quaint little commercial buildings along Adams Avenue. Start from the corner of Adams Avenue and 30th Street and head west on Adams to explore your way through these stores.

You'll encounter a varied collection of furniture, paintings, old photos, license plates, kitchenware, and more at **Zac's Attic** (2922 Adams Ave., 619/284-0400, 10 A.M.–4:30 P.M. Thurs.–Mon.), one of the largest of the shops on this row. It is set in a lovely Craftsman-style building that is accented with river-rock support pillars.

Nostalgic music collectors love **Folk Arts Rare Records** (2881 Adams Ave., 619/282-7833, www.folkartsrarerecords.com, 9 A.M.–5 P.M. Mon.–Fri., 10 A.M.–6 P.M. Sat.–Sun.). This musty shop absolutely crams its little rooms from floor to ceiling with old records.

Just a few doors down is **Antique Cottage** (2873 Adams Ave., 619/281-9663, 10 A.M.–6 P.M. Mon.–Sat., 10 A.M.–5 P.M. Sun.). The furniture practically spills out onto the sidewalk here, with chairs and tables and sofas stacked up like a giant Jenga puzzle. It doesn't make for casual browsing, but the owner knows his stock inside and out and if you have something in mind he is likely to duck into a pile and crawl out with just the thing you're seeking.

Resurrected Furniture (2814 Adams Ave., 619/283-3318, 10 A.M.–6 P.M. Mon.–Sat., 10 A.M.–5 P.M. Sun.) is a lot less crowded with inventory and there are also books, knickknacks, and works of art here. This is a good store for those who like Asian antiques.

Jewelry shoppers should drop in on **Abigail's Antiques and Curios** (2831 Adams Ave., 10 A.M.–5 P.M. Mon.–Sat.), which carries antique costume pieces as well as assorted gold and silver jewelry.

BOOKSTORES

San Diego is home to lots of quirky booksellers who welcome browsers as heartily as buyers. In Seaport Village, **Upstart Crow Book Store and Coffee House** (835 W. Harbor Dr., 619/232-4855, www.upstartcrowtrading.com, 9 A.M.–10 P.M. Sun.–Thurs., 9 A.M.–11 P.M. Fri.–Sat.) brews up a good blend of one-of-a-kind tomes, kitchy souvenirs, and caffeine. Climb up the creaky steps to find a spot overlooking the coffee bar while you flip through their selection.

If you are looking for the kind of musty store you can get lost in for days, then **Wahrenbrock's Book House** (726 Broadway, 619/232-0132, 9:30 A.M.–5:30 P.M. Tues.–Sat.) is a must. This old place is a favorite for local book lovers who come to pore over two stories of stacks that include a lot of antique gems.

On the Orange Avenue strip in Coronado, **Bay Books** (1029 Orange Ave., 619/435-0070, www.baybookscoronado.com, 9 A.M.–9 P.M. Mon.–Sat., 9 A.M.–6 P.M. Sun.) is a good spot to come pick out a summer read before hitting the Silver Strand. This little family-owned shop offers a nice variety of genres, with a special emphasis on children's books and military history and fiction (it is just blocks away from a naval air station, after all).

Comic-Con comes but once a year, but that doesn't mean we can't dork out over the latest issues the rest of the time. **San Diego Comics** (6937 El Cajon Blvd., 619/698-1177, www.san-diego-comics.com) is one of the most established comic book stores in town. Just remember fellas, reading comics on the beach is a real mood killer for those bikini-clad ladies.

Sports and Recreation

Shoehorned between sparkling water and mountainous backcountry, San Diego is a well-placed headquarters for those who like to get out and sweat a little. Unsurprisingly, there are many occasions to strap on some boat shoes and pick up the old rod and reel. The bay and numerous lakes in town make that a no-brainer. The city also lives up to its reputation when it comes to golf, hosting some of the best public courses on the West Coast.

Many of the best rugged recreation options are outside of city limits in the outer edges of the county's consciousness. But it really doesn't take a long drive to satisfy an appetite for sport. There are oodles of wild and seemingly rural pockets right in town that are ready to surprise the unacquainted with opportunities for rock climbing, mountain biking, and hiking.

SURFING AND BOOGIE BOARDING

You'll need to drive to the city beaches or up to North County to find the really good surfing breaks, but occasionally Coronado Island will see some swells that are decent for a little long board action. The best bets are usually within **Silver Strand State Beach.**

Boogie boarders can usually get lucky in the mild waves that lap along **Coronado Beach,** close to Hotel del Coronado and downtown Coronado.

CYCLING
Downtown and Mission Valley

With a very extensive selection of bikes and a central location in the Gaslamp Quarter, **Bike Tours San Diego** (509 5th Ave., 619/238-2444, 8 A.M.–7 P.M. daily, $35 per day for road or mountain bikes) is a great spot for the true cycling enthusiast to rent two wheels for one day or even a week. This is one of the only places in the city that rents proper road bikes to out-of-towners. It also has a stock of high-quality mountain bikes that are capable of taking to the county's more extreme back-country trails.

The business also runs bike tours all over San Diego for multiple skill levels.

On your own, you can take off directly from the Gaslamp and head along the Embarcadero Waterfront on your own if you are cruising. Serious cyclists can continue along Harbor Drive when it turns into Pacific Highway. There is a signed bicycling route along the highway that skirts around the northeastern curve of the airport all the way to the San Diego River, but there are no bike lanes drawn and it can be really hairy in certain places. Exercise extreme caution on this route.

From there it is possible to take the southern path along the river until it hits Friars' Road and take the right on Friars' to head into Mission Valley. Friars' Road has a bike lane that stretches on for many miles, continuing on through its transition to Mission Gorge. It is possible to take this route through Mission Valley and head all the way past city limits into the bedroom community of Santee. There is, however one very dangerous spot a couple miles into the route at the Friars' Road interchange with Rte. 163. The bike lane is interrupted by

FIDO SURFS AT LOEWS

Everyone in San Diego surfs during the dog days of summer, even, well, the dogs. Loews Coronado Bay Resort (619/424-4000) has a surf instruction program designed just for canine companions. Participants in the Su'ruff Camp receive instruction in the long-lost art of dog surfing for $75 per hour. Your fluffy pal will learn how to stay calm atop a longboard in the gentle waves that wash up to Coronado Island.

If Fido is good enough, maybe think about entering him in the annual Surf Dog Competition held by the resort on Imperial Beach.

the on-ramps and impatient and speedy drivers do little to heed the "Share the Road" signage that was futilely erected here. To bypass this mess, hang a right on Fashion Valley Road and a left on the San Diego River Trail that runs beneath the trolley line. This continues for about two miles until Qualcomm Way. There you can take a left and it will spit you back onto Friars' Road, where you can take a right and continue your eastward journey.

Silver Strand State Beach

In Coronado, **Holland's Bicycles** (977 Orange Ave., Coronado, 619/435-3153, 10 A.M.–6 P.M. Mon.–Sat., 11 A.M.–5 P.M. Sun.) has been in the business of pedals and spokes since 1924. This long-standing company offers rentals out of two locations on Coronado Island. The first is its mail location on Orange Avenue and the second is **Bikes and Beyond** at the Coronado Ferry Landing (1201 1st St., Coronado, 619/435-7180, 10 A.M.–6 P.M. Mon.–Sat., 11 A.M.–5 P.M. Sun., $10 per hour, $30 for four hours, $50 per day).

Once you've been outfitted at either location, pedal south along the Silver Strand Bike Path and see how far you can make it. The path is paved and rolling to flat for 8.5 miles all the way down to Imperial Beach, but the wind can create quite a bit of resistance. Just be sure to watch out for cars turning in at the intersections, as drivers can be inattentive to traffic on the trail and the laws of physics dictate that they'll win every time no matter who has the right of way.

Balboa Park

The **Morley Field Velodrome** (2221 Morley Field Dr., www.sdvelodrome.com) is a hit with track cyclists and those who enjoy this fast-paced sport. The velodrome is open for free to all cyclists on road or track bikes on Saturdays from 9 A.M. to noon. On Tuesday nights the facility holds a multi-tiered racing event. The cost to race is $10 and it is free to watch.

BOATING AND FISHING
The Big Bay

On a busy day you'll have to navigate around other pleasure craft and naval ships, but beyond this inconvenience San Diego Bay makes for an ideal body of water to glide along by sail or motor. From downtown, rentals can be found at **Seaforth** (333 West Harbor Dr., Gate 1, 619/239-2628, 9 A.M.–30 minutes prior to sunset daily), which is based out of the Marriott Marina. There you can pick up a range of craft, from small row boats to large sailboats. Seaforth also runs a shop out of Coronado Island (1715 Strand Way, Coronado, 619/437-1514, 9 A.M.–30 min prior to sunset Mon.–Fri., 8 A.M.–30 minutes prior to sunset Sat.–Sun.) that has a similar selection and slightly extended hours on the weekend.

Most of the local saltwater fishing is best found outside of the bay's waters in the open ocean. The majority of the experienced tour guides are based out of America's Cup Harbor (see the *La Jolla and the Beaches* chapter). This is also where the tackle shops closest to downtown are located.

However, if you are looking to go it alone from a rental boat or from your own craft and are seeking a local shop without any touristy vibe, you can venture up to the strip malls of Clairemont Mesa to shop some of the stores there. Two favorites among anglers are **Noah's Tackle Store** (4837 Convoy St., 858/874-0486, www.noahstackle.com, 10 A.M.–6 P.M. Mon.–Fri., 9 A.M.–5 P.M. Sat.) and **JP's Bait and Tackle** (4488 Convoy St., #C, 858/277-7417). These stores can also help facilitate those who wish to shore-fish from the waterfront, which can be done from the **Embarcadero Marina Park Pier.** This structure juts from the southern side of the park and provides anglers with the opportunity to hook bass, croaker, and halibut.

Fly-Fishing

Most traditional fly fishers wouldn't think of San Diego County as a great spot to wave that wand around, but it actually has a host of opportunities for the open-minded. In the high mountains near Palomar there are a couple of crystal-clear lakes for traditional trout fly-fishing. Beyond that, the weather is usually too hot for those cold water–loving species. But the angler who can think of fly-fishing beyond the strict definition of fishing for trout can have a blast on any number of the county's watery sites.

Lower elevation lakes provide a place to cast out to a range of warm-water species such as bass, crappie, and bluegill. And along the coast and the flats of the bays and lagoons there are opportunities to catch a number of saltwater species who would be lured by the dance of the right fly.

In town, you can stock up on flys, leaders, and local knowledge at **Stroud Tackle** (1457 Morena Blvd., 619/276-4822, www.stroud tackle.com, 10 A.M.–6 P.M. Mon.–Sat.), which happens to be headquarters for the San Diego Fly Fishers Club.

On Coronado Island, **Andy Montana's Surfside Fly Fishers** (957 Orange Ave., Coronado, 619/435-9992, www.andymontanas .com, 10 A.M.–6 P.M. Sun.–Fri., 9 A.M.–6 P.M. Sat.) provides tackle and also leads regularly scheduled surf-casting lessons and fishing trips along the coast.

The **San Diego Fly Fishers** (www.sandiego flyfishers.com) club also offers free fly casting lessons at Lake Murray every Sunday from 9 A.M. to noon.

Balboa Park is one of the finest spots in the city for a stroll.

Lake Murray

Located within Mission Trails Regional Park, Murray Reservoir (5540 Kiowa Dr., La Mesa, 619/668-2050, sunrise–sunset daily) is an ideal place to unwind with a fishing pole in hand. It is stocked from November through May with a range of species that include large-mouth bass, bluegill, catfish, black crappie, and trout. There's plenty of shoreline to cast into this 171-acre reservoir, but if you prefer to bob along in a boat, rentals are available on Wednesdays, Saturdays, and Sundays. Don't forget to buy a fishing permit. You can pick them up from the electronic pay station next to the concession building.

WALKING AND RUNNING

The abundance of public open spaces and walkways makes San Diego an ideal town for walkers and runners. For a flat and scenic stroll, the **Embarcadero** along the bay offers exercise and people-watching all at once. Be mindful that the sidewalk can be pretty packed on summer afternoons, so running through the crowd may be frustrating to some. But in mornings, evenings, or in the winter, you can pound the pavement without fear of collision. A good alternative on those busy days is to park and run along the water at Harbor Island Park. Just north of the Embarcadero, this park offers a three-mile walkway that extends along the length of the park. Those with the motivation can actually combine the two together into a longer course, as there is a wide and safe sidewalk that runs all the way from the Embarcadero into Harbor Island.

If you are looking for a little motivation, tie your laces and head over to the **Silver Strand** on Coronado for a little jog. This beach borders the Navy SEAL training facility and if you hit the sand early enough you just might have the pleasure of being lapped by a SEAL out for his morning run.

SAN DIEGO

If the beach is too much for your burning calves, Coronado also has a paved pedestrian path that runs the length of the strand all the way down to Imperial Beach.

Balboa Park is perhaps one of my favorite places in the city to take a stroll, with its level walkways, lush gardens, and beautiful architecture. The park also offers a number of undeveloped canyon trails that are great for exploring leisurely and can also offer a softer surface to pick up the pace a little.

HIKING
San Pasqual-Clevenger Canyon Open Space Park

Just east of Escondido at the northern edge of the city lies San Pasqual and Clevenger Canyon Open Space Park (trailhead on San Pasqual Valley Rd., 5.3 miles past San Diego Wild Animal Park, 858/538-8082) whose trails wind up and down the area mountains and offer fine views of San Pasqual Valley, a rural

Take a break from the shores with a classic hike through the city's chaparral-covered natural parks.

© ERICKA CHICKOWSKI

area that is currently home to avocado, citrus, and palm farmers. The trails are dotted with oak and sycamore and in the late spring hikers will likely encounter a display of wildflowers including the white chamise and the fragrant purple ceanothus. Hikers are able to enjoy the beauty in peace, as bikes and horses are restricted from this trail.

Mission Trails

The trip up Cowles Mountain is the definitive hike within **Mission Trails Regional Park,** but the paths up this peak are just a small part of the trail system here. In fact, the majority of the trails in the park are across Mission Gorge from Cowles on the park's other peak, **Fortuna Mountain.** All of these hikes are moderate to challenging hauls with plenty of elevation change, and the views to match. They run through the chaparral and coastal sage scrub habitats that are so prevalent in this part of the county.

MOUNTAIN BIKING

One of the most popular mashing grounds for fat-tire enthusiasts within city limits is **Mission Trails Regional Park,** which offers a trail system of over 40 miles that is open to mountain bikers. The trails range from challenging single-track to more mild fire roads. Climbs and quick descents are abundant. So are hikers, so please ensure the future of mountain biking in the park by being courteous to pedestrians. Similarly, take heed of bike restrictions posted at certain trails. With so many miles of great terrain to roll through, there is no need to sneak onto forbidden trails.

The elevation gain at Mission Trails may be too much for those faint of heart (and lungs). A flatter alternative is the wildly popular trail in **Los Peñasquitos Canyon Preserve.** This nearly six-mile round-trip can be attacked from either end of the trailheads, one at each end of the trail. The trail runs through oak canopies, swaying grasslands, and a resplendent springtime mix of California poppies, wild radish mustard, and bush mallow flowers. The real highlight of the trail is the scenic set of waterfalls that cascade down a canyon hillside about halfway along the trail. The water flow is best viewed in winter and early spring.

If this trail is not long enough for you, consider starting at the western trailhead and extending the ride by crossing Mercy Road and continuing down Knott Grove Trail, a 1.5-mile path that edges near and crisscrosses over Penasquitos Canyon creek several times and is shaded by willow, sycamore, and toyon.

Only a couple miles away from Penasquitos is another short lung burner on **Black Mountain.** The way up runs over an old jeep road now called Nighthawk Trail (trailhead at 9711 Oviedo Way), a part of the Black Mountain Open Space Park that the city planners wisely carved out of housing development zones that have all but swallowed what was not long ago a rural part of the county. The trail is 1.8 miles to the top, which affords a 360-degree view of the ocean and regional mountain ranges.

ROCK CLIMBING

In town, climbers can limber up at one of several climbing gyms scattered around the city. The most centrally located among them is **Solid Rock** (2074 Hancock St., 619/299-1124, www .solidrockgym.com, 11 A.M.–10 P.M. Mon.– Fri., 9 A.M.–9 P.M. Sat., 11 A.M.–7 P.M. Sun., $12 weekday, $15 weekend adults, $13 weekend youth) in Old Town. The biggest is **Vertical Hold** (9580 Distribution Ave., 858/586-7572, www.verticalhold.com, 11:30 A.M.–10 P.M. Mon. & Fri., 11:30 A.M.–11 P.M. Tues.–Thurs., 10 A.M.–9 P.M. Sat., 10 A.M.–8 P.M. Sun., $15 day pass) in Mira Mesa. Both offer rental equipment and hold classes for climbing newbies.

Fans of bouldering will fall in love with the **Santee Boulders,** located just over the city line near the town of the same name. The field here holds popular routes such as Moby Dick, Dog Pile, and the Bullet Hole.

For traditional and top-rope climbing, head over to the granite cliffs of **Mission Gorge** in Mission Trails Regional Park. Here you'll encounter lines like Rock, Rock On, Knob Job, and Lunch Rock.

In addition to running its gym, Vertical Hold also organizes outings to these and other sites across the county. Visit www.verticalhold .com for details.

GOLF

San Diego is heaven for scratch golfers and duffers alike. Most of the world-class links are located north of the city, but there are still a number of very good, centrally located courses to get your swing on without breaking the bank.

Running through some of the best real estate in Mission Valley, **Riverwalk Golf Club** (1150 Fashion Valley Rd., 619/296-4653, www.river walkgc.com, $95 Mon.–Thurs., $120 Fri.–Sun. and holidays) ripples along the banks of the San Diego River. The riparian setting makes for some challenging golf, with water playing a factor on 13 of the 27 holes. If you can, make it a point to play the Mission course. The third hole there is the course's showpiece with a lake and a waterfall surrounding the green. Just do yourself a favor and play that one conservatively or you'll watch your ball supply dwindle.

The links at **Balboa Golf Course** (2600 Golf Course Dr., 619/235-1184, reservations 619/570-1234, 6 A.M.–sunset daily, $34 Mon.– Fri., $43 Sat.–Sun.) are actually two golf courses in one. There is the 9-hole executive course that plays pretty straightforward and there's the 18-hole championship course that winds through mesas and canyons and can confound the best golfers. This muni is a great course but be prepared: It gets crowded and plays very slowly, especially on the weekends.

It is hard to believe that **Mission Trails Golf Course** (7380 Golfcrest Pl., 619/460-5400, www.americangolf.com, $22 Mon.–Fri., $38 Sat.–Sun.) is still within city limits. Set along the banks of Lake Murray and at the foot of Cowles Mountain, the course has natural vistas aplenty. Owned by the city, this course is privately operated so the grounds are less scrubby than many munis. Watch out for the brush on hole 17. The fairway is short but the scrubs and trees that run across it seem to magnetically attract those dimply fliers.

With glorious views of Glorietta Bay and downtown, **Coronado Golf Course** (2000 Visalia Row, Coronado, 619/435-3121, www .golfcoronado.com, $25 greens fee, $15 cart) is another great municipal course. The problem is that everybody knows it, so tee times are tricky to book.

Wedged between Old Town State Historic Park and Presidio Hill, **Presidio Golf Course** (4136 Wallace St., 619/295-9476, $10) is a laid-back and fun pitch-and-putt course that is ideal for families with kids just learning to golf. The small facility is well maintained for its size and on weekdays it is usually quiet enough for serious golfers to fine-tune their short games before heading out for a round at the more challenging courses in town.

Finally, those with military connections may want to use them to gain access for a round at **Admiral Baker Golf Course** (Friars Rd. and Admiral Baker Rd., 619/556-5521). The 36 holes here are regarded by many as the best military links in the country. If you're a civvy, you'll need to be in the company of a navy friend or relative to play.

SKATING

Washington Skatepark (www.washington streetskateboardpark.org, 9 A.M.–dark daily, free) was built in the true antiestablishment spirit of skating. Back in 1999 when the city had no skate parks at all and city police were encouraged to clamp down hard on those skating in public areas, a few enterprising souls decided to take matters into their own hands and pour concrete ramps away from the scrutiny of authority figures. The spot was below the I-5 Washington Street Bridge.

While the parks founders got quite a few heavy sessions on the set-up, the clandestine park was eventually ferreted out by the city and was shut down despite the howls of unhappy skaters.

They remained persistent, though, and decided to go through official channels to have the park legitimized. The city agreed to let these citizens take over the park if they could wade through a maze of red tape. It took several years, but in 2002 they accomplished their mission and now what stands is one of the most popular free skate parks in SoCal, designed and built by skaters for skaters. The park is directly under I-5 over Washington Street. From I-5 south, exit on Washington Street and go two blocks south until you see the park.

Bill and Maxine Wilson Skate Park (702 South 30th St., 619/527-3596, 2 P.M.–8 P.M. Mon.–Fri., 11 A.M.–7 P.M. Sat.–Sun.) has a good mixture of street, vert, and pool skating, featuring railings, stairs, and a 90-foot-long snake run. It also has a ten-foot key hole and a beginner's bowl for the youngsters. A one-day pass is $5; call to verify hours of operation, which sometimes vary according to the seasons.

LAWN BOWLING

Members of the **San Diego Lawn Bowling Club** (1549 El Prado, 619/238-5457, www .sandiegolawnbowling.com) regularly don their dress whites and take to the grass of Balboa Park for a bit of friendly competition. The club maintains grounds at the park and offers free lessons to any interested bowling novice on Tuesday, Friday, and Sunday at 11 A.M.

It also welcomes guests from bowling clubs around the world to join its members in regularly held fixtures. Even those with no interest in playing might enjoy stopping by to watch a match. Visit the website for times and dates.

SPECTATOR SPORTS

Some cities are football towns and some ain't. San Diego is unequivocally a skip church on Sunday, dye your dog team colors, and scream out loud at the TV kind of football town. **San Diego Charger games** are played in Mission Valley at Qualcomm Stadium (9449 Friars Rd., 619/641-3100, www.chargers.com), a 70,000-seat venue that absolutely roars with excitement when the Chargers (also known as the Bolts, as in lightning bolts) score a touchdown. Tickets can be purchased at any Ticketmaster location or online at www.stubhub.com.

The **San Diego Padres** also have their fair share of loyal baseball fans, but the team has a bit more of a fair-weather friendship with its fan base. When the Pads are tearing it up, the hordes throng to cheer them on at Petco Park (100 Park Blvd., 619/795-5000), but a slump will empty the seats. Whether the Friars are winning or losing, Petco Park is a beautiful ball field and is worth the cost of admission for any baseball junkie who can't get enough of the smell of green grass, leather gloves, and sizzling stadium dogs. Completed in 2004, the park is a stunning visual centerpiece of the Gaslamp Quarter and has done a lot to continue the revitalization of this entertainment district.

OUTDOOR OUTFITTERS

With so many opportunities for outdoor adventure within the city and the region at large, San Diego has plenty of places to pick up gear for rent or purchase that can have you happily wandering the trails, waterways, and cliffsides in no time.

Adventure 16 (4620 Alvarado Canyon Rd., 619/283-2362, www.adventure16.com) is local SoCal chain that specializes in hiking, camping, climbing, and outdoor survival gear.

REI (5556 Copley Dr., 858/279-4400) is one of the largest outdoor outfitters in the county. This is your best bet for rental gear.

Sports Chalet (3695 Midway Dr., 619/224-6777, www.sportchalet.com), particularly this location, is heaven for the outdoors enthusiast. There's a mountain bike shop, a heavy concentration of camping and climbing gear, and a dive shop complete with a training pool.

Road Runner Sports (5553 Copley Dr., 858/974-4475, www.roadrunnersports.com) is the largest running-shoe store in the country and is a runner's paradise for clothes and accessories. The knowledgeable staff can also clue you in on the best routes in town.

Road cyclists and mountain bikers will be pleased at the selection of bikes and accessories at **Trek Superstore** (4240 Kearny Mesa Rd., #108, 858/974-8735, www.treksandiego .com), a major outlet for America's most prolific bicycle maker.

C & C Outdoor Store (3231 Sports Arena Blvd., 619/222-2326, www.ccoutdoorstore .com) is a smaller hiking and camping shop with a particularly good selection of clothes and shoes suited for exploration in the wild.

Aqua Tech Dive Center (1800 Logan Ave., 619/237-1800, www.divecenter.com) is a well-respected dive shop with a good selection of wet and dry dive equipment for rent, as well as a number of dive classes.

Accommodations

As would be expected from a city that sprawls out nearly 73 square miles, there are dozens of lodging options in every neighborhood. Some visitors might find prices to be a bit of a shock, as even cheap chain hotels and motels charge at least $125 during high season. Downtown and Mission Valley are the best bets for bargain hunters. Those willing to pay a premium can find plenty of quaint inns on Coronado Island and near Balboa Park. The high-rise and penthouse set can look to downtown and the waterfront for their digs. In addition to being home to one of the very few tent campsites within city limits, the northern part of the city also plays host to several exclusive resorts.

DOWNTOWN
Under $100

La Pensione (606 W. Date St., 619/236-8000, www.lapensionehotel.com, $90 d) is one of the better hotel bargains in the city. The European-style hotel offers accommodations in Little Italy for a fraction of what most neighboring hotels charge. The hotel is close to the trolley, which is great for fans of public transport but could be a potential disaster for light sleepers who can't snore through late-night train noise.

Those who prefer a true hostel experience can still find it downtown at the **HI-SD Downtown Hostel** (521 Market St., 619/525-1531, www.sandiegohostels.org, dorm bed $19–24, $47–54 d, family room $64–82), which is located in ground zero of Gaslamp Quarter partying. This typical hostel offers 4-, 6-, and 10-person dormitories, as well as a couple of private rooms.

$100-200

Traveling with pets can really limit your lodging options, especially in a busy city center. Typically the only hotels within downtown metropolitan areas that accept furry companions are expensive boutiques or absolute dumps. **Harborview Inn and Suites** (550 W. Grape St., 619/233-7799, www.sdharborview .com, $139 s, $159 d) is a happy exception. It offers clean and decent rooms that you don't have to sneak Rover into.

Like a hostel for grown-ups, ◖ **500 West** (500 W. Broadway, 619/234-5252, www.500westhotel.com, $99 s, $109 d) rents out small rooms with twin and double beds that are well decorated, comfortable, and clean. You pay slightly more than a hostel, but shoot, you don't have to bring your own sheets, you'll never get locked out at night, and you sure as heck don't have to do any chores! Seriously, though, this place offers a chic room and a more mature atmosphere for those who don't need a large footprint to be comfy. A dorm room for four is $84.

Set in the neighborly district of North Park, **Carole's Bed and Breakfast** (3227 Grim Ave., 619/280-5258, www.carolesbnb.com, $109 d and up) has most of the elements that make a good bed-and-breakfast great. It is set in a historic 1904 Craftsman, it is run by a little old lady who is as cute as a button, and the prices are extremely reasonable. The only downside is that breakfast is only an extended continental. But considering the rates, this is really just a minor setback. You can take those hundreds of dollars you'd have spent at a more gourmet bed-and-breakfast and go blow them on a dozen nice meals downtown.

Little Italy Inn (505 W. Grape St., 619/230-1600, www.littleitalyhotel.com, $99–169 d, 2-br suite $199 d) likes to tout itself as European-style, but one advantage it has over those types of places is the option for a room with the comfort of its own porcelain palace. Some even have bathrooms with jetted tubs. Otherwise, this place is as much a throwback to the old country as the neighborhood it's in, and features little architectural flourishes throughout the interior and an elegant decor.

The lobby at the **Horton Grand** (311 Island Ave., 619/544-1886, www.hortongrand .com, $179 s, $199 d) is decorated in Victorian furnishings accented by a 100-year-old oak staircase. Rooms also feature period furniture and each comes with a fireplace to complete the effect. Flickering may not just come from the hearth, though. Legend has it that this hotel is haunted by several ghosts. One of the notables is Roger Whitaker, said to occupy room 309.

$200-300

The **Westin Emerald Plaza** (400 W. Broadway, 619/239-4500, $299 d) is hard to miss in the city skyline. The hexagonal rooftops on this cluster of sleek black towers are rimmed with green lights at night. This is an ideal place for city sophisticates to rest their heads. The rooftop pool area presents a fantastic skyline and bay view to enjoy from the facility's whirlpool tub.

Clad in bright modern furniture and pop art, **The Bristol Hotel** (1055 1st Ave., 619/232-6141, www.thebristolsandiego.com, $299 d) is what you'd get if Andy Warhol did hotels. There's function in the form, too. The hotel is right in the Gaslamp, offers free Internet, and has great big desks for all you stick-in-the-muds who insist on working while on vacation.

When it comes to ◖ **Hotel Solamar** (453 6th Ave., 619/531-8740, www.hotelsolamar .com, king $289 d, suite $609 d), I've got two words for you: leopard-print robes. This boutique hotel cozies up well with its hip and trendy Gaslamp Quarter neighborhood. Bedspreads are bedecked in spunky polka dots and the hotel offers in-room yoga accessories along with a special TV channel to lead you through a routine. Plus, the lobby is fresh and modern without being prickly. It is comfortable enough to hang around to read the paper while enjoying the communal coffee service offered gratis each morning.

Over $300

Lavish, splendid, sumptuous, luxurious, re-splendent…there are only so many words in the thesaurus associated with "opulence," and they're all appropriate to describe the **⟨ US Grant Hotel** (326 Broadway, 619/232-3121 or 866/837-4270, www.usgrant.net, $549 d), a 90-year-old historic hotel in the middle of the Gaslamp. It makes its first impression count with a grand marble lobby and enormous glass chandeliers, and it never stops impressing. Rooms are decorated with French art specially commissioned for the hotel and marble bath-rooms and 300-thread-count linens. Public spaces are decorated with silk carpets, gilded accents, and original paintings and bronze sculptures. Plus, the service is absolutely on par with the environs and the room rate, which is more than some pay for a whole month's rent.

WATERFRONT AND CORONADO ISLAND
Under $100

On-the-go bargain hunters might find **Marina Inn and Hotel Suites** (1943 Pacific Hwy., 619/232-7551, www.marinainnsd.com, $89 s, $99 d) a good buy if they don't plan on spending much time there. Located on a busy thoroughfare, this motel offers humble digs that are centrally located next to the airport, downtown, and the waterfront. Those going on a cruise or using San Diego as a point of departure might consider one of the stay-and-park packages this place offers. Stay a couple of nights and park for seven days while you do your thing elsewhere.

Honestly, though, **Island Inn** (202 Island Ave, 619/232-4138, www.islandinn.net, $89.95 d) is a better bargain. The location is still pretty central—right across the street from the Convention Center and the water—and rooms are a little less threadbare. Plus, if you plan on staying three weeks or longer you can negotiate a rock-bottom weekly rate of $183 per week. Just remember that you get what you pay for.

$100-200

The views of San Diego are top-notch at

Holiday Inn on the Bay (4610 De Soto St., 858/483-9800, $219 s/d) and the location is within easy walking distance of all of the waterfront sights. Rooms are clean and services are what you'd expect from a chain hotel. But bring your earplugs—some nights the train noise is enough to wake a hibernating bear.

Just one street removed from the commotion of Coronado's Orange Avenue, **Cherokee Lodge** (964 D Ave., Coronado, 619/437-1967, www.cherokeelodge.com, $125 s, $175 d) offers one of the island's most affordable lodging options. The simple rooms are designed to appeal to visitors on government and navy business, so this bed-and-breakfast avoids the explosion of Laura Ashley patterns that too often plague the decor of bed-and-breakfasts. Instead, visitors can get in touch with their masculinity as they are greeted with solid-color bedding, wood-paneled walls, paintings of seafaring adventures, and mahogany-hued furniture.

Located close to the Coronado Ferry Landing, **Coronado Inn** (266 Orange Ave., Coronado, 619/435-4121, www.coronadoinn.com, $165 d, with kitchen $249 d) and nearby sister property **Coronado Island Inn** (301 Orange Ave., Coronado, 619/435-0935, www.coronado inn.com, $149 d) are moderately priced and designed to suit the typical traveler. Rooms are average and both establishments offer free parking and complimentary continental breakfasts. On the whole, the property at Coronado Inn is slightly nicer, with the added bonus of a pool and gas barbecues.

Right across the street from the Hotel del Coronado, **El Cordova Hotel** (1351 Orange Ave., Coronado, 619/435-4131, www.el cordovahotel.com, $149 d) is a pleasantly modest hotel built to resemble a small Spanish village. Around the street perimeter of the hotel are a number of boutiques and restaurants, while the room entrances surround the center pool and barbecue courtyard area to create a cozy community atmosphere. The exterior is decorated with fluted roof tiles, the interior with hand-fired Mexican tile from Tecate. Rooms are small, even the suites, but that is just part of the appeal at this charming little inn.

Crown City Inn (520 Orange Ave., Coronado, 800/422-1173, $139 s, $149 d) is a warm and inviting establishment that welcomes travelers with pets and children. Every room comes outfitted with a microwave and refrigerator and each afternoon the innkeepers set out a spread of cookies, shortbread, and iced tea in the lobby.

$200-300

Villa Capri by the Sea (1417 Orange Ave, Coronado, 619/435-4137, www.villacapriby thesea.com, $219 d, with kitchen $349 d) is an endearing mid-century-modern hotel that has aged reasonably well since it opened in the late 1950s. The well-cared-for rooms surround the itty-bitty pool in the courtyard. Its major attraction can also be its biggest downside, as it is right on a busy stretch of Orange Avenue. Coronado shuts down early, though, so nighttime traffic noise isn't too bad.

Fans of historic inns should book a room in **The Mansion at Glorietta Bay Inn** (1630 Glorietta Blvd., Coronado, 619/435-3101, www.gloriettabayinn.com, $175 d, mansion room $275 d) in Coronado. The beautifully restored Edwardian home was built by sugar baron John D. Spreckels in 1908 and is slavishly faithful about keeping architectural and decorative details as authentic as possible. Only eleven of the inn's 100 rooms are in the mansion itself, so be sure to book early to get a special room.

Even if you don't stay at the **Manchester Grand Hyatt** (1 Market Pl., 619/232-1234, www.manchestergrand.hyatt.com, $280, suites start at $350), the lobby alone is worth a look during a walk along the San Diego waterfront. The entrance is imposing, with windows that creep up four stories, all the way to the top of the towering ceilings. The sun streams through to bathe the marble floors and pillars with sunlight and further illuminate the floor-to-ceiling Spanish Colonial Revival murals.

Rooms and beds are comfortable and even though the two-towered hotel was designed with the business traveler in mind, it is a nice place for families due to its waterfront location,

the large and welcoming pool and tennis courts, the full-service spa, and the on-site babysitting offered to guests.

Over $300

The red gable roofs of the █ **Hotel del Coronado** (1500 Orange Ave., Coronado, 619/435-6611, www.hoteldel.com) are as vibrant as the day she opened in 1888. Even after more than a century of use, this landmark hotel remains one of the most prominent luxury spots in town. Guests here can stroll the adjacent beach, whack a few rounds of balls on the tennis courts, have themselves rubbed down at the full-service spa, or simply sit with a drink at one of the oceanfront pools. The resort has modernized a bit, with contemporary ocean-themed rooms in its cabana and ocean-tower expansion buildings. But in the main building itself rooms match the Victorian architecture, with traditional furnishings and elegant linens. The resort is designed to be extremely family-friendly,

Hotel del Coronado has drawn statesmen and starlets to the region since 1888.

running a number of summertime kids camps. It also hosts special programs and a game room for teens.

Hidden away from downtown Coronado, **Loews Coronado Bay Resort** (4000 Coronado Bay Rd., Coronado, 619/424-4000) has long played second fiddle to the reputation of the legendary Del. But this "other" resort on Coronado deserves more respect than it gets. The property features three heated swimming pools and three bayside tennis courts, a full-service spa, pet-friendly policies, an 80-slip marina, and a secluded atmosphere. Guests can access Silver Strand State Beach via an underpass beneath Rte. 75 and they'll have amazing views of the downtown skyline and the Coronado Bay Bridge.

RV Camping
Camping options are sparse near the city, but RV owners can find shelter on Coronado Island at **Silver Strand State Beach** (5000 Rte. 75, Coronado, 619/435-5184, $30 per night per site). The park allows RV campers to stay overnight for "en route" camping. There are no hookups and campers are required to sleep in their RVs at night, as the park bans tent camping of any kind. The park is pretty strict about this policy and it will turn away any vehicles that aren't completely self-contained. Also be mindful of the fact that the gates close early—at 7 P.M. in winter, 8 P.M. in spring and fall, and 9 P.M. in summer—so don't be late or you won't get in for the evening.

Beyond the strict rules, the campground makes an excellent base from which to explore the dunes of Silver Strand.

BALBOA PARK, UPTOWN, AND MIDCITY
Under $100
Head east of Midcity to find the best bargains. Less than a mile away from San Diego State University, **Best Western Lamplighter Inn** (6474 El Cajon Blvd., 800/545-0778, www.lamplighter-inn.com, $89 d) is a good value for family in town to visit students, or music fans staying the night for a big concert at

Cox Arena. The facility and rooms are absolutely spic-and-span, and the grounds include a modestly sized heated pool. An expanded continental breakfast, including a make-your-own-waffle station, is included in the room rate. In addition to fostering a kid-friendly atmosphere, Lamplighter also accepts pets.

Just over the edge of city limits, **Santee Inn** (10135 Mission Gorge Rd., 619/258-2020, www.thesanteeinn.com, $79 s, $89 d) is an average motel in the little town of Santee. The inn is close enough to the freeway to make the drive downtown reasonable and it has a small kidney bean–shaped pool. It is also pet friendly and includes a limited continental breakfast.

Hotel Occidental (410 Elm St., 619/232-1336, www.hoteloccidental-sandiego.com, twin beds $69 d, double bed $79 d, queen suite $139 d) tries to follow a similar model to 500 West (described in *Accommodations Downtown*). The rooms are not quite as nice as 500 West, however, and the Uptown location is slightly less central to downtown and waterfront attractions. It is close to Balboa Park, however, and the neighborhood is safe.

$100-200
Literally right across the street from Balboa Park's northern edge, **Balboa Park Inn** (3402 Park Blvd., 619/298-0823, www.balboaparkinn.com, $99 d, suite $179–219 d) is a quiet alternative to the typical downtown lodging options. Set in a complex of four Spanish colonials, the inn has a quiet patio that can be mighty inviting after a crowded day at the zoo. Be sure to take a walk around the surrounding neighborhood, which was home to San Diego's affluent families in the early 20th century.

Lafayette Inn and Suites (2223 El Cajon Blvd., 619/296-2101, www.lafayettehotelsd.com, $139 d, more for poolside rooms) is a last-resort kind of hotel. Rooms could be better maintained and the old building doesn't hide its age in spite of recent renovations. But the neighborhood is safe and it is close to Balboa Park and Hillcrest.

$200-300

As the name suggests, all of the rooms at **Park Manor Suites** (3167 5th Ave., 619/296-0057, www.parkmanorsuites.com, $199 s, $219 d) feature full kitchens and dining areas. Located on the west edge of Balboa Park, this stately 80-year-old brick structure has a hint of neoclassical in its exterior accents and inside is decorated with a European flair. Marble floors, ornate chandeliers, bronze sculptures, and damask arm chairs welcome guests in the lobby. Located in Hillcrest, this hotel is a particular favorite among gay and lesbian travelers. On Friday evenings between 5 and 10 P.M. the rooftop bar here hosts a gay cocktail party.

Sommerset Suites Hotel (606 Washington St., 619/692-5200, www.sommersetsuites .com, studio suite $214 d, one-bedroom suite $234 d) offers bare-bones rooms that are large enough to give a big family the space it needs to peaceably survive a vacation. One-bedroom suites come with a fully equipped kitchen and a pull-out sofa bed. Rate includes a continental breakfast each morning.

Over $300

The opulent rooms at **€ Britt Scripps Inn** (406 Maple St., 619/230-1991 or 888/881-1991, www.brittscripps.com, $371–511 d) are an example of Victorian extravagance, with ornate floral bedspreads, rich tapestry, and elegant furniture. Built in 1888 by a man named James Britt for the Scripps family, this gorgeous Queen Anne served as a townhouse for San Diego's favorite benefactors when they ventured from La Jolla to do business in the city. Breakfast is served daily on the wraparound porch and an afternoon wine and cheese service is laid out in the parlor.

MISSION VALLEY AND OLD TOWN

Located a few minutes away from the partiers at the beach and the hustle and bustle of downtown and Balboa Park, the Mission Valley and Old Town corridor is the epicenter of affordable, family-oriented hotels and motels. This is especially true in Mission Valley, which is home to Hotel Circle, a cluster of hotels and motels that line a stretch of I-8. Chain hotels are usually the name of the game here, but there are a few independent establishments as well.

Under $100

Other than Motel 6 and its ilk, **Old Town Inn** (4444 Pacific Hwy., 800/643-3025, $79 d, efficiency $125 d) is one of the least expensive establishments in this area. Accommodations are spartan, but clean. Staff is friendly. And the location is pretty hard to beat, as it is located just a short walk away from Old Town State Historic Park and the Old Town Transit Center. This is a great choice for the budget-conscious family or starving student who plans on taking advantage of the public transit system.

$100-200

Two of the nicer places along Hotel Circle are on the north side of the freeway, abutting the lush greenery of Riverwalk Golf Club. The largest of the two is the 1,000-room **Town and Country Resort** (500 Hotel Circle N., 619/291-7131, www.towncountry.com). This locally owned resort has a large convention center on-site, so its amenities are designed to keep business folk satisfied. The big bonus from this setup is the fact that when there are no large events happening, rates go down. The downside is that the rooms are inconsistent here. Some are new and others look worn. If you can, try to snag one of the Royal Palm Tower rooms, which are some of the better of the bunch.

Next door, the **Crowne Plaza San Diego** (2270 Hotel Circle N., 619/297-1101, www .cp-sandiego.com) is decidedly tourist friendly. The hotel's schtick is its Polynesian theme, so waterfalls, tropical foliage, and tiki decorations abound. The atmosphere borders on the edge of cheesiness without completely teetering over to the tacky side, and honestly kids will love it, especially the pool area. Some of the rooms can be a little dated, and those inexperienced in San Diego hotel rates might think they aren't getting the best deal during high season. Trust me, the rates are fair for the area—especially if you catch a good deal with a third-party online seller.

Across the freeway from the Crowne Plaza on the south side of the hotel circle is **Kings Inn** (1333 Hotel Circle S., 619/297-2231, www.kingsinnsandiego.com, $160 d), a motel that is sufficient when you just can't find a reservation anywhere else in town. Rooms are adequate but lack much of anything beyond a bed, a TV, and a tiny little bathroom. As a plus, it does offer guests free Wi-Fi, the staff is nice, and you get vouchers to eat at the Amigo Spot and Waffle Spot located on the premises.

Located in the center of Old Town activity, **◖ A Victorian Heritage Park Inn** (2470 Heritage Park Row, 619/299-6832, www .heritageparkinn.com, $170 d) is located within the Christian House, a restored Queen Anne in Heritage Park. This pretty building's signatures are its two-story turret and a wraparound veranda. The innkeepers have done justice to the old dame by outfitting her in period furniture and decor. Guests are served a full breakfast at the dining room's candlelit table, and with many an international guest staying here you are sure to hear fascinating travel tales over the fine comestibles.

Nearby **◖ Hacienda Old Town** (4041 Harney St., 619/298-4707, www.haciendahotel -oldtown.com, $175 s/d) is a cute place that has a number of Spanish-style buildings scattered over a hillside that overlooks Old Town and the downtown skyline. The hotel is centrally located in Old Town—in fact it is hard to miss from the shopping district due to the distinctive architecture—which makes it a great base of operation for sampling the margaritas at all of the nearby Mexican joints without worrying about a drive back to the hotel. Don't expect to get too rowdy, though, as the Hacienda is still very family-oriented.

NORTH CITY
$100-200

The northern outposts of town tend to either be bedroom communities or open spaces,

limiting lodging options more than within city limits. Most of the available accommodations up here are luxury resorts, but the **Best Western Inn Miramar** (9310 Kearny Mesa Rd., 858/578-6600 or 800/827-2635) does have affordable rooms that can work in a pinch for those in the neighborhood on business or to visit family.

Over $300

Rancho Bernardo Inn (17550 Bernardo Oaks Dr., 858/675-8500, www.rancho bernardoinn.com,$289 s, $259 d) manages to dazzle guests with the amenities of a large resort—golf course, spa, gardens, and tennis courts—while maintaining the intimate atmosphere of a small inn. Rooms and suites are decorated in an elegant but casual Spanish Revival motif and are all equipped with huge 42-inch plasma TVs, deep soaking tubs and Aveda bath products, and a private patio overlooking some type of greenery, be it gardens or the on-site golf course. The room rate includes a full breakfast at the resort's patio restaurant, the Veranda.

Another option for a golf retreat is **Doubletree Golf Resort** (14455 Penasquitos Dr., 858/672-9100, $269 d), which is not nearly as nice and lacks a spa but still sports a championship golf course, tennis courts, and a more kid-friendly pool area.

Camping

Tent campers will typically need to drive out of the city in order to find a decent campsite, but there is a notable exception in the north part of the city. **Kumeyaay Lake Campground** (2 Father Junipero Serra Tr., 619/668-2748, www .mtrp.org/campground) in Mission Trails Regional Park offers 46 primitive sites with picnic tables, a firebox, tent pad, and bathrooms with hot-water showers on premises. First-come, first-serve camping is available, but I'd highly recommend making an online reservation during high season. Camping costs $14 per site per night with one vehicle; $4 each additional vehicle. One camping unit per site; pets are $3 each.

Food

Even a couple of decades ago, San Diego wasn't well known for its culinary lineup. Things have changed, as the city has attracted many a top-notch chef to lead the new era of dining in San Diego. In addition to many new (and not-so-new) fine dining establishments, there are plenty of casual spots to find a messy burger, barbecue, or a simple sandwich.

DOWNTOWN
Cafés and Casual Eats

If Maverick, Goose, and Iceman are names that mean something to you, then you better plan on making a landing at **Kansas City Barbeque** (610 W. Market St., 619/231-9680, www.kcbbq.net, 11 A.M.–2 A.M. daily, $12). This long-running establishment was an on-location set for the piano scene and the final jukebox scene in the 1986 schmaltz classic *Top Gun*. The bar still sports a collection of *Top Gun* memorabilia, including the fighter helmet worn by Tom Cruise as Maverick. Come for the movie memorabilia, but be sure to stay for some barbecue, which is sweet and smoky.

The fish-and-chips at **Shakespeare Pub** (3701 India St., 619/299-0230, www.shakespeare pub.com, 11 A.M.–midnight Mon.–Thurs., 11 A.M.–1 A.M. Fri., 7 A.M.–1 A.M. Sat., 8 A.M.–midnight Sun., entrée $8) come with a chunk of cod the size of a log. With a splash of vinegar this crispy treat is to die for, but if fried seafood isn't your thing Shakespeare also plates a number of other English favorites such as bangers and mash and steak-and-kidney pie. The bar is a favorite with soccer fans, who often crowd in to watch the football matches streamed through satellite here.

If you are planning a romantic picnic at any of the hundreds of green spots in town and you like cheese, stop—do not pass Go, do not collect $200—and immediately head to **Venissimo Cheese** (754 W. Washington St., 619/491-0708, www.venissimo.com, 10 A.M.–6 P.M. Mon.–Sat.). This is the temple at which cheese worshippers of San Diego prostrate

themselves. It sells cheddars, Bries, Stiltons, chèvres, and everything in between from all over the world. To complete that picnic basket it also has a selection of fruits, nuts, olives, and crackers, plus a few selected aged meats. You'll have to go elsewhere for the wine, though.

My suggestion for wine to complement your picnic is **Wine Steals** (1243 University Ave., 619/295-1188, www.winesteals.com, 4–11 P.M. Mon., 11 A.M.–11P.M. Tues.–Wed., Sun., 11 A.M.–midnight Thurs.–Fri.), which is only about a mile away from Venissimo—take Washington Street east and veer right when the road forks into University Avenue. The store has a varied selection of vino that suits just about any budget and taste. If you ask nicely, the knowledgeable staff can probably even help you pair with your cheeses.

California Cuisine

Toast to the service, toast to the food, but most of all, toast to the views at **Bertrand at Mister A's** (2550 5th Ave., #406, 619/239-1377, www.bertrandatmisteras.com), one of San Diego's finest rooftop eateries with views of the glittering San Diego skyline and the waterfront. The menu is California cuisine at its best, a touch of French flavor here, a dash of Japanese inspiration there, and a supreme respect for fresh meat and seafood throughout. Don't dare leaving without dipping your spoon through the glassy crust of the house's crème brûlée, a must-have dessert.

Late-night diners will love the brooding and seductive atmosphere at **Modus** (2202 4th Ave., 619/236-8516, www.modusbarlounge.com, 5 P.M.–1:30 A.M. Tues.–Sun.), a sophisticated supper club for those who occasionally like some food with their drink. The food is tasty, but the real allure here is the atmosphere. If this restaurant were a woman, she'd be wearing dark eye shadow and a slinky black cocktail dress.

Chive (558 4th Ave., 619/232-4483, www.chiverestaurant.com, 5–10 P.M. Sun.–Thurs., 5–11 P.M. Fri.–Sat., $13), on the other hand, would be donning a chic white sundress. The design is every bit as hip as Modus, but the atmosphere is a lot more airy and bright. Entrées come tapas style. Be prepared to be wowed by the presentation, which is as painstakingly attended to here as the flavors.

Many long-time San Diegans agree that Ingrid Croce was one of the most instrumental pioneers in the Gaslamp Quarter revitalization. Wife of folk crooner Jim Croce, Ingrid opened **Croce's** (802 5th Ave., 619/233-4355, www.croces.com, 5:30 P.M.–midnight Mon.–Fri., 10 A.M.–midnight Sat.–Sun., $28) in 1985 when the Gaslamp was still a bad part of town. This fine-dining restaurant is now at the core of the area's food and entertainment scene, serving a mix of pastas, steaks, seafood, and salads to the diners who come just as much for the food as they do for the nightly jazz shows.

Also in the Gaslamp is **JSix** (616 J St., 619/531-8744, www.jsixsandiego.com, 11:30 A.M.–10 P.M. Sun.–Wed., 11:30 A.M.–11 P.M. Thurs.–Sat.), which serves a Coastal California menu that's heavy on seafood and fresh produce. Its chef is a big proponent of sourcing ingredients from local and sustainable farms, ranches, and fisheries, so the only thing you'll feel guilty about after a meal here is your bulging waistline. The extended hours and eclectic atmosphere also make it a nice hangout for an appetizer and a glass of wine before the rest of the Gaslamp's fine-dining establishments open up after the break between lunch and dinner.

Steak and Seafood

Carnivores will leave **Rei Do Gado Brazilian Steak House** (939 4th Ave., 619/702-8464, www.reidogado.net, 11 A.M.–10 P.M. Sun.–Thurs., 11 A.M.–11 P.M. Fri.–Sat., $40) more than sated. This Brazilian restaurant serves customers an all-you-can-eat feast of savory meats supplemented by a large selection of salads and hot sides from its buffet spread. The choices are unbelievable—17 different kinds of meats, from filet mignon to leg of lamb, are sliced off of the skewer on which they've just been roasting and placed on your plate for as long as your stomach can take it. At $40 per person it is on the pricey side, but you can save a few dollars

by eating here in the middle of the day for the largely unchanged $15 lunch feast.

Those craving a traditional steakhouse dinner should check out **Georges on 5th** (835 5th Ave., 619/702-0444)—or G5, as some of the locals like to call it. The ambience is livened up with a bit of Wyatt Earp memorabilia spread around the dining room and the steak is as good as the prices suggest. This is one of the last remaining holdouts in this rumpled town to enforce a dress code, so men need to be sure to bring a dinner jacket. Please be kind to the chefs and do yourself a favor in the process: Don't order anything well-done. Nobody likes to see a tender piece of prime mangled that way.

At **Turf Supper Club** (1116 25th St., 619/234-6363, 5 P.M.–midnight Mon.–Tues., 5 P.M.–2 A.M. Wed.–Fri., 1 P.M.–2 A.M. Sat.–Sun.), you can cook your meat any way you want it. This trendy establishment lets patrons put the sizzle in their own steak at the communal grill. The buzz of cooking around the grill stimulates a lot of social action, making the scene a blast for groups of singles looking to hit it off with a potential Mr. or Ms. Right.

Italian

Little Italy is an obvious choice to find *cibo italiano.* There are a number of restaurants that offer a range of dining experiences, but the informal trattorias are where Little Italy excels.

One excellent choice in this category is **Mimmo's** (1743 India St., 619/239-3710, www.mimmos.biz, lunch 10 A.M.–3 P.M. Mon.–Sat., dinner 5–9 P.M. Mon.–Thurs., 5–11 P.M. Fri.–Sat., noon–9 P.M. Sun., $12). Lunch is served deli-style, while dinner is served on the patio or in the informal dining room. The food rivals some of the more expensive Italian joints in town, without the stuffy atmosphere or the earth-shattering bill at the end.

Zagarella's (1655 India St., 619/236-8764, www.zagarellarestaurant.com, lunch 11 A.M.–2 P.M. Mon.–Fri., dinner 5–10 P.M. Mon.–Sun., $15) is another fine trattoria in the neighborhood. The menu is more diverse than Mimmo's, and also a little more expensive.

Stock up to make your own homemade

Italian meal at **Assenti's Pasta** (2044 India St., 619/239-5117), which sells the genuine article when it comes to fresh pasta. On weekend afternoons you'll see little old ladies streaming in and out of the shop in preparation for their family feasts.

Venture out of Little Italy for some of the city's better Italian fine-dining experiences. In the Gaslamp are two of the best Tuscan restaurants in the city. Right in the middle of the Gaslamp excitement is **AquaAl2** (322 5th Ave., 619/230-0382, www.aquaal2.com, lunch 11:30 A.M.–2 P.M. Mon.–Fri., dinner 5 P.M.–2 A.M. daily), the sister restaurant to a popular restaurant in Florence that has been frequented by international stars for almost 30 years. Opened in 2000, the American version imported many of the restaurant's signature dishes, including Fileno al Mirtilio, filet mignon topped with a blueberry sauce, a surprisingly complementary pair.

Like a woman who knows she's beautiful without needing to constantly preen in front of the mirror, **Trattoria La Strada** (702 5th Ave., 619/239-3400, www.trattorialastrada.com, 11 A.M.–11 P.M. Sun.–Thurs., 11 A.M.–12:30 A.M. Fri.–Sat. $23) is a little less pretentious than AquaAl2. The food is just as rich, though, with veal, chicken, and seafood playing the starring role in the best entrées here. If you really want to taste the quality of the meats, the restaurant serves a well-rounded selection of carpaccio.

Asian

For a West Coast town, San Diego is sadly a bit bereft of a well-rounded mix of Asian cuisine. It is possible to find it; you just have to search a lot harder than you should have to.

Most of the town's very best Far Eastern restaurants are located north of I-8 on Kearny Mesa, but downtown does have the best Indian. One of the perennial favorites is **Monsoon** (729 4th Ave., 619/234-5555, www.monsoonrestaurant.com), an upscale restaurant that elevates Indian cuisine beyond the simple pleasures of tandoori and vindaloo. The selection on the six-page menu is staggering. Before you even start your meal you'll have to

choose between eight different kinds of naan (leavened flat bread) and an equal number of chutneys and pickles. If you don't think you'll be able to choose between the mint curry or the mango ($14.50 for vegetarian, more with meats), the *roghan ghosht* (lamb with spiced yogurt, mint, and mustard seeds) or the Calcutta shrimp simmered in spiced cream and cardamom pods, consider coming during a weekday lunch ($13.95) or Monday dinner ($19.95), when a self-serve buffet is laid out.

Trendy sushi bars are quite plentiful in the Gaslamp, but beware—there are a few stinkers out there that try to skate by on decor alone. Not so at **Taka** (555 5th Ave., 619/338-0555, www.takasushi.com), where the sashimi is fresh and delicate and the wasabi is nose-clearingly spicy. The place has killer *anmitsu* ($5) for dessert; that's green-tea ice cream with sweet red beans and fruit jelly covered with black sugar syrup.

Mandarin House (2604 5th Ave., 619/232-1101, 11 A.M.–10 P.M. Mon.–Thurs., 11 A.M.–11 P.M. Fri., noon–11 P.M. Sat., 2 P.M.–10 P.M. Sun., $8) on Bankers Hill serves up very good, albeit slightly Americanized, Chinese food. The house specialty is the must-have: salt-pepper chicken dredged in seasoned flour and pan-fried with mounds of garlic, green onion, and spicy red peppers.

Dessert

Gelato is easy to find in Little Italy, but the best is served at **Gelato Vero Caffe** (3753 India St., 619/295-9269, www.gelatovero.net, 6 A.M.–midnight Mon.–Thurs., 6 A.M.–1 A.M. Fri., 7 A.M.–1 A.M. Sat., 7 A.M.–midnight Sun.). Try the spumoni—its rich and creamy base is studded with pistachios, cherries, and chocolate and is heavenly on a summer day.

Speaking of divinity, **Heaven Sent Desserts** (3001 University Ave., 619/793-4758, www.heavensentdesserts.net, 11 A.M.–11 P.M. Tues.–Thurs., 11 A.M.–midnight Fri.–Sat., 11 A.M.–10 P.M. Sun.) offers a number of desserts that transcend earthly delights. The house's strong suit is its cakes.

Probably no dessert joint in town can match the atmosphere and the selection of

SAN DIEGO

⟨ **Extraordinary Desserts** (www.extra ordinarydesserts.com). It's the secret weapon of many a local Casanova, a place where you'll be seated in a quiet nook and waited on hand and foot by servers clad all in black who seem to be able to produce just about any sugary concoction that has ever been dreamed up. The menu has tortes, tarts, custards, cookies, ice cream, iced cakes, and cupcakes galore. This café runs two locations: The original is on Bankers Hill (2929 5th Ave., 619/294-2132, 8:30 A.M.–11 P.M. Sun.–Thurs., 10 A.M.–midnight Fri.–Sat.) and the second spot is in Little Italy (1430 Union St., 619/294-7001, 8:30 A.M.– 11 P.M. Mon.–Thurs., 8:30 A.M.–midnight Fri., 10 A.M.–midnight Sat., 10 A.M.–11 P.M. Sun.).

WATERFRONT AND CORONADO
Cafés and Casual Eats

Coronado village is filled with great little cafés from which you can sip coffee, munch on sandwiches, and watch a streaming procession of amblers poke and prod their way through adjoining gift shops and boutiques.

For prime people-watching, nothing beats the patio at **Tent City** (1100 Orange Ave., Coronado, 619/435-4611, www.tentcity restaurant.com). Named for the resort of candy-striped canvas tents that would be pitched at the foot of Hotel del Coronado each summer in the early 20th century, this café is run by the Coronado Historical Association and abuts their quaint history museum. It is situated on a well-traveled section of Orange Avenue and there are lots of places to pull up a chair outside. The patio is also dog friendly—if they aren't busy the nice staffers might even bring your pooch a bit of water to lap up while you eat.

Occupying that culinary ground somewhere between a bistro and a fine restaurant, **Rhinocerous Cafe and Grille** (1166 Orange Ave., Coronado, 619/435-2121, www.rhinocafe .com, lunch 11 A.M.–2:30 P.M. daily, dinner 5 P.M. to close daily, $17) takes its food a bit more serious than the average café—it must be that extra "e" that they tacked on to the end of "grill." Casual diners will feel most comfortable during lunch,

Nibble on a sandwich and watch the people stream by from the patio of Tent City.

© ERICKA CHICKOWSKI

but at dinnertime rumpled beachwear is discouraged and reservations are recommended.

No such formalities are required at **Night and Day Café** (847 Orange Ave., Coronado, 619/435-9776, 24 hours daily, entrée $7), which is the closest thing to a dive-y diner you'll find in Coronado. It is actually quite nice and the food is less heavy than most all-night greasy spoons.

After the kind of night that might require a stop in Night and Day Café, a little restorative grub might be in order once the sun shines again. **Bino's** (120 Adella St., Coronado, 619/522-0612, www.binosbistro.com, 7 A.M.– 5 P.M. Mon.–Wed., 7 A.M.–8 P.M. Thurs.–Sun., entrée $8) is the perfect kind of out-of-the-way café to nurse a hangover on one of those dreaded mornings-after. Nestled away from the rush of Orange Avenue, this little coffee shop specializes in scrumptious crepes.

On the other side of the bay there are precious few cafés of much merit along the San Diego waterfront. The best bet may be to go looking further inland in the Gaslamp Quarter or near Balboa Park.

California Cuisine

An eclectic blend of California cuisine with hints of Italian, French, and Mediterranean influence, **Molly's Restaurant** (333 W. Harbor Dr., 619/230-8909, www.mollysfinedining.com, 5:30–9 P.M. Sun.–Thurs., 5:30–10 P.M. Fri.–Sat., entrée $30) sits by the pool at the Marriott Hotel and Marina. This is a dinner-jacket sort of place, without the stuffy inevitability of actually being required to wear one. The chef's daily selection of freshly made pasta is melt-in-your-mouth delectable and entrée meats and seafood are all juicy and well prepared. The real treat here is the amazing selection of artisan cheeses, which span the spectrum of creamy mild flavors to sharp and strong, and are paired on plates with honeycomb, raisin bread, and seasonal fruits and nuts. My recommendation is to share the six-cheese selection plate ($20) and eat lighter entrées.

Seafood

San Diego has a cornucopia of waterfront-view restaurants, but none tops the skyline sight lines of **Peohe's** (1201 1st St., Coronado, 619/437-4474, www.peohes.com, $26). This Coronado favorite serves up sea critters tropical style, with Polynesian decor and indoor waterfalls to match. Be sure to ask your server to bring over one of their signature Pupu platters.

Those who'd like their seafood with a heaping helping of history should visit **Coronado Boathouse** (1701 Strand Way, Coronado, 619/435-0155, 5–10 P.M. Sun.–Thurs., 5–11 P.M. Fri.–Sat.). It's the distinctive Victorian set on Glorietta Bay that looks a bit like a "mini Del." Some make the mistake of fingering the boathouse as a send-up of the famous hotel, but the building was actually erected a year before Hotel del Coronado. The restaurant lives up to its splendid setting with a fresh and flavorful selection of seafood.

Speaking of the Del, the famous hotel also hosts its own lineup of fine seafood at **1500 Ocean** (1500 Orange Ave., Coronado, 619/435-6611, www.hoteldel.com, 5:30–10:30 P.M. daily, bar 5:30–midnight daily, $26). The res-

taurant overlooks the resort's beachfront and serves a menu that relies on local Southern Californian ingredients.

Not to be confused with the one on Coronado, **The Boathouse** on Harbor Island (1220 El Carmel Pl., 858/488-6242, www.boathouse restaurant.com, $21) offers traditional seafood and steak, with a healthy dose of pasta as well.

Also on the mainland side of the bay are a pair of eateries over at Seaport Village. Set on stilts over the bay, **San Diego Pier Café** (885 W. Harbor Dr., 619/239-3968, www.piercafe.com) wins out in terms of nautical ambience. The restaurant is set in a Coastal New England–style building, with a menu to match. But **Harbor House** (831 W. Harbor Dr., 619/232-1141, www.harbor housesd.com) has it beat in terms of food. While you are there, make your taste buds tingle with one of their beer oyster shooters, served with local suds made by Karl Strauss Brewery.

French

There are several charming French restaurants to choose from in the heart of downtown Coronado.

Chez Loma serves some of the best French onion soup in town.

© ERICKA CHICKOWSKI

Antique Row Café is best known for its ample breakfasts, but it can also be a tasty lunchtime rest stop for shoppers in Normal Heights.

Right along the main drag, **Crown Bistro** (520 Orange Ave., Coronado, 619/435-3678, www .crownbistro.com, breakfast 8 A.M.–2 P.M. daily, lunch 11 A.M.–2 P.M. daily, dinner 5–9 P.M. daily, Champagne Breakfast 8 A.M.–2 P.M. Sun., $15) serves a heavily Americanized version of French food. On Sundays the bistro cancels lunch altogether in favor of its Champagne Brunch, served until 2 P.M. Reservations are recommended for this weekly event, as well as for dinner.

Set within a cute little Victorian on a village side street, **◖ Chez Loma** (1132 Loma Ave., Coronado, 619/435-0661, www.chezloma .com, $27) offers more traditional French cuisine. If you go, be sure to supplement your meal with a cup of the onion soup—it is some of the best I've ever tasted, with big, delicious cuts of onion that taste as if they've been caramelizing for days. Bargain hunters may want to go early: Chez Loma offers an early-bird three-course prix fixe menu for $24.95 between 5 and 6 P.M. every day. The special also stands all evening on Tuesday.

BALBOA PARK, UPTOWN, AND MIDCITY
Breakfast and Brunch

By day **Rudford's** (2900 El Cajon Blvd., 619/282-8423, www.rudfords.com, 24 hours daily, entrée $7) is the kind of place where you can get a filling breakfast even when the sun has risen well above its highest point. By night you can still get the breakfast, along with a host of other American diner faves such as chicken-fried steak and patty melts with fries.

Only a few blocks north there is also the popular **Antique Row Café** (3002 Adams Ave., 619/282-9750, 6 A.M.–10 P.M. Mon.–Fri., 6 A.M.–3 P.M. Sat.–Sun., entrée $8). This quaint little breakfast spot is right in the middle of Antique Row in Normal Heights and is itself awash in old bric-a-brac and curios. Servings are huge and known to have cured more than one hangover over the years. Just get there early on the weekend or you'll encounter a long line. On the plus side, the diner offers coffee and cinnamon roll bites for those patient enough to wait.

Cafés and Casual Eats

Right in the center of Balboa Park, the **Tea Pavilion at the Japanese Friendship Garden** (2215 Pan American Plaza, 619/231-0048, 10 A.M.–4 P.M. daily, summer weekends 10 A.M.–5 P.M.) is a great place to rest between museum tours and garden walks. The café serves a light menu of sushi, rice bowls, noodles, and salads.

Painted in the bright red, green, and white colors of the Mexican flag, **Frutilandia** (3647 University Ave., 619/282-0774, 7 A.M.–8 P.M. Mon.–Fri., 8 A.M.–8 P.M. Sat., 8 A.M.–7 P.M. Sun.) is what those south of the border call a *frutería*. It specializes in drinks, dishes, and treats made with fruits of all stripes. Fill up on a fruit salad made with a mix of standard and exotic fruits, quench your thirst with an *agua fresca*—fruit mashed into water with a splash of lemon or lime and a dash of sugar—or satisfy both urges with a *licuado*—a milkshake made with fresh fruit and milk.

The **Egyptian Tearoom** (4644 College Ave., 619/265-7287) provides sustenance and relaxation for SDSU students starved for both. Not far from campus, the Tearoom is usually a quiet spot in the afternoons and early evenings, doling out hummus and pita ($4.95), vegetarian couscous ($4.95), and gyro sandwiches ($5.95) to customers as they work on their homework. In the evening the social butterflies drop in to share a hookah packed with tobacco flavored with fruity aromas.

DZ Akins (6930 Alvarado Rd., 619/265-0218, www.dzakinsdeli.com, 7 A.M.–9 P.M. Sun.–Thurs., 7 A.M.–10 P.M. Fri.–Sat.) is one of the few delis in town that can satisfy someone with a hankering for a true New York–style corned-beef sandwich. DZ has all of the morning-through-night traditional deli fare many East Coasters miss out on in SoCal, including blintzes, bagels and lox, and matzo-ball soup.

On the east side of North Park, **Caffe Forte** (3139 University Ave., 619/283-4710) presents the standard independent-coffee-shop vibe—edgy decor, friendly regulars, and a revolving circus of staff that can vary from cheerful and upbeat to efficiently morose. The coffee is tasty and if you are feeling social it is a good place to strike up a conversation with one of the locals.

The lighting is dim, the plates are industrial grade, and food is served off a cart, but the **Chicken Pie Shop** (2633 El Cajon Blvd., 619/295-0156, 10 A.M.–8 P.M. daily) is still a great place. For $6 you get a chicken or beef pie served up with soup, potatoes, veggies, coleslaw, a roll, a slice of fruit pie, and bit of friendly banter from the waitresses that roll those carts up and down the dining room. The menu also offers fried chicken, sandwiches, and other such sundries, but trust me and order the pie meal—it's what everyone else is having.

Vegetarian and Vegan

As would be expected in health-conscious Southern California, most restaurants in town offer something tasty for vegetarians. But if you are looking for a restaurant or store that caters strictly to the vegetarian and vegan palate, your best bet is probably the Uptown and College neighborhoods.

One well-known spot is **Spread** (2879 University Ave., 619/543-0406, www.spreadtherestaurant.com, 5:30–11 P.M. Tues.–Fri.,11 A.M.–3 P.M. and 6–11 P.M. Sat., 9 A.M.–3 P.M. Sun.), a North Park eatery that bills its fare as "Nouveau Comfort Food." It is completely organic, with offerings for both vegans and vegetarians, and an emphasis on creativity. Because the menu changes based on the local produce offerings, the menu varies. Some past items include macadamia rosemary grits, Thai veggie pizza, and wild-mushroom ragu.

Another spot in nearby Normal Heights is **Jyoti-Bihanga** (3351 Adams Ave., 619/282-4116, www.jyotibihanga.com, 11 A.M.–9 P.M. Mon.–Tues. and Thurs.–Fri.,11 A.M.–3 P.M. Wed., noon–9 P.M. Sat.), which is run by the students of the spiritual leader Sri Chinmoy. The menu features a variety of salads, sandwiches, and wraps that rely on fresh produce and house-made veggie protein patties.

Vegans who'd like to pick up a few snacks would do well to visit **All Vegan Store** (4669 Park Blvd., 619/299-4669, www.allvegan shopping.com, 11 A.M.–7 P.M. Tues.,

11 A.M.–8 P.M. Wed., 2–8 P.M. Thurs.–Fri., 10 A.M.–9 P.M. Sat., 1–6 P.M. Sun.) in University Heights. Similarly, vegetarians and vegans especially appreciate the organic produce and healthy packaged food offered at the specialty grocer **Henry's** (4175 Park Blvd., 619/291-8287, www.henrysmarkets.com, 7 A.M.–10 P.M. daily). This local chain is a subsidiary of Whole Foods and can be found throughout the city. There is a location in North Park that is very close to Balboa Park.

Contemporary

I hesitate to write about ◖ **Adams Avenue Grill** (2201 Adams Ave., 619/298-8440, www .adamsavenuegrill.com, breakfast from 9 A.M. Sat.–Sun., lunch 11 A.M.–2 P.M. daily, , dinner from 5 P.M. daily, $19) because I feel like this little spot is my own personal dining room and I'd hate to wait for a seat—but for you, dear reader, I have an obligation. Hidden away in a non-commercial stretch of Adams Avenue, this intimate restaurant serves a mixture of home-style dishes, such as the daily pot roast ($16.95), and daring experimental meals such as the saffron-infused poached salmon with peach chutney ($19.95). This is the type of place that warrants a full meal: appetizers through dessert and a wheelbarrow to roll you out in. Be sure to get a taste of the goat-cheese-and-walnut fritters ($8.25) before filling up on dinner, and save room for desserts such as the pecan caramel triangle ($5.95).

Another neighborhood fave, farther southeast in North Park, is **The Linkery** (3382 30th St., 619/255-8778, www.thelinkery.com, 5–11 P.M. daily, $10), which makes up a fresh menu of gourmet homemade sausages each day. You can order them in a tasty picnic plate along with cheese and a spinach salad, in tacos, or as an add-on to one of their other entrée items. This progressive eatery is serious about buying meats and produce from organic and sustainable sources—a list of its vendors is printed on the menu. It is also unique in that waiters work for a higher salary and do not accept tips. If you leave behind a gratuity it will be donated to a rotating list of charities chosen by the owners.

Southern

Those headed to Balboa Park for an afternoon should make time for a leisurely lunch at **Gulf Coast Grill** (4130 Park Blvd., 619/295-2244, www.gulfcoastgrill.com, lunch 11 A.M.–2 P.M. Mon.–Sat., brunch 9 A.M.–2 P.M. Sun., $18) before they hit the museums. Just blocks away from the park, this eatery fuses flavors of the South and the Southwest to create a happy blend of fresh and spicy flavors. Their blackened seafood is tops on the menu. Try the shrimp atop their Gulf Greens Salad ($9.95) for a refreshing midday meal.

Literally steps away from the Euclid Avenue trolley stop, **Magnolia's** (342 Euclid Ave., 619/262-6005, www.magnoliasdining .com, $15) serves Cajun cooking with that special Southern hospitality. This is the real deal. You'll find authentic filé gumbo, jambalaya, and cornmeal-crusted fried oysters here. The only downside is the location—it is smack dab in the middle of a sterile-looking strip mall. However, its owners have done a good job of dressing up the interior to liven up the Southern ambience and the restaurant features a secluded garden patio in back that completes the effect.

Not far away, **Bonnie Jean's Soul Food** (1964 54th St., 619/262-8854, 11:30 A.M.–7 P.M. Tues.–Thurs., 11:30 A.M.– 9 P.M. Fri.–Sat., 11:30 A.M.–6 P.M. Sun.) has the atmosphere part of the equation down to an art. Its owners like to promote good morsels and good morals—they've decorated the little house the restaurant is set in with Christian artwork, and soulful gospel music is piped through the speakers. Real salvation comes here by way of a full stomach, which should easily be attained with a menu that's packed with old Southern comforts such as ribs, fried chicken, oxtail, and collard greens.

Spanish

Set amid the flourishes of Balboa Park's Spanish Revival architecture, **The Prado** (1549 El Prado, 619/557-9441, dinner 5–9 P.M. Tues.– Thurs., 5–10 P.M. Fri.–Sat., and 4–8 P.M. Sun., entrée $23) delivers food to match the surrounding ambience. As an added bonus, the restaurant operates a food and wine school for nonprofessionals, with observational cooking classes and wine seminars.

Asian

Consistently voted as the best Thai food in San Diego in local publications, **Lotus Thai** (3761 6th Ave., 619/299-8272, www.lotusthai cuisine.com) in Hillcrest has some of the lightest, crispiest spring rolls on the planet and its pad thai is the perfect blend of sweet and spicy that too many other places are unable to balance.

If Asian fusion cuisine is your kind of thing, **Kemo Sabe** (3958 5th Ave., 619/220-6802) is a fun option in Hillcrest. The chef here unites Pacific Rim and Southwestern flavors in combinations that are surprisingly complementary. For example, blackened *satay* chicken breasts are served with chile corn cakes and melon salsa, and onion cake enchiladas are stuffed with *moo shu* pork and Szechwan plum salsa.

MISSION VALLEY AND OLD TOWN
Breakfast and Brunch

Step into a time warp at **Perry's** (4620 Pacific Hwy., 619/291-7121, 6 A.M.–2 P.M. daily), a 1960s-era breakfast joint that has buffeted the attacks of California health consciousness to continue serving the same greasy-spoon goodness that the locals have been enjoying for decades. Mexican and American breakfasts are equally good here and the cups of coffee are strong and bottomless. Don't be scared off by the wait on the weekends. The staff is swarming the place to efficiently usher customers toward gluttonous satisfaction. Just step up to the register, scribble your name on the notepad, and it'll be no time at all before you're elbows deep in a hearty breakfast.

Steak and Burgers

The vibe at **Hunter Steakhouse** (2445 Hotel Circle N., 619/291-8074, www.paragonsteak .com, 11:30 A.M.–9 P.M. Mon.–Fri., 11:30 A.M.–10 P.M. Sat., 4–9 P.M. Sun., entrée $21) is that of an old college club or the well-appointed den of a stately manor. You'll sink down into the comfortable plush booths and relax under the diffuse lighting that glows around the dark woods that accent the walls. The steaks are prime cuts and sides are as thoughtfully prepared as the meat.

Listen up, pilgrim. **Longhorn Café** (6519 Mission Gorge Rd., 619/283-0831) has some manly size burgers—if you are lucky you can eat them under the squinty gaze of the Duke himself. This burger joint in Mission Valley has a whole room dedicated to John Wayne memorabilia for those who are into his films. In addition to burgers with all the fixin's, you can sink your teeth into the juicy steak sandwiches.

For some of the best pub grub in Mission Valley, head over to **McGregor's** (10475 San Diego Mission Rd., 619/282-9797, 11 A.M.–2 A.M. Mon.–Fri., 10 A.M.–2 A.M. Sat.–Sun., $9). Set in an inauspicious strip mall, this restaurant and bar is a favorite watering hole for locals. It is located very close to Qualcomm Stadium, making it a good place to continue the festivities after the Chargers hit the gridiron.

Fondue

Kids will love to dunk their bread, meats, and fruits into the pots at **Forever Fondue** (6110 Friars Rd., 619/295-7792, 5–10 P.M. Sun.–Thurs., 5–11 P.M. Fri.–Sat., entrée $30) in Mission Valley. This classy but casual eatery equips diners with traditional fondue gear and lets them choose their flavors. The all-inclusive meals come with a cheese fondue pot of your choice with breads, veggies, and apples; a salad; and a brothy entrée pot in which to cook one of seven assortment trays of meats and vegetables. It is all capped off with a dessert pot—there are ten chocolatey concoctions to choose from—served with fruit, pound cake, cheesecake, and Rice Krispie treats.

Mexican

The stars of **Old Town Mexican Café** (2489 San Diego Ave., 619/297-4330, www.oldtown mexcafe.com, 7 A.M.–2 A.M. daily, entrée $10) are the "Tortilla Ladies of Old Town" who pat and form over 7,000 corn and flour tortillas every day. Passersby can watch them do their thing through the big picture windows that face the street. So can expectant diners, who line up in an eager crowd—the wait is an hour or longer at dinnertime in the summer and during the Christmas to New Year's rush. To beat the crowds try to plan a visit at lunchtime or even in the morning for a filling Mexican breakfast. In the morning, the huevos rancheros or the *machaca* (eggs scrambled with shredded beef, onions and bell peppers) are best. Tops on the lunch and dinner menu is the *carnitas* feast that can be shared among everyone at the table.

Rockin' Baja (3890 Twiggs St., 619/260-0305, 11 A.M.– 9 P.M. Sun.–Thurs., 11 A.M.–10:30 P.M. Fri.–Sat., entrée $20) buzzes with fun. This Mexican seafood restaurant specializes in Baja-style slipper lobster tails, which are flash-fried and served up in the place's signature tin pails. These buckets can also come with shrimp, chicken, and carne asada. All of the meals here come with rice, beans, and tortillas, as well as unlimited rights to pile your plate with the green stuff over at the salad and salsa bar.

Those interested in practicing their Spanish without eating yet another taco can saunter over to **Berta's** (3928 Twiggs St., 619/295-2343, www.bertasinoldtown.com, 11 A.M.–10 P.M. Tues.–Sun., $15). This restaurant dishes out flavors from all over Latin America and beyond, and the menu bursts with empanadas, paellas, fricassees, and flans.

NORTH CITY
Breakfast and Brunch

TV geeks should insist on stopping by **Studio Diner** (4701 Ruffin Rd., 858/715-6400, 24 hours daily, $10), set on the lot of Stu Segall Productions, a working movie and TV studio that produced shows like *Renegade, Silk Stockings,* and *Veronica Mars.* This nostalgic restaurant is decorated inside with film memorabilia and the shiny chrome exterior adds an impressive touch of authenticity. The fare here is typical diner grub, served up around the clock.

94th Aero Squadron (8885 Balboa Ave.,

858/560-6771 or 858/560-6953, 94thsd @sbcglobal.net) re-creates the feel of a WWI-era French farmhouse in its architecture and decor. The ambience is enhanced by the fact that the restaurant borders the airstrip at Montgomery Field, so you can watch small aircraft take off and land as you sip mimosas and listen to period music piped through the sound system. Brunch is served between 9 A.M. and 3 P.M. on Sundays and the spread here has enough food to keep you full for a whole week. The buffet includes prime rib, ham, peel-n-eat shrimp, crab legs, salads, breads and pastries, an omelet and waffle station, and a whole smorgasbord of desserts. The place is packed during brunch, so be sure to make reservations well in advance.

French

If you've been exploring the northern reaches of the county, there is no reason to stick out the traffic on I-15 south in order to enjoy a fine meal. Barely within the northernmost fingers of city limits, Rancho Bernardo has several venerable French establishments worth stopping for.

Just off the Rancho Bernardo Road exit, **Bernard'O** (12457 Rancho Bernardo Rd., 858/487-7171, www.bernardorestaurant.com, lunch 11:30 A.M.–2 P.M. Wed.–Fri., dinner 5:30–9 P.M. Mon.–Thurs., 5–9:30 P.M. Fri.–Sat., 5–8:30 P.M. Sun. , $25) serves a California French menu that mixes French cooking traditions with fresh California ingredients. A particular favorite is the Californian Bouillabaisse, a medley of seafood in a Rouille lobster sauce.

About a mile away in the posh Rancho Bernardo Inn, ◖ **El Bizcocho** (17550 Bernardo Oaks Dr., 858/675-8550, entrée $35) is regarded by many critics as one of San Diego's best. In 2007, Chef Gavin Kaysen became the first chef from a San Diego restaurant to earn the honor of being named Best New Chef by *Food & Wine* magazine. Choose between such entrées as Seven Spice Lamb en sous vide ($36), with cucumber-mint yogurt and zucchini flower; or grilled swordfish ($39) with summer cranberry beans. Or entrust your taste buds—and your wallet—to the chef for a $110-per-person tasting menu.

SAN DIEGO

The neighborhood around **WineSellar & Brasserie** (9550 Waples St., #115, 858/450-9557, www.winesellar.com, lunch 11:30 A.M.–2 P.M. Thurs.–Sat., dinner from 5:30 P.M. Tues.–Fri., from 6 P.M. Sat., $35) is hardly anything to speak of—in fact it is more of an office park than a neighborhood—but this North City restaurant draws a crowd with its incredibly diverse wine selection and expert food pairings. Located just north of Marine Air Station Miramar on Sorrento Mesa, it frequently changes the menu to match the whims of the chef and the wine.

Asian

San Diego's Asian residents are well assimilated into the general citizenry so there are very few neighborhoods with concentrated Asian populations the way there are in other Californian cities such as Los Angeles or San Francisco. However, San Diego's thriving Korean community is particularly active amid the strip malls of Clairemont and Mira Mesa. Adventurous diners can't do wrong picking their way through the restaurants here that sometimes are not even labeled in English.

Many of the best restaurants are on Convoy Street. Here you can find **Korea House** (4620 Convoy St., #A, 858/560-0080), one of the best of the Korean barbecue places south of L.A. Also nearby is **Noodle Town** (4647 Convoy St., #105, 858/565-0403), which specializes in every variety of Korean noodles from cold buckwheat *nehngnyum* to spicy *jam-bong*.

The Convoy area isn't exclusively Korean, either. **Emerald Chinese Seafood** (3709 Convoy St., #101, 858/565-6888, www.emerald restaurant.com) offers the most authentic Cantonese cuisine in the county. Visit Sunday for dim sum, but be prepared to open the wallet wide as those little morsels add up.

The best Japanese is on Convoy, too. **€ Izakaya Sakura** (3904 Convoy St., #121, 858/569-6151, 11 A.M.–10 P.M. daily, entrée $10) is a hidden place that doesn't even have a sign out front, but it is well worth the hunt. It is located in the same shopping center as Wings and Things and the Original Pancake House. Step inside and see if you can find one of the few English menus floating around the place. Izakaya is like Japanese tapas, small entrées ordered as you go. Don't forget the beverages—the place has an assortment of sake that rivals a fine steakhouse's wine selection.

Information and Services

MAPS AND TOURIST INFORMATION
Visitors Centers
The International Visitor Information Center (1040⅓ West Broadway at Harbor Dr., 619/236-1212 or 619/230-7084, 9 A.M.–5 P.M. daily June–Sept., 9 A.M.–4 P.M. daily Oct.–May) along the Embarcadero is one of two major visitors centers run by the San Diego Convention and Visitors Bureau within San Diego County. Staff members at the center can provide visitors with a stack of useful guides and maps and should be able to answer questions or suggest activities based on individual needs. This location also has attraction and tour tickets available, sometimes at reduced rates.

In Coronado, the local chamber of commerce runs a **visitors center** (1110 Orange Ave., Coronado, 619/437-8788, 9 A.M.–5 P.M. Mon.–Fri., 10 A.M.–5 P.M. Sat.–Sun.) that is geared specifically to island activities.

Maps
San Diego is an easy county to get your bearings in, but it sure helps when you have the right map. **Map Centre** (7576 Clairemont Mesa Blvd., 858/278-7887, 858/278-7847, or 888/849-6277, www.mapworld.com, 10 A.M.–5:30 P.M. Mon.–Fri., 10 A.M.–5 P.M. Sat.) in Clairemont sells local, regional, and international maps. It is also a clearinghouse for nautical maps and electronic GPS units.

Members of AAA can also find service at two **Auto Club** locations: one in Mission Valley (2440 Hotel Circle N., 619/233-1000) and the other in Clairemont (4973 Clairemont Dr., Ste. C, 858/483-4960).

EMERGENCY SERVICES

San Diego's central police department is located northeast of downtown. It operates numerous community stations, including a **Balboa Park station** (non-emergency 619/685-8206, 9 A.M.–4 P.M. Mon.–Thurs.) at 1549 El Prado.

As a separate municipality, Coronado Island has its own police force. Coronado police headquarters are at 700 Orange Avenue.

There are two major hospitals in the core of the city. **Scripps Mercy Hospital** (4020 5th Ave., 619/260-7022) is in Hillcrest. The **University of California-San Diego Medical Center** (200 W. Arbor Dr., 619/543-6222) is in Mission Valley.

MONEY AND COMMUNICATIONS
Banks

Downtown there are a number of banks west of 4th Avenue along West Broadway. In Hillcrest near Balboa Park, the largest and most convenient is **Bank of America** (737 University Ave., 858/452-8400). Coronado visitors can look to the local **Coronado First Bank** (801 Orange Ave, Ste. 101) for service.

Post Offices

On Coronado Island, you can mail your postcards from the post office (1320 Ynez Pl.) in the village. Across the bay, there are several post offices downtown, including one inside of Horton Plaza (51 Horton Plaza) and a freestanding post office at 815 E Street. North of I-8, try the post office (5052 Clairemont Dr.) on Clairemont Mesa.

Internet Access

San Diego is very friendly to roaming computer users, with lots of free Wi-Fi hotspots across the city. Tourists armed with laptops can start looking for access at any of the libraries, all of which offer free wireless Internet. Those without their own computers can also take advantage of the free computer access provided at all of these public branches. Another very convenient option for those traveling without a laptop is **The Internet Place** (193 Horton Plaza, 619/702-4643, www.tipsd .com, 10 A.M.–9 P.M.), which offers computers for $5.50 per hour. Those downtown can also wander anywhere on India Street from Cedar to Fir in Little Italy. The business district there beams out free wireless from an antenna on India and Date Streets.

Similarly, Normal Heights is constantly working on its NHWiFi Project to provide free wireless Internet access to as much of the neighborhood as possible. The most reliable free hotspot here is at the corner of Adams and Bancroft Avenues.

For Balboa Park explorers, stop off near the Plaza de Balboa on the east side near the fountain. The Reuben H. Fleet Science Center's Galileo Café has a free hotspot there, and if it isn't busy they won't chase you away from their tables in the plaza outside.

Libraries

The facilities at San Diego's **Central Library** (820 E St., 619/236-5800, www.sandiego.gov/ public-library, noon–8 P.M. Mon. and Wed., 9:30 A.M.–5:30 P.M. Tues. and Thurs.–Sat., 1–5 P.M. Sun.) can hardly compete with some of the municipal showpiece buildings that other cities boast. But the collection is decent and it is a good central spot for free computer and Internet access. Where the San Diego library system excels is in its wide network of branch libraries—there are 33 in all. Some of the smaller libraries have spotty hours of operation, but there are still plenty that are open nearly every day.

The **University Heights branch** (4193 Park Blvd., 619/692-4912, 12:30–8 P.M. Mon. and Wed., 9:30 A.M.–5:30 P.M. Tues. and Thurs.– Fri., 9:30 A.M.–2:30 P.M. Sat.) serves the area near Balboa Park. The **Mission Valley branch** (2123 Fenton Parkway, 858/573-5007, 12:30–8 P.M.

Mon. and Wed., 9:30 A.M.–5:30 P.M. Tues. and Thurs.–Fri., 9:30 A.M.–2:30 P.M. Sat., 1–5 P.M. Sun.) is convenient to Hotel Circle. And those in the north end of the city will feel comfortable in the well-appointed **Rancho Bernardo branch** (17110 Bernardo Center Dr., 858/538-8163, 12:30–8 P.M. Mon. and Wed., 9:30 A.M.–5:30 P.M. Tues. and Thurs.–Fri., 9:30 A.M.–2:30 P.M. Sat., 1–5 P.M. Sun.).

Newspapers

The *San Diego Union-Tribune* is the paper of record in town. For information on upcoming concerts and activities, your best bet is to find a copy of either the *San Diego Reader* or *San Diego CityBeat,* both of which are free weekly alternatives that offer comprehensive entertainment calendars.

LAUNDRY

Tending to a laundry emergency is twice as tedious when the San Diego sun is shining. Those looking for full-service laundry or dry cleaning should consider **Continental Cleaners and Laundry** (450 10th Ave., 619/232-3598), which offers cheap and fast full-service dry cleaning and laundering.

If you'd rather not have someone else handle your unmentionables, **Lucky Launderland** (4009 30th St., 619/280-8183) has one of the cleanest and friendliest self-serve facilities in the city.

Getting There and Around

ARRIVING BY AIR

San Diego's major airport is San Diego International Airport, right in the middle of downtown. The centralized location makes it easy to find a suitable transportation option to relay you to your hotel from here. The airport is small, with only two international terminals and one commuter terminal. The international terminals are adjacent to one another and the airport operates a short shuttle called the Red Bus from both of them over to the commuter terminal. These run punctually every 10 minutes and can be caught at the curb near the big red signs marked The Red Bus STOPS HERE.

Airport Transportation

The San Diego public transit system operates the Airport Flyer (Rte. #992) between all three terminals to downtown. This bus takes approximately ten minutes to make the route one-way. Cost is $2.25 one-way.

Taxis are available at the airport's Transportation Plaza. Follow the signs and wait in line for the transportation coordinator on-site to direct you to the next available taxi. Numerous private shuttle services also offer van pickup from both terminals. These include **Xpress Shuttle** (800/900-7433) and **Cloud 9 Shuttle** (800/974-8885).

Airport Car Rental

Because of its central location San Diego International has limited real estate, so there are no car rentals on site. However, most major rental companies have lots within a mile of the airport and they all run convenient and very frequent shuttles from the transportation islands located at each terminal. Phone kiosks are located in the baggage terminals in order to call ahead.

Rental companies located close by include **Alamo** (2942 Kettner Blvd., 619/297-0311), **Avis** (3180 N. Harbor Dr., 619/231-7171), **Dollar** (2499 Pacific Hwy., 619/234-3389), **Enterprise** (1691 Hancock St., 619/225-8881), **Hertz** (3202 N. Harbor Dr., 619/220-5222), and **National** (3280 N. Harbor Dr., 619/497-6777).

Airport Parking

Compared to many major international airports, parking at this one is cheap. Short-term parking in the main lots is only $1 per hour and there are free "cell phone" lots available to those who are meeting friends or family at the airport. Drivers simply pull into the lot and can wait up to an hour there until they make contact with arriving passengers and agree on a spot for pick-up on the main terminal drive.

There are three major long-term parking lots around the airport, but the largest and the cheapest is **SAN Park Pacific Highway** (3302 Pacific Hwy.), which costs $10 per day. Be sure to arrive at least ten minutes earlier than you normally would in order to account for the shuttle ride to the terminal.

ARRIVING BY TRAIN AND TROLLEY

San Diego is serviced by Amtrak at the downtown **Santa Fe Depot** (1050 Kettner Blvd., 619/239-9021, 5:15 A.M.–10 P.M. daily).

Before you rush off to the beaches, museums, or the waterfront, take a look around the station. The depot is an amazing Mission Revival building that is in the Historic American Buildings Survey, San Diego's Historical Site Board Register, and the National Register of Historic Places. Like Balboa Park, it was built for the Panama-California Exposition in 1915–1916.

This busy station is also the southernmost stop for San Diego Northern's Coaster commuter train. Validated Coaster tickets can be used for a free transfer to the **Airport Flyer** (city bus #992) to the San Diego International Airport, which departs from the station at the northeast corner of Kettner and Broadway every 12 to 15 minutes between 5 A.M. and 12:52 A.M. It should take 10 minutes to get to the airport from the train station.

In addition, the depot is home to the hub of the San Diego Trolley System, which can provide transport to other areas in the city upon arrival at the station.

ARRIVING BY BUS

Those arriving by Greyhound bus will find themselves dumped at the downtown **bus station** (120 W. Broadway, 619/239-6737). Unlike many a metropolitan Greyhound station, this is in a pretty safe neighborhood. Gaslamp hostels and other lodging options are within walking distance and there is usually a queue of taxis waiting to whisk you off to wherever you choose.

Mexicoach bus lines are an option for those traveling to and from Mexico. The downtown Mexicoach station is at the Santa Fe Depot.

DRIVING

Like most of Southern California's cities, San Diego is undeniably a driving town. The city is very easy to navigate, though sometimes difficult to explain due to its geographical size. Major freeways running north–south are I-5, I-805, and I-15. I-5 and I-805 run parallel to one another between La Jolla in the north and San Ysidro to the south, at which points they merge together. I-15 begins at the interchange with I-8 in Mission Valley.

Other minor freeways running north–south are Rte. 163 (running from an I-5 interchange in Balboa Park until it crosses paths with I-15 in Miramar), Rte. 15 (from I-5 downtown until it transitions into I-15 at I-8), and Rte. 75, of which the Coronado Bridge is a part and which runs the length of the Silver Strand down to Imperial Beach.

East to west the major freeway is I-8, which rolls along from the ocean at Ocean Beach, through Mission Valley, and all the way across the county and the rest of the state. Other lesser freeways include Rte. 52 from I-5 at La Jolla, past Miramar and through the town of Santee, and Rte. 94 running through Midcity.

Parking

Parking is usually ample in areas such as Mission Valley and North City. Spots are scarce downtown on any given day, and during tourist season Balboa Park and Old Town can be a nightmare.

One of the best bets downtown for an open stall is the expansive garage servicing Horton Plaza. Save yourself the aggravation and cough up the $6 per hour to park here, rather than circling the block and worrying about feeding quarters into the streetside meters. Not that I've ever done this, but I hear the cheapskate trick is to park in this lot and stop by Longs Drugs in the plaza to pick up a candy bar and a three-hour parking validation for your troubles.

In Old Town the lots directly surrounding the state park fill up first. One lot that many tourists miss is the large parking area that services Old Town Transit Center. Park here and venture through the underpass tunnel that takes you directly to the park's boundaries.

Most days you'll be able to find a spot in one of Balboa Park's numerous lots, but when there is an event going on, things can get hairy. Unfortunately, what you see here is what you get. Keep circling the lots, as people come and go frequently. Perhaps one of the least utilized lots is the one at Inspiration Point, just across Park Boulevard on the southeast side of the park. From this location it's a trek into the center of the park, but it is serviced by a tram that runs along President's Way all the way to Plaza de Panama.

PUBLIC TRANSIT

Though it probably has some of the best public transit in the region, there are still often quite a few concessions and compromises that will need to be made when traveling without a set of wheels. Those who plan to stay in the city center and stick to attractions along the waterfront, downtown, and around Balboa Park may find that they can get away with skipping a car rental and rely on buses and trolleys instead. Rather than paying full fare each time you ride, it might make sense to pick up a transit pass. For $5 you can ride unlimited for one day, $9 for two days, $12 for three days, and $15 for four. Passes can be purchased at the **Transit Store** (102 Broadway, 619/234-1060, www.sdcommute.com).

Bus

Downtown most of the major routes run along Broadway between Front Street and 9th Avenue. This is also where the Transit Store is located. Go there for timetables and maps and unlimited-ride passes.

The major bus hub is located at the Old Town Transit Center, which acts as a transfer point between the trolley, many of the buses that shuttle from downtown and parts south to those in the northern part of the city, and the beach communities. This center also has ample

parking, making it a good option for park-and-ride users who may want to avoid parking hassles in high-traffic areas such as the beaches.

Trolley

The San Diego Trolley system has over 55 trolley stations throughout city limits and more beyond, reaching south all the way down to the border. This light rail system is by no means as complete as the New York subway system, but it does act as a decent means of conveyance between centrally located sights, lodging, and spectator sports venues such as Petco Park and Qualcomm Stadium.

The one gaping hole in the trolley system is its lack of service to the city beach communities. In order to get there via public transport you'll have to catch the trolley to Old Town Transit Center and transfer to a bus headed northwest.

For more information and maps, visit www.sdcommute.com or stop by the Transit Store (102 Broadway, 619/234-1060).

Ferry

Coronado Island has been easily reachable from downtown by car since the construction of the Coronado Bridge in 1969. However, it is still possible to take to the water the old-fashioned way and ride over on a ferry (619/234-4111, www.sdhe.com, $3 one way, $3.50 with bicycle). The ferry leaves downtown at the Broadway Pier (1050 N. Harbor Dr.) every hour on the hour starting at 9 A.M. and arrives at Coronado's Ferry Landing Marketplace (1st St. and B Ave.) about a half hour later. Similarly, the ferry departs from Coronado on the half hour every hour starting at 9:30 A.M. During the week, the last ferry departs from downtown at 9 P.M. and from Coronado at 9:30 P.M. Operation is extended by one hour on Fridays and Saturdays.

TOURS
Bus and Trolley Tours

Old Town Trolley Tours (4010 Twiggs St., 800/213-2474, $30 adults, $15 children 4–12, free under 4) is one of the most complete guided trips in the city. These bright-orange trolley buses start from Old Town and wind their way along the waterfront, through downtown and the Gaslamp, over the Coronado Bay Bridge and into downtown Coronado, back over the bridge and up to Balboa Park, returning to Old Town after two hours. The dandy part about the arrangement is that there are eight stops along the way at key tourist destinations and riders are encouraged to hop off their current bus to eat or sightsee and hop back on any of the other buses that come by every half hour. Tours run daily between 9 A.M. and 4 P.M., until 5 P.M. in the summer.

It's corny, it's fun, and your teenagers will hate you for taking them on a **SEAL Tour** (619/298-8687, www.sandiegoseals.com, 10 A.M.–4 P.M. Oct.–May, 10 A.M.–5 P.M. June–Sept.). These off-the-wall land and sea tours are taken aboard a colorfully painted amphibious bus that guides you through the nature, history, and culture of San Diego's Big Bay. The tours start from Seaport Village and go along the Embarcadero and up through Point Loma to take to the water from Shelter Island. In total you'll be exploring for about 90 minutes. A lightweight jacket is recommended.

Boat Tours

The San Diego shoreline is a beautiful sight from the water. There are a number of boat tours on the Big Bay to choose from.

San Diego Harbor Excursions (www .sdhe.com) offers a number of different kinds of trips from its dock on the Embarcadero. Its signature boat ride is the Dinner Cruise ($58 adults, $36 children ages 4–12), a two-and-a-half-hour trip around the bay that departs at 7:30 P.M. daily, even on holidays. In addition the company offers whale-watching trips hosted by naturalists from the Birch Aquarium, nature trips to the uninhabited Los Coronados Islands off the Mexican coast, and one- to two-hour harbor tours.

Boat lovers can also choose to take similar tours with **Hornblower Cruises** (1066 N. Harbor Dr., 888/467-6256, www.hornblower .com), which offers nightly dinner dance cruises for $65 as well as its very own whale watching cruises.

To feel the wind in your hair, hop aboard the **Maritime Museum of San Diego's *Californian*** (1492 North Harbor Dr., 619/234-9153), a topsail schooner that is designated the official Tall Ship of the State of California. The museum runs daily sailing trips at 1 P.M. These four-hour trips can be as interactive as you want them to be, as the ship's skipper allows riders young and old to help sail the boat if they are interested.

Walking Tours

Learn about the booms and busts of the Gaslamp Quarter on Saturdays at 11 A.M., when the **Gaslamp Foundation** (www.gaslamp quarter.org) runs a walking tour that starts at the William Heath Davis Historic House Museum and passes by some of the best examples of Victorian-style commercial buildings that still stand in the district. The walk costs $10, $8 for seniors, students, and members of the military.

The Black Historical Society of San Diego also runs its own Gaslamp walking tour called the **Harlem of the West Tour** (520 E. St., www.harlemofthewest.com), which departs from the lobby of the Gaslamp Plaza Suites Hotel every Saturday at 11 A.M. This 45-minute tour will take you to sites of some of the most historic black businesses, jazz and blues establishments, and community gathering spots. Cost is $5, free for those 16 and younger.

An informative pre-recorded audio guide can be rented from the **Balboa Park Visitors Center** (1549 El Prado, 619/239-0512, 9:30 A.M.–4:30 P.M. daily, $5 adults, $4 seniors, students, and active military, $3 children 3–11). The hour-and-a-half walking tour offers a breezy and fun look at the park's architectural, horticultural, and cultural attractions.

The state park runs free guided tours of Old Town State Historic Park at 11 A.M. and 2 P.M. every day. The tour departs from the Robinson-Rose House Visitor Center and will give you a rich understanding of the cultural and historical background of San Diego's oldest community.

LA JOLLA AND THE BEACHES

In a little under twenty miles of ocean shoreline, the city beaches of San Diego offer varied landscapes that appeal to a variety of sensibilities. Hidden cove beaches provide a space for solitude and lonesome meditation, while open sandy shores attract crowds and bring out the social animal in all of us. Sandstone cliffs encourage pensive thought. Rocky tidepools delight curiosity.

The diverse scenery is reflected in the assortment of people it attracts. In a beachside café you're just as likely to cross paths with a crusty old fisherman as you are with a well-manicured yacht owner. Buzz-cut Marines are as likely to toss their blanket on the sand next to yours as dreadlocked hippies. At a stoplight it is possible to see a Rolls Royce pull up behind a rusted-out pickup with a surfboard hanging out of the tailgate. Look over to the sidewalk while you wait and you just might see a middle-aged skateboarder rolling side-by-side with his teenaged son.

All of these disparate characters create the fabric of a community that celebrates its differences. The diversity doesn't create friction; instead it is a testament to the welcoming atmosphere found here.

PLANNING YOUR TIME

You can easily drive through all of the city beach neighborhoods in under an hour, but as many transplant residents will tell you, it can take a lifetime to explore the beaches and the streets that surround them. Because of the accessibility between each neighborhood, plan your itinerary around your interests rather than

© ERICKA CHICKOWSKI

HIGHLIGHTS

🌙 **Birch Aquarium at Scripps Institution of Oceanography:** The ocean research and animals studied by Scripps are put on display here. Be sure to bring the kids to the re-created tidepool to see how it tickles to hold a sea anemone (page 108).

🌙 **La Jolla Cove:** This gorgeous little beach sits in a nook pushed into the sea cliffs of San Diego's northernmost beach neighborhood (page 111).

🌙 **La Jolla Village:** Mingle with millionaires in this posh district, a magnet for fine cuisine, shopping, and the arts (page 111).

🌙 **The Strand:** Find the quintessential Southern California beach along this two-mile length of sandy seashore (page 123).

🌙 **Mission Bay Park:** What was once mudflats is now a little slice of heaven for boaters and picnickers at the largest man-made aquatic park in the country (page 124).

🌙 **SeaWorld:** Parked on the shores of Mission Bay, this adventure park has something for animal lovers and thrill-seekers alike (page 125).

🌙 **Cabrillo National Monument:** Perched on top of the very tip of Point Loma, the views of San Diego Bay and the ocean are unparalleled here. Named after the first explorer to discover the area, it is also home to several historical curiosities and a national cemetery (page 137).

🌙 **Shelter Island:** Shimmied up next to the eastern side of the Point Loma peninsula, this island is home to marinas, hotels, and restaurants. Unwind in the city-view park that stretches along its entire length (page 138).

LOOK FOR 🌙 TO FIND RECOMMENDED SIGHTS, ACTIVITIES, DINING, AND LODGING.

worrying about sticking to a particular area of town on any given day.

Don't don your bathing suit until you've spent some time wandering the high-class storefronts in **La Jolla Village.** Art lovers will enjoy the dozens of galleries there, as well as the Museum of Contemporary Art San Diego. The Village overlooks **La Jolla Cove,** a pristine inlet that inspires many of the resident artists who sell their work here. It is also home to some of the only fine-dining restaurants in this casual region that actually require a jacket.

From there you can venture to Point Loma, which acts as a complementary southern bookend to La Jolla's artistic charms to the north. As one of the oldest neighborhoods in the city,

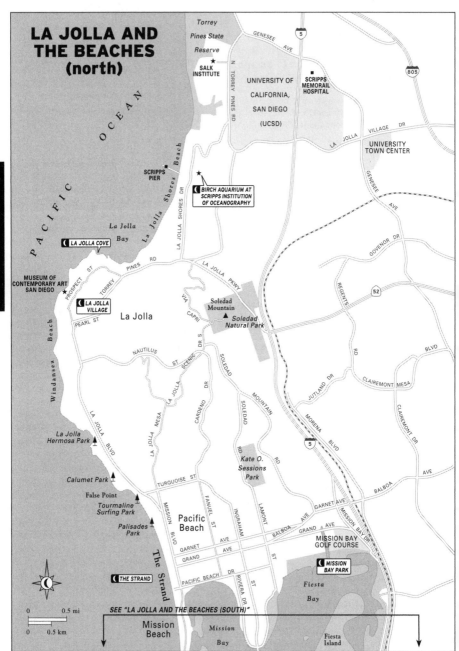

LA JOLLA AND THE BEACHES (north)

Torrey Pines State Reserve

SALK INSTITUTE

UNIVERSITY OF CALIFORNIA, SAN DIEGO (UCSD)

SCRIPPS MEMORIAL HOSPITAL

GENESEE AVE

5

805

N TORREY PINES RD

LA JOLLA VILLAGE DR

UNIVERSITY TOWN CENTER

GENESEE AVE

GOVENOR DR

REGENTS RD

52

JUTLAND DR

CLAIREMONT MESA BLVD

CLAIREMONT DR

SCRIPPS PIER

La Jolla Shores Beach

La Jolla Shores Dr

BIRCH AQUARIUM AT SCRIPPS INSTITUTION OF OCEANOGRAPHY

La Jolla Bay

LA JOLLA PKWY

LA JOLLA COVE

P A C I F I C   O C E A N

PINES RD

PROSPECT ST

TORREY

MUSEUM OF CONTEMPORARY ART SAN DIEGO

LA JOLLA VILLAGE

PEARL ST

La Jolla

VIA CAPRI

Soledad Mountain

Soledad Natural Park

MORENA BLVD

5

NAUTILUS ST

SCENIC DR S

SOLEDAD

SOLEDAD MOUNTAIN RD

Windansea Beach

LA JOLLA MESA

CARDENO DR

LA JOLLA BLVD

La Jolla Hermosa Park

Kate O. Sessions Park

BALBOA AVE

Calumet Park

False Point

Tourmaline Surfing Park

Palisades Park

TURQUOISE ST

MISSION BLVD

FANUEL ST

INGRAHAM ST

LAMONT ST

BALBOA AVE

GRAND AVE

GARNET AVE

Pacific Beach

MISSION BAY DR

MISSION BAY GOLF COURSE

GARNET AVE

GRAND AVE

MISSION BAY PARK

THE STRAND

The Strand

PACIFIC BEACH DR

RIVIERA DR

Fiesta Bay

0   0.5 mi
0   0.5 km

SEE "LA JOLLA AND THE BEACHES (SOUTH)"

Mission Beach

Mission Bay

Fiesta Island

LA JOLLA

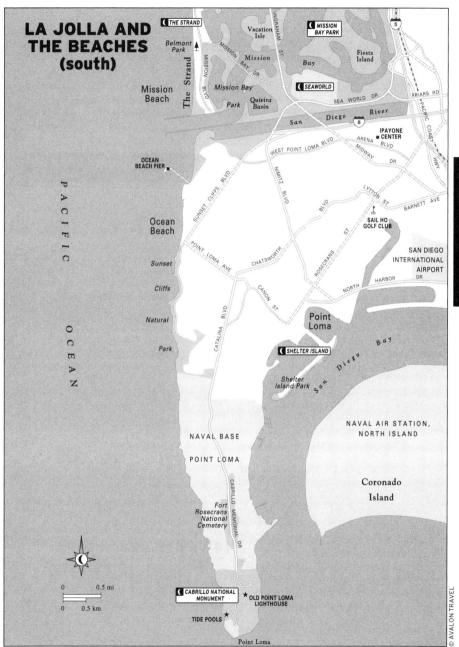

LA JOLLA AND THE BEACHES (south)

THE STRAND

Belmont Park

Mission Beach

The Strand

MISSION BLVD

MISSION BAY DR

Vacation Isle

INGRAHAM ST

Mission Bay

Mission

Bay

Fiesta Island

MISSION BAY PARK

5

SEAWORLD

SEA WORLD DR

FRIARS RD

PACIFIC COAST HWY

Mission Bay Park

Quivira Basin

San   Diego   River

8

IPAYONE CENTER

WEST POINT LOMA BLVD

ARENA BLVD

MIDWAY DR

NIMITZ BLVD

SUNSET CLIFFS BLVD

OCEAN BEACH PIER

Ocean Beach

Sunset

Cliffs

Natural

Park

POINT LOMA AVE

CHATSWORTH

CANON ST

CATALINA BLVD

BLVD

ROSECRANS ST

LYTTON ST

BARNETT AVE

SAIL HO GOLF CLUB

NORTH   HARBOR   DR

SAN DIEGO INTERNATIONAL AIRPORT

PACIFIC

OCEAN

Point Loma

SHELTER ISLAND

Shelter Island Park

San   Diego   Bay

Bay

NAVAL AIR STATION, NORTH ISLAND

Coronado Island

NAVAL BASE

POINT LOMA

CABRILLO MEMORIAL DR

Fort Rosecrans National Cemetery

0   0.5 mi

0   0.5 km

CABRILLO NATIONAL MONUMENT

OLD POINT LOMA LIGHTHOUSE

★ TIDE POOLS

Point Loma

© AVALON TRAVEL

LA JOLLA

this area features highlights of San Diego's past. Be sure to visit **Cabrillo National Monument,** which features historic coastal gun emplacements and the Old Point Loma Lighthouse. If you are an antique hunter, stop off at the Ocean Beach Antique District on your drive south.

There are also innumerable opportunities for adventure seekers. Learn to surf at Tourmaline Surfing Park or La Jolla Shores. Or zip around **Mission Bay** on a personal watercraft. Scramble around the precipices that make up Sunset Cliffs Natural Park. Or simply take a stroll along the Mission Bay Boardwalk. All of these activities are in such close proximity that it is easy to hit several in a single day. Just try not to cram too much in, or you won't fit in with the locals. No matter which beach you're near, stress should never be on the schedule.

La Jolla

Spanish for "The Jewel," La Jolla is one of San Diego's most affluent neighborhoods. It is home to some of the region's best restaurants and most lavish shops. But the area isn't all about flashy cars and expensive jewelry; it features a wealth of natural beauty, too. Tucked away in the northeasternmost corner of San Diego city limits, La Jolla lives up to its sparkling moniker with a breathtaking shoreline that squeezes together a number of different beach landscapes in just a few miles—rocky tidepools, sandstone precipices, and gentle sandy beaches.

The magnificent landscape is a major source of inspiration for the renowned and thriving arts community in the area. La Jolla is home to dozens of galleries, museums, and world-class performing arts organizations.

From a sightseeing perspective, La Jolla is primarily broken up into two distinct areas. To the north and east is **La Jolla Shores** and University Town Center, which surrounds the University of California–San Diego (UCSD). Farther south and closer to the rest of San Diego is **La Jolla Cove** and the adjacent **La Jolla Village.** Along the water the Shores and the Cove are less than a mile apart, but the shoreline between the two beaches is rocky and inaccessible, making it necessary to make the ten-minute drive along Torrey Pines Road to shuttle between them. On the map, the distance is relatively short, but plan on some form of transportation because the road is a busy thoroughfare and very steep.

SIGHTS
La Jolla Shores

All of the geological stars aligned to make La Jolla Shores Beach an idyllic place for family outings. This particular stretch of coast is protected from the fiercer SoCal waves by a cavernous 500-foot-deep underwater canyon. The canyon ends up deflecting much of the break farther north, which is also likely the reason why the pristine white sand has been able to accumulate over the mile-long section of seashore. All of this adds up to a peaceful beach perfect for sunbathing, building sandcastles, and wading with the little ones.

The beach also shares space with **Scripps Pier.** Built for oceanographic research at the nearby Scripps Institution of Oceanography, the pier is not open to the public. However, it is a landmark structure in La Jolla and makes a great background for vacation snapshots.

If you'd like to get the sand out of your shorts without losing sight of the ocean, grassy **Kellogg Park** runs parallel to the beach. The park also features barbecue grills, picnic tables, and a playground for kids to swing and climb on.

(Birch Aquarium at Scripps Institution of Oceanography

San Diego has long been a hub for oceanographic studies, primarily due to the early development of the Scripps Institution of Oceanography in 1903. Now a part of UCSD, Scripps Institution is the one of the world's leading centers for marine studies.

Part of the establishing endowment plans stipulated that the organization operate an aquarium for the public, and since 1905 it has maintained four successive aquarium and museum facilities. Its most recent facility is the Birch Aquarium (2300 Expedition Way, 858/534-3474, www.aquarium.ucsd .edu, 9 A.M.–5 P.M. daily), which rests on a hillside overlooking the Shores, the institution's campus, and its research facilities on Scripps Pier.

Birch Aquarium's marine and museum exhibits bring to light much of the work that the institute does to protect oceanic ecosystems worldwide. Though the aquarium is designed to be enjoyed by visitors of all ages, it is particularly accessible to the inquisitive minds of the younger set. If you have children, you'll want to check out the facility's centerpiece: three artificially constructed tidepools placed on a patio with a view of **La Jolla Bay.** Kids are encouraged to get their hands wet and

© AVALON TRAVEL

MISS SCRIPPS

Few families made as much of an impact on San Diego development as the Scripps clan did. And among the Scripps, no member was quite as generous or as beloved as Miss Ellen Browning Scripps.

Miss Scripps moved to La Jolla in 1896 after amassing an enormous amount of money through her work to help build her family's national chain of newspapers. In a time when few women had careers, Ellen Scripps worked side by side with her brothers James and Edward Willis ("E. W.") to build a newsmaking empire. She was a talented journalist and to her last days continued to write a syndicated column.

It is said that a journalist provides a voice to those who have none, and renders aid to those who cannot help themselves. It is very possible that the same traits that led her into the trade that would make her a wealthy woman also spurred her on to become one of the greatest philanthropists the city has ever seen.

In 1924 she wrote, "The most important and beautiful gift one human being can give to another is, in some way, to make life a little better to live." She did that by giving money and support to hundreds of civic efforts throughout San Diego. Miss Scripps was responsible for saving the rare Torrey pine tree, found only on the San Diego coast, by buying a parcel of land north of La Jolla and donating it to the state with the condition that it never be developed. She provided funds to Balboa Park for buildings, and to San Diego Zoo to build the world's largest aviary.

Because she firmly believed that there were no two betterments of life than science and art, many of her contributions flowed into organizations that followed these pursuits.

She founded Scripps Memorial Hospital and Scripps Clinic. Her money helped open doors at The Athenaeum Music & Arts Library and La Jolla Public Library. And with her brother E. W., she provided the seed money to start the Scripps Institution of Oceanography.

She wasn't the type to give her money for recognition, and perhaps because of this, Miss Scripps was fondly thought of by her fellow citizens. *Time* called her "the most beloved woman in Southern California" in 1926, when she graced the cover of the magazine at the age of 89.

As her nephew Thomas Scripps wrote in a memoir about her, "Aunt Ellen had the heart of a nurse, the courage of an astronaut and a capacity to give both generously and wisely."

touch the sea anemones, starfish, and other tidal creatures on display.

For admission to the aquarium, adults pay $11, seniors $9, college students $8, and kids 3–17 $7.50; those younger get in free.

Salk Institute for Biological Studies

Less than two miles from Birch Aquarium and the Scripps Institution is another world-class research outfit. Founded by the man who cured polio, Jonas Salk, the Salk Institute (10010 N. Torrey Pines Rd., 858/453-4100, ext. 1287, www.salk.edu) is a private scientific center focused on biological research that can improve the human condition. When Salk first dreamed up his organization, he was determined to build it a home that was as inspiring and creative as the work that would be done there.

In 1959 he teamed up with the already well-known architect Louis Kahn to create what would become one of Kahn's greatest masterpieces. Built on land gifted by the city, the campus centerpiece is its civic plaza, bounded on each side by two angular buildings that mirror one another and point to an expansive blue sky that leads to the ocean.

The free guided tour, offered Monday, Wednesday, and Friday at noon, will offer you an appreciation for the award-winning architecture and the work it has inspired over the years. Call for reservations.

La Jolla Cove

Nestled under sandstone cliffs, the beach at La Jolla Cove is minimal—the winter high tide often washes over the first few steps that lead up to the street. But it isn't the sand that keeps visitors coming. The water that washes up is part of the **San Diego-La Jolla Underwater Park,** a 6,000-acre sanctuary that extends north all the way to Del Mar. Water visibility is usually very good, making the cove a favorite among swimmers, snorkelers, and scuba divers who all vie for a peak at the sealife that teems below. With good visibility it is possible to spot fish such as Garibaldi, rockfish, and sea bass. The 533 acres of the cove's water are also an ecological reserve, so you can look at but not touch the sealife. Taking marinelife or rocks from the site is unlawful.

You needn't get wet to enjoy the cove's natural beauty, though. Overlooking the cove is **Ellen Browning Scripps Memorial Park** (1133 Coast Blvd.), a 5.2-acre park that offers lots of grassy space to toss a blanket and watch the hubbub in the water below. Perched on the green at Scripps Park, you'll be able to see the craggy line of San Diego County's northern coast stretch for miles. And in the more immediate distance you can see the crowds of sunbathers at La Jolla Shores Beach.

Just out of view from Scripps Park are a string of hidden jewels tucked into the sandstone that stretches from the Cove to the Shores: the La Jolla Caves. Nearly all of these seven oceanside caves are only accessible by water. The lone exception is open to the public through the **Cave Store** (1325 Cave St., 858/459-0746, www.cavestore.com, 10 A.M.–5 P.M. Mon.–Fri., 9 A.M.–5 P.M. Sat.–Sun., $4 adults, $3 children 16 and under), a short walk away from the Scripps Park. Sunny Jim Cave is accessible through a long, steep set of stairs that start in the shop, so keep that in mind if you're traveling with someone with mobility limitations. Hours are extended Memorial Day through Labor Day, when the cave opens at 9 A.M. and closes at 7 P.M. on weekdays and at 8 P.M. on weekends. Visitors are advised to call in advance because hours fluctuate.

La Jolla Village

The beating heart of La Jolla's bustling arts, dining, and shopping scene, La Jolla Village is located right next to La Jolla Cove. Much of the activity is centered around Prospect, Girard, and Herschel Streets, but there are plenty of sites tucked away throughout this 30-block neighborhood.

Among them is **The Athenaeum Music & Arts Library** (1008 Wall St., 858/454-5872, www.ljathenaeum.org, 10 A.M.–5:30 P.M. Tues. and Thurs.–Sat., 10 A.M.–8:30 P.M. Wed., free), a private library dedicated solely to the arts. It has one of the largest collections of classical music in the United States and hosts art exhibits featuring rising new talent throughout the year.

Walk a few blocks south and you can learn how La Jolla became a magnet for the arts at the **La Jolla Historical Society** (7846 Eads Ave., 858/459-5335, www.lajollahistory.org, 10 A.M.–4 P.M. Mon.–Fri., free). Located in a quaint turn-of-the-20th-century beach cottage, the society's home is packed with memorabilia, photos, and documents that illustrate the area's vibrant past. The cottage is also the jumping-off point for its annual Secret Garden Tour in the spring, which highlights some of the most beautiful private homes and gardens hidden in and around the village. Call in advance for reservations, as this crowd-pleaser sells out every year.

Also within walking distance is the La Jolla branch of the **Museum of Contemporary Art San Diego** (MCASD, 700 Prospect St., 858/454 3541, www.mcasd.org, 11 A.M.–5 P.M. Fri.–Tues., 11 A.M.–7 P.M. Thurs.). Initially established in 1941 as a La Jolla community art center, MCASD boasts a combined collection of more than 3,000 works of art created from 1950 onward. After many decades of success, MCASD La Jolla, housed in the remodeled 1915 home of Ellen Browning Scripps, is one of two museum locations to feature its collection, which includes works in all different media and genres. Of particular note are its minimalism and Pop art pieces, as well as its collection of regional art.

Admission to the museum is $6 for adults and $2 for students, members of the military, and seniors. Admission is free on the third Tuesday of every month. Museum members and children under 12 are always free.

Across the street from the museum's back door is Coast Boulevard, which offers an excellent opportunity for strolling alongside the ocean. The promenade along Coast Boulevard winds all the way to the Cove, with plenty of greenery and a couple of notable parks along the way. Directly across the street from MSCAD is **Cuvier Park** (intersection of Coast Blvd. and Cuvier St.), sometimes called the Wedding Bowl. This grassy spot is sometimes missed because it is a few steps below street level. If there isn't a wedding being held there, it is sometimes possible to have the oceanview lawn to yourself.

Closer to the Cove along Coast Boulevard is **Children's Pool,** an artificially protected beach made possible by Ellen Browning Scripps. Miss Scripps donated the money to build a curving wall to protect the area from buffeting waves and create a safe spot for children to swim. However, in the intervening years her plans have been upset by Miss Mother Nature. It seems that some of the local marine mammals took a shine to the protected beach, and they told their friends. Now the sand is a favorite resting spot for local seals and their pups, particularly during pupping season. Seals are very territorial, so it isn't an ideal spot for swimming or sunbathing anymore, but Children's Pool still benefits kids. They love watching the antics of resident seals from the walkways overlooking the beach.

Bird Rock

Just out of the hustle of La Jolla's busier neighborhoods is Bird Rock, which acts as a gateway to Pacific Beach farther south. Along the oceanside streets, Bird Rock is home to some of La Jolla's most stunning residences, as well as a few hidden parks worth a stop.

This includes my favorite stretch of shore, **Windansea Beach.** Windansea has a sandy beach, but it is broken up by numerous sandstone formations that make for good eye candy and

Windansea Beach and the iconic "sugar shack"

© ERICKA CHICKOWSKI

can provide secluded spots for sunbathing. Its trademark formation is its Polynesian-style *palapa* hut, called the "sugar shack," first built by surfers in the 1940s and now a structure on the historical register.

ENTERTAINMENT AND EVENTS
Performing Arts

Philanthropist Ellen Browning Scripps set the tone early on for La Jolla generosity. La Jolla's elite plays patron to a wide variety of artistic endeavors, particularly in the performing arts. Tops in this category is the Tony Award–winning **La Jolla Playhouse** (2910 La Jolla Village Dr., 858/550-1010, www.lajolla playhouse.com). Founded in 1947 by Gregory Peck, Dorothy McGuire, and Mel Ferrer, the playhouse operates three facilities to perform an average of six shows each season. The playhouse also shares its stages with the UCSD theater department, an award-winning entity in its own right.

Musically, the **La Jolla Music Society** is the preeminent classical-music concert producer in San Diego. The Society puts on shows at intimate local venues such as the stage at The Neurosciences Institute (10640 John Jay Hopkins Dr., 858/626-2000, www.nsi.edu) and MCASD La Jolla's auditorium (700 Prospect St., 858/454-3541), as well as other larger facilities in the county.

Another cozy concert setting is the venue at the **Athenaeum Music & Arts Library** (1008 Wall St., 858/454-5872), which seats only 150 people. The Athenaeum's shows are extremely popular with music enthusiasts due to the snug atmosphere—buy tickets early because shows regularly sell out.

The university also plays host to numerous musical acts throughout the year. **La Jolla Symphony & Chorus Association** (858/534-4637, www.lajollasymphony.com) is a performance ensemble affiliated with the school. It performs six concert weekends each year at **UCSD's Mandeville Auditorium** (UCSD campus on Muir College Dr. near lot 207, 858/534-8497), and the **RIMAC Arena** (9500

Gilman Dr., 858/534-6467) on campus is a frequent stop for big-name artists on their national tours. Check www.ticketmaster.com for updated show calendars and pricing.

Nightlife

You'll have to fight the urge to sing a sea shanty when raising your glass at **The Whaling Bar and Grill** (1132 Prospect St., 858/454-0771, 7 P.M.–midnight Wed.–Sun). Located at La Valencia Hotel, this longtime bar is decked out with harpoons, lanterns, and fishing murals. The cozy pub decor is completed with dark leather banquettes and mahogany accents for an atmosphere that invites you to stay for "just one more round."

For jet-setting hipsters, **Koi Lounge** (7660 Fay Ave., 858/454-4540, 6 P.M.–1 A.M. Thurs.–Sat.) is a spot for the fashionably dressed-down. The raw bar there serves sushi favorites from Zenbu, just two doors down.

Another stylish location to sip a few is **Clay's La Jolla** (7955 La Jolla Shores Dr., 858/551-3620, www.clayslajolla.com, 5–11 P.M. daily, no cover), which features jazz shows Wednesday through Sunday night, usually starting around 7 P.M.

If it's laughter that you're seeking, **The Comedy Store** (916 Pearl St., 858/454-9176, www.thecomedystore.com, 7 P.M.–midnight Wed.–Sun) is selling it. Operated by Mitzi Shore, mother of the Hollywood flash-in-the-pan Pauly Shore, this comedy lounge features up-and-coming and established talent.

Those who want to try a little salsa dancing should find the hidden **La Jolla Marriott bar** (4240 La Jolla Village Dr., 858/587-1414), where the locals flock on Friday and Saturday night for lessons and dancing. The cover charge is around $10. Lessons and dancing usually start at 8:30 P.M.

Events

A blend of the area's love affair with art and cuisine, the **La Jolla Festival of the Arts and Food Faire** (www.lajollaartfestival.org) held in June is a favorite for all San Diegans. Similarly, the **La Jolla Gallery & Wine Walk** in the fall is a good chance to get a taste of art, wine, and fine cheeses in one glitzy evening.

La Jolla also hosts a number of well-regarded sporting events. Held continuously for over three quarters of a century, the **La Jolla Rough Water Swim** at La Jolla Cove is the nation's largest rough-water swimming competition. By land, the **La Jolla Half Marathon** is another popular test of fitness. The route runs from Del Mar through La Jolla's most scenic roads with the finish at the Cove.

SHOPPING
University Town Center

University Town Center (4545 La Jolla Village Dr., 858/546-8858, 10 A.M.–9 P.M. Mon.–Fri., 10 A.M.–8 P.M. Sat., 11 A.M.–7 P.M. Sun.) is one of the largest shopping centers in the city. Known simply as UTC by the locals, this mall has 187 stores, a food court, and even an ice-skating rink. The lineup of stores includes Abercrombie & Fitch, Nordstrom, The Limited, and Pottery Barn.

Art Galleries

La Jolla Village's streets are packed with dozens of art galleries that feature collections ranging from the beautiful to the downright bizarre. Serious art collectors and lookie-loos alike can easily fill an entire afternoon studying artwork in the neighborhood.

Much of the action is on Prospect Street and Girard Avenue. On Prospect, **Morrison Hotel Gallery** (1230 Prospect St., 858/551-0835, www.morrisonhotelgallery.com, 11 A.M.–7 P.M. Sun.–Thurs, 11 A.M.–9 P.M. Fri.–Sat.) is named after The Doors album *Morrison Hotel*. As the name suggests, music is the motif here, with collectible fine-art photography featuring musicians and moments in music. A few steps away is **Galeria JAN** (1250 Prospect St., #B21, 858/551-2053, www.galleriajan.com, 11 A.M.–7 P.M. Sun.–Thurs, 11 A.M.–9 P.M. Fri.–Sat.), which was originally established in Europe in 1986 and moved to La Jolla a decade later. Visitors strolling through over the years have been delighted by originals created by masters such as Max Ernst, Miró, Chagall, Jean Pierre

Rousseau, and Roy Lichtenstein. The work at **Emilia Castillo La Jolla** (1273 Prospect St., 858/551-9600, www.emiliacastillolajolla.com, 10 A.M.–6 P.M. Mon.–Sat., 11 A.M.–5 P.M. Sun.) is only by one master, the great Mexican silversmith Emilia Castillo. Here you'll see the largest exclusive collection of her silver jewelry and houseware, along with work in other mediums such as gold and porcelain.

On Girard, **Molloy Gallery** (8008 Girard Ave., Ste. 190, 858/729-9909, www.molloygallery.com, 11 A.M.–6 P.M. Tues.–Sun.) is a unique specialty gallery that sells Australian Aboriginal fine art. **Bartram Gallery** (7874 Girard Ave., 858/459-9797, www.bartramgallery.com, 10 A.M.–7 P.M. Mon.–Thurs., 10 A.M.–9 P.M. Fri.–Sat., 11 A.M.–6 P.M. Sun.) has a collection of fine photography that captures the natural world. The medium at **La Jolla Fiber Arts** (7644 Girard Ave., 858/454-6732, www.lajollafiberarts.com, 10 A.M.–6 P.M. Tues.–Sat., 11 A.M.–4 P.M. Sun.–Mon.) is anything textile. The collection includes handwoven tapestry, baskets, quilts, and even book arts. Contemporary crafts are displayed and sold at **Gallery Eight** (7464 Girard Ave., 858/454-9781, 10 A.M.–5 P.M. Mon.–Sat.), including jewelry, ceramics, glass, furniture, and apparel.

Village Boutiques

When price is no object, La Jolla Village's boutiques should be the first place you look for apparel, jewelry, and one-of-a-kind items for the home. For those with a lighter pocketbook, these trendy shops are still fun to browse through and dream a little.

Fashionistas should start their spending spree at **Pomegranate** (152 Prospect St., 858/459-0629, 10 A.M.–6 P.M. Mon.–Wed., 10 A.M.–9 P.M. Thurs.–Sat., 11 A.M.–6 P.M. Sun.), which features unique wardrobe items that you'll never see someone else wearing. Pick through the shop's selection of antique jewelry or continue on to **Artful Soul** (7660 Fay Ave., Ste. A, 858/459-2009, www.artfulsoul.com, 10 A.M.–5:30 P.M. Mon.–Sat., 10 A.M.–4 P.M. Sun.), which has a stunning collection of jewelry and handbags created

© ERICKA CHICKOWSKI

La Jolla Cove is a favored spot among recreational and competitive swimmers.

by La Jolla artists. Before making a jewelry decision, be sure to also stop in on **Suzan's Silver & Amber Jewelry** (1298 Prospect St., Ste. 1N, 858/454-9808), which has interesting pieces in their own right.

The men in your party don't have to be left out in the cold. **The Ascot Shop** (7750 Girard Ave., 858/454-4222, 9 a.m.–6 p.m. Mon.–Sat.) is bound to have the perfect tie to spiff them up for a night on the town.

If your home is your castle, why not choose decor that makes you feel like royalty? Shop at **Nestlife** (7636 Girard Ave., 858/454-4220, www.nestlife.com, 9:30 a.m.–5 p.m. Mon.–Sat., 10 a.m.–5 p.m. Sun.) and you'll likely find something that fits the bill. The shop specializes in fine china, crystal, linens, and well-crafted home accessories.

SPORTS AND RECREATION
Surfing and Swimming

La Jolla Shores' consistently gentle break makes it an ideal place for beginning surfers to test their mettle. If you're the adventurous type,

you can paddle right on in and pick it up as you go. Numerous shops on nearby Avenida de la Playa will rent you a beginner's board and a wetsuit, including **La Jolla Surf Systems** (2132 Avenida de la Playa, 858/456-2777, www.lajollasurfsystems.com), which will rent a board and a suit for $11 per hour. The shop also offers lessons for those who would prefer a little guidance.

For even more structure, consider a surf camp. **Surf Diva** (2160 Avenida de la Playa, 858/454-8273, www.surfdiva.com) specializes in surf instruction for the sport's underrepresented sex. But beginners of either gender (and any age, for that matter) are welcome at many of Surf Diva's camps and clinics.

Advanced surfers and those with an appreciation for surf culture have to put **Windansea Beach** (6800 Neptune Pl.) on their must-visit shortlist. A reef just offshore provides a consistent break that has acted as home base for some of Southern California's most renowned surfers. The beach gained lasting literary notoriety when in 1965 Tom Wolfe wrote about some of the local characters that frequented the beach board-in-hand in *The Pumphouse Gang*.

Surfing isn't allowed at La Jolla Cove, but it serves as a major focal point for the purest of water sports, swimming. Competitive swimmers flock from around the world to freestyle in the Cove's clear and scenic waters. The beach serves as prime practice grounds for a close-knit but welcoming community. On any given morning there are usually swimmers out for a dip, but to be safe consider contacting the **La Jolla Cove Swim Club** (www.lajollacoveswim club.org) or the **Triathlon Club of San Diego** (www.triclubsandiego.com) before your stay to arrange for a local swim buddy to join you. If you have what it takes, earn bonus points with the locals by forgoing the wetsuit in the winter months. The water is so frequented by hardcore swimmers that it's likely you won't be the only one out there without the neoprene.

Kayaking

Almost all of the La Jolla Caves are accessible by water, making these secret grottos a paddler's treasure. Several Shores-area touring outfits offer kayak tours of the cliffside caves, including **La Jolla Kayak** (2199 Avenida de la Playa, 858/459-1114, www.lajollakayak.com, single kayak $45, double $70).

Other specialty firms also offer a twist on the usual kayak experience, teaching anglers the art of fishing on a kayak. **La Jolla Kayak Fishing** (619/461-7172, www.kayak4fish.com) offers an all-day fishing excursion from La Jolla Shores that will teach participants basic kayak skills, surf survival, kayak setup, and fishing techniques—all while hunting for trophy fish such as yellowfin tuna and thresher sharks. The trip is $175 per person and includes a kayak and fishing gear.

Scuba and Snorkeling

Some of La Jolla's best features are underwater at the **San Diego-La Jolla Underwater Park** in La Jolla Bay. Both experienced and beginning scuba divers can benefit from a trip to **Ocean Express** (2158 Avenida de la Playa, 858/454-6195, www.oexcalifornia.com), which

offers equipment rentals, instruction, and dive tours of the underwater park.

In the summer some of the best wildlife isn't deep at all. A snorkel, mask, and fins are all that are needed to see the annual influx of Leopard Sharks in the shallows of La Jolla Bay. These spotted sharks come close to shore in the late summer months to give birth to their young. They are completely harmless to humans and fascinating to watch in their own element. One reliable spot to get the right gear is **Hike Bike Kayak** (2246 Avenida de la Playa, 858/551-9510, www.hikebikekayak.com), which offers rentals and also conducts snorkel tours when the sharks come into the bay.

Golf

One of the nation's finest sets of municipal links is found at **Torrey Pines Golf Course** (11480 N. Torrey Pines Rd., 800/985-4653, www.torreypinesgolfcourse.com). Built in 1957, this oceanview course is home to the PGA Buick Invitational each January and host to the 2008 U.S. Open.

It features two 18-hole golf courses, North and South, that can challenge even the most experienced player. You'll contend with long yardage, tricky wind patterns, and even sneakier course formations, so pick your tee wisely—the black tees are for pros and masochists only. Realistic golfers should choose the North course, as it is the easier of the two. It is also cheaper, with full greens fees of $85. The South course fees are $135.

Biking

Touring the streets of La Jolla on a bike can be really rewarding, but the killer hills are a deal-breaker for most casual riders. **Hike Bike Kayak** (2246 Avenida de la Playa, 858/551-9510, www.hikebikekayak.com) solves this problem with a bike tour that it likes to call the La Jolla Plunge. Riders are shuttled up to the top of La Jolla's highest peak, Mount Soledad, which features a park with a monument to local veterans and a 360-degree view of San Diego. From there it is downhill through La Jolla for 3.5 miles. The two-to-three-hour tour also rides through Pacific Beach and Mission Beach before heading back to Hike Bike Kayak's shop at the Shores.

Ice Skating

For a cool moment out of the sun, **IceTown** (4545 La Jolla Village Dr., 858/452-9110, www.icetown.com, 10:30 A.M.–5:30 P.M. Mon., 10:30 A.M.–4:30 P.M. Tues., 10:30 A.M.– 5 P.M. Wed.–Thurs., 10:30 A.M.–4:15 P.M. and 7–10 P.M. Fri., 12:30–4 P.M. and 8–10:30 P.M. Sat., 1:30–4 P.M. Sun.) at University Town Center is just the ticket. The Olympic-size rink is set within the mall's food court, making it a favorite rest stop for families shopping with kids in tow. General admission is $11 and kids 5 and under get in for $6 with a paying adult. Skate rentals are $2, free for seniors and those with military or student ID. Families might consider making this a Sunday activity, as a family four pack with skates is just $40.

ACCOMMODATIONS

La Jolla lodging ranges from the elegantly simple to the sumptuously opulent. Be prepared to pay for the scenery—and the bragging rights— that come with staying in the area. During high season most accommodations will not be available for less than $200 per night. Beachfront and oceanview properties often charge many times that rate. Travelers who prefer more spartan beach accommodations or simply wish to save a buck are advised to look a few miles south in Pacific Beach.

Under $100

Located in Bird Rock, **La Jolla Biltmore Motel** (5385 La Jolla Blvd., 858/459-6446, $76 d) is reasonably close to both La Jolla and Pacific Beach. Facilities are more "motel" than "Biltmore," but the low price includes a room that will be serviceable and clean.

$100-200

Located within a short walk of the Village's boutiques and restaurants, the **Inn by the Sea** (7830 Fay Ave., 800/526-4545 or 800/462-9732 from California or Canada, www.lajollainn bythesea.com) offers an affordable alternative to some of the neighboring luxury hotels. On-line reservations are significantly less expensive than booking by phone, with singles and doubles starting at $139 during high season.

Built on one of the Village's busiest street corners, **La Jolla Inn** (1110 Prospect St., 858/454-0133, www.lajollainn.com, $200 d) offers well-appointed European-style accommodations. Rooms either overlook the ocean or the busy shops below. Rates include a continental breakfast served to your room and afternoon refreshments served in the hotel's library.

$200-300

Frequently voted as the best bed-and-breakfast by national media outlets, **Bed and Breakfast Inn at La Jolla** (7753 Draper Ave., 858/456-2066, www.innlajolla.com) features fifteen unique rooms in a 1913 home designed by the famous Cubist architect Irving Gill. Rooms start at $199 d and include a gourmet breakfast and a wine-and-hors d'oeuvres reception in the evening.

Another hotel with historical architectural highlights is ◖ **The Grande Colonial La Jolla** (910 Prospect St., 858/454-2181, www .thegrandecolonial.com, $245 d). Built in 1926, the building's architecture features colonial accents and a colorful palette, highlighted by the front facade's sunburst-style windows. Rooms are European-style and include evening turndown service.

Over $300

Formerly known as the SeaLodge Hotel, ◖ **La Jolla Shores Hotel** (8110 Camino Del Oro, 866/392-8762, www.ljshoreshotel.com) is one of the precious few hotels in San Diego that is positioned directly on the beach. The hotel is right next door to Kellogg Park and all rooms have patios that either overlook the ocean or the hotel's center courtyard, a hacienda-style garden area that features lush greenery, fountains, lattice work, and several comfortable spots from which guests can enjoy the scenery. Many of the gardenview rooms without kitchenettes can be reserved in the summer for around $280 d, but the majority of the hotel's rooms are well above $300 d.

Referred to as "The Pink Lady" by the locals, **La Valencia** (1132 Prospect St., 858/454-0771 or 800/451-0772, www.lavalencia.com) is a luxury hotel with a long history of accommodating the rich and famous. The lobby features signed photos with best wishes to the hotel from classic greats such as Lon Chaney and Greta Garbo. The hotel is built into a hill overlooking the ocean. One of the legendary quirks of the place is that the lobby level is referred to as the eighth floor. When the first building was opened in 1926 the plan was to dig down seven floors below street level. Developers only made it three floors down, but the numbering for the floors lived on. No two rooms are alike at the hotel, making each stay a unique one. The ocean villas by the pool (from $695 d) come with an on-call butler to do your bidding, but many of the rooms and suites (from $350 d) in the other two towers have a better view. Although you're largely paying hefty prices for the beachfront locale, the hotel does have a number of first-class amenities. Facilities include a swimming pool, children's wading pool, spa, and sauna. Beach accessories are also available free of charge.

If you've ever wondered what it is like to belong to an exclusive country club, satisfy your curiosity with a stay at the **La Jolla Beach and Tennis Club** (2000 Spindrift Dr., 800/624-2582, www.ljbtc.com). The 14-acre club is one of the city's most elite, with a four-and-a-half-year waiting list and an initial price tag of $60,000 to join its ranks. As a patron in one of the club's 90 guest rooms, you'll be entitled to all of the perks enjoyed by full-fledged members. This includes access to the club's private beach, championship tennis courts, and nine-hole pitch-and-putt golf course, plus admittance to the club dining room and permission to use club meeting spaces. The property features eight different kinds of rooms with rates from $299 d a night up to $1,179 d per night. The most common, the beachfront two-bedroom suite, runs $879 d per night.

FOOD

La Jolla's fine comestibles are enough to win over even the snobbiest of foodies. Though fine dining is the area's forte, there is no shortage of comfortable spots for a casual meal.

Cafés and Casual Eats

La Jolla has an abundant supply of quaint cafés. Among the standouts is **Rudy's Café** (2168 Avenida de la Playa, 858/454-5665, www.rudyscafeca.com, 6 A.M.–7 P.M. daily, $5), which is one of the first eateries to open on the Shores' main drag. Stop in for an early cup of joe or enjoy a sandwich or salad later in the day when the people-watching is at its best.

Over in the Village, **Goldfish Point Café** (1255 Coast Blvd., 858/459-7407, 8 A.M.–8:30 P.M. daily, $6) offers a stunning view of the ocean and a friendly atmosphere. Situated across the street from the Cave Store, this little establishment rarely frowns on lingering customers.

If you find yourself in Bird Rock, try the **French Pastry Café** (5550 La Jolla Blvd., 858/454-9094, 10 A.M.–3 P.M. Mon., 8 A.M.–6 P.M. Tues.–Wed. and Sun., 8 A.M.–10 P.M. Thurs.–Sat.). Its pastries and breads are baked daily. They're delicious on their own, but even more impressive when accompanied by a meal in the café's dining room. Breakfast and lunch are served until 3 P.M. daily and dinner is served Thursday through Saturday between 5 and 10 P.M.

Beach Fare

Jeff's Burgers (2152 Avenida de la Playa, 858/454-8038, 10 A.M.–9 P.M. Mon.–Fri., 8:30 A.M.–9 P.M. Sat.–Sun., $7) serves typical beach-day treats just a walk away from La Jolla Shores. Its specialty is in the name, with plenty of other sandwich and ice cream choices also available.

For those who prefer picnicking on the beach, **La Jolla Shores Market** (2259 Avenida de la Playa, 858/459-3465, 7 A.M.–8 P.M. daily) is a clean, well-stocked spot to pick up groceries, ice, and charcoal.

If you work up an appetite surfing Windansea, swing by **Bird Rock Pizza** (5737 La Jolla

Blvd., 858/456-2473, www.birdrockpizza.com, 11 A.M.–9 P.M. Sun.–Thurs., 11 A.M.–10 P.M. Fri.–Sat., $6) for a Bird Rock Special Pizza. Served with pepperoni, sausage, mushrooms, green peppers, onions, and black olives, this house specialty can quiet even the loudest growls of hunger.

Contemporary

Most San Diegans regard the 🅒 **Marine Room** (2000 Spindrift Dr., 858/459-7222, www.marine room.com, 5:30–9 P.M. Sun.–Wed., 5:30–10 P.M. Thurs.–Sat., $35) as the "go-to" place for special events such as birthdays or anniversaries. Set directly on the beach, this restaurant sets the bar for cuisine across the region. Its award-winning dinner menu never fails to please, but for a really unique experience, try to arrange a reservation for one of its High Tide brunches. Held just a few times a year when the tide crashes against the restaurant's ocean-facing walls, these brunches offer the best tastes of breakfast nibbles, seafood, and desserts.

One of the finest views of the cove can be found at **George's at the Cove** (1250 Prospect St., 858/454-4244, www.georgesatthecove .com, 11 A.M.–9 P.M. Sun.–Thurs., 11 A.M.–10 P.M. Fri.–Sat., $36), which is actually two restaurants in one. George's Ocean Terrace serves fresh and casual fare on a patio facing the cove, while George's Modern California offers a dynamic menu that focuses on seafood and seasonal produce offered locally.

The patio at **Top of the Cove** (1216 Prospect St., 858/454-7779, www.topofthecove .com, lunch 11:30 A.M.–3 P.M. Mon.–Sat., 10:30 A.M.–3 P.M. Sun., dinner 5:30–10:30 P.M. daily) also has a great view of the Cove. The contemporary cuisine here incorporates the best elements from France, northern Italy, and the Pacific Rim. Try the Muscovy duck served with a mushroom potsticker and ponzu sauce ($29) to get a taste of the fusion.

A relative up-and-comer in the La Jolla scene is **Nine-Ten** (910 Prospect St., 858/964-5400, www.nine-ten.com, 11:30 A.M.–2:30 A.M. and 6 P.M.–10 P.M. daily, $30), based out of the Grande Colonial Hotel. Serving classic California cuisine, this restaurant uses produce selected daily from the harvests of local farms to create a fresh menu. For the best of what Nine-Ten has to offer, ask for the Mercy of the Chef ($70, $110 with wine pairings), a multi-course dining experience you won't soon forget.

Steakhouses

Grab a friend and dress down for a quality hunk of meat at **Bully's** (5755 La Jolla Blvd., 858/459-2768, 11 A.M.–10 P.M. Sun.–Thurs., 11 A.M.–11 P.M. Fri.–Sat.). Located south of the Village bustle in the quiet Bird Rock neighborhood, this unpretentious establishment serves the author's favorite prime rib deal in town. For $30, two people split a 22-ounce slab, served with a side and salad or soup for each diner.

For finer cuts and white-glove service, **Donovan's Steakhouse** (4340 La Jolla Village Dr., 858/450-6666, www.donavanssteakhouse .com, 5–10 P.M. Sun.–Thurs., 5–11 P.M. Fri.–Sat., $38) near UTC is one of the West Coast's finest steakhouses and the only one in La Jolla to win a prestigious Distinguished Restaurants of North America Award. The restaurant also features an award-winning wine selection with over 800 bottles, and a knowledgeable staff and sommelier to help you choose between them. All of the food is first-rate at Donovan's, but the meat easily steals center stage. Donovan's is one of only five restaurants in the country to receive prime-grade beef in every shipment, and every single steak served at the restaurant is prime grade.

French

The intimate dining room at **The Sky Room** (1132 Prospect St., 858/454-0771, 6:30–10 P.M. daily) only has twelve tables, assuring that each diner will be well attended. Located on the top floor of the La Valencia tower, the restaurant juts up and out of the cliff on Prospect Street and has wraparound windows to give an unobstructed coastal view to the north and south. At night you can see the lights on Scripps Pier twinkle over the water as you savor entrées such as the trio of duck ($44) or the elk loin with parsnip potato croquette ($45).

Italian

La Jolla Shores features two delicious choices for Italian fare only a couple of doors from one another. Checkered tablecloths and hanging prints depicting Italian villages are meant to evoke the community feeling of a European town square at **Osteria Romantica** (2151 Avenida de la Playa, 858/551-1221, www .osteriaromantica.com, 11:30 A.M.–2:30 P.M. and 5 P.M.–10:30 P.M. Mon.–Fri., 11:30 A.M.–10:30 P.M. Sat.–Sun., $16). This little bistro is informal, but the entrées are not. Try the seafood dishes—particularly good is the bow-tie pasta with salmon, vodka, and asparagus.

Two doors east, **Barbarella** (2171 Avenida de la Playa, 858/454-7373, 11:30 A.M.–10 P.M. Sun.–Thurs., 11:30 A.M.–10 P.M. Fri.–Sat., $16) is a chic little spot that adds a touch of French cuisine to its Italian favorites. The French onion soup is, in fact, one of the best items on the menu. The owner is an avowed wine enthusiast and offers a robust selection of vino for very reasonable prices, so don't forget to pair your meal with a glass or two.

Moroccan

Bring a hearty appetite and a sense of adventure to **Marrekesh** (634 Pearl St., 858/454-2500, www.marrakeshrestaurant.com, 11:30 A.M.–3 P.M. and 5–11 P.M. daily). Stepping into the dining room with its brocade and tapestries and the nearly floor-level plush seating you'll feel as if you've been whisked off to a well-appointed North African tent. The vibrant decor is highlighted by an oversized Moroccan mural on its largest wall. The couscous is phenomenal and you'll have a chance to taste it through one of seven five-course feasts ($28). Don't forget to bring some single dollars, too. The restaurant features belly dancing nightly, so you'll want a couple of bucks to tip the dancers.

Sushi

Styled after the hippest restaurants in Tokyo, **Roppongi Restaurant and Sushi Bar** (875 Prospect St., 858/551-5252, www.roppongi usa.com, 11 A.M.–11 P.M. daily, $25) offers a creative selection of sushi and Asian-fusion cuisine. Adventurous diners should try the Albacore Jalapeño Roll. Made with albacore, jalapeños, cucumber, garlic ponzu sauce, it is spicy and refreshingly cool at once.

Vying for accolades with Roppongi is the nearby **(Zenbu Sushi Bar and Restaurant** (7660 Fay Ave., Ste. 1, 858/454-4540, 5 P.M.–9:30 P.M. Sun.–Wed., 5 P.M.–1 A.M. Thurs.–Sat.), which features sushi so fresh it is practically still wiggling. The restaurant is owned by a family that also owns a local sea-food distribution company, giving it exclusive access to the freshest fish in the city. In addition to some traditional sushi rolls, this place makes some off-the-wall concoctions. Those with a slight sweet tooth should definitely try the Wind-N-Sea Roll with freshwater eel, tempura banana, avocado, and cucumber. Another fun item is the Hot Rock, which comes with wafer-thin slices of fresh beef and a steaming-hot chunk of volcanic rock to sear them on.

INFORMATION

The **La Jolla Visitor Center** (7966 Herschel Ave., 619/236-1212, www.sandiego.org) is one of two regional centers operated by the San Diego Convention and Visitors Bureau. Situated in the middle of La Jolla Village, this location employs a multilingual staff and stocks a complete collection of brochures and maps. It's open daily year-round, but hours vary widely by season. Call for hours.

The local branch of the **public library** (7555 Draper Ave., 858/552-1657, www.lajollalibrary .org, noon–8 P.M. Mon. and Wed., 9:30 A.M.–5:30 P.M. Tues., Thurs., and Fri., 1–5 P.M. Sat.) has free wireless Internet.

Look for both of La Jolla's free weekly newspapers, *The La Jolla Light* and *La Jolla Village News,* at local establishments.

SERVICES

In the Village, the nearest post office is at 1140 Wall Street. There is also a post office closer to the Shores and UCSD at 3298 Governor Drive. Numerous banks dot the main Village streets of Girard and Herschel.

Medical services are available at **Scripps**

Memorial Hospital (9888 Genesee Ave., 858/626-4123, www.scripps.org).

GETTING THERE AND AROUND

La Jolla is accessible by public transit on bus routes 30, 150, and 50. From downtown San Diego and Old Town, the most scenic bus route is 30, which winds along the coast all the way to UCSD.

From downtown, the easiest driving route is on I-5 north. Take the La Jolla Village Drive exit and turn left on Torrey Pines Road to take you to either La Jolla Shores or La Jolla Village.

If you want to enjoy the area like some locals do, **San Diego Prestige** (5605 La Jolla Blvd., 858/551-6001, www.sandiegoprestige .com) rents exotic cars such as Lamborghinis, Ferraris, and Lotuses starting at $350 per day. Hourly rates are also available.

Mission Bay

Sandwiched between the ocean's swells and Mission Bay's glassy waters are two prototypical California neighborhoods that draw an eclectic crowd of locals, transplants, and wayfarers with one common bond: love of sand, surf, and sun. The combination of these three magic ingredients seems to be the perfect cocktail to lull visitors into the easy frame of mind so typical of the locals in Mission Beach and Pacific Beach.

Cruising down Mission Boulevard, the main drag that strings the two beach neighborhoods together, you'll see all the things you expect to see in coastal Southern California: sun-bleached surfer dudes, Royal Palms reaching skyward, and a glimpse out to sea at every cross street. But it's the things—and the people—you don't expect that really define the area: a hotel perched up on a pier, paunchy old men skipping across the street with longboards under-arm, couples riding skateboards side-by-side holding hands, and toddlers swinging playfully from Mom and Dad's tattoo-covered arms.

Driving south from La Jolla, you'll hit Pacific Beach first. Affectionately called "PB" by the locals, it's larger than its neighbor Mission Beach, and is generally where beach residents rest their heads each night. Consequently, there are many more hidden restaurants and bars to be found on quiet streets out of the main commercial districts.

Mission Beach, on the other hand, is hardly more than water and sand with Mission Boulevard running through both elements. The neighborhood is long and skinny on the map, at some points only a couple of blocks wide. The narrow grid of streets between bay and ocean are organized chaos—a collection of beach shacks and luxury rentals, restaurants and bars, all built upon one another with no seeming borders. The funny thing is, it doesn't seem cluttered. The coexistence just adds to the charm and vitality of the area.

SIGHTS
Belmont Park

The seaside rides at Belmont Park (3146 Mission Blvd., 619/491-2988, 11 A.M.–8 P.M. Mon.–Thurs., 11 A.M.–10 P.M. Fri.–Sun. Oct.–Apr.; 11 A.M.–11 P.M. Sun.–Thurs., 11 A.M.–midnight Fri.–Sun. May–Sept.) are a blend of old-school carnival thrills and newer rides. Its longtime jewel is the Giant Dipper roller coaster. Originally built in 1925, the wooden coaster still packs enough punch to keep most adventure-seekers happy.

Prices on rides vary, but visitors can buy unlimited-ride wristbands to avoid the hassle and expense of ride tickets. Those under 50 inches tall pay $13.95, while taller riders pay $19.85.

Also within Belmont Park are two stationary wave machines operated by **Wavehouse** (3127½ Ocean Front Walk, 858/228-9283), including **Bruticus Maximus** (noon–10 P.M.

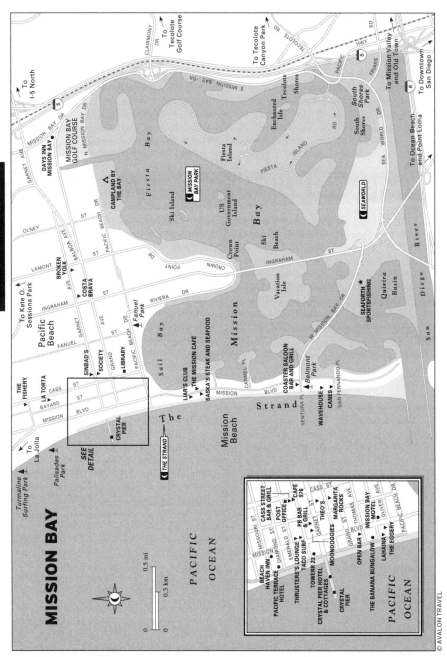

MISSION BAY

To I-5 North
To Tecolote Golf Course
To Tecolote Canyon Park
To Mission Valley and Old Town
To Downtown San Diego
To Ocean Beach and Point Loma
To Kate O. Sessions Park
To La Jolla

DAYS INN MISSION BAY
MISSION BAY GOLF COURSE
CAMPLAND BY THE BAY

Fiesta Bay
Ski Island
US Government Island
Fiesta Island
Enchanted Isle
Tecolote Shores
South Shores Park

MISSION BAY PARK
SEAWORLD

Crown Point
Ski Beach
Vacation Isle
Sail Bay
Mission Bay

San Diego River
Quivira Basin

Pacific Beach

THE FISHERY
LA TORTA
SINBAD'S
SOCIETY
LIBRARY
LIAR'S CLUB
THE MISSION CAFÉ
SASKA'S STEAK AND SEAFOOD
COASTER SALOON BAR AND GRILL
WAVEHOUSE
CANES
Belmont Park

SEAFORTH SPORTSFISHING

Mission Beach
The Strand

CRYSTAL PIER
Palisades Park
Turmaline Surfing Park

SEE DETAIL
THE STRAND

PACIFIC OCEAN

0 0.5 mi
0 0.5 km

Detail

BEACH HAVEN INN
PACIFIC TERRACE HOTEL
THRUSTER'S LOUNGE
TACO SURF
TOWER 23
CRYSTAL PIER HOTEL & COTTAGES
CRYSTAL PIER
THE BANANA BUNGALOW
LAHAINA
THE EGGERY
OPEN BAR
MOONDOGGIES
PB BAR & GRILL
THEO'S
CAFÉ 976
CASS STREET BAR & GRILL
POST OFFICE
MARGARITA ROCKS
MISSION BAY MOTEL

PACIFIC OCEAN

© AVALON TRAVEL

© ERICKA CHICKOWSKI

Giant Dipper at Belmont Park

Mon.–Thurs., noon–11 P.M. Fri.–Sat., noon–9 P.M. Sun.). Bruticus simulates some of the sickest tube waves that have challenged and bested the most talented surfers in the world. A crack at Bruticus's beginner wave requires a one-time registration fee of $10 and costs $20 per hour. Advanced waves are double that: $20 initially and $40 per hour.

Crystal Pier

Sitting like a sentry at the terminus of the happening Garnet Avenue, Crystal Pier (sunrise–sunset, free) is a good place to break out a rod and reel or to just look oceanward in contemplation. Some of the more talented local surfers like to stake out a spot in the water just north of the pier, so this PB landmark also makes a good vantage point to watch their snaps, floaters, and cutbacks when big swells roll in.

◖ The Strand

Spanning several miles through both Mission Beach and Pacific Beach, the Strand is San Diego's quintessential stretch of sand. In the summer you can just let your nose carry you through the sights. The smells of brine, hot asphalt, lighter fluid, sizzling burgers, football leather—they all mix with the sweet tropical scent of SPF collectively rising off sunbathers' lotioned bodies.

Typically, families and couples will head down the steep wooden steps from the streets of Pacific Beach to find a spot out on the sand north of Crystal Pier. The atmosphere is more subdued here.

Head south for crazier fun closer to Mission Beach. At about Grand Avenue the beach slopes up right to street level, making it easy to drag a keg out to the beach. During the summer the volleyball courts south of the pier are always hopping, and you can usually find at least a few college kids playing football in board shorts and backwards caps nearby.

Even farther south, close to Belmont Park, the scene calms down again. This is an excellent spot for families who aren't staying in the beaches area, as it is close to the only free public parking lot on the Strand.

Mission Beach Boardwalk

One of the best places to soak in the character of San Diego's beaches isn't on the sand, but instead the paved walkway of the Mission Beach Boardwalk. Winding three miles from **Palisades Park** in Pacific Beach down to the jetty at Mission Bay's inlet, the boardwalk is lined by vacation rentals and little motels, and occasionally peppered with restaurants, coffee stands, and beach vendors.

Heading south from Palisades, the walkway starts on a cliff overlooking the beach. After about a half a mile you'll pass Crystal Pier and get a peek up Garnet Avenue before reaching a point where the terrain levels out and the boardwalk is even with the sand on the beach. Meandering farther, the walkway will likely be more congested with revelers as you reach the bars and restaurants near Oliver and Reed Streets. From there it is full-steam ahead until you reach Belmont Park, which is the last concentration of commerce along the walkway before reaching its final point at the jetty.

The walk is populated with a diverse cast of characters, including some amusing regulars that you should keep your eyes peeled for. This includes Slo-Mo, an older man who goes so slowly on his inline skates it's a marvel he doesn't fall over. He's usually carrying an old boom box with him to share his tunes with the rest of the boardwalk—shout out his nickname and he'll give you a wave. For years a man known as The Flash has streaked by on the holidays in inappropriately appropriate garb—one Easter he was roller-skating in a bunny get-up of costume ears, a thong bikini bottom, and '80s-style rollerskates. Sandman, as he's known locally, is a little more G-rated and far more stationary. He'll use his broom to design cool sketches in the sand that blows onto the boardwalk.

Tourmaline Surfing Park

If you want to learn a little bit about the spirit of surfing, spend some time in the parking lot at Tourmaline Surfing Park (Tourmaline St. and La Jolla Blvd.), just north of the Strand. The asphalt is a staging ground for the park's beach, but it's almost a social scene in its own right. There you'll find old-timers and "kooks" (new surfers) chatting while waxing their boards, dancing their way into wetsuits, and scanning the horizon to figure out a good paddle-in route.

Here new arrivals mingle with their dripping-wet "bros" in arms, who skip back toward the lot's bathrooms and shower off after a good session. The whole area has the electricity of a schoolyard at lunchtime, only without the bullies. Old friends crack jokes, newcomers make small talk, and it seems like the good times will never end.

◖ Mission Bay Park

At 4,600 acres, Mission Bay Park (best access from E. Mission Bay Dr., Ingraham St., and W. Mission Bay Dr.) is the largest man-made aquatic park in the country. Once a salt marsh consisting primarily of mudflats, the bay was dredged in 1944 to create the palm-lined recreational paradise that it is today. Most of the 27 miles of shoreline along this irregularly shaped bay is beach with adjacent grass, giving picnickers, kite flyers, and sunbathers plenty of room to spread out. The bay itself has a number of little inlets and coves, and even a couple of islands that are navigated by an endless stream of boats and personal watercraft.

One of those islands, **Fiesta Island,** is particularly noteworthy. This 485-acre mass of land was created with the extra soil acquired from dredging the bay. The land has a paved road looping through it, but it has largely been left unimproved, giving visitors a less manicured but more natural space to visit. All of Fiesta Island is leash free, and in one corner of the island there is a large area fenced for dogs, making this a particularly great stop for those traveling with pets. Access is easy: Take Fiesta Island Road from East Mission Bay Drive.

The well-manicured beaches around the bay are easily toured via **Bayside Walk,** a wide and largely wheelchair-accessible path that leads around much of the park. Easiest access to the walkway is at the Crown Point lot along Crown Point Drive with ample free parking.

By water, the bay can also be explored by

the boatless aboard the *Bahia Belle* (3999 Mission Blvd., 858/539-7779), a Mississippi-style sternwheeler that hosts evening cruises around the bay.

■ SeaWorld

Perhaps San Diego's most recognized attraction, SeaWorld (500 SeaWorld Dr., 800/257-4268, www.seaworld.com, from 9 A.M. daily mid-summer through fall, 10 A.M. daily the rest of year, closing times vary) offers families a mix of animal fun and amusement-park action. This 189-acre park on the shores of Mission Bay offers smaller kids a chance to see Shamu, has a couple of heart-thumping rides for teens, and even has a beer-tasting pavilion for adults looking for a little refreshment. Admission for guests 10 years and over is $56, kids 3–9 $46, and toddlers 2 and under get in free.

Other Parks

Hidden away in one of PB's quieter neighborhoods, the hillside **Kate O. Sessions Park** (Lamont St. and Soledad Rd.) offers incredible views of Mission Bay and the beaches. Picnic tables and barbecues are scattered, but the best spots are on the oft-blanketed lawn.

The park also features a more natural section on its north side, with a short but satisfying little trail that winds through native chaparral.

Palisades Park is a scenic little park perched atop the cliffs overlooking the Pacific Beach shoreline. The park is the northernmost point on the boardwalk and is a great spot to cuddle with a loved one while watching the sunset.

Near Mission Bay, **Fanuel Street Park** is a good place to start a stroll down Bayside Walk. The park is right next to the path and has a small parking lot. The park also features a fun jungle gym for the kids, a large lawn for picnicking, restrooms, and a fish-cleaning station for lucky anglers fishing the bay.

ENTERTAINMENT AND EVENTS
Garnet Avenue Bars

The singles scene in Pacific Beach is legendary among college-age kids in Southern Califor-

nia and beyond. Walking through the area, it sometimes seems as if the entire local economy is fueled by bars, tattoo parlors, and smoke shops. Much of the partying is centered in the commercial district of Garnet Avenue, though there are also plenty of watering holes along the beach and scattered over side streets as well.

On Garnet, **PB Bar and Grill** (860 Garnet Ave., 858/272-4745, www.pbbarandgrill.com, 11 A.M.–1:45 A.M. Mon.–Sat., 9 A.M.–1:45 A.M. Sun.) is a popular stop for those celebrating

LA JOLLA

GETTING INKED

Body art is de rigueur in Mission Beach and Pacific Beach, with tattoo parlors almost as plentiful as the bars that jam the area's storefronts. These establishments are all part of a San Diego culture of acceptance that celebrates the artistry of "tats." No one knows for sure exactly what it is that has made San Diego such an inky city, but it probably has to do with a mix of factors, including the area's long seafaring history and its counterculture surf-and-skate scene.

If you decide to commemorate your trip with something as permanent as a tattoo, be sure to take some time between the trip to the bar and the one to the tattoo seat. Drunken tattoo decisions are rarely good ones, especially considering that the truly professional artists will turn you away if you're inebriated.

Experts recommend that you shop around a little for both the right shop and the right artist. By visiting a couple of shops, you can compare levels of cleanliness and professionalism. Ask to see pictures of an artist's past work to see if their style matches what you have in mind.

Some of the most popular and well-regarded shops are located on Garnet Avenue, including **Guru Tattoo** (1122 Garnet Ave., 858/270-1070, noon-9 P.M. Sun.-Thurs., noon-10 P.M. Fri.-Sat.) and **Chronic Tattoo** (1253 Garnet Ave., #B, 858/274-9140, noon-10 P.M. daily), which only inks original designs.

their 21st birthdays. Undeniably the most aggressive "meat market" in the entire city, it can be fun if you just loosen up and embrace it for what it is, cheesy pick-up lines and all.

Right next door, **Moondoggies** (832 Garnet Ave., 858/483-6550, 11 A.M.–2 A.M. daily) has its fair share of college co-eds, but the atmosphere is a little more relaxed.

A few blocks farther from the beach, **Sinbad's** (1050 Garnet Ave., 858/866-6006, 11 A.M.–2 A.M. Sun.–Thurs., 11 A.M.–4 A.M. Fri.–Sat.) not only offers refreshments, but also the opportunity to share a measure of flavored tobacco with your pals in one of its ornate hookah pipes. The tobacco is mild, imbued only with the fruit flavor of choice, so even non-smokers can enjoy this communal activity.

Because it is hidden away from the traffic of Garnet Avenue, **Cass Street Bar and Grill** (4612 Cass St., 858/270-1320, 10 A.M.–2 A.M. Mon.–Fri., 9 A.M.–2 A.M. Sat.–Sun.) is frequently missed by tourists. Too bad, because the patrons who frequent this place can be a breath of fresh air compared to the homogenous crowds a few blocks away. Salty old men with their dogs tied up out front, married couples on a night out away from the kids, and young professionals all mingle in this relaxed, open-air establishment. In addition to being a good bar, its food is also head and shoulders above typical pub fare. Bring a wad of bills, though, because the grub is cash only.

Mission Boulevard Bars

If they were holding red plastic cups you'd think the crowds at **Open Bar** (4302 Mission Blvd., 858/270-3221, 1 P.M.–2 A.M. Mon.–Fri., 10 A.M.–2 A.M. Sat.–Sun.) were at a college kegger. On big nights the rowdy crowd absolutely jams the deck for some raucous fun.

By day, probably the most in-demand barside property in either PB or Mission Beach is on the deck at **Lahaina** (710 Oliver Ave., 858/270-3888, 9 A.M.–9 P.M. daily). Tacked onto an oceanfront beach shack, this veranda is standing-room-only in the summertime,

with crowds often spilling out onto the adjacent boardwalk.

Because the Mission Beach neighborhood is situated on such a small amount of land—the bulk of which is taken up by rental properties—the range of watering holes is a little more limited than in Pacific Beach. But there are definitely a couple of notable highlights. Right across the street from the Big Dipper, **Coaster Saloon Bar and Grill** (744 Ventura Pl., 858/488-4438, 9 A.M.– 2 A.M. Mon.–Fri., 8 A.M.–2 A.M. Sat.–Sun.) absorbs a bit of the carnival atmosphere with a sometimes-rowdy tourist crowd blowing off steam away from home.

A few blocks away from the hustle of Belmont Park, **Liar's Club** (3844 Mission Blvd., 858/488-2340, www.liarsclubsd.com, 11 A.M.–midnight daily) is a locals joint in the truest sense of the word. Its selection of beer on tap is a veritable tour of San Diego breweries, and its jukebox selection heavily favors local bands.

Nightclubs

Outside of the Gaslamp District downtown, the beaches have the best collection of nighttime entertainment in the region.

Visit **Club Tremors** (860 Garnet Ave., 858/272-4745, 9 P.M.–1:30 A.M. Tues.–Sat.) to get your groove on. The beach area's only dance club, Tremors is run by the management at PB Bar and Grill.

For trance, hip-hop, and other thumping tunes mixed by a skilled DJ, **Thruster's Lounge** (4633 Mission Blvd., 858/483-6334, 1 P.M.–2 A.M. daily) is a surprising venue. Little more than a shoebox with mirrors (including a comically small dance floor), Thrusters still has a loyal following of techno enthusiasts who pack the place on weekends.

Just a couple of blocks away from Garnet, **Margarita Rocks** (959 Hornblend St., 858/272-2780, 1 P.M.–2 A.M. Mon.–Fri., 9 A.M.–2 A.M. Sat.–Sun.) has a multilevel dance floor and hires a staff of go-go dancers and bikini-clad waitresses to appease the sometimes puerile crowd. For refreshment, its five bars and multiple beer tubs keep the pack sufficiently lubricated to stay on the dance floor no matter how rusty their moves are.

It's a musical free-for-all at **710 Beach Club** (710 Garnet Ave., 858/483-7844) in Pacific Beach, which hosts live music sets nearly every night.

Near Belmont Park, **Cane's** (3105 Ocean Front Walk, 858/488-1780, 11 A.M.–2 A.M. Mon.–Fri., 9 A.M.–2 A.M. Sat.–Sun.) specializes in bringing in cover bands that can rip out uncannily similar tributes to their title groups.

If you're looking for something different, visit **Wavehouse Bar and Grill** (3127½ Ocean Front Walk, 858/228-9283, 11 A.M.–midnight Sun.–Wed., 11 A.M.–12:30 A.M. Thurs.–Sat.) to watch the waterworks. It's a hoot to watch surfers try their hand on the barrel wave machine, Bruticus Maximus. When they're good it is very exciting, and when they're not, well, sometimes its kind of funny.

Finally, those who enjoy a bit of friendly competition can invite their friends out for a little nine-ball action at **Society** (1051 Garnet Ave., 858/272-7665, noon–2 A.M. Mon.–Fri., 11 A.M.–2 A.M. Sat.–Sun.). This high-class pool hall features well-maintained tables and has a full-service bar and kitchen.

Events

San Diegans are awfully proud of the softball-derived sport Over the Line (OTL). Invented right in town, this beach pastime is so popular here that kids learn how to play it in P.E. class. The peak of OTL competition comes each summer at the annual **Over the Line Tournament** that has been organized by the Old Mission Beach Athletic Club for over half a century. Part athletic contest and part toga party, the weekend-long event draws more than 20,000 people at a time to its Fiesta Island digs each year. The event is a bit of a bacchanalia, so parents are strongly encouraged to leave their kids at home.

Fourth of July is the apex of high season

in the beach area, one of the few times of the year when almost every square inch of beach is taken up by blankets, bodies, and surfboards. Families tend to converge on the Strand, while singles and the younger set congregate on the bayside beaches to watch the annual fireworks over SeaWorld.

In the fall, Pacific Beach celebrates its sense of community with **Pacific Beach Fest.** Bring a bundle of single dollars and try a taste from each participating restaurant in the festival's Taste of Pacific Beach.

SHOPPING
Surf Shops and Beach Essentials

If you're looking to pick up a new board for your quiver, or just want to do a little wistful window shopping, the strip along Mission Boulevard has a healthy bounty of surf shops to choose from.

Pacific Beach Surf Shop (747 Pacific Beach Dr., 858/373-1138, 9 A.M.–7 P.M. daily) is one of the best shops on the north end for both beginners and lifelong surfers. The shop is in a plaza with ample underground parking. The staff is friendly and the store has a good selection of new and used boards, as well as beachwear, sandals, and sunglasses. It also has a wide selection of boards, wetsuits, and other beach toys for rent in the shop and in its nearby rental shack on the boardwalk.

Down in Mission Beach you can also check out **Endless Summer** (2888 Mission Blvd., 858/488-8983, www.surfmissionbeach.com). In addition to surf and beach accessories, the store also specializes in skate gear.

Ladies who can't find something girly enough at the surfshops should browse at either **Gone Bananas** (3785 Mission Blvd., 619/488-4900, 10 A.M.–8 P.M. Mon.–Fri., 10 A.M.–6 P.M. Sat.–Sun.) in Mission Beach or **Sun Splash** (979 Garnet Ave., 858/581-3400, www.sunsplashswimwear.com, 10 A.M.–8 P.M. Mon.–Fri., 10 A.M.–7 P.M. Sat.–Sun.) in Pacific Beach. Both are high-end swimsuit boutiques that sell suits designed to attract heaps of attention.

SPORTS AND RECREATION
Beaches and Surfing

Though there are better breaks in the county, the central location and easy access to amenities make the waters along Mission Beach and Pacific Beach very popular with surfers.

At **South Mission** just north of the jetty, the waves are very rideable even on days with the smallest waves. To rent a board nearby, visit **Hamel's Action Sports Center** (704 Ventura Pl., 858/272-2828, 9:30 A.M.–6:30 P.M. daily) across the street from Belmont Park. You can't miss it; it's in the building shaped like a castle right on the boardwalk.

North of the pier is also a popular spot for shredders. Just be aware that, typically, the closer to the pier you get the more aggressive and serious the surfers. If you are a beginner, try not to get in their way.

Another favorite location is **Tourmaline Surfing Park** (Tourmaline St. and La Jolla Blvd.), which is completely closed to swimming and wading. Longboarders especially dig the long, languid waves here, which give them plenty of time on deck to practice cross-stepping and hanging a few toes over the nose.

In Pacific Beach there are plenty of places to rent surfing equipment. **Pure Life** (4466 Mission Blvd., 858/274-2468, 10 A.M.–5 P.M. daily) has the best deal on the Mission Boulevard strip, with an all-day board-and-wetsuit combo running you one cool Alexander Hamilton ($20).

Most rental shops will only rent out beginner foamies (boards made entirely of foam) because they are more forgiving and buoyant. If you are an advanced surfer who would rather have the maneuverability of a traditional fiberglass board, you can rent one from **Pacific Beach Surf Shop** (4150 Mission Blvd., #161, 858/373-1138, 9 A.M.–7 P.M. daily) in the Pacific Beach Promenade mall.

Swimming

The shore along the strand is obviously one of the best places to go for a dip. In the summer be sure to keep your eyes peeled for the sandwich

SURFING ETIQUETTE

As free-flowing as surfing is, it might come as a surprise to newcomers that there are a few rules to follow. There aren't many – but the ones that exist are ironclad. Because you aren't likely to find these laws of wave riding on any sign on the beach, I'll lay them out for you.

First, never jump in on a wave that someone else has caught. This sin, called "dropping in," is on par with baby 'napping to a surfer.

The person who is closest to the peak of the wave has right of way, so if you see someone closer than you making an attempt don't bother paddling. Just pull back and wait your turn.

Try not to paddle out right where the waves are rolling in. Spend a moment on shore to see where they are breaking and plan your route on the edges of the breaks to avoid obstructing someone else's ride. Not only is this the polite thing to do, it also makes it a heck of a lot easier to make it out to the line.

A surfer limbers up before paddling out.

boards set out on the beach by the lifeguards; they'll tell you which areas are for surfers and which areas are for swimmers. They'll typically have a yellow-and-black checkered flag flying on them.

For calmer waters, Mission Bay is another good bet. Lifeguards staff swimming beaches around the bay in the spring and summer, including those at **Sail Bay** (4000 Fanuel St.), **Crown Point** (3700 Crown Point Dr.), and **Tecolote Shores** (1600 East Mission Bay Dr.).

If the thought of sea creatures creeps you out a little, you can doggie paddle through the clear and chlorinated water at **The Plunge,** an indoor pool at the Wavehouse (3146 Mission Blvd., 858/228-9283) whose deck has hosted more than its fair share of children's birthday parties during the more than eight decades it has been open.

Boating and Fishing

Situated at the entrance to Mission Bay, **Quivira Basin** is the hub of boating activity in the area. Visitors can rent a range of motorized craft at the docks of **Seaforth Boat Rentals** (1641 Quivira Rd., 619/223-1681, www.seaforthboat rental.com, 8 A.M.–30 minutes before sunset Mon.–Fri., 7 A.M.–30 minutes before sunset Sat.–Sun.) in the marina at Quivira. Next door, the affiliated **Seaforth Sportsfishing** (1717 Quivira Rd., 619/224-5447, www .seaforthlanding.com, 5 A.M.–5 P.M. daily) provides a selection of frozen and live bait, as well as tackle designed for bay fishing.

Anglers with a sense of adventure can also depart from Quivira with either Seaforth's chartered trips or with the boats of **Islandia Sportfishing** (1551 West Mission Bay Dr., 619/222-1164, www.islandiasportfishing.com), which runs overnight trips in the spring and summer that start at $150.

To splash down in the water, there are six boat ramps circling Mission Bay Park. The two with the best access and parking are at **South Shores** (Mission Bay Pkwy. and Sea-World Dr.) and **Ski Beach** (Ingraham St. and Vacation Rd.). These spots are also a

good place to launch personal watercraft, which are a popular form of propulsion on the waters of Mission Bay. To rent your own for the day, visit **San Diego Jet Ski Rentals** (2830 Grand Ave., 858/272-6161, 8 A.M.– 5 P.M. daily).

Cycling and Running

The three-mile **Mission Beach Boardwalk** is an excellent spot to steer a beach cruiser if you don't mind using your feet to slow you a little when the crowds occasionally get in the way. It shouldn't bother you, because this ride is more about seeing the sights than working up a sweat.

To continue the ride, try cutting over on one of Mission Beach's surface streets to the bay and ride north on **Bayside Walk.** Except on very busy days, this path is less crowded and more easily navigated on wheels. It continues for five miles before coming to an end at the nature preserve on the northeast corner of the bay. It is possible to ride all the way around the park by hanging a right on Pacific Beach Drive, a left on Olney Street, and a right on Grand Avenue. Continue along Grand as it curves toward the northeast entrance of the park. There you can recommence on the bay-side path.

Much of the boardwalk and the bayside path are constructed with concrete, which can be murder on the knees when running long distance. The obvious alternative is taking the sandy beaches, but another low-impact choice is heading a few miles inland to **Tecolote Canyon Park** (5180 Tecolote Rd., 858/581-9944). This park spreads its fingers through the canyons that lie under the mesas overlooking Mission Bay. Follow the main trail for an enjoyable run or walk that'll keep your joints intact.

Golf

The Mission Bay area has a couple of very family-friendly golf courses that can offer a leisurely afternoon for any level of player.

Within Mission Bay Park, the municipal **Mission Bay Golf Course** (2702 N. Mission

LA JOLLA

LA JOLLA

Bay Dr., 858/581-7880, 18 holes $23, 9 holes $14, carts $10) is an 18-hole executive course that promotes a very friendly environment where few people get stuck on stuffy conventions. You'll be as comfy in board shorts as in khakis, and rarely will you have a pushy party behind you rushing your strokes. Most notably, this course is the only fully lighted course in San Diego, offering night golfing until 10 P.M. every night. The course also has a lighted driving range and a modest practice green and bunker area.

Just up the hill from the bay, **Tecolote Canyon Golf Course** (2755 Snead Ave., 858/279-1600, greens fees $25, carts $12) is a challenging executive course that can sometimes catch even the scratch golfers off guard at first. Don't be fooled by the short yardage as the tricky course winds within canyons, and the scattered hazards force a high level of accuracy to reach par on any given hole. This course also has a nighttime driving range and a practice facility open during daylight hours.

ACCOMMODATIONS

Beach- and bay-area lodging lies on a spectrum from flophouses to the hippest of hotels. Pricing might shock some travelers expecting more for their money—in the end you are paying for location more than anything else.

Under $100

The Banana Bungalow (707 Reed Ave., 858/273-3060, www.bananabungalowsandiego .com, $20–25 dorm bed, $65–105 d) youth hostel bumps right up against the boardwalk and is a favorite for international travelers who would like to mingle with like-minded wanderers. Quarters are tight, with most guests sleeping in the bunk beds that crowd the hostel's dormitories. Private rooms are also available. Most guests don't mind the lack of personal space in the dorms, spending most of their time on the hostel's large deck overlooking the beach.

$100-200

Those looking for a crash pad with more privacy than the hostel can stay at the **Mission Bay**

Crystal Pier Hotel and Cottages

© ERICKA CHICKOWSKI

Motel (4221 Mission Blvd., 858/483-6440, www
.missionbaymotel.com, $110 d). It is across the
street from the beach and the boardwalk and
within easy walking distance from Pacific Beach's
bar scene. There is a modest pool area and rooms
are fairly well kept. The crowd here is fairly young
during high season, so come prepared to be put
up in a room next to a group of not-so-quiet
partiers. These walls, they are thin.

Beach-lovin' families stretching their dollars will be delighted with **Pacific Shores Inn**
(4802 Mission Blvd., 858/483-6300, www
.pacificahost.com, $118 d), one of the cheap-
est and cleanest motels you'll find in Pacific
Beach. There's no ocean view, but there is
a small pool and it is only a block from the
beach. Plus the beds are comfy and staff stays
at the desk all night, which is not always the
case at competing motels nearby.

Days Inn Mission Bay (4540 Mission Bay
Dr., 858/274-7888, $134 d) is not in the most
scenic part of the neighborhood, but it is an
easy drive from SeaWorld and has painless freeway access to reach the rest of the city. This dis-
count motel is designed to be a launching pad
for families who will spend most of their time
at the beach and SeaWorld anyway and would
prefer not to spend a bundle on their room.
The pool is a good spot to lounge when there
isn't time to hunt for parking on the Strand.

Beach Haven Inn (4740 Mission Blvd.,
858/272-3812, www.beachhaveninn.com,
$150 d) offers budget-minded travelers a good
compromise between weather-beaten motels
and uber-luxury hotels. The inn is tidy and
well cared for, with an appealing pool and
spa area with a barbecue for those times when
you'd just rather not go out to eat. Plus, it's a
stone's throw from the Pacific Beach commercial district, as well as the boardwalk.

$200-300

You can't get any closer to the ocean than in the
rooms at ▐ **Crystal Pier Hotel and Cottages**
(4500 Ocean Blvd., 858/483-6983, www
.crystalpier.com, $289 d). Stay here and you'll
be sleeping right on top of the ocean, as the cottages are actually built on the pier itself.

Pacific Terrace Hotel

© ERICKA CHICKOWSKI

Over $300

Pacific Terrace Hotel (610 Diamond St.,
858/581-3500 or 800/344-3370, www.pacific
terrace.com, $329 d) has one of the best ocean-
front pools in the entire region. The hotel sits
atop the bluff that overlooks Pacific Beach, and
the pool bumps right up against the boardwalk.
Watch the surfers rip it up without even leaving
the heated pool. Rooms are spacious and well
appointed, and continental breakfast and afternoon refreshments are included in the rate.

Two blocks down along the boardwalk,
▐ **Tower 23** (723 Felspar St., 858/270-
2323, www.tower23hotel.com, $389 d) is
another scenic option for singles and young
couples. The hotel caters to well-manicured
partiers with its hip architecture and cheeky
atmosphere. Its signature feature is the
Tower Deck, from which you can look over
the boardwalk and pier while being warmed
by the deck's huge open-flame fireplace.

Camping
Campland by the Bay (2211 Pacific Beach

Dr., 800/422-9386, $39 no RV hook-ups, $65 full hook-ups per site, per night) is centrally located right on Mission Bay in Pacific Beach. This RV-friendly mega-campsite has a full slate of amenities for visitors, including two pools, a whirlpool tub, an arcade, laundry facilities, and a market and deli.

FOOD
Breakfast and Brunch

If you're still recovering from last night's bender at Garnet's bars, visit █ **Broken Yolk** (1851 Garnet Ave., 858/270-9655, www.thebroken yolkcafe.com, 6 A.M.–3 P.M. daily, $7) for a little hair of the dog: Tableside mimosas are served with a jug of freshly squeezed OJ (the best in town), a bottle of champagne, and a brace of flutes. The Broken Yolk is also known for its gustatory challenge. The café serves a 12-egg omelet dish that is only $1.99 if you can finish it yourself in an hour. Winners also walk out the door with a celebratory T-shirt and the honor of having their name engraved on the restaurant's wall-of-fame plaques. Losers leave with a very full stomach and 20 fewer dollars in their pocket for the privilege of trying.

Closer to the beach, the patio at **The Eggery** (4150 Mission Blvd., #121, 858/274-3122, www .theeggery.com, 7 A.M.–2 P.M. daily, $7) affords a view of the river of people streaming by on the nearby boardwalk. The country-style breakfasts will fill you up practically until dinner, making this a good pit stop before going to see Shamu.

The Mission Café (3795 Mission Blvd., 858/488-9060, 7 A.M.–3 P.M. daily) is also steps to the beach, though it only has streetside views. That's OK, though, because it serves what most locals regard as the best-tasting breakfast in either of the beach neighborhoods. If you like rosemary, try the roast beef hash and eggs ($8.95) served with rosemary potatoes. And if you're an adventurous java lover, wash it down with a Vincent Vega. This unique coffee cocktail includes a shot of espresso and a dash of vanilla syrup poured over an icy glass of Coca-Cola.

Cafés and Casual Eats

The coffeehouse-and-café scene thrives in the beach area. Visit █ **Café 976** (976 Felspar St., 858/272-0976, www.cafe976.com, 7 A.M.–11 P.M. daily) and snag a spot in their shady garden. The menu runs from healthy to indulgent at all times of day, with a number of vegetarian choices mixed in throughout. Whether you are a meat eater or not, the breakfast burrito with soy chorizo is darned tasty ($7.95).

Beach Fare

Sometimes there's no better way to cap off a trip to the beach than with a salty or sugary treat that would land you in hot water with a nutritionist. Pizzas, burgers, sandwiches, and ice cream are all easy to find, with a few notable eateries that stand out above the crowd.

Don't let the line wrapping around the building at **Kono's Cafe** (704 Garnet Ave., 858/483-1669, 7 A.M.–3 P.M. Mon.–Fri., 7 A.M.–4 P.M. Sat.–Sun., $4) scare you off on busy days. The

along the strip, West Mission Bay Drive across from Belmont Park

© ERICKA CHICKOWSKI

kitchen crew is mighty speedy and the cheap eats are well worth the queue.

Near the intersection of Garnet and Cass in PB, **Olde City Grill** (967 Garnet Ave., 858/483-4624, 8:30 A.M.–4 P.M. Mon.–Fri., 8:30 A.M.–5 P.M. Sat.–Sun., $8) is an excellent spot to find authentic Philadelphia cheesesteaks, as well as pizza and Italian ice.

If you're in Mission Beach near Belmont Park, stop by **Gaglione Brothers Cheesesteaks** (724 Ventura Pl., 858/488-1690, 11 A.M.–9 P.M. daily, $7). The steak sandwiches there aren't Philly-style, but they're still smothered in meat and melted cheese. You can top that off with an ice cream cone at Kojacks just two doors down. Just don't forget to ride the Big Dipper *before* you eat.

For sandwiches outside the realm of cheesesteaks, saunter around the block to **Sully's** (4508 Cass St., #C, 858/483-3322, 11 A.M.–8 P.M. daily, $6). The shop puts a California twist on old-school deli favorites, the vegetarian Reuben being a good example of some of the bolder interpretations. There are plenty of classics, too, like the meatball sub that practically splits at the seams with sauce and meat.

There are lots of little markets and liquor stores that sell quick beach snacks, but to really stock up, stop at the **Ralph's** (4315 Mission Blvd., 858/273-0778, 24 hours daily) on Mission Boulevard. The full-service grocery has ample parking in its underground lot to make it a convenient shopping trip.

Contemporary

Pacific Beach isn't exactly known for fine dining, but **JRDN** (723 Felspar St., 858/270-5736, www.jrdn.com, lunch 7 A.M.–4 P.M. daily, dinner 5–10 P.M. Sun.–Thurs., 5–11 P.M. Fri.–Sat., $22) makes a good attempt at breaking the mold. The fresh interior (reminiscent of Miami Beach) and scrumptious menu items are worth the visit. And the setting is hard to beat, with most diners getting at least a little peek at the beach from this boardwalk restaurant. Just be prepared to look oceanward for a long time—the servers are notoriously slow.

Steak

Late at night, pass Denny's by in favor of **Saska's Steak and Seafood** (3768 Mission Blvd., 858/488-7311, www.saskas.com, lunch 11 A.M.–3 P.M. Mon.–Fri., 10 A.M.–3 P.M. Sat.–Sun., dinner 4 P.M.–2 A.M. daily, $17), which serves a full menu every night until the bars close at 2 A.M. Saska's was the first real steakhouse to open in the beach neighborhoods, propping its doors wide open for customers back in 1951. Today the signature steaks are joined on the menu by loads of fresh seafood.

Seafood

Unlike some seafood restaurants on the beach's boardwalk, the food is as good as the view at **World Famous** (711 Pacific Beach Dr., 858/272-3100, 7 A.M.–11 P.M. daily). The menu here highlights the best in California coastal cuisine, with an emphasis on dishes featuring mahi mahi, shrimp, lobster, and crab. Entrées are reasonably priced, around $18 a pop on average.

There aren't any beach views at **The Fishery** (5040 Cass St., 858/272-9985, 11 A.M.–10 P.M. daily, $23), but the menu does show off the variety of fresh fish displayed and sold in the fish market that is integrated into the restaurant. Tucked into the quiet north end of Pacific Beach, this restaurant is a perfect find for travelers who like to live as the locals do. The market is closed during dinner hours, but during lunch there is a steady procession of neighborhood regulars streaming in and out of this place to pick up tidy white packages of seafood.

Mexican

For authentic Mexican grub with a decidedly local vibe, check out ◖ **Taco Surf** (4657 Mission Blvd., 858/272-3877, 9 A.M.–10 P.M. Sun.–Thurs., 9 A.M.–midnight Fri.–Sat., $5). The eats are cheap, tasty, and filling at this paper-plates-and-plastic-forks hole-in-the-wall. Try the fish tacos. In a town that practically made this treat a national phenomenon, these are the best ones served. The fish is battered and fried as you wait and served up on hot corn tortillas with cabbage and a tangy white sauce.

While the cooks do their magic, check out the collection of vintage surfboards hanging from the walls and ceiling.

Facing the quiet streets of North PB, **La Torta** (4864 Cass St., 858/272-2077, www.latorta.com, 10:30 A.M.–8 P.M. Mon.–Sat., 10:30 A.M.–6 P.M. Sun., $6) is a unique find amid the many taquerias in the neighborhood. This Mexican sandwich shop serves dozens of signature sandwiches on fresh *telera* buns. For a satisfying lunch, split a sandwich and an order of chicken tortilla soup between two people.

French

Don't let the delicious desserts waiting for you at ◖ **The French Gourmet** (960 Turquoise St., 858/488-1725, www.thefrenchgourmet .com, 10 A.M.–8:30 P.M. Tues.–Thurs., 8 A.M.–9:30 P.M. Fri.–Sat., $23) make you rush through your meal. The food at this tiny restaurant is just as delicious as the dazzling array of breads and pastries baked fresh each day.

Spanish

It is easy to whiz past ◖ **Costa Brava** (1653 Garnet Ave., 858/273-1218, www.costa bravasd.com, 11 A.M.–midnight daily, $19) when you're driving along Garnet Avenue toward the ocean. The restaurant is about a block away from the main concentration of eateries in PB and its door is camouflaged by a thick set of shrubs that act as a patio border between the restaurant and the street. But if you like paella bursting with seafood and saffron, it is definitely worth slowing down to find. Owned by a restaurateur straight from Madrid, Costa Brava also serves creative tapas dishes and potent sangria.

INFORMATION

For more information on Pacific Beach restaurants, hotels, and shops, stop by the offices of **Discover Pacific Beach** (1503 Garnet Ave., 858/273-3303, www.pacificbeach.org, 9 A.M.–5 P.M. Mon.–Fri.). Located within Mission Bay Park, the **Mission Bay Information Center** (2688 East Mission Bay Dr., 619/276 8200, 9 A.M.–5 P.M. Mon.–Sat., 9:30 A.M.–4:30 P.M.

Sun.) also provides information on establishments and services throughout San Diego.

SERVICES

For non-emergency police issues, there is a neighborhood **police station** (4439 Olney St., 858/581-9920) in Pacific Beach.

If you need to tear yourself away from beach or bay to check your email, or if you're just looking for a good place to nurse a sunburn, the **public library** (4275 Cass St., 858/581-9934, 12:30 P.M.–8 P.M. Mon. and Wed., 9:30 A.M.–5:30 P.M. Tues., Thurs. and Sat., 12:30 P.M.–5:30 P.M. Fri., 1 P.M.–5 P.M. Sun.) is within a few blocks of both. The **post office** (4680 Cass St., 858/272-1948) is a block away from Garnet Avenue.

Pacific Beach Urgent Care (4490 Fanuel St., Ste. 208, 858/274-9116, www.pburgentcare.com, 8 A.M.–8 P.M. Mon.–Fri., 8 A.M.–4 P.M. Sat.–Sun. and holidays) is off of Cass Street and can take care of most non-trauma medical issues.

GETTING THERE AND AROUND

Because of its unusual location, both beach neighborhoods are a bit isolated from the rest of the city with a few arterials over the bay acting as major choke points. When jetting across town for dinner reservations, just remember that it always takes longer than you think to get into and out of the beaches due to traffic and parking concerns.

Speaking of parking, in the summer it can be quite a game of chance to find a good spot near the beach. The only free public parking lot along the strand is at Belmont Park.

If you'd like to forgo a car altogether, the #30 bus services the beach area. If you're staying out of the immediate area, think seriously about public transportation on busy beach days such as the Fourth of July. For example, you can park at the **Old Town Transit Center** and hitch a ride on the #30 to get to the beach in only about 15 minutes. That is probably at least as long as you'll be walking from your parking spot anyway, unless you're really lucky or willing to pay some college kid $50 to park on his landlady's lawn.

Point Loma and Ocean Beach

Visitors can leave the pretension behind when they travel through Ocean Beach (just call it OB—the locals do) and Point Loma. These funky little communities are home to love children and military folks alike, all harmoniously united through the same laid-back attitude toward life.

OB sports a unique beach scene at the southwest corner of land where the San Diego River and Pacific Ocean meet. The beachside streets are a maze of unique local shops and eateries, and the neighborhood attracts bohemians and beatniks with its distinct counterculture vibe.

Point Loma tends to be a little less irreverent, but just as easygoing. Named for the peninsula that juts out at the entrance of San Diego Bay, this area understandably has a long relationship with the sea and a storied naval history. After all, it is surrounded by towering coastal cliffs on one side and a steady procession of boats in the bay on the other.

Nearly five centuries ago it was the landing point for Juan Rodriguez Cabrillo, the first European to set foot on the West Coast, who arrived in 1542. Over the region's history the neighborhood has been home to numerous Navy installations. The area is also a haven for fishing boats and pleasure craft, with marinas crowding the harbors that line the neighborhood on its east side.

SIGHTS
Ocean Beach Park
Keep your ears open for the sound of guitars astrummin' from the dreadlocked denizens at Ocean Beach Park. The mile-long beach extends from the OB Pier all the way to the mouth of the San Diego River. Unlike the bronzed and buff regulars up in Mission Beach and Pacific Beach, the crowd here is more concerned with enjoying the scenery than showing off.

At the north end of the park is **Dog Beach,** an off-leash area that runs next to the river.

It is fun to watch the dogs dance like whirling dervishes in the sand here, dodging and roughhousing with each other while their owners either socialize or watch amusedly. Just be sure to keep your sandals on, as some owners aren't always responsible about picking up messes. If you are an owner, be sure not to set that bad example. There are complimentary bags stands and garbage cans scattered over the beach.

Also, remember that Fido can't drink the water here. The river water is brackish once it gets this far downstream. For hangin' tongues, visit the parking lot where there is a water fountain made just for mutts.

Ocean Beach Pier
At 1,971 feet long, Ocean Beach Pier (5091 Niagara Ave., 24 hours daily) is the longest concrete pier on the West Coast. The massive concrete structure extends far enough out to give anglers a chance at deeper waters and fish within the Point Loma kelp beds. And the T-shaped deck at the end of the pier gives passersby enough room to look out to sea without worrying about getting caught in someone's line. On quiet winter days this is a great place for a smooch with your sweetheart.

Sunset Cliffs Natural Park
Sunset Cliffs Natural Park (Sunset Cliffs Blvd., 619/235-1169) certainly earns its name. When the sun kisses the ocean each day these sandstone cliffs glow orange. The cliffs are unstable, though, so be careful where you step when you're hunting for a snapshot. There are parking lots sprinkled along Sunset Cliffs Boulevard for access up top. The adventurous can trek from the parking lot at the pier around the cliffside bend farther south to explore the small beaches and tidepools hidden within the cliffs' nooks and crannies. Just be sure to bring a tide chart and be aware of the time so as not to get trapped during high tide.

LA JOLLA

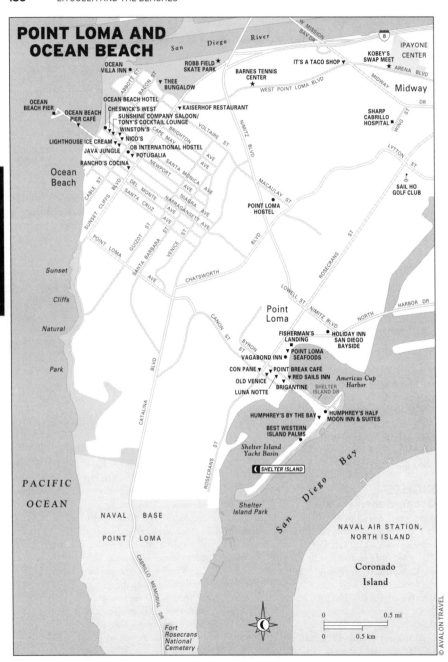

POINT LOMA AND OCEAN BEACH

© ERICKA CHICKOWSKI

LA JOLLA

Old Point Loma Lighthouse at Cabrillo National Monument

(Cabrillo National Monument

Right on the tip of Point Loma is Cabrillo National Monument (1800 Cabrillo Memorial Dr., 619/557-5450, 9 A.M.–5:15 P.M. daily), a 144-acre park featuring tidepools teeming with sealife, a historic lighthouse open for tours, a historical museum, and the best view of downtown and San Diego Bay in the city.

The entrance is midway up the steep hill that leads to the top of Cabrillo Monument. As you drive past the gatehouse, you can veer right to wind down to the tidepools that face the Pacific. Put on some sandals with traction and clamber down for a look at the tiny crustaceans, fish, and other sealife that live in the craggy fissures that make up these pools. Just be sure to tread lightly and take only pictures—the ecology here is fragile and will only persevere with your cooperation.

Continue up the main road to the top, which holds the other highlights of the park. Be sure to bring your binoculars in the winter, because this 350-foot peak affords great views of migrating grey whales to the west.

Named after Juan Rodriguez Cabrillo, who discovered San Diego Bay nearly five centuries ago, the park features a 150-foot statue of the explorer at the summit. Steps away is a museum that commemorates his exploration and his interaction with the Kumeyaay natives.

Also within walking distance of the parking lot is the **Old Point Loma Lighthouse.** Towering 422 feet above the sea, the lighthouse opened in 1855 as a major disappointment to the sailors it was intended to guide. Most lighthouses work best when placed on high, but engineers had not factored in the marine layer that often plagues San Diego in the summertime. After a couple of decades trying to make it work, authorities built another lighthouse farther down the cliffs of the peninsula in order to get the light under the fog. But the old lighthouse stands today, restored and opened for visitors to tour at their leisure.

On your way up you will probably notice a cemetery on the left side of the road, a

LA JOLLA

© ERICKA CHICKOWSKI

The marina at Shelter Island is a forest of masts and rigging.

seemingly endless sea of marble gravestones rolling over green grass. The park is also home to **Fort Rosecrans National Cemetery,** where 88,826 souls from armed services are interred. On Memorial Day, the navy works with other branches of the military to hold a moving ceremony on the grounds to pay respects to those who have fallen to protect our freedom.

🅒 Shelter Island

Shelter Island isn't actually an island anymore, but it has an isolated hideaway feel to it nonetheless. Once nothing more than a shoal off of Point Loma's shores on San Diego Bay, the island's land level was raised and a causeway was added in the 1940s when the Port Authority dredged between the island and mainland to provide better marina space there.

In the 1950s, when GIs returning from the Pacific brought back with them an excitement for all things Polynesian, many resort and restaurant developers decided to take advantage of the newly connected piece of land to build a sanctuary that pays homage to the tropics.

Today the decor still persists, with many of the hotels, restaurants, and shops on the west side of the island sporting a tiki motif and lush gardens reminiscent of Hawaii and other far-flung islands. Behind all of this is a forest of sailing masts in the marinas that sit between the island and the rest of Point Loma.

All of the buildings overlook **Shelter Island Park,** which spreads along the entire east side of the island. The 1.2-mile park has few obstructions, lending an incredible view of San Diego Bay, with downtown San Diego in the distance and north Coronado Island in the more immediate foreground.

ENTERTAINMENT AND EVENTS
Performing Arts
The Shelter Island marinas offer a scenic backdrop for the stage at **Humphrey's by the Bay** (2241 Shelter Island Dr., 619/523-1010). In the summer Humphrey's hosts a perpetually sold-out concert series in its open-air venue of 1,350. It has hosted popular

LA JOLLA

musicians such as Chris Isaak, B. B. King, and Lionel Richie.

For edgier artists and up-and-coming bands from the San Diego music scene, try **SOMA** (3350 Sports Arena Blvd., Ste. I, 619/226-7662). A smaller venue in this same vein is **Winston's** (1921 Bacon St., 619/222-6822), which is located near the beach. This popular bar hosts live music every night on its well-equipped, though small, stage.

Festivals

Come summertime, the biggest festival this side of the San Diego River is the **Ocean Beach Street Fair.** Tents overwhelm the beach's streets with vendors selling arts and crafts by local artists, while bands rock out on the stage near the pier, and pots roil nearby as amateur chefs duke it out for bragging rights at the event's annual chili cook-off.

Bars

The best bars in this neck of the woods are on Ocean Beach's main drag, **Newport Avenue.** Most of them are rowdy affairs, with revelry reaching its peak during football season. **Sunshine Company Saloon** (5028 Newport Ave., 619/222-0722, 11 A.M.–2 A.M. Mon.–Fri., 10 A.M.–2 A.M. Sat.–Sun.) is one of the largest of the bunch, with two stories to mingle through with pint in hand. Clear days are particularly pleasant on the second-story open-air patio, from which you can catch a glimpse of the beach.

Another OB classic is a couple of doors down at **Cheswick's West** (5038½ Newport Ave., 619/225-0733, 11 A.M.–midnight Mon.–Sat., 10 A.M.–midnight Sun.), a particular favorite among leather-clad bikers. Snag a stool near the open-shuttered window to watch passersby wander to and from the beach.

For something stronger than beer swing by **Tony's Cocktail Lounge** (5034 Newport Ave., 619/223-0558, 11 A.M.–2 A.M. Mon.–Fri., 10 A.M.–2 A.M. Sat.–Sun.) for a martini. The drinkslingers here pour them stiff and neat. The atmosphere isn't snooty, either. The leather booths are about as formal as it gets in this place.

SHOPPING
Kobey's Swap Meet

On the weekends, bargain hunters take over the parking lot at iPay One Center for **Kobey's Swap Meet.** Running continuously since 1976, Kobey's is San Diego's largest market and is the third-largest on the West Coast. Each weekend over 1,000 sellers put out their clothing, electronics, fresh produce, and assorted other items for the 30,000 shoppers that come to pick through their wares.

Newport Avenue Antiques

San Diego is a great city for antique hunting, and one of the best strips of antique shops in town is in Ocean Beach. Newport Avenue's 4800 block features an antique district with an assembly of shops that sell treasures from all different time periods and geographies.

The largest and most eclectic selection can be found at **Newport Avenue Antique Center** (4864 Newport Ave., 619/222-8686, 10 A.M.–6 P.M. daily), which offers space to vendors in its warehouse-like space. There you'll be able to find items from the early 1800s all the way up to the mid-20th century. Collectors of 1950s-era memorabilia will find a visit there particularly fruitful.

The center also features Asian antiquities, but the better bet for these items is across the street at **Oriental Treasure Box** (4847 Newport Ave., 619/221-9071, 11 A.M.–5 P.M. Tues.–Sun., closed Mon.). This smaller shop has a very strong selection of kimonos, hand-carved woodwork, and ceramics, among other Asian curiosities.

Vignettes (4828 Newport Ave., 619/222-9244, 10:30 A.M.–5 P.M. Mon.–Sat., 11 A.M.–5 P.M. Sun.), on the other hand, is better suited for collectors of Western antiques. Its vintage Paris souvenirs are particularly fun to browse through and it has a medley of elegant furnishings and decorative accessories.

SPORTS AND RECREATION
Surfing and Swimming

While swimming is certainly allowed at Ocean Beach, those looking for a place to

LA JOLLA

jump in the water without a board can find cleaner agua at the beaches farther north. The San Diego River empties out at Ocean Beach, and as a result the water here sometimes catches the dirty runoff that collects on the river's traverse downstream.

Unless it has rained, however, the water is far from dangerous, and because of the good breaks that occur here, the surfers are not deterred. The area south of the pier is good for all levels of surfers. For board rentals, visit **Cheap Rentals** (3689 Mission Blvd., 858/488-9070, 9 A.M.–6 P.M.) just across the West Mission Bay Drive Bridge in Mission Beach. In addition to hourly and daily rentals, this place also loans out equipment by the week.

North of the pier all along **Sunset Cliffs** there are reef breaks that lifelong surfers dream about. However, this area is only for the advanced surfer. The rocks leading up and down the cliffs are unstable and dangerous, and the tricky tides can easily create conditions that can quickly pin the inexperienced to the cliff sides. The bottom line is this: Don't paddle in here unless you have the chops for it, and always bring a buddy.

Fishing

The rails of the Ocean Beach Pier offer some of the best land-based saltwater fishing in the county. **Ocean Beach Pier Bait Shop** (5091 Niagara Ave., 619/226-3474, 7 A.M.–9 P.M. daily) can help you find something enticing to put on the end of your hook.

To ply deeper waters, wander over to Point Loma, from which a number of deep sea tours depart. **Point Loma Sportfishing** (1403 Scott St., 619/223-1627, www.pointloma sportfishing.com) offers a range of trips: half-day, three-quarter-day, full-day, overnight, and multi-day outings. For a fishing trip to really brag about back home, try one of the overnight squid fishing trips and hunt giant squid the size of peewee-league linebackers.

Fisherman's Landing (2838 Garrison St., 619/221-8506) also offers chartered trips of varying length. In addition, the Fisherman's shop has an extensive line of rods and tackle for those looking to pick up some supplies for a trip out on their own.

Sailing

The well-protected waters of San Diego Bay are a haven for sailing enthusiasts from 'round the world. If you're sailing into San Diego on your own craft, Point Loma's the best bet for guest slips and boating-related amenities. The sanctuary provided by Shelter Island and Harbor Island offers refuge to dozens of private marinas, as well as the **Harbor Police's guest marina** (1401 Shelter Island Dr.) on the south end of the Shelter.

This facility has 22 slips for boats up to 40 feet and end ties for longer boats, as well as water, shore power, restrooms, and parking. No reservations are taken, but you can reach the Harbor Police on VHF 16 to ask if space is available.

Additionally, if you belong to a yacht club, you may have reciprocal privilege at the numerous clubs that make their home in Point Loma. This includes the grand-daddy of them all, the **San Diego Yacht Club** (1011 Anchorage Ln., 619/221-8400). Call ahead for specifics.

For those who don't have their own boat, there is still plenty of opportunity to sail the Big Bay from Point Loma. **Sail San Diego** (955 Harbor Island Dr., Docks A–D, 619/297-7426, www.sailsandiego.com) has morning, afternoon, and sunset sails from Harbor Island each day.

And for a truly unique vacation experience, **Harbor Island Yacht Club** (Marina Cortez, 1880 Harbor Island Dr., 619/291-7245 or 800/553-7245, www.harboryc.com) offers five-day live-aboard, learn-to-sail vacations. For $1,695 you'll stay aboard a Catalina slipped at the yacht club while you learn the art of catching wind.

Golf and Tennis

Originally constructed by the navy in 1925, the **Sail Ho Golf Course** (2960 Truxtun Rd., 619/222-4653, www.sailhogolf.com, greens

LA JOLLA

fees $15) has a long and storied history for such a small course. When it was in the hands of the military, the course was just four holes, used as part of a physical fitness and well-being program for recruits. At some point Sam Snead acted as head golf professional there when he served in the navy.

In later years the course was expanded to nine holes and eventually transferred to the city, where it was especially popular for junior tournaments. San Diego natives Craig Stadler and Phil Mickelson both played here as kids. In recent years the course was renovated. As a part of the redesign, a clubhouse with a pro shop and a restaurant was added, making this a comfortable course for all comers.

If you prefer racquets over clubs, **Barnes Tennis Center** (4490 West Point Loma Blvd., 619/221-9000, www.tennissandiego.com) is a world-class tennis facility just a few minutes away from the beach. Catering to the highly competitive youth tennis movement in San Diego, Barnes lets kids hit around for free. Adults can play here too, for a nominal fee. Hard courts are $6 per hour and clay courts are $8.50 per hour, with a $4 light fee at night.

Cycling
For a true test of strength and stamina, turn your quads to jelly on **Cabrillo Memorial Drive,** which climbs steeply up to Cabrillo National Monument. The views are your reward—as is the ride down—and the $3 walk-in and bicyclist entrance fee is less than if you enter the monument in a car.

A more leisurely (and flat!) ride can be had along both banks of the San Diego River. The north-side path leads up to Friars Road, which has a protected bike lane leading into Mission Valley. The south-side path leads to Pacific Highway, which provides easy street access to the haciendas of Old Town.

Bike rentals are difficult to find in Point Loma and Ocean Beach if your hotel doesn't provide them. The closest shop is **Bike Tours San Diego** (509 5th Ave., 619/238-

2444, 8 A.M.–7 P.M. daily) in the downtown Gaslamp District.

Skating
To get a taste of the gnarly San Diego skate scene, visit **Robb Field Skate Park** (2525 Bacon St., 619/525-8486, 1 P.M.–sunset Mon.–Fri., noon–sunset Sat.–Sun., day pass $5). The 40,000-square-foot facility was planned with the help of local skate pros and features a street-course design with a number of bowls, handrails, ledges, and blocks. All skaters must wear protective gear, and minors must have a liability waiver signed by their guardians.

Spectator Sports
Known by the locals simply as "Sports Arena," **iPay One Center at the San Diego Sports Arena** (3500 Sports Arena Blvd., 619/224-4171) is one of the larger venues in the city for headlining artists making the national tour circuit. The iPay One arena is also equipped for sporting events. It is home to the **San Diego Gulls,** a minor-league hockey team, and plays host to the Los Angeles Lakers and Los Angeles Clippers for the occasional preseason basketball game.

ACCOMMODATIONS
Under $100
International travelers, educators with proper credentials, and those with a current hostel card from any of the big chains are welcome at the **OB International Hostel** (4961 Newport Ave., 619/2237873 or 800/339-7263, www .californiahostel.com, $19 dorm bed). The friendly rooming house provides dorm rooms with a reservation and offers a couples room on a first-come, first-serve basis.

A more restrained crowd frequents the **Point Loma Hostel** (3790 Udall St., 619/223-4778, www.sandiegohostels.org, $22 dorm bed, $55 d, $65 t) just a few miles away. Run by Hostelling International, this clean hostel also offers advanced reservations for its private rooms and its special family-size private room.

Ocean Beach Hotel is a favorite among bohemian travelers looking to soak up the local vibe.

$100-200

The ho-hum accommodations at **Vagabond Inn** (1325 Scott St., 619/224-3371, reservations 800/522-1555, $134 d) aren't going to spark much excitement, but they'll do the job. The motel is located between Shelter Island and Harbor Island, only two miles from the airport and within walking distance of several good seafood restaurants. The property has a heated pool and room rates include continental breakfast and a morning paper.

Prices might seem a bit high for the state of the rooms at **Ocean Villa Inn** (5142 West Point Loma Blvd., 619/224-3481 or 800/759-0012, www.oceanvillainn.com, $149 d), but dog lovers should be willing to pay the premium. The motel abuts Dog Beach, the only 24-hour off-leash space in San Diego County. For an extra $25 the hotel will let up to two pets stay with you. The property also has a dog comfort station to take your puppy to the bathroom on the property, a dog wash, and a pool (for human comfort only). Rates include continental breakfast.

Ocean Beach Hotel (5080 Newport Ave., 619/223-7191, www.obhotel.com, $169 d) is positioned on the most happening corner on the beach, Newport Avenue and Abbott Street. Singles and free-spirited couples enjoy this hotel, as it is within stumbling distance of Ocean Beach's best bars. Ocean-facing rooms cost quite a bit extra, but if you spring for one you'll have a fantastic view of the pier and the hippies who frequently stroll on the boardwalk across the street.

Holiday Inn San Diego Bayside (4875 N. Harbor Dr., 619/224-3621 or 800/345-9995, www.holinnbayside.com, $169 d) sits along the gateway arterial to Point Loma from downtown and the airport. Rooms are above average for a franchise hotel and the grounds are so well protected by building placement and foliage that it is hard to tell that it is on a fast-moving thoroughfare. Amenities include a 9-hole putting area, a heated pool, and a deck area that features a billiards table, shuffleboard court, and table tennis. The deck area is home to outdoor movie screenings in the summer. Bike rentals are complimentary, as is the shuttle to and from the airport.

$200-300

The most obvious choice for lodging on Shelter Island is (**Humphrey's Half Moon Inn and Suites** (2303 Shelter Island Dr., 619/224-3411 or 800/542-7400, www.halfmooninn.com, $209–219 s, $279 and up d). Located at the end of the island's causeway, the Polynesian-style architecture, gardens, and pool and spa facilities replete with poolside bar all add to this luxury inn's charm. The open-air concert venue and well-regarded restaurant put things over the top for visitors.

If you are seeking a truly secluded hotel on Shelter Island away from the noise of concerts, partiers, and giddy kids, try (**Best Western Island Palms** (2051 Shelter Island Dr., 619/222-0561, www.islandpalms.com, $179 d) for a more relaxed atmosphere. The character of this property is low-key, with a lot of good amenities in its own right, including two pools, tennis courts, and a comfortable bar and grill by the marina.

FOOD
Cafés and Casual Eats

You'll have to weigh your priorities before visiting **Ocean Beach Pier Café** (5091 Niagara Ave., 619/226-3474, 8 A.M.–8 P.M. daily, $8). On one hand, the café is as much a landmark as the pier itself, the view is great, and the food is tasty. On the other hand, cleanliness is not exactly top of mind for the managers here. If you aren't picky, ask for a wet rag to wipe up your sticky table and chow down. If you like seafood, be sure to try the house's special lobster tacos. These succulent treats are a favorite with adventurous taco fans.

Only a block away from the beach, **Jungle Java** (5047 Newport Ave., 619/224-0249, www.junglejavaofob.com, 7 A.M.–8 P.M. daily Sept.–May, 7 A.M.–10 P.M. daily June–Aug.) offers a garden sanctuary to sip a cup or two. While you're there, browse through the unique crafts and handiwork items displayed for sale.

If you're in the beach area but would prefer

something cooler, try **OB Smoothie Bar** (5001 Newport Ave., 619/222-0293) a few blocks east. This small no-nonsense shop blends up a whole array of frozen and fruity concoctions and also makes healthy sandwiches for those who'd like something solid.

In Point Loma, **Con Pane** (1110 Rosecrans St., 619/224-4344, 7 A.M.–6 P.M. Mon.–Tues. and Thurs.–Fri., 8 A.M.–6 P.M. Sat., 8 A.M.–4 P.M. Sun., $5) and **Point Break Café** (2907 Shelter Island Dr., 619/758-9870, 6:30 A.M.–3 P.M. daily, $8) are both good choices. Con Pane bakes fresh rustic breads and serves up food in a coffee-shop atmosphere, while Point Break offers hearty and healthy meals made for diners seeking a sit-down type of restaurant.

Beach Fare

Before you head back from the beach to your hotel or car, be sure to stop off at **Lighthouse Ice Cream** (5059 Newport Ave., #102, 619/222-8600, 11:30 A.M.–10 P.M. daily) for some of the best sweet stuff in town. The shop is less than a block away from the pier. If you're not worried about the waistline, try the fresh waffle sandwich ($2.50). Made with two squares of Belgian waffles sizzled right in front of you, they're so good you'll want to have two.

If your tummy is grumbling for something more substantial, (**Hodad's** (5010 Newport Ave., 619/224-4623, 10:30 A.M.–8:30 P.M. daily, $8) is the ideal place for a giant burger and a plate of onion rings. This place's name is surfer parlance for a poser, someone who dresses and acts the part but can't actually surf very well. The atmosphere is just as silly as a hodad walkin' the beach with a never-used surfboard. License plates line the walls, there's a table set in a car, funny pictures and memorabilia, and, yes, surfboards on the ceiling.

Seafood

Point Loma is probably one of San Diego's best neighborhoods for those in search of some tasty creatures of the deep. At America Cup

LA JOLLA

© JOANNE DIBONA/SAN DIEGO CVB

Point Loma Seafoods, right on the water, always has fresh fish and seafood.

Harbor, stop off for a quickly prepared meal at the fish-market deli **Point Loma Seafoods** (2805 Emerson St., 619/223-1109, 9 A.M.–6:30 P.M. Mon.–Sat., 11 A.M.–6:30 P.M. Sun., $9). Fish and seafood is plucked from the huge display cases and fried fresh while you wait.

Near the entrance to Shelter Island, **Brigantine** (2725 Shelter Island Dr., 619/224-2871, www.brigantineseafood.com, lunch 11:30 A.M.–2:30 P.M. Mon.–Fri., 11:30 A.M.–3 P.M. Sat., dinner 5–9 P.M. Sun.–Thurs., 5–10 P.M. Fri.–Sat., $32) is a Point Loma institution. The restaurant is a local chain now with six locations, but this is the original. Try the signature swordfish, a staple of Brigantine meals since it opened in 1969.

If Brigantine is packed, amble over to **Red Sails Inn** (2614 Shelter Island Dr., 619/223-3030, 7 A.M.–11 P.M. daily, $22) across the street. Also a longtime favorite, this restaurant not only has good seafood selections but also some savory steaks.

Mexican

For the finest taco grub north of Imperial Beach, **Nico's** (4918 Newport Ave., 619/223-

0230, 7 A.M.–9:45 P.M. daily, $5) in Ocean Beach is a tasty place to stop for a big and juicy California burrito. Stuffed with carne asada and freshly fried potatoes, these beauties will fill you up for the day.

In the Point Loma area, the brightly colored **It's a Taco Shop** (3910 W. Point Loma Blvd., 619/223-6330, 7 A.M.–1 A.M. Mon.–Fri., 24 hours Sat.–Sun., $6) is honest about its intentions right off the bat. This bright-yellow establishment is all about Mexican fast food, specifically the taco but also burritos and other quick eats. For those who love authentic Mexican comfort food, this place serves *menudo* (tripe stew).

Healthier Mexican choices can be found at OB's **Rancho's Cocina** (1830 Sunset Cliffs Blvd., Ste. H, 619/226-7619, 8 A.M.–10 P.M. daily, $8), which prepares a number of vegetarian and vegan renditions of typical dishes.

French

Whatever you do, don't leave **◖ Thee Bungalow** (4996 W. Point Loma Blvd., 619/224-2884, 5:30–9:30 P.M. Mon.–Thurs., 5–10 P.M. Fri.–Sat., 5–9 P.M. Sun., $25) without trying the dessert soufflés. These light and fluffy desserts ($15 for two), served in chocolate or orange liqueur flavors, are the perfect cap to the rich continental meals served here. Because they take time and care to rise properly, order the soufflés when you pick out your dinner entrées—my favorite is the roast duck, served with your choice of savory sauces.

German

There aren't any tubas here, but **Kaiserhof Restaurant** (2253 Sunset Cliffs Blvd., 619/224-0606, lunch 11:30 A.M.–3 P.M. Fri.–Sun., dinner 5–10 P.M. Tues.–Sat., 4:30–9 P.M. Sun., $15) puts a little oompah on your plate with its authentic German food. Located right at the foot of the Sunset Cliffs Boulevard Bridge as you enter Ocean Beach, this bar serves up schnitzels and sausages in a myriad of different ways. The outdoor *biergarten* is also a very comfortable place to put away a few mugs of the authentic German beer on tap here. It's particularly great for soccer fans, who are invited to watch the week's biggest games on the *biergarten*'s wide-screen television.

Portuguese

Portugalia (4839 Newport Ave., 619/222-7678, 11 A.M.–midnight Tues.–Thurs., 11 A.M.–2 A.M. Fri.–Sat., 11 A.M.–11 P.M. Sun., $18) is one of the few eateries in San Diego that serves up Portuguese and Brazilian eats. The location is hard to miss—the exterior is adorned with a two-story-high painted cross. Inside, the restaurant serves such favorites as beef Madeira and *linguica* (Portuguese sausage). It also acts as a social meeting space for the Portuguese-speaking community.

Italian

Good Italian is hard to come by in Point Loma and Ocean Beach, but there are two pearls in the rough only a couple of blocks from one another near Shelter Island. **Old Venice** (2910 Canon St., 619/222-5888, 11 A.M.–9:30 P.M. Sun.–Thurs., 11 A.M.–10:30 P.M. Fri.–Sat.) is a cozy and elegant place to find dependable favorites like veal saltimbocca ($19) and chicken

piccata ($16.75). The interior is lit with elegant sconces and a flickering fireplace, and on the weekend evenings there is live piano music.

Luna Notte (2833 Avenida de Portugal, 619/523-1301, 5–9 P.M. daily, $16), on the other hand, is a more relaxed bistro that serves Italian Mediterranean cuisine, blending French and Spanish cooking traditions into its Italian dishes. Families with young children will feel more comfortable at Luna Notte, without sacrificing flavor.

INFORMATION AND SERVICES

Visit **Ocean Beach Mainstreet Association** (1868 Bacon St., #A, 619/224-4906, www.oceanbeachsandiego.com, 9 A.M.–5 P.M. daily) for the skinny on neighborhood happenings and recommendations on where to eat, drink, or stay.

The headquarters for **San Diego Police Department's Western District** (5215 Gaines St., 619/692-4800) is in Ocean Beach. There is also a storefront neighborhood **police station** (3750 Sports Arena Blvd., Ste. 3, 619/531-1540, 8:30 A.M.–4:30 P.M. Mon.–Fri.) in Point Loma near the Sports Arena.

Several banks can be found along Sunset Cliffs Boulevard, which crosses by Newport Avenue in Ocean Beach. The **public library** (4801 Santa Monica Ave., 619/531-1532, 9:30 A.M.–5:30 P.M. Tues. and Thurs.–Sat., noon–8 P.M. Mon. and Wed., 1 P.M.–5 P.M. Sun.) and the **post office** (4833 Santa Monica Ave., 619/224-3570) are only a block from Newport Avenue.

GETTING THERE

The Ocean Beach and Point Loma areas are accessible from the northern beach areas by two bridges over the San Diego River. However, the area has good access to the rest of the city. On the north end, I-8 reaches its end in Ocean Beach, with easy access to parts east. To the south, North Harbor Drive has quick and painless access to the airport and downtown.

By bus, Ocean Beach is served by routes 35 and 923. Point Loma has access to the 28 A, B, and C lines.

NORTH COUNTY

Dubbed North County by resident San Diegans, the territory between northern city limits and the county line is home to an array of quirky sights. Meander the roads here and you're bound to encounter world-class horse racing, marshy lagoons, a couple of secluded nudist beaches, and even a school for trapeze artists.

North County is best known for its coastal communities. These small towns dot the historic Coast Highway 101 (U.S. 101), a notable strip of pavement that was once San Diego's major link to Los Angeles and the rest of the state. The highway was decommissioned when I-5 was built in the 1960s, but the stretch through North County remains the lifeblood of its oceanview towns.

Each has its own particular flair. Del Mar is home of the ponies as the longtime host of the Del Mar Thoroughbred Club. Solana Beach is a quiet bedroom community with artistic flair. Encinitas was built by the surfers who flocked here since the inception of the sport to try their skills on some of the best breaks on the West Coast. Carlsbad also attracts its fair share of surfers, along with loads of families who come for the long stretch of sandy beach at South Carlsbad State Beach and the amusement park fun offered at Legoland. The northernmost coastal town in the county, Oceanside, butts up against the sprawling Camp Pendleton Marine Corps Base. This military-friendly town attracts water lovers and anglers, who flock to the Oceanside Pier to cast from and surf near what is the longest pier on the West Coast.

North County isn't just about the ocean breezes, either. Heading inland to Escondido,

© ERICKA CHICKOWSKI

HIGHLIGHTS

◖ **Torrey Pines State Reserve:** Officially in La Jolla, visit this state reserve for a glimpse of the rare Torrey pine tree, ocean vistas from the sandstone cliffs, and beachcombing on secluded beaches (page 150).

◖ **Downtown Encinitas:** Founded as an enclave for hippies and surfers, this community offers small-town, coastal charm with quaint historic sights and friendly walkways (page 165).

◖ **Leo Carrillo Ranch Historic Park:** A hidden favorite among local picnickers and strollers, this 10-acre city park is a preserved piece of what was once a sprawling ranch owned by Hollywood actor Leo Carrillo, best known for his role as Pancho in *The Cisco Kid* (page 173).

◖ **Legoland:** Any kid who has spent hours on the living room floor in front of a pile of Legos will appreciate this amusement park dedicated to those clickable bricks (page 176).

◖ **Mission San Luis Rey:** Once known as the King of Missions, Mission San Luis Rey features beautiful gardens, a fascinating museum and a church painstakingly rebuilt according to historical literature (page 183).

◖ **San Diego Wild Animal Park:** This expansive wildlife preserve run by the San Diego Zoological Society is a fun place to check out majestic creatures such as elephants, zebras, rhinoceros, and antelope mingled together on a range that best approximates their habitat in the wild (page 189).

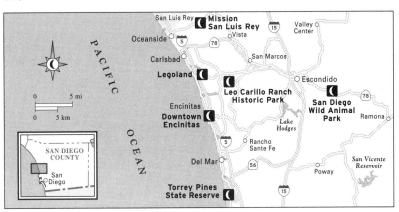

LOOK FOR ◖ TO FIND RECOMMENDED SIGHTS, ACTIVITIES, DINING, AND LODGING.

NORTH COUNTY

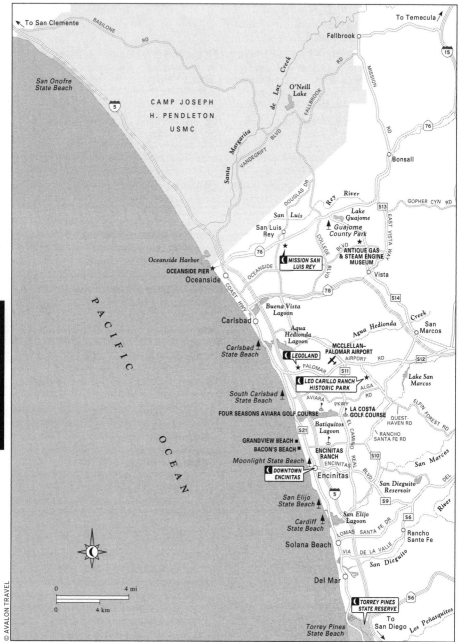

NORTH COUNTY

To San Clemente

BASILONE RD

San Onofre
State Beach

CAMP JOSEPH
H. PENDLETON
USMC

To Temecula

Fallbrook

O'Neill
Lake

de Luz Creek

FALLBROOK RD

MISSION RD

Bonsall

Santa Margarita

VANDEGRIFT BLVD

DOUGLAS DR

Rey River

GOPHER CYN RD

S13

EAST VISTA WAY

Lake
Guajome

Guajome
County Park

San Luis

San Luis
Rey

COLLEGE BLVD

★ MISSION SAN
LUIS REY

★ ANTIQUE GAS
& STEAM ENGINE
MUSEUM

Vista

Oceanside Harbor

OCEANSIDE PIER

Oceanside

COAST HWY

OCEANSIDE BLVD

78

S14

P A C I F I C

Buena Vista
Lagoon

Carlsbad

Aqua
Hedionda
Lagoon

Agua Hedionda

Creek

San
Marcos

Carlsbad
State Beach

LEGOLAND

MCCLELLAN-
PALOMAR AIRPORT

S12

★ PALOMAR

AIRPORT RD

511

Lake San
Marcos

★ LEO CARILLO RANCH
HISTORIC PARK

ALGA RD

ELFIN FOREST RD

South Carlsbad
State Beach

AVIARA PKWY

LA COSTA
GOLF COURSE

QUEST-
HAVEN RD

FOUR SEASONS AVIARA GOLF COURSE

521

Batiquitos
Lagoon

EL CAMINO REAL

RANCHO
SANTA FE RD

San Marcos

O C E A N

GRANDVIEW BEACH

BACON'S BEACH

Moonlight State Beach

ENCINITAS
RANCH

ENCINITAS BLVD

510

DOWNTOWN
ENCINITAS

Encinitas

San Dieguito
Reservoir

DEL

San Elijo
State Beach

5

S9

River

Cardiff
State Beach

San Elijo
Lagoon

S6

Rancho
Sante Fe

Solana Beach

LOMAS SANTA FE DR

VIA DE LA VALLE

San Dieguito

Del Mar

Torrey Pines
State Beach

TORREY PINES
STATE RESERVE

To
San Diego

S56

Los Peñasquitos

N

0   4 mi

0   4 km

© AVALON TRAVEL

NORTH COUNTY

CASTLE CREEK COUNTRY CLUB & RESORT

OLD CASTLE RD

★ **WELK RESORT**

Valley Center

Lake Wohlford

Dixon Lake Recreation Area

Dixon Lake

Escondido

SAN DIEGO WILD ANIMAL PARK

San Pasqual Battlefield State Historic Park

HARMONY GROVE RD

Elfin Forest Recreational Reserve

Kit Carson Park

San Pasqual

SAN PASQUEL RD

★ **ORFILA VINYARDS & WINERY**

Olivenhain Reservoir

Lake Hodges

THE VINEYARD AT ESCONDIDO GOLF COURSE

BLACK MOUNTAIN RD

POWAY

Poway

Creek

Coast Highway is the scenic byway of choice.

© ERICKA CHICKOWSKI

visitors will find hidden in the craggy hillsides the San Diego Wild Animal Park, one of the West's most impressive zoological preserves.

PLANNING YOUR TIME

If you plan to visit some North County sights while staying close to downtown San Diego, be sure to build in enough drive time. Many locations up north take at least a half-hour to 45 minutes to reach from downtown, and when traffic strikes the drive can stretch out to an hour—especially when trying to reach spots like the Oceanside Pier and the San Diego Wild Animal Park. Traffic is the worst in the summer during the county fair and race season in Del Mar.

If you decide to visit more than a couple of sights in North County, it might make sense to spend a few nights up there rather than trying to commute from downtown.

The towns in North County can take as little as one day to wander through and up to a week or more to really explore. Many of the biggest draws up here, such as the **San Diego Wild Animal Park** and **Legoland** are full-day adventures in and of themselves. If time is limited, be sure to at least plan one day to cruise Coast Highway through all of coastal towns to really experience the California beach vibe.

NORTH COUNTY

Del Mar and Solana Beach

Best known for its horse racetrack, Del Mar boasts a number of natural attractions for visitors. The quaint village of Solana Beach also makes for a fine stop for those heading up U.S. 101, especially shoppers who dig antiques and unique housewares.

Farther inland is Rancho Santa Fe, an enclave of the super-wealthy that is also home to several exclusive resorts.

SIGHTS
◖ Torrey Pines State Reserve
The golden sandstone cliffs of San Diego's wildest natural beachscape ripple by the ocean like earthen corduroy. Chaparral dotted with stands of windswept Torrey pine, the rarest pine native to the United States, clings to the cliffs.

In addition to the pines themselves, the natural wonders of Torrey Pines are plentiful. A series of short oceanview trails wind under the pines, and rabbits are frequently seen scampering through the underbrush and wildflowers that bloom in springtime. Several of these trails lead to the foot of the cliffs, where a wide and peaceful beach sits unmarred by development. Also down at sea level is the marshy Los Penasquitos Lagoon. Here Great Blue Heron swoop by flitting Western Meadowlark, Black-necked Stilts, and Killdeer.

A stop at the visitors center can yield trail maps and a bit of extra information about local flora and fauna.

Torrey Pines State Reserve and Torrey Pines State Beach is officially in La Jolla, but it is sandwiched between La Jolla and Del Mar in such a way that parking and most access is closer to Del Mar. It is open between 8 A.M. and sunset, and it costs $8 to pass through the access parking gate.

Seagrove Park
Perched on a bluff at the foot of 15th Street and only a few blocks from the Del Mar shopping district, Seagrove Park (Coast Blvd.) has a well-maintained green from which to watch the dolphins that frequent the breakers just off the shore below. This picturesque spot is a favorite among wedding planners who fall in love with the undulating lawn, the shady pines, and the vibrant brick walkways. Just below the train tracks there is a fenced-in playground area with swings.

Powerhouse Park
Walking north from Seagrove over the railroad crossing, the park transitions into Powerhouse Park, so named for the circa-1928 power station on premises. Originally built to provide heat for the legendary Stratford Inn,

---

HISTORIC COAST HIGHWAY

Before city leaders cut the ribbon on I-5 in 1968, there was just one major route from Los Angeles down to San Diego: Pacific Coast Highway, also known as U.S. 101.

Running just a few blocks from the ocean for much of the route in the county, this major arterial was responsible for much of the growth of towns like Carlsbad and Encinitas during the middle part of the 20th century.

Though I-5 supplanted much of the old U.S. 101 in the southern part of the county, it completely bypassed the decommissioned highway for a more inland route in North County. That left behind the two-lane whisper of highway history, one that cruisers and cyclists love to stroll along to this day. Though it isn't the major north-south arterial anymore, it is still an important link between North County's coastal communities. And it is definitely a much more colorful route on this stretch than I-5. If you have the time and are traveling up through Del Mar, Solana Beach, Encinitas, Carlsbad, and Oceanside, do yourself a favor and take the detour. Your sense of nostalgia will thank you.

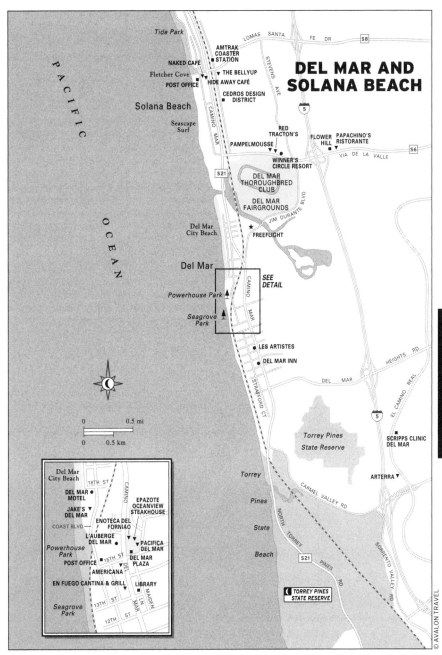

DEL MAR AND SOLANA BEACH

PACIFIC OCEAN

Tide Park

LOMAS SANTA FE DR
S8

AMTRAK COASTER STATION

NAKED CAFE
Fletcher Cove
POST OFFICE

THE BELLYUP
HIDE AWAY CAFÉ

CEDROS DESIGN DISTRICT

Solana Beach

Seascape Surf

STEVENS AVE
CAMINO DEL MAR
I-5

RED TRACTON'S
PAMPELMOUSSE
FLOWER HILL
PAPACHINO'S RISTORANTE

VIA DE LA VALLE
S6

WINNER'S CIRCLE RESORT

S21

DEL MAR THOROUGHBRED CLUB

DEL MAR FAIRGROUNDS

JIM DURANTE BLVD

Del Mar City Beach

★ FREEFLIGHT

Del Mar

SEE DETAIL

Powerhouse Park

Seagrove Park

CAMINO DEL MAR

LES ARTISTES
DEL MAR INN

HEIGHTS RD

DEL MAR

STRATFORD CT

EL CAMINO REAL

I-5

SCRIPPS CLINIC DEL MAR

ARTERRA

Torrey Pines State Reserve

Torrey

Pines

State

Beach

CARMEL VALLEY RD

NORTH TORREY PINES RD

SORRENTO VALLEY RD

S21

TORREY PINES STATE RESERVE

0   0.5 mi
0   0.5 km

NORTH COUNTY

Detail inset

Del Mar City Beach

18TH ST
CAMINO DEL MAR

DEL MAR MOTEL
JAKE'S DEL MAR

EPAZOTE OCEANVIEW STEAKHOUSE

COAST BLVD
ENOTECA DEL FORNIAO
L'AUBERGE DEL MAR

PACIFICA DEL MAR

Powerhouse Park
POST OFFICE
15TH ST
AMERICANA
DEL MAR PLAZA

EN FUEGO CANTINA & GRILL
LIBRARY

13TH ST
12TH ST

DEL MAR LN
MAIDEN

Seagrove Park

© AVALON TRAVEL

© ERICKA CHICKOWSKI

Powerhouse Park in Del Mar

the building has been repurposed many times over its lifespan and its smokestack serves as a symbol of civic pride for the surrounding community, which is probably why Del Mar converted the building into a community center after acquiring the land for a public park. Visitors can veg out on the expansive lawn or venture down the nearby dirt path to the beach below.

Del Mar City Beach

The Del Mar City Beach is best known for the stretch below Seagrove and Powerhouse, a wide, sandy section that attracts every type of beach denizen due to the convergence of circumstances: a couple of grassy parks, nearby parking lots, and a lifeguard tower staffed from 9 A.M. to dusk. But the beach actually extends all the way from Torrey Pines State Beach up to Solana Beach city limits.

South Beach is a little more secluded due to limited access. Intermittent cliffsides tower over this section of sand, so the easiest way to

get here is via a walk on the beach from Torrey Pines or from Seagrove Park.

As the beach meanders north of 29th Street, the shoreline goes to the dogs. Sometimes called North Beach by local residents, most of San Diego calls this stretch Dog Beach, in honor of its tolerance of wet and waggin' tails. Rover can romp freely through the surf and the river here between October and May. The rest of the year, dogs are still allowed, but leashes are required. This popular beach is also known as Rivermouth due to the creek estuary on its south edge.

Fletcher Cove

Here's a trick question for you: Where in the so-named town can you find Solana Beach? The answer: It doesn't exist. Unlike similarly named beach towns and neighborhoods in San Diego, Solana doesn't have a corresponding beach.

Oh, sure, it has its fair share of coastal stretches, and even a few nice places to pound an umbrella in the sand. It's just that none of them are actually called Solana Beach.

If locals were forced to name one of their beaches after the town, it would probably be Fletcher Cove (Lomas Santa Fe Dr., Solana Beach, 858/755-1569, parking lot open 6 A.M.–10 P.M. daily), a pretty little inlet at the base of Solana's sandstone cliffs. The cove, like all of Solana's beaches, is facing an onslaught of erosion that can sometimes wash almost all the sand away, leaving cobblestones behind. That's OK, though, because the park above can still be a nice green spot to lay out and enjoy views of the surf. The park also has a playground that is usually equipped with at least a few kiddos ready to welcome newcomers for a game of tag.

Other Solana Beaches

Several of Solana Beach's shoreside parks are hidden at the foot of cliffs topped by houses and condos. Access may be provided via narrow sidewalks shooting between private property and down public stairs to the waterfront below.

This is the case with **Seascape Shores,** which is a few blocks south of Fletcher Cove. Access is granted through the condos at the 500 and 700 blocks of South Sierra Avenue. This is a nice secluded beach that is often enjoyed by surf fishers, boogie boarders, and snorkelers.

Tide Beach Park is north of Fletcher at the foot of the stairs leading from Pacific Avenue and Solana Vista Drive. This beach tends to have the least erosion problems of all of the Solana beaches. During low tide here the tidepools on this beach are teeming with visible sealife.

During summer months lifeguards staff both of these beaches between 10 A.M. and 6 P.M. Parking on nearby streets is free.

Freeflight

If you've been under the sun a little too long and are looking for a shady activity before the races, head over to **Freeflight Aviary** (2132 Jimmy Durante Blvd., Del Mar, 858/481-3148,

10 A.M.–4 P.M. daily). Run by a local animal hospital, the tropical setting at Freeflight is barrier-free. Parrots, macaws, cockatoos, and other exotics can fly wherever they like within the confines of the aviary.

The best part is that visitors are welcome to pet and feed the birds if the animals are willing to allow it. Admission for adults is $5, $2.50 for children 13 and under.

ENTERTAINMENT AND EVENTS
Del Mar Thoroughbred Club

Bing Crosby was nothing if not a self-promoter, so it's no surprise that when he partnered with Jimmy Durante, Pat O'Brien, and Charles Howard to open up the **Del Mar Racetrack** (2260 Jimmy Durante Blvd., Del

NORTH COUNTY

OPENING DAY AT OL' DEL MAR

Every day of Del Mar's short summer race season is special, but if you really want to feel the electricity of beautiful people, social maneuvering, and galloping ponies, battle through the traffic and the crowds to experience the rush of opening day.

Held on a Wednesday in mid-July each year, this kick-off party for the races is a day for pageantry and partying at the track. The locals dust off their finest duds for the event, with the ladies sporting sleek summer dresses and stylish hats, a tradition that is continued in honor of the track's early days. In fact, besides the races themselves the biggest competition on this day is among these fillies in the annual "One and Only Truly Fabulous Hats Contest."

Opening day also brings a procession of celebrities, a big party in the track's center field, and some of the best gambling action of the season. Be sure to get there early to stake out a seat and consider taking the train if you aren't already staying in Del Mar – traffic from downtown San Diego is brutal.

NORTH COUNTY

Race season is the high point of the year in Del Mar.

Mar, 858/755-1141, www.delmarracing.com, mid-July–early Sept., $5–25), he wrote a song about his brand-new place:

> There's a smile on every face
> and a winner in each race
> where the turf meets the surf
> down in old Del Mar.

Ol' Bing might have been a little biased, but this racetrack where the surf meets the turf really is a special place. The ocean breeze is ever-present and fans get a glimpse of the ocean from the grandstands. The setting is perfect for a place with a storied racing history. This was where Seabiscut beat Ligaroti in 1938, and it was a magnet for Hollywood stars and wealthy gadflies. Today the diminutive jockeys still sport their colorful garb and gallop over the track for the benefit of a whole new generation of gamblers and socialites.

The season runs from July to early September. First post is at 2 P.M. every day except Tuesday, when the track goes dark, and Friday, when first post is at 4 P.M. Each week these Friday races are followed by raucous concerts on the center green.

As for Bing, his memory lives on: His tribute song is played every day the ponies run.

Del Mar Fairgrounds

The racetrack is actually part of the Del Mar Fairgrounds, a complex that holds the San Diego County Fair every year. Run every year in June, the county fair might seem out of place in such a suburban community as Del Mar. But it really hasn't been more than a decade since this area was built up with luxury homes and condos. If you look east of I-5 you can still see plenty of open space tilled for the flowers and produce that are coveted by people all over the West Coast.

The fair is a good mix of carnival rides, animal shows, and gluttonous eating. Be sure to plan ahead, as the traffic down I-5 can be intense.

Del Mar Horsepark

Del Mar pulls in a lot of visitors enamored

with equines through the racetrack, making it an obvious place to host the 65-acre Del Mar Horsepark (14550 El Camino Real, Del Mar, 858/794-1171, 7 A.M.–4 P.M. daily). This championship equestrian facility is about three miles away from the racetrack and features a pair of jumping stadiums, four show rings, and a dressing ring. When there isn't a big event going down, horse enthusiasts are welcome to stop by to watch the riders and horses train.

San Diego Polo Club

Even if you can't afford to live there, you can still get a taste of the ritzy Rancho Santa Fe lifestyle at the San Diego Polo Club (14555 El Camino Real, Rancho Santa Fe, 858/481-9217, www.sandiegopolo.com, Sun. June–Oct., entry $5, buffet $35). It only costs $5 to watch a whole day of *chukkers,* or match periods, at the polo grounds during the season. These Sunday events are like a picnic at the park, only with galloping ponies and mallets a'swinging amid a churn of flying grass. For an extra $35 you can actually make it a picnic—the club offers a buffet lunch at every match.

Nightlife

Del Mar and Solana Beach aren't well-known for a hoppin' bar scene, a fact that makes **The Bellyup** (143 S. Cedros Ave., Solana Beach, 858/481-9022) such a pleasant surprise for many newcomers. Locals with the inside scoop know this club well—many of them will tell you that it is probably in the top five of all music venues in the county.

Del Mar's nightlife tends to skew toward the middle-aged double-date crowd, but **En Fuego Cantina & Grill** (1342 Camino del Mar, Del Mar, 858/792-6551, 11:30 A.M.–10:30 P.M. Sun.–Thurs., 11:30 A.M.–12:45 A.M. Fri.–Sat.) usually has a boisterous mix of young singles packing the patio on the weekend evenings.

The patio at **Enoteca del Forniao** (1555 Camino del Mar, Del Mar, 858/755-8639, 10 A.M.–10 P.M. Sun.-Thurs., 10 A.M.–11:30 P.M. Fri.–Sat.) makes an excellent spot to sip a glass of wine and puff a fine cigar while watching the sun dip down into the ocean. Set

on the second floor of the Del Mar Plaza, this wine and coffee bar serves a whole cellar full of Northern Italian wines and an expertly poured espresso, *crema* and all. In addition to the great views, there is plenty of fun people-watching, with lots of interactions between Del Mar's elite: self-satisfied men hitting on surgically enhanced fortune hunters, Hawaiian-shirted retirees reminiscing, and businessmen loosening their ties with prospective clients.

The bar is open until 1 A.M. on Fridays and Saturdays during the summer.

SHOPPING

Del Mar's shopping is on par with La Jolla in quality, if not quantity. The action is centered around the corner of 15th and Camino del Mar, which is the unofficial "downtown" of this small community.

On the southwest corner, Stratford Square is the remaining vestige of the famous Stratford Inn. This half-timbered, stucco Tudor square is peppered with local shops that sell curios, clothes, and collectibles. These include **Frustrated Cowboy** (1444 Camino del Mar, Del Mar, 858/755-7963, www.frustrated cowboy.com, 10:30 A.M.–5:30 P.M. daily), which has all nature of Western knick-knacks and doodads; **Earth Song Book Store** (440 Camino Del Mar, Del Mar, 858/755-4254, www.earth songbooks.com, 10 A.M.–6P.M. daily), a new-agey purveyor of books, cards, and gifts; and **Marquis Jewelers** (1448 Camino Del Mar, Del Mar, 858/792-1826, 11 A.M.–4 P.M. Mon.–Tues., Thurs.–Sat., closed Wed. and Sun.), a place of many shiny baubles.

The shopping scene's other centerpiece is Del Mar Plaza. Diagonal from Stratford Square, this upscale center is a cozy, open-air complex designed to convey a town-center feel. It features three stories that blend into the Del Mar cliffsides with 22 shops and luxury boutiques, designer hair salon and spa facilities, and a number of gourmet restaurants. Most stores at the plaza are open 10 A.M.–9 P.M. Monday–Saturday and 11 A.M.–6 P.M. Sunday.

Some of the designer chain stores include **White House/Black Market** (858/794-4038, www.whiteandblack.com, 10 A.M.–9 P.M. Mon.–Sat., 11 A.M.–6 P.M. Sun.), **Georgiou** (858/481-1964, www.georgioustudio.com), and **Banana Republic** (858/350-0847, www.bananarepublic.com).

The plaza also has several one-of-a-kind boutiques such as **Jolie Femme** (858/792-1222), a lingerie and accessory shop; **Shoetique 101** (858/350-7642, www.shoetique101.com), which features handmade shoes; and **Bayley Boutique** (858/792-9002), a designer store that sells contemporary fashion for twenty- and thirtysomethings.

Del Mar Plaza also has an underground parking lot, a big plus in the parking-poor Del Mar.

Away from the tourist beach zone off the I-5 ramp to the racetrack is the less glamorous **Flower Hill Promenade** (2720 Via de la Valle, Del Mar, 858/481-7131, 10 A.M.–6 P.M. Mon.–Sat., noon–5 P.M. Sun.), a more weathered shopping mall that actually has an abundance of decent independently owned stores hidden away in that dingy exterior. Notable highlights include a bath and body store, **Bathe** (2670 Via de la Valle, Ste. A220, 858/794-9069); an upscale kitchen shop, **Silver Skillet** (2690 Via de la Valle, Ste. 150, 858/481-6710, www.silverskillet.com); and one of the best toy stores in San Diego, **Thinker Things** (2670 Via de la Valle, 858/755-4488, www.thinkerthings.com).

Artisan furnishings, handcrafted home accessories, and assorted works of art are the major draws in Solana Beach's **Cedros Design District.** This funky strip is checkered with '50s-style homes and old Quonset huts converted into showrooms, studios, and cafés. Pick up a wrought-iron wall accent at **Cokas-Diko** (412 South Cedros, Solana Beach, 858/481-4341, www.cokasdiko.com). Or choose between the bouquets of pretty silk flowers at **Flora & Ambiance** (415 S. Cedros Ave., Ste. 140, 858/259-6730, www.flora-ambience.com, 10 A.M.–5 P.M. Tues.–Sat., noon–5 P.M. Sun.). Other notable temptations include the Latin American furniture at **Laura y Laura** (404 N. Cedros Ave., 858/345-1286, www.lauraylaura.com, 10 A.M.–5 P.M. Tues.–Sat.)

and the original paintings by local artists that are on display at **Cedros Village Fine Art Gallery** (348-E S. Cedros Ave., 858/720-1838, 11 A.M.–5 P.M. Tues.–Sun.).

If you want some perspective on all that cool stuff you're looking at, stop in at **SoLo** (309 S. Cedros Ave., 858/794-9016, www.solocedros.com, 10 A.M.–6 P.M. Mon.–Sat., 11 A.M.–5 P.M. Sun.) and page through the architecture and design books they sell.

Bookworms can take a break at **The Bookworks** (2670 Via de la Valle, Del Mar, 858/755-3735, 10 A.M.–9 P.M. Sun.–Thurs., 10 A.M.–11 P.M. Fri.–Sat.), which is located at the Flower Hill Promenade.

SPORTS AND RECREATION
Surfing
Located on Torrey Pines State Beach, the break off of **Black's Beach** is probably just about the only place in San Diego where it is socially acceptable to surf naked. But the popularity of this surf spot doesn't hang on this novelty factor. It is actually known to be the best beach break in the entire county. The powerful and clean waves here are formed by a deepwater canyon located far offshore. On big days it is an experts' only area, due to dangerously strong rip tides and the isolated nature of the beach. To get there you must hike about a mile down the beach access trail from Torrey Pines State Reserve.

If Black's is closing out or too small to do anything with, chances are luck can be found farther north at **15th Street's reef break.** Accessible from the section of Del Mar City Beach just below Seagrove Park, the reef here is an island of rocky sea floor amid Del Mar's mostly sandy-bottom beaches. This is known as one of the county's very best breaks, producing a long and well-defined left-breaking wave.

Rusty Surfboards (201 15th St., Del Mar, 858/259-3200, Mon.–Fri. 10 A.M.–6 P.M., Sat. 9 A.M.–6 P.M., Sun. 9 A.M.–5 P.M.) is just two blocks away from this break. This is a convenient place to make a pit stop for wax, combs, rashguards, and even a new stick if you've got a wad of cash to burn.

When there's a south swell and the Santa

BARING IT ALL AT BLACK'S BEACH

Whisper the words "Black's Beach" to the typical San Diegan and you'll likely get a wink and a smile in return. This well-known spot at Torrey Pines State Beach is oft-regarded as the best clothing-optional beach in all of SoCal. Tucked below the sandstone cliffs of Torrey Pines State Reserve, Black's is a secluded place of pilgrimage for those who'd hate to let a tan line ruin their bronzed complexion.

If you plan to visit, be sure to cross into state park territory. Part of Torrey Pines Beach is on city property and those who make the mistake of disrobing on the city side will likely be cited. Though it is technically banned at the state beach as well, long-standing California State Park policy is to overlook nudity when it occurs at out-of-the-way beaches that have a long tradition of nude sunbathing. The only exception is if someone complains to the ranger station – then a ranger can ask anyone on the beach to put their clothes back on for the remainder of the day.

In addition to Black's Beach, this policy also stands at the section of sand at San Onofre State Beach that lies adjacent to Camp Pendleton. This other nude beach is at the end of Trail 6 in this northernmost state park in the county.

also has a better selection of surf shops, including **Surf Ride Board Shop** (325 N. U.S. 101, Solana Beach, 858/755-0858, 10 A.M.–6 P.M. Sun.–Fri., 9 A.M.–6 P.M. Sat.) and **Mitch's Surf Shop North** (363 N. U.S. 101, Solana Beach, 858/481-1354, 10 A.M.–6 P.M. Mon.–Sat., closed Sun.).

Cycling

Serious cyclists can always be found cruising the bike lanes on U.S. 101 along the North County shoreline. Del Mar is a rational starting point for riders heading north, as the road flattens out at the entrance of Torrey Pines State Reserve after a huge hill that leads down from La Jolla.

Cyclists can pick up spare tubes, apparel, and other accessories in Solana Beach at **B&L Bikes** (211 N. U.S. 101, Solana Beach, 858/481-4148, 10 A.M.–6 P.M. Mon.–Fri., 8 A.M.–6 P.M. Sat., 10 A.M.–4 P.M. Sun.). Due to its very knowledgeable staff of gearheads this store is popular with the strong contingent of triathletes who train along U.S. 101. B&L also owns a rental shop two doors down called 101 Rentals that can hook riders up with high-tech steeds that even Lance might be a little jealous of.

Recreational riders who might be intimidated by riding along the highway can find refuge on the **Coastal Rail Trail** that starts in Solana Beach. This paved bike path unfolds along an easement provided by the railroad that runs parallel to the highway. The Solana stretch goes 1.7 miles in total and the plan is to eventually hook this up to other sections in Carlsbad and Oceanside, but there have been permit problems in Encinitas that have been holding up that last section.

Balloon Rides

Float over the racetrack, the polo grounds, the palatial estates, and the farms that surround Del Mar on a hot-air-balloon ride from **Panorama Balloon Tours** (800/455-3592, www.gohotair.com). The colorful envelopes fill up and lift the baskets away two hours before sunset. You'll sail through the dusky sky and return back to terra firma in the gloaming light. The cost is $169 on

NORTH COUNTY

Ana winds blow from the northeast, conditions are ripe for a good session off of the Del Mar sandbars. One popular area known as **Rivermouth** is located on the north end of the beach. Just beware: If it has rained within 72 hours you need to give this spot a wide berth no matter how appealing the waves look. This is a high-pollution area when runoff is flowing out after a storm.

In Solana Beach, **Fletcher Cove** is a fun all-purpose wave that all levels of surfers will paddle out for. The real draw, though, is Seaside. Located to the north of town, this features a reef affectionately known as **Table Tops.** Solana weekdays and $189 on weekends and includes hors d'oeuvres and drinks.

ACCOMMODATIONS
$100-200

There is not much about **Winner's Circle Resort** (550 Via de la Valle, Solana Beach, 858/755-6666, www.winnerscircleresort.com, two-person studio $140, four-person 1-br $190, six-person 2-br $245) that screams luxury other than the price tag. The facilities and rooms are about on par with a suite in a well-cared-for chain hotel with the added bonus of tennis courts and a heated pool. But, and this is a big one for race fans, this property is literally across the street from Del Mar Race Track.

Each of the ten rooms at the eccentric **Les Artistes** (944 Camino del Mar, Del Mar, 858/755-4646, www.lesartistesinn.com, $115–195 d) is named for a famous artist and designed using that person's style for inspiration. Remington is done up in rough-hewn pine, cowboys, and cattle skulls; Furo offers Shoji screens and a Japanese-style soaking tub; and O'Keefe is accented with Santa Fe highlights and floral displays. Many of the rooms offer patios facing the inn's gardens and the entire place is pet-friendly, which can be a real benefit to those who wish to take Fluffy for the short walk down to Dog Beach.

$200-300

The Tudor Revival stylings of **Del Mar Inn** (720 Camino del Mar, Del Mar, 858/755-9765, www.delmarinn.com, queen $225 d, double $265 d) pay homage to the town's legendary but no longer running Stratford Inn, which was also accented by the pitched roofs and half-timbered framework seen here. The interior plays it up further with traditional floral bedspreads over a poster bed frame. Don't bother paying extra for an "ocean view" here as it really is a partial view with buildings obstructing the way. While this is the nicest Clarion Inn I've ever seen, it is still a Clarion nevertheless. The price is for the location, which is easy walking distance from the center of Del Mar's shopping district. Continental breakfast is included.

You've got to hand it to ◖ **Del Mar Motel** (1702 Coast Blvd, Del Mar, 858/755-1534, www.delmarmotelonthebeach.com, king $269 d, double $289 d, oceanview $299 d). In a town that is as completely wrapped up in appearances as this one, the temptation had to be high to rename the place an "Inn" or a "Cottage" or *anything* but the seemingly low-brow title of "motel." The name continues to stick, practicing a little truth in advertising. This white cinderblock motel is a seaside relic from the past and a breath of fresh air amidst all of the fancy resorts in town. Paint is fresh and the linens are new, but these rooms are extremely basic. So why's it so expensive? Well, this place is parked literally right on the beach. Sand drifts over the wooden deck patio and barbecue area that overlooks the ocean not more than a couple yards away. There's a lifeguard shack right there as well, giving a little peace of mind to parents with rambunctious little ones.

Over $300

If your first name is an initial, you frequently tie your cashmere sweaters around your neck, or you carry your dog in a handbag, the help just might let you darken the doorstep at **L'Auberge Del Mar** (1540 Camino del Mar, Del Mar, 858/259-1515 or 800/245-9757, www.laubergedelmar.com, $445 d). This exclusive luxury property is the centerpiece of the Del Mar village. The handsome tudor buildings hold an even more beautiful interior—dark woods line the lobby and the rooms are accented with marbled bathrooms, plush beds, and artwork framed with gilded edges. Along with the country-club atmosphere comes the attitude as well. Unless you've clearly just inherited a large trust fund you may receive a somewhat aloof reception from the staff.

What's a ritzy enclave without a cream-of-the-crop luxury resort in its backyard? Rancho Santa Fe more than lives up to its tony reputation with two incredible resorts.

Set on a lush 40-acre property, ◖ **Rancho Valencia** (5921 Valencia Cir., Rancho Santa Fe, 858/756-1123 or 800/548-3664, www.ranchovalencia.com, king $550 d, studio

© ERICKA CHICKOWSKI

Solana Beach's secret lunch spot, Hide Away Café, isn't so hard to find if you know where to look.

suite $725 d, one bedroom suite $790 d) welcomes guests to get a treatment at its full-service spa, take lessons from the staff tennis pro on its pristine courts, or play on its croquet lawn. The resort also features gardens and two heated pools, as well as access to tee times from five of Rancho Santa Fe's most exclusive golf courses.

Morgan Run Resort & Club (5690 Cancha De Golf, Rancho Santa Fe, 858/756-2471, www.morganrun.com) has golf right on the premises. This set of links is a part of the very private, very extravagant Morgan Run Country Club. Guests at the resort are afforded access to club facilities, including a group exercise studio, a spa, championship tennis courts, a lap pool, and private dining facilities.

FOOD
Beach Fare
Between Del Mar and Solana Beach, Solana has the lock on the best casual beach grub. There's an ample supply of breakfast cafés, sandwich joints, taco shops, and pizza parlors

there that'll never ask you to shake the sand from your shorts before strolling in.

Before heading out to the beach, fuel up on the home-style breakfasts served at **Hide Away Café** (150 S. Acacia Ave., Solana Beach, 858/755-3388, 6 A.M.–2 P.M. Mon.–Fri., 7 A.M.–2 P.M. Sat.–Sun., $6). The name says it, but this ivy-covered little cinderblock building is really easy to miss. It is concealed in a shopping center less than half a block to the northeast of Fletcher Cove.

◖ **Naked Café** (106 S. Sierra Ave., Solana Beach , 858/259-7866, 7:30 A.M.–2:30 P.M. daily) is even closer to Solana's main shoreside haunt, Fletcher Cove—right across the street, in fact. The café's name should probably be preceded by "Feel Good…" what with all of the healthy meals served here.

Area surfers will break bread, er…tortillas, at **Rudy's Taco Shop** (524 Stevens Ave., Solana Beach, 858/755-0788, 7 A.M.–8:45 P.M. Mon.–Sat., 7 A.M.–7:45 P.M. Sun., $5) between sessions at Fletcher Cove. Even some of the most voracious among them can't finish the

NORTH COUNTY

monster carne asada burritos. With a drink this trademark vittle costs about $9 and can probably feed a family of rabid wolverines.

After a long day at the beach, or a tiring drive through Del Mar race traffic, **Pizza Port** (101 N. Hwy. 101, Solana Beach, 858/481-7332, www.pizzaport.com, 11 A.M.–10 P.M. Sun.–Thurs., 11 A.M.–11 P.M. Fri.–Sat., $12) makes an excellent harbor for a melty slice of pie and pint of craft beer. This boisterous canteen is the go-to hot spot when locals want to get the crew together for a casual get-together.

Del Mar beachgoers can find soda, ice cream, and other nibbles at the snack shack in the parking lot adjacent to the 18th Street lifeguard headquarters.

For something a bit more substantial near the Del Mar City Beach, make yourself presentable and head up to the corner of 15th Street and Camino del Mar to ◖ **Americana** (1454 Camino del Mar, Del Mar, 858/794-6838, 7 A.M.–3 P.M. daily, 5:30 P.M.–9P.M. Tues.–Thurs., 5:30 P.M.–10 P.M. Fri.–Sat., $15), which is shorts-casual, not wet-bathing-suit-and-bare-feet casual. If a classed-up diner and a cute little farmhouse met and had kids, this would be their offspring. Open for breakfast, lunch, and dinner, this place is decorated with black-and-white checkered flooring, petite plants potted in rustic tin, and café curtains. The front room is dominated by a lunch counter lined with chrome and black cushioned chairs and the back has table seating. The menu is California home-style: a mix of rib-sticking classics and healthy meals featuring gourmet greens, meats, and cheeses.

Contemporary Californian

With its proximity to quality local farms and to some of the richest communities in Southern California, Del Mar is a hotbed of haute cuisine.

Situated on a serpentine road that rolls by the estates of rural Rancho Santa Fe, ◖ **Mille Fleurs** (6009 Paseo Delicias, Rancho Santa Fe, 858/756-3085, www.millefleurs.com, 6–9:30 P.M. Mon.–Fri., 5:30–10 P.M. Sat.–Sun., $27) is probably the most decorated of

them all. *Food & Wine* magazine cited it as "Top 25 in America" and the *New York Times* calls it the best restaurant in all of San Diego. The cuisine here is French with California influences, with a frequently changing menu that usually sprinkles exotic dishes featuring ingredients like frog legs and veal tongue in with traditional favorites like lobster and filet mignon. You'll be dining alongside Rancho Santa Fe residents whose net worth is more than some developing countries, so don't embarrass your mom by showing up in anything less than Sunday best.

Pamplemousse Grille (514 Via de la Valle, Del Mar, 858/792-9090, www.pgrille .com, dinner nightly 5 P.M.–10 P.M., lunch 11:30 A.M.–2 P.M. Fri.) is as much a restaurant as it is a fashion show during horse-racing season, when the well-heeled come to be seen, dressed in their chic hats and Italian threads. The crowd is drawn by the excellent fare here, a blend of Asian and Continental flavors that generates dishes like Ahi Tuna Tartare and Korean Marinated Pork Chop with plum wine sauce ($20). The restaurant sits in an unlikely business park across Via de la Valle from the horse track, a location that belies its homey Country French interior. Once summer passes it is actually a much quieter environment conducive to an intimate night out with that special someone.

A relative new kid on the block, ◖ **Arterra** (11966 El Camino Real, Del Mar, 858/369-6032, www.arterrarestaurant.com, breakfast 6:30–9:30 A.M., lunch 11:30 A.M.–2 P.M., dinner 5:30–9:30 P.M. daily $33, tasting menu $65–72, pairings $45–52) is an open secret that some regular diners would probably hate me to advertise too much. The restaurant is inauspiciously located at the Del Mar Marriott, which itself is tucked on a side street away from Del Mar's core tourist areas. Once you make it in, though, it is clear that this is not your average hotel restaurant. The spacious dining room's high-back chairs, oak flooring, and floor-to-ceiling drapes are dressed in a warm palette that echoes the name, which means "art of the earth." The food is the true expression, though—marrying locally grown produce with the best California meat and seafood. The seasonal menu changes to suit the harvest, but the tuna and lamb dishes are almost always stunners no matter how they are prepared.

Steak and Seafood

Red Tracton's (550 Via de la Valle, Del Mar, 858/755-6600, www.theredtractons.com, 11 A.M.–3:30 and 4 P.M.–10 P.M. Mon.–Sat., 4 P.M.–10 P.M. Sun., $27) has been slicing up cuts of its signature prime rib since men wore fedoras and ladies wouldn't be caught dead wearing slacks on a night out. Though this place has the den-like setting, the menu, and the prices of a traditional steakhouse, diners today get away with a more casual look there than they could elsewhere.

Eating at **Jake's Del Mar** (1660 Coast Blvd., Del Mar, 858/755-2002, www.jakes delmar.com, 11:30 A.M.–3:30 P.M. and 4:30 P.M.–9 P.M. Tues.–Sat., 10 A.M.–2 P.M. and 4:30 P.M.–9 P.M. Sun., $30) is the quint-essential Del Mar dining experience. Snuggled up to the Powerhouse, this waterfront restaurant has a bank of windows overlooking the surf and sand. The seats farther away from the windows are elevated so that there is no bad seat in the house to watch the sun set over the water. Seafood is the specialty, but the meat dishes aren't neglected either. Try the osso bucco and you'll find that the tender meat surrenders at the slightest push of a fork tine.

Pacifica del Mar (1555 Camino del Mar, Del Mar, 858/792-0476, www.pacificadel mar.com, 8 A.M.–11 P.M. daily) is an energetic seafood bistro that sits atop Del Mar Plaza's second story. The oceanfront patio affords a great view over the shopping district and the water beyond. This is a lively spot even on the weekends with the din of social chatter punctuated by fork-on-plate clatter as diners dig into dishes like the salt-and-pepper prawns with *udon* noodles and petrale sole paupiette stuffed with lobster ($29).

Right next door the terrace at **Epazote**

Oceanview Steakhouse (555 Camino del Mar, Ste. 322, Del Mar, 858/259-9966, www .epazotedelmar.com, 11:30 A.M.–9 P.M. Sun.–Thurs. 11:30–10 P.M. Fri.–Sat., $30) is an intimate date-night spot with the same great view as its neighbor. This is a steakhouse for the young, a hip location with banquettes and tables facing the ocean and a lively bar inside that is a hit with the happy-hour crowd. The food doesn't suffer from the mediocrity that some trendy places do, either. Salads are farm-fresh and all of the cuts here are Certified Premium Sterling Silver. They come with the choice of seven different toppings, including traditional béarnaise and a daring peppered blue brûlée. Family-style sides are equally delicious, especially the sautéed wild mushrooms, which doesn't skimp on the chanterelle and porcini.

Italian

Papachino's Ristorante (2650 Via de la Valle C-210, Del Mar, 858/481-7171, www .papachinos.com, 11 A.M.–10 P.M. Sun.–Thurs., 11 A.M.–11 P.M. Fri.–Sat., $12) is a casual option for dinner after an afternoon at the races. Hidden away in the Flower Hill Promenade, it is convenient to the freeway and to the Del Mar Fairgrounds. This Italian American eatery serves up pasta like ravioli and spaghetti, along with a huge menu of pizzas. Diners have the options to order a pie with traditional ingredients, or to go for others like shrimp, pesto, or barbecue chicken.

Scalini (3790 Via de la Valle, top floor, 858/259-9944, www.scalinisandiego.com, 5:30–10 P.M. Sun.–Thurs., 5:30–11 P.M. Fri.–Sat., $26) caters to a more refined palate with a menu of authentic Italian dishes. The dining room is elegant, featuring a classy piano bar and a patio lit by strings of lights hanging from the canopies. It is only open for dinner and reservations are highly recommended, especially during race season, as this is a neighbor to the racetrack.

Farmers Markets

East of I-5, Del Mar still clings to its rural

NORTH COUNTY

identity with a patchwork of farms that produce a bumper crop of plump fruit and vegetables. Most famous of them all is **Chino Farms** (6123 Calzada del Bosque, Rancho Santa Fe, 858/756-3184), a farm stand revered by the high-profile chefs who flock here daily to stock their kitchens for the dinner rush. The flavorful produce here is so delectable that even the titans of L.A.'s dining community will make the one-and-a-half-hour drive every day to get their hands on fresh delicacies like the dainty French strawberries, the Heirloom tomatoes, and the squash blossoms that have made Chino Farms a culinary legend. The farm stand is open 10 A.M.–4 P.M. Tuesday–Saturday, 10 A.M.–1 P.M. Sunday in fall and winter; and 10 A.M.–5 P.M. Tuesday–Saturday, 10 A.M.–1 P.M. Sunday in spring and summer.

INFORMATION AND SERVICES

There's a **police station** (858/565-5200) at 175 N. El Camino Real. **Scripps Clinic Del Mar** (12395 El Camino Real, Ste. 317, 858/794-1250) can handle most non-emergency illnesses and injuries. Probably the most convenient drugstore to get those prescriptions filled is the **Longs Drugs** on Coast Highway (U.S. 101) in Solana Beach. Emergency medical care can be found one town north in Encinitas at Scripps Memorial Hospital.

In downtown Del Mar, the **post office** (122 15th St., 858/755-1509) is less than a block from Seagrove Park. Within walking district is the **public library** (1309 Camino del Mar, 858/755-1666, 10 A.M.–6P.M. Tues., 10 A.M.–8 P.M. Wed.–Thurs., 10 A.M.–5 P.M. Fri.–Sun.), which offers free wireless Internet.

GETTING THERE AND AROUND
Public Transit

The North County Transit System operates a commuter train service called **Coaster** that rumbles from Oceanside to downtown San Diego. There is a Coaster station in Solana Beach at 105 North Cedros Avenue, which

offers morning and afternoon service both north and south. Riders can park their cars up to 24 hours in the adjacent lot.

Amtrak operates on the same tracks as Coaster, shuttling in passengers on the **Surfliner.** This Amtrak line runs from San Luis Obispo all the way south to downtown and stops at the Solana Beach station.

Solana Beach Train Station is also serviced by two bus routes run by the North County Transit Department. The #101 runs north to south from Oceanside to University Town Center in La Jolla. The #308 runs east to west from the station to the Escondido Transit Center.

There is no public transit service to Del Mar, but the city contracts **British Bus Company** (619/251-5074) to operate free shuttles from the Solana Beach station during racing season.

Driving
Car rentals are available in Del Mar from the **Enterprise-Rent-A-Car** (15575 Jimmy Durante Blvd., Del Mar, 858/350-1050) location adjacent to the racetrack. Another company, **Delmartrain.com** (858/481-7099), offers a third-party service that arranges for rental through one of several major chains and drops the car off at the Solana Beach Train Station.

Those driving from downtown San Diego should be mindful of the Del Mar traffic jams that lock up I-5 in the summertime. The county fair in June and the races from July through September create such an influx of people to the Del Mar Fairgrounds that the freeway frequently backs up all the way to La Jolla. It is not unheard of for it to take two hours to traverse I-5 from Pacific Beach to the Via de la Valle exit.

A potential workaround to bypass this snarl is to drive on North Torrey Pines Road through La Jolla, which will wind down past Torrey Pines onto Coast Highway. Depending on the conditions this can be a way to sneak into Del Mar and Solana Beach or farther on to the other North County coastal areas. If you are going to the races it may or may not help you, as the side streets are likely to also be a mess as you approach the track.

Encinitas

Encinitas is home to one of the most famous surf breaks on the west coast, Swami's. Named in honor of the Self-Realization Fellowship spiritual center that rises above the cliffs overlooking the water at the break, Swami's was forever memorialized in the Beach Boy's tune "Surfin' USA". While the water is certainly inviting there and at the eleven other beaches in Encinitas, you can enjoy the town without getting wet. The city is made up of three distinct neighborhoods, surfer-friendly Cardiff-by-the-Sea to the south, downtown Encinitas, and the artist's enclave of Leucadia.

SIGHTS
San Elijo Lagoon
This wetland has long provided natural resources to the people of San Diego County. Archeologists have found ancient landfills known as shell middens that are full of fish bones, shell fragments, and refuse left behind by Native Americans as many as 8,000 years ago. These people came to San Elijo to hunt and fish the marshland and ocean that surrounds this waterway.

Today most of the surrounding land and its wildlife is protected as a part of the San Elijo Lagoon Ecological Reserve (2710 Manchester Ave., Encinitas, www.sanelijo.com), a 1,000-acre plot of protected land. The ecological diversity here is wide. Terns, cormorants, coots, and gulls all scour the water here for fresh and brackish water fish. Trails wind through grasses and the coastal shrub along the lagoon. And the waves crash into the vibrant tidal zone of this wetland.

In addition to the trails, the San Elijo Lagoon Conservancy runs a nature center that celebrates the flora and fauna of San Elijo through interpretive displays and literature.

Even if you don't get a chance to stop at the lagoon, you can witness its beauty as you drive from Solana Beach to Encinitas on Coast Highway (U.S. 101). The road connects the

© ERICKA CHICKOWSKI

Moonlight Beach in Encinitas is a hot spot.

NORTH COUNTY

two towns with a bridge that passes through the lagoon just behind the surf zone.

Moonlight Beach
Moonlight Beach is by far the most popular park in Encinitas, and with good reason. This white-sand beach features volleyball courts, playgrounds, a well-staffed lifeguard station, a snack shack, and beach-toy rental, plus a copious amount of parking in nearby lots and street parking. All of this is located just a few blocks from downtown Encinitas.

Other Parks and Beaches
The banks, reefs, and cays of Encinitas are her strongest selling points. In Cardiff-by-the-Sea, the best shoreline is at two state beaches. Farthest south is **Cardiff State Beach,** which runs adjacent to the San Elijo Lagoon. The sloping sand is good for beachcombing and the shore is frequented by anglers who cast their long surf

NORTH COUNTY

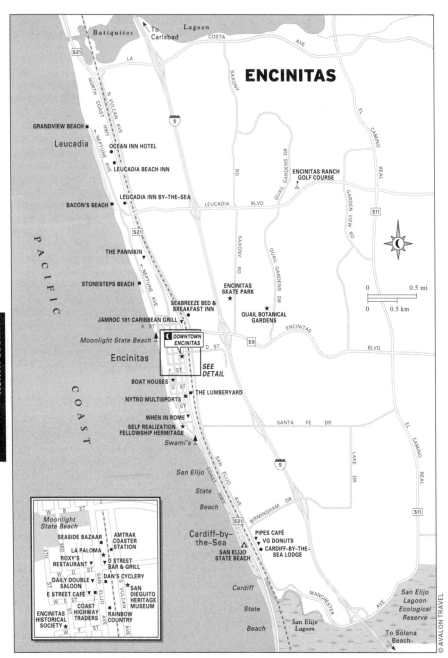

ENCINITAS

Batiquitos   Lagoon
To Carlsbad
COSTA   AVE

SAXONY

S21
LA
NORTH COAST HWY
N VULCAN AVE
NEPTUNE AVE

5

GRANDVIEW BEACH ■
Leucadia
● OCEAN INN HOTEL
RD
QUAIL GARDENS DR
● LEUCADIA BEACH INN
ENCINITAS RANCH
GOLF COURSE
EL CAMINO REAL
GARDEN VIEW RD

BACON'S BEACH ■   ● LEUCADIA INN BY-THE-SEA
LEUCADIA   BLVD
S11

S21
THE PANNIKIN ▼
SAXONY RD
QUAIL GARDENS DR

PACIFIC
STONESTEPS BEACH ■
NEPTUNE AVE
ENCINITAS
SKATE PARK ★
0   0.5 mi
0   0.5 km

SEABREEZE BED &
BREAKFAST INN ●
QUAIL BOTANICAL
GARDENS ★
ENCINITAS
59
BLVD

JAMROC 101 CARIBBEAN GRILL ●
A ST
Moonlight State Beach ▲   ☾ DOWNTOWN
ENCINITAS ★   D ST
Encinitas   SEE
DETAIL
F ST
COAST
BOAT HOUSES ★
G ST   ● THE LUMBERYARD
NYTRO MULTISPORTS ■
G ST
WHEN IN ROME ▼   SANTA FE   DR
SELF REALIZATION ★
FELLOWSHIP HERMITAGE
Swami's ▲
San Elijo
SAN ELIJO COAST HWY
5
LAKE DR
EL CAMINO REAL
State
Beach
BIRMINGHAM DR
S21
S11

Cardiff-by-
the-Sea
PIPES CAFÉ ▼
▼ VG DONUTS
● CARDIFF-BY-
THE-SEA LODGE
SAN ELIJO
STATE BEACH
Cardiff
MANCHESTER   AVE
San Elijo
Lagoon
Ecological
Reserve
State
Beach   San Elijo
Lagoon
To Solana
Beach

DETAIL INSET:

Moonlight
State Beach
W   B   ST
SEASIDE BAZAAR ■   AMTRAK
COASTER
STATION
LA PALOMA ★
4TH   3RD
ROXY'S
RESTAURANT ▼   D   ST
D STREET
BAR & GRILL ▼
DAILY DOUBLE
SALOON ▼   DAN'S CYCLERY ■
E STREET CAFÉ ▼   SAN DIEGUITO ★
HERITAGE MUSEUM
ENCINITAS
HISTORICAL
SOCIETY ★
COAST
HIGHWAY
TRADERS ■   RAINBOW
COUNTRY ■
W   F   ST
VULCAN AVE
SAN
ELIJO

© AVALON TRAVEL

rods here for ocean fishing. The adjacent reef here is popular among snorkelers and divers as well. Just north of this beach, past the lagoon's outlet, is **San Elijo State Beach.** This beach is similar to Cardiff with the added benefit of a campground that is equipped with a supply store that also rents beach equipment.

North of Moonlight, **Beacon's Beach** is named for a WWII-era military signal station. The beacon is gone now, but this Leucadia beach still draws surfers who come for the waves.

🄲 Downtown Encinitas

You might not know it from a trip to Encinitas, but surfer dudes are not an indigenous people. Learn about the real locals at the **San Dieguito Heritage Museum** (561 S. Vulcan Ave., 760/632-9711, noon–4 P.M. Wed.–Fri., $4 adults, $3 seniors, $2 children under 14). It offers a quiet little repository of artifacts and photos that chronicle the regional heritage of Diegueño, Luiseño, and Kumeyaay tribes, as well as the local history behind the Ranchero period and the transition to U.S. sovereignty.

La Paloma (471 S. U.S. 101, 760/436-7469) is a historic symbol of Encinitas's thriving art and music scene. The theater was built in 1928, a time when vaudeville acts preceded movies that screened here. Not only does the theater have a rich history of cinema, airing movies from Laurel and Hardy to Warren Miller, but it is also a storied small venue for music concerts and poetry slams. The building itself is visually intriguing with Spanish Colonial flourishes and a barrel tile roof that has inspired many artists to take pen or brush to capture its beauty on paper.

The oldest structure in town also happens to be the home of the Encinitas Historical Society. This **historic school house** (390 W. F St., 760/753-5726, noon–4 P.M. Wed., Fri., and Sat.) is located just four blocks from Coast Highway. The society houses a number of events here; on every second Saturday at 10:30 A.M. the house is the starting point of a 90-minute historical walk of downtown.

While you are stopping by the schoolhouse, be sure to turn the corner on 3rd Street heading south. Less than halfway down that first

HEAVEN'S GATE IN RANCHO SANTA FE

The wealth factor of Rancho Santa Fe's elite residents puts them in another world compared to San Diego at large. But that wasn't enough for a certain group of people who called this small town home in the mid-1990s. Tucked away on a quiet street of this quiet community, 38 people lived in a mansion as part of a cult that believed they would be taken off the planet and into interdimensional Nirvana on the Hale-Bopp Comet.

Led by their wide-eyed leader, Marshall Applewhite, this group called itself Heaven's Gate. It shocked the tightly knit Rancho Santa Fe community when in 1997 almost every single one of its members was found dead in the mansion as part of a mass suicide meant to trigger their ride into the stars.

The town has tried to distance itself from the event. The street that the mansion stood on has changed names, and after being sold several times the mansion itself was torn down. Nevertheless, this bizarre event remains a morbid footnote in the town's mostly unremarkable history.

block you'll come across two of the city's most curious structures. There at 726 and 732 3rd Street stand two beautiful boats, blue and white gleaming in the sunlight, looking like they are ready to float down the street and head out to sea momentarily. These craft are "moored" a block away from the ocean and have never had the pleasure of feeling waves lap at their sides. Known simply as **the boat houses,** they were built expressly as dry-land habitation by an eccentric Encinitas native in 1928.

Self-Realization Fellowship

Surfers and locals call it Swami's but this cliffside spiritual compound that is known by its gilded onion-domed towers is really named the Self-Realization Fellowship Ashram Center

(215 K St., Encinitas, 760/753-2888, www .yogananda-srf.org). The center was founded in 1937 by Paramahansa Yogananda, a charismatic spiritual leader from West India who taught a blend of Christian, Hindu, and Yoga philosophies that still captivates followers worldwide today.

The fellowship runs a lovely property that is open to the public regardless of religious belief. Most attractive are the Hermitage (2–5 P.M. Sun.) and meditation gardens (9 A.M.–5 P.M. Tues.–Sat., 11 A.M.–5 P.M. Sun.), a peaceful sanctuary that includes several stunning ocean views, a waterfall, and a koi pond.

Quail Botanical Gardens

Quail Botanical Gardens (230 Quail Gardens Dr., Encinitas, 760/436-3036, 9 A.M.–5 P.M. daily, $10 adults, $7 seniors, students, and active cilitary, $5 children 3–12, free 2 and under) is a source of inspiration for any aspiring botanists who are convinced there is no hope for their out-of-season garden. Amid the parched native coastal scrub, these gardens are an oasis of tropical foliage and other plant life from around the world.

The 30-acre grounds are almost like a zoo for plant matter. Trails connect various exhibits that display collections from exotic regions like the Himalayas, the Canary Islands, and South Africa. Other themed gardens include a subtropical fruit garden, two desert gardens, and a bamboo garden. There's even a rain forest here, for crying out loud!

The gardens were first cultivated in the early part of the 20th century by a pair of Boy Scout leaders who grew their plants from clippings and seeds collected during their worldwide travels. The couple left their estate to the county in 1957 in order to continue teaching children about botany in perpetuity. Be sure to bring a little extra change for parking; it'll cost you a dollar here.

ENTERTAINMENT AND EVENTS
Bars

Normally you go on vacation to get away from

the office, but you should make an exception when visiting Encinitas. **Duke's Cardiff Office** (110 A Aberdeen Dr., Encinitas, 760/753-7766, 10 A.M.–2 A.M.) is a classic windowless dive, hidden away in a tiny strip mall, with a name that offers a ready-made excuse for liquid lunch libations when local spouses ask how their sweetie's day at work went. You're as likely to see the pool tables racked by surfers as you are business peeps, as all types of drinkers are drawn by the easy, breezy atmosphere here.

Competing with the Office for the title of Best Encinitas Dive is **Daily Double Saloon** (546 S. U.S. 101, Encinitas, 760/753-1366, 11 A.M.–2 A.M. daily) in downtown Encinitas. The floors are sticky, the furniture is worn, but the Saloon keeps drawing a rough-and-ready crowd with its cheap, stiff drinks. Ladies on the prowl will especially dig the eye-candy here. This is a congregating temple of the Holy Order of Hot Surfer Dudes.

D Street Bar and Grill (485 S. U.S. 101, Encinitas, 760/943-9101, 11 A.M.–1:30 A.M. daily) is another all-purpose favorite. This classed-up sports bar is a comfortable spot to enjoy a pitcher or three with a group of friends. The scene is lively, but not so loud that you can't shoot the breeze with pals.

Events

The biggest shindig in Encinitas goes down in April, when the roadways are flooded with vendors and artists for the **Encinitas Street Fair.** The event typically features live music and dance scattered on outdoor stages, a special performance at the historic La Paloma Theater, and a beer garden with its own dedicated music stage.

This event also kicks off the annual **Arts Alive Banner Project,** a cooperative effort between city government and local artists to create unique fine-art banners to hang in the city during the spring until they are auctioned off just before summer.

Held on the third Thursday of each month from June through September, the **Rods & Woodies Classic Car Show** series is a tribute to the historic Highway 101 and the cars that used to roll by. The event is a spectacle of vintage vehicles mostly from the 1930s through the '50s, all in mint and shiny condition.

Encinitas is the world's most prolific producer of that scarlet holiday harbinger, the poinsettia. The city honors its leafy flower with the **Poinsettia Festival,** a street fair held downtown each year in mid-November.

SHOPPING

Well-heeled shoppers flock to Del Mar's shops and showrooms to express their individuality through a flashy display of conspicuous spending. The frugal and the eccentric go to Encinitas.

Here they can still convey their style—only through a bargain hunt in and out of the bazaars, thrift shops, and art studios downtown. This is bohemian shopping at its best.

Encinitas's hippie artist roots have flowered with a good crop of new-age shops sprinkled about town. You can smell the patchouli for miles at **Rainbow Country** (633 S. U.S. 101, Encinitas, 760/943-8006), a rasta-reggae affair that is heavy on the incense and tie-dye and none too discreet with the smoking accessories.

Coast Highway Traders (530 S. Coast Hwy. 101, 760/944-1381, 10 A.M.–6 P.M. daily) has an incredible collection of Día de los Muertos (Day of the Dead) skeleton dolls along with folk art from around the world.

Home-spun knitters can spend hours picking through the natural and exotic fibers for sale at **The Black Sheep** (1060 S. Coast Hwy. 101, 760/436-9973, www.theblacksheep.biz, 10 A.M.–6 P.M. Mon.–Sat., noon–5 P.M. Sun.). And **Seaside Bazaar** (459 S. U.S. 101, Encinitas, 760/753-1611, 10 A.M.–4 P.M. Sat.–Sun.) is a weekend open-air market that features antiques, linens, and funky clothes and jewelry.

While Encinitas does maintain strong ties to its non-conformist hippie heritage, the fact of the matter is that the average house here costs well over $500,000 and most hippies here have grown up to live flashier lifestyles than their parents ever dreamed up. If Ben and Jerry didn't have their palaces in Vermont, they'd be in Encinitas. **The Lumberyard** (8525 Gibbs

Dr., Ste. 200, Encinitas, 858/292-8989) betrays the real dual nature of Encinitas. In the no-man's-land between Cardiff and downtown Encinitas, this cookie-cutter strip mall has a concentration of 20 or so shops that pretty effectively sum up the confused, sometimes guilty psyche of the locals. On one hand, there are stores like **Magical Child** (967 S. Coast Hwy. 101, 760/633-1326, 10 A.M.–5:30 P.M. Tues.–Sat., 10 A.M.–5 P.M. Sun., closed Mon.) and **SoulScape** (765 South Coast Hwy 101, Ste 106, 760/753-2345, www.soulscapeonline.com, 9:30 A.M.–9 P.M. daily), which promise to get shoppers in touch with their inner spirit if only they lay down enough smackers for some nature of cosmic merchandise. Then there are others like **Bella Moda Boutique** (967 S Coast Highway 101 Ste 104, 760/479-9879, 10 A.M.–5:30 P.M. Mon.–Sat., 11 A.M.–4 P.M. Sun.) and **Chuao Chocolatier** (937 S. Coast Highway 101, Suite C-109, 760/635-1444, 10 A.M.–6 P.M. Mon.–Thurs., 10 A.M.–7 P.M. Fri.–Sat., 10 A.M.–5 P.M. Sun.), which are upscale without even pretending to be in touch with their karmic centers. If you really want to be mean, slip into one of these stores and whisper the epithet of the flower-child: "Bourgeoisie!" I dare you to see what happens. You might want a getaway car running in the parking lot.

SPORTS AND RECREATION
Swimming and Surfing

Besides at Moonlight Beach, the shoreline in Encinitas is typically pocked with ragged reefs or littered with cobblestones, cliffside shores whose beach is mostly submerged come high tide. Not so great for family wading or sunbathing, but perfect for paddling out and tucking into that perfect curl.

The reefs are particularly plentiful on the southern edge of town. At Cardiff State Beach's middle section, **Cardiff reef** offers a consistent set of waves that are enjoyed by kooks and aggro types alike. On the northern part of this state beach by the outlet of San Elijo Lagoon is **Suckouts,** a steep section that can give the experienced surfer an opportunity to get tubed if they don't go over the falls first.

San Elijo State Beach is just north of Cardiff State Beach, right in front of Cardiff-by-the-Sea. Here the best-known break is called **Pipes.** This is another of North County's trademark left-breaking waves, best firing in the winter at low tide with a medium swell.

The most famous of them all, though, is **Swami's,** which is named for the temple with the onion-domed turrets that rise on the cliff above this legendary reef-break. Swami's breaks the rules of Encinitas surf spots. The wave breaks right and it doesn't lose its form

SURF LINGO

Surf culture is full of colorful slang and lingo meant to describe riders, equipment, conditions, and emotions. The lexicon could probably fill a whole book of its own.

The following are some of the most common terms you might hear around town.

Aggro: An adjective used interchangeably to describe aggressive surfing and angry behavior.

Bro: A good friend or buddy. Also heard as "brah."

Dawn Patrol: As a noun, this is the crew that shows up to ride the waves in the early-morning hours while the waves are still glassy and free of wind interference. As a verb it is the act of waking up early to enjoy the good conditions.

Drop-in: Also referred to as "snaking a wave," dropping-in is the act of catching a wave that is already occupied by a rider. This is surfing's number one no-no.

Duck dive: A method of pushing your body and your surfboard under a wave so that it washes over you rather than sending you back to shore. This is the preferred technique to get past the breakers.

Getting Tubed: A perfect moment in surfing when the lip of a steep wave curls over the surfer as he or she rides to create a cylindrical tunnel of water around the rider. Sometimes called "getting shacked."

Goofy Foot: Surfing with your right foot forward.

Grommet: A young surfer. Often abbreviated to just "grom."

Hang Ten: Longboarding trick where the rider stands with all ten toes dangling off the nose of the board. Takes a great deal of practice and agility. Also known as "toes on the nose."

Hodad: A non-surfer who hangs out at the beach. Often used as a negative term for surfing wannabes.

Impact zone: The point where most of the waves are crashing down.

Inside: Anywhere between the breaking waves and the shore. To be "caught inside" is to be unable to make it past the crashing waves to the lineup. The best bet is to wait for a calm time between sets to paddle out.

Kook: A derisive term for beginner surfers.

Leash: A piece of tubing fixed to the back of a board that attaches the board to the surfer's ankle or knee. Keeps the board from hurtling toward shore upon wiping out. Some surfers pride themselves in their ability to surf without a leash, but it is generally considered bad manners to others around them.

Lineup: The group of surfers bobbing just outside the breakers waiting to catch a wave.

Quiver: A surfer's collection of boards.

Regular Foot: Surfing with your left foot forward.

Set: A group of waves.

Soul surfer: A surfer who sees the art of wave riding as a spiritual unity with the elements and who loves to share the joy of surfing with any bro or wahine willing to listen.

Stick: Another word for a surf board.

Turtle roll: An alternative to the duck dive, surfers do this by flipping upside down with the board so that the wave washes over the underside. This method is used by those with longboards who can't push these buoyant sticks under for a duck dive.

Wahine: A female surfer, generally a term of affection.

Whitewash: The foamy leftovers from a wave that has already broken. This is where many beginners first learn to ride waves.

Surf and skate essentials can be found at shops throughout Encinitas.

when the monster swells come in—in fact, that is when this titan really shines, which makes this spot a SoCal magnet in the winter. Even on the mellowest days, though, the parking lot above this beach is likely to be buzzin', full of barely running VW busses, sensible Hondas, and snazzy BMWs, all with one thing in common: an empty surf rack.

The lineup at Swami's can become as crowded as that parking lot, so if you get there and feel like you need your space, another nearby alternative is **Boneyards,** a reef break that is only accessible by walking north from Swami's.

The beach break at **Moonlight Beach** is fickle, but it can be cooperative during its fair share of swells. The whitewash here is a friendly spot to bring out a foam board to learn how to surf, which is probably why Encinitas's most popular surf instruction outfit, **Kahuna Bob's** (760/721-7700, www.kahunabob.com), chooses Moonlight as one of two beaches on which to instruct first-timers. The other beach is **Beacon's** farther north.

One of the most popular spots in the northern Leucadia area is **Grandview Beach,** which features a mix of beach and reef break that makes for good all-purpose riding at all ability levels. This particular section of shoreline is home to another popular surf academy, **Leucadia Surf School** (760/685-7873, www.leucadiasurfschool.com).

Cycling

Riding south to north on Coast Highway, the first sight as you descend the rise from Solana Beach is a breathtaking vista of Cardiff Beach to the left and San Elijo Lagoon to the right. The views don't let up the rest of the way, which will bring you past the gilded domes of the Self-Realization Fellowship, the slow bustle of downtown Encinitas, and the artists enclaves in Leucadia.

Two of the most convenient spots to pick up supplies or have those derailleurs tuned are **Nytro Multisports** (940 S. U.S. 101, Encinitas, 760/632-0006, www.nytro.com, 10 a.m.–6 p.m. Mon.–Sat., 10 a.m.–5 p.m. Sun.) and **Dan's Cyclery** (553 1st St., Encinitas, 760/753-5867).

Golf

The golf options are thin in Encinitas compared to its neighbors to the north and south. If you are looking to tee up within city limits your best bet is at **Encinitas Ranch** (1275 Quail Gardens Dr., Encinitas, 760/944-1936, $77 weekday, $82 Friday, $97 weekends and holidays, $10 cart), which is set on a plot of former flower fields. The course is designed with the windswept look of a coastal sea ranch. Hole 11 is the signature. Surrounded by a constantly blooming ring of plants, "The Flower Hole" pays tribute to Encinitas's agricultural roots.

SK8 TOWN

San Diego's anti-establishment board culture has long substituted smooth concrete for watery waves when the inclination or the need arises. The region is a hub for the skateboarding community, an incubation tank for home-grown legends like Tony Hawk and a mecca for dozens of other pros who have come to settle down in the area to have a chance to grind next to like-minded athletes. Especially popular is the North County area, which boasts one of the best public skate parks in the country at the Encinitas YMCA. The following is a roster of some of the skate legends that call the area home:

- Tony Hawk
- Bucky Lasek
- Andy MacDonald
- Rob Lorifice
- Bob Burnquist
- Mathias Ringstrom
- Chad Muska
- Jamie Thomas

Don't be surprised if you see these pros, or any others for that matter, when you shred the rails and ramps at local skate parks. This town is crawling with skate legends.

Skateboarding

The north-county skate scene is as legendary as its surf. In fact, when the swells aren't rolling in, many of the area surf rats will join their brothers in boards at the **Encinitas YMCA Skatepark** (200 Saxony Rd., Encinitas, 760/942-9622, regular hours 3:30–6 P.M. Mon.–Fri., 10 A.M.–6 P.M. Sat.–Sun., summer hours 2:30–7:45 P.M. Mon.–Fri., 9 A.M.–5 P.M. Sat.–Sun., $10 per 2.5-hour session). The facility gets major props for its 80-foot-wide, 13-foot-tall vert ramp, designed by the Birdman himself, Tony Hawk.

This massive park also has a double-hipped keyhole pool, numerous mini-ramps, and a street course packed with skateable surfaces.

ACCOMMODATIONS
Under $100

A cute little motel by the Coast Highway, **Leucadia Beach Inn** (1322 N. U.S. 101, Encinitas, 760/943-7461 or 800/706-7461, www.leucadiabeachinn.org, $85–145 d) is reminiscent of your first apartment out of college. Sure, the rooms are spartan and the furniture isn't new. But every colorful wall is painted with care, decorations are lovingly placed, and the vibe is friendly and cheerful. The place is spotless; it really has some of the best bargain lodging in all of North County. The downside is that it has only a handful of rooms so vacancy can be hard to come by in the summer months.

$100-200

Nuzzled up against one of the winding cliffside roads leading from the freeway down to the Encinitas coast, **SeaBreeze Bed & Breakfast Inn** (105 N. Vulcan, Encinitas, 760/944-0318, www.seabreeze-inn.com, $120 s, $175 d) has four homey rooms and a comfortable oceanview garden with koi pond and waterfall, all in a pet-friendly setting. If you can afford it, try to book the Penthouse Suite, which has a private spa on a patio with ocean vistas. During the week breakfast is more limited than what some frequent bed-and-breakfast visitors might expect.

Ocean Inn Hotel (1444 N. Coast Hwy., 760/436-1988 or 800/546-1598, www.ocean innhotel.com, $199 d) is another Coast Highway hotel popular with beachgoers—it is only a block away from Grandview Beach. All rooms come with a microwave and a mini-fridge and the patio has barbecues available for those who'd like to save a bit of cash by grilling up a few meals.

$200-300

Cardiff-by-the-Sea Lodge (142 Chesterfield, Cardiff-by-the-Sea, 760/944-6474, www .cardifflodge.com) isn't on the beach, but it is within walking distance. The pretty building is across the railroad tracks from Cardiff State Beach. The rooms here are a bit worn down, though, and the breakfast at this bed-and-breakfast is more of an extended continental than a full meal. However, it does offer a few rooms with a whirlpool tub and accommodations closest to the beach in Cardiff-by-the-Sea.

For a more authentic bed-and-breakfast experience, visit **Black Orchid Bed and Breakfast** (653 Requeza St., Encinitas, 760/753-0584, $275 s, $300 d). This inviting and well-decorated place is located away from the beach, but the quirky and fun-loving innkeepers pour their heart into being gracious hosts. A full breakfast each morning is included.

Camping

You'd better book early if you want to save a spot at the **San Elijo State Beach** (2050 N. U.S. 101, 760/753-5091) campground. This is the county's southernmost beachfront campground that allows tent camping and its qualities are hardly a secret. The 30 campsites are shielded from one another by coastal scrubs and accented by the occasional palm tree. The beach is just a quick scamper down the low bluff's wooden staircase.

This is a developed campground that has full restrooms with hot showers, an RV dump station, and cold outdoor showers for rinsing off after a surf. In the summer the park store has supplies, ice, and beach equipment rentals.

FOOD

Just the aroma wafting out of **VG Donuts** (106 Aberdeen Dr., 760/753-2400, www.vgbakery .com, 5 A.M.–9 P.M. Mon.–Thurs., 5 A.M.–10 P.M. Fri.–Sat., 5 A.M.–7 P.M. Sun, $2) is enough to widen your hips, but who can think of that when there are creamy, fresh donuts waiting to be gobbled up? You can munch on your sugary treat and a cuppa joe on the patio that overlooks Cardiff reef surf break just beyond the railroad tracks.

No café is as revered by the wave-riding set as ◖ **Pipes Cafe** (121 Liverpool Dr., 760/632-0056, 7 A.M.–3 P.M. daily, $6), though. This Cardiff eatery has the three essential elements that make up a truly classic breakfast joint: flavorful food, huge portions, and cheap prices.

Surfers famished after a session at the famed surf spot near the Self-Realization Fellowship will often stop for a gorge-fest of healthy grub at **Swami's Café** (1163 S. U.S. 101, 760/944-0612, 7 A.M.–8 P.M. daily, $6). The menu is very veggie-friendly, with lots of salads, options with tofu, and smoothies. Breakfast is hearty, featuring big breakfast burritos, French toast, pancakes, and granola. Don't come here in a hurry, though. The food's good, but it takes a while to get it.

The cookies at **E Street Cafe** (130 W. E St., 760/230-2038, 7 A.M.–10 P.M. daily, $7) make for an excellent pick-me-up after a day of shopping for art and incense in downtown Encinitas. This large coffee house and Internet café has a dizzying selection of teas and coffees to warm those bones on the days that the marine layer never quite burns off, as well as a selection of iced drinks for the real scorchers.

Also downtown is **The Pannikin** (510 N. U.S. 101, Encinitas, 760/436-0033, 6 A.M.–6 P.M. daily, $5), a distinctive café that makes itself at home in a historic train station from the 1880s. Pannikin is part of a small chain that has two other locations sprinkled in Del Mar and La Jolla, but the location in Encinitas can't be beat for its historic setting and friendly vibe. The place continues the railroad theme with its decor inside. The coffee is robust and full-flavored, the pastries are fresh-made by the store,

NORTH COUNTY

and the menu also features a slate of quiche, egg steamers, and lunchtime sandwiches.

Eat to the beat of steel drums and rasta-fari rhythms at **Jamroc 101 Caribbean Grill** (101 N. U.S. 101, Encinitas, 760/436-3162, 11 A.M.–8:30 P.M. Mon.–Thurs., 11 A.M.–9:30 P.M. Fri.–Sun., $10), which is probably the only place in North County that you can get your hands on authentic jerk chicken and fried plantains. Open for lunch and dinner, Jamroc features most entrées in two sizes: "Likkle" or "Bigga," making it a good pit stop for a quick family meal without draining vacation coffers.

Roxy's Restaurant (517 S. Coast Hwy. 101, 760/436-5001, 11 A.M.–10 P.M. daily, $14) sounds like the name of a greasy-spoon diner, but this Encinitas eatery is actually a refuge for health-food nuts and vegetarians. The menu here is a blend of Mediterranean and vegetarian classics, with a good dose of salads mixed in with other specialties like homemade spanakopita and a falafel plate.

The glut of cafés and grills can wear on a poor traveler who just wants a restaurant where napkins are placed gently in the lap, rather than dispensed from a chrome box on the table. **When in Rome** (108 S. U.S. 101, Encinitas, 760/944-1771, www.wheninrome.signonsandiego.com, 5:30 P.M.–9:30 P.M. Tues.–Sat., 5 P.M.–9 P.M. Sun., closed Mon., $23) offers that respite with its fine Italian dining. The dining room feels like a classic Roman atrium; it is covered by a retractable roof, so when the weather is fine diners eat al fresco. In addition to the usual pasta favorites such as linguine and ravioli, you'll also find items such as chicken cacciatore and veal saltimbocca.

INFORMATION AND SERVICES

Get the skinny on the ins and outs of Cardiff-by-the-Sea, Leucadia, and downtown Encinitas at the **Encinitas Visitor Center** (138 Encinitas Blvd., Encinitas, 760/753-6046, www.encinitaschamber.com, 9 A.M.–5 P.M. Mon.–Fri.), run by the Encinitas Chamber of Commerce.

Part bohemian, part yuppie, Encinitas is united by a sense of community – and the surf.

© ERICKA CHICKOWSKI

If you run into problems, there is a **police station** (175 N. El Camino Real, Encinitas, 760/966-3500), and **Scripps Memorial Hospital** (354 Santa Fe Dr., Encinitas, 760/633-6501) has an around-the-clock emergency room.

There are two **public libraries,** one in Cardiff-by-the-Sea (2081 Newcastle Ave., Cardiff-by-the-Sea, 760/753-4027) and another farther north at 540 Cornish Drive (760/753-7376) in Encinitas.

The **post office**(760/753-1415) is located at 1150 Garden View Road in Encinitas.

GETTING THERE AND AROUND

Encinitas is serviced by the **Coaster** commuter train at the station (25 East D St., Encinitas, 800/262-7837) located in downtown Encinitas. This station is not a stop for Amtrak. The closest Amtrak station is in Solana Beach.

The station is also a stop for several bus lines, including the north–south #101 from Oceanside to La Jolla's University Town Center, the #309 running north–south to Oceanside, and the #386 running east–west to the Wild Animal Park and Ramona.

Carlsbad

No, there are no caverns here (they're in New Mexico), but Carlsbad is still pretty darned cool. The town is home to a state beach, several ecological preserves, and a handful of museums and historical sights. It also plays host to the world-class Aviara Golf Resort, which regularly holds PGA events on its links.

SIGHTS
Carlsbad Historical Sights
Carlsbad got its start as a jerkwater town along the California Southern Railroad that first chugged its way south in the 1880s. At that time it was just known as Frazier's Station, named for John Frazier, the man who dug the first well in town to keep the steam engines well-supplied with water to keep the trains on schedule. The water supply still couldn't keep up with railway demands, so Frazier plumbed the earth again in 1883.

This time he stumbled upon something more valuable than the skunky engine water he dredged up from the first well. The new discovery was mineral water, with chemical composition so good that it matched the water at the best European health spa of the time, located in Karlsbad, Bohemia.

From the well sprang forth the town's name and newfound prosperity from the hotel and bottleworks that surrounded the water.

Located in the heart of Carlsbad Village, Frazier's Mineral Well is on display today in front of **Alt Karlsbad Spa,** which still draws visitors to its healing waters more than a century after the well was dug.

The original train station that started it all was constructed by the **Old Santa Fe Depot** in 1907, and acted as the community's hub for almost 60 years. At one time it operated as a telegraph office, a post office, a Wells Fargo Express office, and a general store. The cross-gabled Stick building is beautifully renovated and now acts as the Carlsbad Visitor Center.

North of the depot Magee Park is home to another well-maintained relic of Carlsbad's early years, the **Smith-Shipley-Magee House** (258 Beech Ave.). This Craftsman-style house is known for its wraparound veranda accented by railings set with a herringbone balustrade. The house is decorated in period furnishing and is also the headquarters for the Carlsbad Historical Society, which runs tours from noon to 4 P.M. on Saturday.

◖ Leo Carillo Ranch Historic Park
One of Carlsbad's best historical properties is nowhere near the village. Recessed in a chaparral-covered canyon that is encroached by ever-multiplying tract homes, Leo Carillo Ranch (6200 Flying LC Ln., 760/476-1042,

© ERICKA CHICKOWSKI

Leo Carillo Ranch Historic Park preserves a piece of North County's rural past.

9 A.M.–5 P.M. Tue.–Sat., 11 A.M.–5 P.M. Sun., closed Mon., free) is one of Carlsbad's last links to its wild ranching days. This property was owned by Leo Carillo, the famous Hollywood actor who starred as Pancho on the TV version of *The Cisco Kid.* Carillo was a descendent of two of the most famous Californio families in Southern California, the Bandinis and the Carillos, and he was very proud of his heritage. In spite of his privileged lifestyle, Carillo worked the ranch personally with the rest of his staff and helped to build the adobe home and pool that stands there today.

The property is but an echo of its former self, just a 10.5-acre sliver of what was once over 2,500 acres. But it is still a beautiful place to stroll and the house and surrounding ranch structures are in fantastic shape. The outdoor pathways and plazas are scattered with beautiful peacocks, succulents, citrus trees, and floral gardens.

Beaches

With flat and level sand, and lined with seawalls and smooth sidewalks, **Carlsbad State Beach** is the picture of a classic beach scene. Joggers, inline skaters, and stroller mommies huff-and-puff their way along the sand-swept path. Multi-colored umbrellas flutter in the wind as happy nappers snooze underneath. Their uncovered neighbors soak in the rays, some breeze through trashy beach novels, others chatter with their friends about nothing in particular. Babies jam their sandy hands into baggies full of cereal while their older siblings take a break to munch on smooshed-up peanut butter sandwiches. They all watch as the waves wash in waders, surfers, boogie boarders, and the occasional clump of seaweed onto the foamy shore.

This five-mile stretch of sand is most populated along the section known as Tamarack Beach, named for the nearby roadway that acts as the unofficial gateway to Carlsbad Village. Tamarack is easy walking distance for the visitors and locals who rest their heads nearby.

For a little more serenity, try **South Carlsbad State Beach,** where Carlsbad meets Encinitas. This beach is overlooked by a state-run campsite and tends to see a lot fewer people kicking through the sand due to its more isolated location. It is also a better spot to cast for fish without fear of hooking a diaper with the baby still in it.

Museum of Making Music

Drums, tambourines, player pianos, harps, and guitars—in untrained hands they make noise. In the deft fingers of an artist they are all mediums for the magical powers of music.

The Museum of Making Music (5790 Armada Dr., 877/551-9976, www.museumofmaking music.org, 10 A.M.–5 P.M. Tues.–Sun., $5, $3 seniors, students, and military, free for 3 and under) puts these instruments and many others on display to give context to the craft of composing and the art of jamming. The exhibits here chronicle the history of American popular music and the instrument manufacturing business from 1890 to today. There are over 450 vintage instruments on display in total, but

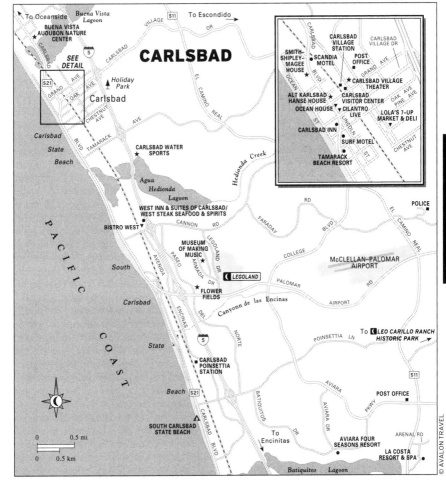

NORTH COUNTY

© AVALON TRAVEL

perhaps the coolest exhibit of all is the hands-on display that allows visitors to take a crack at the music-making process themselves.

The Flower Fields

Springtime visitors have the opportunity to walk through a real live Monet painting at the Flower Fields (5704 Paseo del Norte, 760/431-0352, www.theflowerfields.com). Here, along the undulating Carlsbad hillsides, a sea of colorful Ranunculus blossoms whisper in the breeze that blows from the real ocean just a few miles away.

The fields originally started decades ago strictly as a commercial farm. But beach-bound visitors continued to stop off of the freeway to get a closer look at the blooming beauties, and the 50-acre farm became a tourist destination in and of itself.

The Flower Fields are open 9 A.M.–6 P.M. daily from early March through the middle of May. Admission is $9 for adults, $8 for seniors, and $5 for children between the ages of 3 and 10. A wagon ride through the property costs $4 for adults and $3 for kids.

◖ Legoland

Legoland (1 Legoland Dr., 760/918-5346, www.legoland.com, 10 A.M.–5 P.M. Thurs.–Mon. Nov.–mid-June, 10 A.M.–6 P.M. daily mid-June–July, 10 A.M.–8 P.M. daily July–Aug., 10 A.M.–6 P.M. daily Sept.–Oct., $57 ages 13–59, $44 3–12 and 60-plus) is an opus to those clickable bricks that have entertained generations of kids around the world. I was one of 'em, scheming up all the buildings and cars and spaceships that I could possibly conjure from the mound of plastic Legos that littered my bedroom floor. If you were like me, the inner kid in you will squeal at the sight of what I consider the park's best section: Miniland. This amazing spectacle of ingenuity is a mini-iature-scale depiction of some of the nation's largest cities. Washington, DC, New York, San Francisco, Las Vegas—they're all there and the details that the professional bricklayers built into these little dioramas are amazing.

Legoland is a park best visited by families with kids between about two and twelve. The park is scattered with rides and shows geared toward that age range. Though the promotional literature shows impressive roller coasters, the pictures are a bit misleading in my opinion. The coasters here are zippy little tracks, perfect for making the little ones squeal without losing their lunch, but not enough to excite the teens in the crowd.

Lagoons

Carlsbad is dotted with estuaries and lagoons that are a source of natural serenity and aquatic fun.

Located between Encinitas and Carlsbad, **Batiquitos Lagoon** is one of the better-preserved coastal wetlands still remaining in Southern California. At one point in time this delicate ecosystem was doomed to be filled like 90 percent of the waterways destroyed in the county, with several cockamamie development plans that included a glut of tract housing and even a theme park.

Luckily it was saved for prosperity and now the 610-acre lagoon and the surrounding wetland it rests in is open for gentle exploration. Hiking trails line the shores and a bird-watcher prepared with binoculars has a good chance of spotting the protected least tern that nests here. The lagoon is closed to watercraft, but shore-based anglers are welcome to take a crack at the fish that swim here. The foundation that champions the lagoon's health and future also runs a nature center for those curious about the wildlife and the history of Batiquitos.

Next there's **Agua Hedionda,** a favorite recreational retreat for water sports fans. In Spanish, Agua Hedionda means "stinky water," a moniker earned by the brackish odor emitted by the marshy environs. If you can get over the slight smell you'll be well rewarded with opportunities to kayak, wakeboard, water-ski, and ride personal watercraft at this lagoon.

Finally, between Carlsbad and Oceanside is **Buena Vista Lagoon.** This special marsh has long been a sanctuary for hundreds of species of birds. The area became California's first ecological preserve in 1939 when a young man, Maxton

Brown, secured the agreement of local municipalities to ban shooting birds around the lagoon. He then headed off to war and eventually died in World War II, but his legacy lives on today. After development threatened the lagoon in the 1950s and 1960s, concerned citizens formed the Buena Vista Lagoon Foundation to acquire lagoon property and head off destruction. The foundation managed to save 223 acres of the wetland and 19 acres of watershed.

The wetland here is headquarters for the Buena Vista Audubon Nature Center, which has a collection of interpretive displays on plants and animals and holds classes and guided nature walks.

ENTERTAINMENT AND EVENTS
Carlsbad Village Theatre

This multi-purpose venue is the cat's meow for all types of performing arts events: theater, cinema, stand-up comedy, music, dance, and even the occasional beauty pageant. This is no third-rate kiddie auditorium, either. Plush velvet seats and rich red curtains greet audience members as they file in before the lights go off and the curtains go up.

Events

Carlsbad usually kicks off its event season with a little hustle at the **Carlsbad 5000** on the first Sunday in April. This 5K run is one of the most popular in the nation because of the ultra-flat course. Many professional runners are known to have attained their PR (personal record) here. Unlike many recreational runs, the Carlsbad 5000 holds its elite races at the end, that way all of the joggers can huff and puff their way to the finish, grab a brew from the beer garden, and cheer on the pros in style.

On the first Sunday in May, Carlsbad shuts down to welcome revelers for the **Carlsbad Village Faire.** This all-day event features arts and crafts vendors, music, and carnival treats. Can't make it in May? No worries. This event is so popular that the city holds it again on the first Sunday in November.

Come summer time, local parks are covered

in blankets and picnic spreads on Friday evenings in preparation for the weekly **free jazz concerts.** The city has put these concerts on for more than 20 years, rotating the schedule between several parks each week between late June and the end of August. For schedule information call 760/434-2904.

On the second Sunday in August, the village is taken over by 200 arts and crafts vendors to showcase their sculptures, paintings, photos, ceramics, and handmade jewelry, furniture, and clothing.

And in September, art of another stripe hits the streets for **Art Splash.** This fun event features the best in mural and street arts, arming local and national artists with chalk and setting them loose on the streets near the Flower Fields to show that chalk art isn't just for kids.

One of the longest-running events in Carlsbad is held in October. The **Carlsbad Rotary Oktoberfest** celebrates beer, sausage, and, of course, oompah music at Holiday Park. Come in lederhosen or board shorts, it doesn't matter—just be prepared to wipe that sudsy mustache from your lips many times over.

SHOPPING

Fashionistas with dollar sense like to swerve off the Palomar Airport Road exit on I-5 to stop at **Carlsbad Premium Outlets** (5600 Paseo del Norte, 760/804-9000, 10 A.M.–8 P.M. daily) before hitting the beach. This chic outlet mall has all the brand-name stores that keep the fashion world ticking, including Kenneth Cole, Juicy Couture, Bebe, and Brooks Brothers. Shhh…I won't tell anyone you bought it at the outlet if you don't.

The busy streets of Carlsbad Village have tons of unique shops to browse while letting your stomach settle between meal time and beach time. **Carlsbad Village Art and Antique Mall** (2752 State St., 760/730-9494, www.carlsbadartandantiques.com, 10:30 A.M.– 5 P.M. daily) is a warren of antique dealers and art peddlers. Unique labels and vintage clothes can be found at shops like **Clothing Cottage** (620 Grand Ave., 760/720-5219, www.clothing cottage.com, 10 A.M.–6 P.M. Mon.–Sat.,

11 A.M.–4 P.M. Sun.), **Janika Designs** (2969 State St., 760/729-1840, www.janikadesigns .com, 10 A.M.–5:30 P.M. Mon.–Sat., 11 A.M.– 5 P.M. Sun.), and **OBJ's Collections** (630 Grand Ave., Ste. A, 760/730-9827, 11 A.M.– 6 P.M. Mon.–Fri., 11 A.M.–5 P.M. Sat.–Sun.). If you actually like your mother-in-law, skip the grain of rice etched with her name and go straight for the good stuff. **The Bwarie Gift Basket Company** (100 Carlsbad Village Dr., Ste. 104, 760/730-1456, 11 A.M.–5 P.M. Mon.– Sat., closed Sun.) makes really cool custom baskets. For example, you can get her a "day at the beach" with a basket that includes a beach chair, flip-flops, goodies, and even a bottle of wine to sip during sunset. If you're really set on personalization, have her name etched in the wine bottle instead.

SPORTS AND RECREATION
Surfing
Carlsbad's natural beach landscape doesn't lend itself to consistent surf conditions. It is miles of flat sandy bottoms and not a reef in sight, a bitter pill for the wandering surfer.

But Carlsbad's natural beach landscape isn't completely natural.

In their concern for saving local lagoons from silt deposits and oxygen depletion, government agencies built two different sets of rocky jetties into the ocean to improve the flow between waterways. Those environmental enhancements yielded unintended benefits for surfers, because with that improved flow also came the build up of sandbars surrounding the jetty outlets. And sandbars underfoot means better waves on the surface.

The better of the two spots is at a place called **Ponto** near the Batiquitos Lagoon outlet. The pair of jetties here creates two different breaks depending on the season. By summer the waves break left from the north jetty and by winter they peel right from the south.

Drive north up the 101 to reach the second spot, **Tamarack.** The break here isn't as consistent as Ponto, but it is known to send a stretch of left-handed curl off of the north jetty pretty consistently with a moderate swell and tide.

In the summer the rest of the beach breaks along Carlsbad's strand are not the kind that the seasoned surfer writes home about. But they can be perfect for the beginner to learn the art of the pop-up. **Carlsbad Surf School** (4095 Harrison St., #3, 760/845-2272) offers lessons locally that will run you $60 for two hours of semi-private instruction. This results-oriented school is so convinced that it can get you stoked about surfing that it offers a money-back guarantee. If you don't stand up in the first two hours it'll return your cash.

Those simply interested in rentals can try the gear at **Raw Skin Surf** (2796 Carlsbad Blvd., 760/434-1122, www.rawskinsurf.com, 10 A.M.–6P.M. Tues.–Sat., 10 A.M.–5 P.M. Sun.–Mon.).

Other Water Sports
Agua Hedionda, sometimes just known as Carlsbad Lagoon, is the best place to dip a paddle or rotor in the water. Due to restrictions on the lagoon, the only access available is through **Carlsbad Water Sports** (2002 S. U.S. 101, Oceanside, 760/434-8686), so don't plan on bringing your own equipment. This shoreline vendor is well equipped with rentals and lessons. You'll be able to choose between wave runners, wakeboard and water-ski equipment, kayaks, pedal boats, and aqua cycles.

Spas
Inside the Bavarian-style Alt Karlsbad Hanse House, **Carlsbad Mineral Water Spa** (2802 Carlsbad Blvd., 760/434-1887, 9 A.M.–6 P.M. daily, 60 minute massage $85) taps into the same naturally carbonated mineral water that John Frazier drilled into in 1883. The house specialty is a dip in the healing waters infused with an herbal concoction. The spa also offers massages, mud baths, and facials.

In additional to the more traditional treatments offered elsewhere, the **Four Seasons Aviara Spa** (7100 Four Seasons Pt., 760/603-6800, 5:30 A.M.–9 P.M., 50 minute massage $150) also offers Ayurvedic treatments, based on thousands of years of East Indian health traditions. These ritualistic treatments utilize natural oils and herbs in a method designed to improve the health of mind, body, and spirit.

The Spa at La Costa (2100 Costa del Mar Rd., 800/729.4772, www.lacosta.com/spa, 9:30 A.M.–7:30 P.M. Mon.–Fri., 7:30 A.M.–7:30 P.M. Sat.-Sun., 100-minute massage $265) has one of the most comprehensive facilities in the county and staff there encourages visitors to stick around long after their treatments are over. The peaceful common area includes a pool, whirlpool, and a thundering roman bath, which showers a cascade of water from above to massage the neck and shoulders. Separate male and female facilities have the added benefit of steam rooms, saunas, additional whirlpools, and quiet lounge areas. The signature treatment here is the Spanish Herbal Treatment, a nearly two-hour affair that starts with a wrap in olive oil steeped in lavender and sage and concludes with a massage that will leave you feeling like a very contented limp noodle.

Golf

Carlsbad is home to the best golf in the county, period. The Arnold Palmer signature design at **Aviara Golf Course** (7447 Batiquitos Dr., 760/603-6900, 6 A.M.–sunset daily, $245) has garnered it many accolades, including being named as the top golf resort in Southern California by *Golf* magazine in 2006. Though not directly on the coast, this 18-hole course does overlook Batiquitos Lagoon and the water hazards are designed as visual extensions of the estuary environment.

Only a few miles from Aviara is **La Costa Golf Course,** (2100 Costa del Mar Rd., 800/854.5000, 6 A.M.–sunset daily, $205) which has a storied past as the host of numerous PGA events. The course currently holds the World Golf Championships Accenture Match Play Championship each year. As a club and resort, La Costa balances the use of its two 18-hole courses between members and guests. The resort alternates access to each course every other day.

Plane Rides

Imagine yourself as Snoopy, imagining himself as the Red Baron, on a biplane ride through **Barnstorm Adventures** (800/759-5667, www.barnstorming.com). The rush is very real when you take to the open cockpit of its 1920s-era biplanes over the North County coastline. The company also offers flights on its restored WWII-era fighter craft and warbirds.

ACCOMMODATIONS
Under $100

Scandia Motel (2550 Carlsbad Blvd., 760/729-3585, $70 d) is located on the outskirts of Carlsbad and should inhabit a similar position on a potential hotel shortlist for anyone seeking anything more than a roof over their head and a bed to snooze on.

There's a reason that **Surf Motel** (3136 Carlsbad Blvd., 760/729-7961, www.surfmotelcarlsbad.com, $139 s, $149 d) doesn't show a picture of its rooms on its website—nobody wants to advertise a train wreck. However, and this is a big caveat, this motel is right in the middle of the village and across the street from the beach. It is one of the cheapest places in the village and can make a most excellent crash pad for a couple of surf pals interested in splitting the rate, which is still a bit high for what you get.

$100-200

Set right along to the beach closest to Carlsbad State Park, **Carlsbad Inn** (3075 Carlsbad Blvd., 760/434-7020, www.carlsbadinn.com, $195 d) is a resort complex that consists of a hotel and beach condominiums sharing a pool area and beach cabana. The buildings are a funky mix of mock Tudor and Spanish Revival architecture, but these schizophrenic styles are no matter to the families that flock here for the location smack dab in the middle of Carlsbad Village. The inn is right next door to several low-key restaurants that are geared towards family dining. Another big draw is the inn's daily schedule of activities, with everything from games to crafts to karaoke led by resort staff.

The property at **Tamarack Beach Resort** (3200 Carlsbad Blvd., 760/729-3500, www.tamarackresort.com, $169 d pool view, $199 d

NORTH COUNTY

ocean view) is not as large as Carlsbad Inn and it is across the street from the beach instead of sitting right on the sand. But the rooms here are cleaner and less cluttered than the ones up the street. Tamarack also offers activities and has a welcoming pool area in its center courtyard. It also features a games room with a pool table and table tennis.

$200-300

Like a secret handshake, tales of a stay at **(La Costa Resort and Spa** (2100 Costa Del Mar Rd., 760/438-9111, www.lacosta.com, $400 d) are likely to elicit a knowing wink or a smile among the jet-setting crowd. This is one of San Diego's best-known destination resorts. The resort was built in the 1960s and has been a holiday getaway ever since. Its golf course has hosted several high-profile PGA events over the years. The resort really does live up to its reputation, especially after a $140 million renovation in 2003. Tee times are still coveted at the storied golf course and the spa here invites guests to stay and relax under the thundering roman showers, the steam baths, and the pool well after their treatment is over. This is no stick-in-the-mud resort that looks down on kids, either. The main pool area features a kiddie wading pool and a water park–size slide. And a daycare and activity center provides a full day of activity for the young'uns while Mom and Dad strut their stuff on the golf course or tennis courts. Similarly, teens are kept busy in a teen game room that includes a pool table, video games, and computer access.

Perhaps the only San Diego resort that can compete with such lavishness is just a couple of miles down the road. **Four Seasons Aviara** (7100 Four Seasons Pt., 760/603-6800, www .fourseasons.com) also sports its own championship golf facilities, these designed by Arnold Palmer, and an oceanfront view. Rooms are luscious, with fine linens, a deep soaking tub, and private patios and terraces. Kids are also made welcome here, with nightly milk-and-cookie service delivered to the room and a family pool area. But couples who want to get away from the screeching are afforded that luxury

as well with an adults-only pool area. The spa here is also one of the tops in the county.

Halfway between Legoland and Carlsbad Village, **(West Inn & Suites of Carlsbad** (4970 Avenida Encinas, 760/448-4500, www .westinnandsuites.com, $209 d) has the easygoing and family-friendly atmosphere of a chain hotel with the amenities and rich decor of a high-class establishment. Rooms are equipped with plasma TVs, Egyptian-cotton linens, and pillow-top beds. This independently owned boutique invites furry family members as well as kids, hosting a number of pet-friendly services such as dog-walking and -sitting. The room rate includes a full buffet breakfast, free Wi-Fi access, and complimentary shuttle service through Carlsbad—a big plus on days when beach parking will be limited.

Camping

Set on a bluff above the beach, **South Carlsbad State Beach Campground** is a sprawling 222-campsite facility with nooks for tent and RV campers. Sites are pretty standard, equipped with a picnic table and metal fire ring, and nearby restrooms have flush toilets, spigots, drinking fountains, and pay showers with hot water. There's also a beach store and laundry facilities on-site. Dogs are allowed at the campground but not down on the beach. These $12-per-night sites are a hot item year-round, so don't expect to set your stakes down without a reservation.

FOOD

It's never easy sticking to a vegan lifestyle on the road. **Cilantro Live** (300 Carlsbad Village Drive, No. 106, 760/585-0136, noon–8:30 P.M. Sun.–Thurs., noon–9:30 P.M. Fri.–Sat., $20) can help smooth out the bumps in the road with a selection of hearty entrées that rely solely on vegetable and fruit ingredients.

Joey's BBQ (6955 El Camino Real, Ste. 107, 760/929-1396, 11 A.M.–9 P.M. Sun.–Thurs., 11 A.M.–9:30 P.M. Fri.–Sat., $8) smokes its meat long and slow over hickory, divvying up ample portions of sweet and smoky ribs, chicken, and hot links. The meat is paired with all the usual suspects—beans, coleslaw, and cornbread—for a tangy and messy meal that'll have you reaching for the paper towels.

Set in one of the most distinctive Victorian mansions in Carlsbad, **Ocean House** (300 Carlsbad Village Dr., 760/729-4131, www .oceanhousecarlsbad.com, 11 A.M.–midnight Mon.–Wed., 11 A.M.–2 A.M. Thurs.–Sat., 9:30 A.M.–2 A.M. Sun., $14) is hard to miss as you drive U.S. 101 through Carlsbad Village. The vintage Queen Anne it occupies is a landmark in the area, built as the home of the president of the very first hotel and spa in town. Flanked by palm trees and processions of beachgoers hustling to the shore, this classic building has the charm of an old seaside resort. Inside, the restaurant serves up a mixture of burgers, pastas, and salads.

Get an authentic plate of tamales, chiles rellenos, or rolled *taquitos* to go from **Lola's 7-Up Market and Deli** (7 A.M.–6 P.M. Mon.–Fri., 7 A.M.–5 P.M. Sat., closed major holidays), in the heart of the Carlsbad Barrio. The Hispanic community here helped build the Carlsbad flower empire and in the center of it all, the Jauregui clan that owns Lola's has run a market here on this street for more than 70 years.

The hardest part about dining at 🄲 **Bistro West** (4960 Avenida Encinas, 760/930-9008, 11 A.M.–10 P.M. Sun.–Fri., 11 A.M.–11 P.M. Sat., $16) is making up your mind. The menu is extensive; each section could make up a full menu at any other place. There's a selection of burgers that could satisfy J. Wellington Wimpy himself, homemade soups, and entrée-size salads. If you've got a craving for pasta, take a crack at the puttanesca, a zippy little dish that features anchovies, olives, and capers. The braised meat is some of the best I've tasted, falling off the bone while maintaining all of its flavor.

For a more formal meal, right across the parking lot is the Bistro's intimate and posh sister restaurant, **West Steak Seafood & Spirits** (4980 Avenida Encinas, 760/930-9100, 4:30 P.M.–10 P.M. Sun.–Thur., 4:30 P.M.– 11 P.M. Fri.–Sat., $65). This 20-table steakhouse serves prime cuts and doesn't nickel and dime you with the sides—they're included with your meat. Stick around for dessert here. The apple tarte tatin cheesecake is a unique twist on that traditional French upside-down tart that is worth a visit all on its own.

INFORMATION AND SERVICES

The **Carlsbad Visitor Center** (400 Carlsbad Village Dr., 760/434-6093, www.carlsbadca .org, 9 A.M.–5 P.M. Mon.–Fri.) is located in Carlsbad Village at the Old Santa Fe Station. Mail can be sent from two post offices in town: in the village (2772 Roosevelt) or near Four Seasons Aviara (1700 Aviara Pkwy.).

Depending on where you are in Carlsbad, medical emergencies are best taken care of in Oceanside to the north or Encinitas to the south. In Encinitas visit Scripps Memorial Hospital. In Oceanside, Tri-City Medical Center. The Carlsbad Police Station (2560 Orion Way) is located near the municipal airport just off El Camino Real.

Carlsbad City Library operates two branches: the **Georgina Cole Library** (1250 Carlsbad Village Dr., 760/434-2870, 9 A.M.– 9 P.M. Mon.–Thurs., 9 A.M.–5 P.M. Fri.–Sat., 1 P.M.–5 P.M. Sun.) and the **Dove Library** (1775 Dove Ln., 760/602-2049, 9 A.M.–9 P.M. Mon.–Thurs., 9 A.M.–5 P.M. Fri.–Sat., 1 P.M.– 5 P.M. Sun.). Both are appropriate stops for a respite from the sun and to borrow a computer for a few moments.

GETTING THERE AND AROUND

McClellan-Palomar Airport is the only airport besides San Diego International that offers daily flights from any of the major commercial airline services. United Express flies to and from LAX about seven times each day and US Airways operates a daily shuttle between Palomar and Phoenix.

Three car-rental agencies are based out of this small airport: **Avis** (760/931-1393), **Budget** (760/438-5527), and **Enterprise** (760/603-0240). Taxi service is available from **Coach Cab** (760/722-5100), **Coastal Cab**

(760/722-7472), and **Yellow Cab** (760/722-4214). **Cloud Nine** (800/974-8885) offers a shuttle bus service as well.

The Coaster commuter train stops at two stations in Carlsbad, the **Carlsbad Poinsettia Station,** which primarily serves local bedroom communities, and the **Carlsbad Village Station** downtown. The closest Amtrak station is located north in Oceanside.

Bus route #310 will carry you down to University Town Center in La Jolla, where you can transfer to get downtown. It also travels north to Oceanside. Route #322 circulates through Carlsbad and #320 will take you east to Escondido.

Oceanside

The northernmost coastal town in San Diego County, Oceanside is invariably influenced by the massively sprawling Camp Pendleton Marine Corps base just north of city limits. Flat-tops are de rigueur in town, but recruits are well behaved. In fact, the number of military families that live close by probably helps to foster the family-friendly atmosphere in Oceanside. Also inland is Vista, a bedroom community that is a gateway to several regional parks as well as the foothills of the county's northern mountains.

SIGHTS
Museums
It has been called trivial, vulgar, and even a menace to youth, but at this point no one can deny that the surf culture in California has been a positive influence on the state's coastal way of life. Learn about the legends of wave riding at the **California Surf Museum** (223 N. U.S. 101, 760/721-6876, www.surfmuseum.org, 10 A.M.–4 P.M. daily, free) in downtown Oceanside. This quirky museum exhibits boards, photos, and memorabilia that chronicle the sport's transition from 11-foot balsa-wood logs to the potato-chip shortboards of today.

On the grounds of **Guajome Park** (3000 Guajome Lake Rd.) there stands one of the best examples of Californio architecture in the county. The Rancho Guajome adobe home was built in the 1850s by Cave Johnson Couts, a former U.S. Army lieutenant turned wealthy rancher, for his new wife Ysidora Bandini, a member of Old Town San Diego's influential Bandini clan who received the rancho's 2,200-acre plot as a wedding gift from her brother-in-law. Their 28-room home was a palatial estate in the mid-19th century and it became legendary for the parties and balls that the Couts family would host there. Today it stands as a State and National Historic Landmark and visitors can tour through the home on Saturday and Sunday at 11 A.M. and 2 P.M.

The adobe is only a part of Guajome Park's allure. Tramping on foot or clopping by on horseback, nature-loving explorers can look for more than 186 species of birds flitting across the miles of trails that crisscross the 557-acre park. Tread softly and there's a chance to come across long-tailed weasels, rabbits, and even bobcats. Also on the property is Guajome Lake, a pleasant spot to cast for fish or to dig into a picnic basket.

Near Guajome, the little-known **Antique Gas and Steam Engine Museum** (2040 N. Santa Fe Ave., 800/587-2286, www.agsem.com, 10 A.M.–4 P.M. daily, $3 adults, $2 seniors, $2 dids 6–17, free kids under 6) can make for a fascinating day trip for families and gear heads. This living-history museum is a 55-acre collection of old engines, a working farm, and antique farm equipment all bundled into one package. The best time to visit is on the museum's "show days" during the third and fourth weekends in June and October. Hordes of volunteers descend on the facility to fire up the tractors and the blacksmith forge and to work the farm for the benefit of visitors. Even on non-show days you are likely to see a volunteer running an odd piece of machinery here and there in the course of maintaining the property and the farm.

Oceanside Pier

Oceanside Pier (250 N. Pacific St., 760/966-1406, 24 hrs. daily) has been a landmark for generations of citizens and visitors, even though the pier itself has had multiple reincarnations. This, the sixth in the succession of water-bound structures, juts out to 1,954 feet, making it the longest wooden pier on the West Coast. The concrete approach is the oldest part of the pier, dating back to 1925; the wooden part was replaced in 1988.

It is a favorite among strolling couples, waddling toddlers, and the throngs of fishermen who flock here every day. The end of the pier is a good place to spot mischievous sea lions who enjoy stealing fish off anglers' lines. Or simply look out to sea and try to catch a glimpse of Catalina Island to the north and Los Coronados islands to the south. Visitors can also get a bite to eat at Ruby's Diner, located at the pier's terminus.

Below deck the pier is also frequented by surfers, who regard this as the best structurally improved break in the county.

《 Mission San Luis Rey

Called the "King of Missions," Mission San Luis Rey was one of the last of the 21 California missions to be founded by the Franciscans, but it ended up being the largest and wealthiest of all. At its height, this massive religious, farming, and ranching operation spanned over 1,000 square miles.

The church that was at the center of it all still rests within Oceanside city limits and is one of the few mission parishes still run by the Franciscans. The friars welcome visitors to meander through the sunken gardens, to look at the first pepper tree planted in California, and to hike through the trails that wander through the property's 56 acres.

The church itself is mostly a reconstruction, but the Catholic Church has taken care to painstakingly follow old design patterns found in books and textiles that have been maintained over the centuries.

There is also a museum on the property that contains exhibits on mission life, art work, and historical artifacts that document the rise, fall, and reconstruction of San Luis Rey.

San Onofre State Beach

Like the fertile crescent of Southern California beach culture, San Onofre (entrance fee $10 per car) has enticed beach revelers to its gentle shorelines since the days when surfers carved their own boards out of balsa wood.

This state beach is three and a half miles of untouched shoreline that represents everything the region has to offer. The bluffside campgrounds and beach connector trails are covered in coastal scrub and chaparral, with the occasional bunny hopping through the brush here and there. From the bluffs you can often see gray whales and dolphins swimming off shore. On the weekends the campground is packed with scouts, partying twentysomethings, and with retirees in RVs with plates from all over the country.

San Onofre State Beach in the off-season

© ERICKA CHICKOWSKI

NORTH COUNTY

NORTH COUNTY

It's the friendly type of place where campers share their ice and their road-trip stories.

Meander down the trail and you'll find seclusion if you want it. Or you can join the crowds off the beach closest to the day-use parking. Guitars are a-strummin' here, barbecues sizzle, and people slip in and out of their wetsuits to hit the surf whenever they feel like it. Watches and schedules have no place here.

On the far northern end of the park is the San Mateo Creek Preserve, a marshland ripe for exploration via the nearby trails starting in San Mateo Canyon.

ENTERTAINMENT AND EVENTS
Bars

There's not a martini bar in sight in Oceanside. Nope, this town is pub and tavern territory through and through.

Young hotheads should be aware that if they're looking for a fight they might just find it in O'side and probably a trip to the hospital to boot. The majority of the marines in town are respectable soldiers, but there are a few bad apples and they are drawn to the seedier bars like flies on a wheelbarrow full of manure. Keep your wits about you and your tone respectful to avoid a whuppin'.

With that said, there are a couple of mellow establishments that can provide a nice nightcap after a day on the water. The pirate-themed **Haunted Head Saloon** (207 N Tremont St., 760/231-7600, 11 A.M.–2 A.M. daily) is festooned with Jolly Rogers and equipped with a pool table, foosball, and a giant TV. The place can get boisterous on the weekends but the vibe is still pretty chilled out.

The Rusty Spur (406 Pier View Way, 760/722-2216, 10 A.M.–2 A.M. daily) used to be one of the rowdier bars in town, but when new owners took over this 50-year-old bar they cleaned up the joint and banned a lot of the troublemakers who were ruining it for everyone. If you've got a hankering for pool, this place has the most tables of all the bars in town.

The entertainment at **McCabe's Beach Club** (1145 South Tremont St., 760/439-6646,

10 A.M.–1:30 A.M. daily) is a grab bag of live country-and-western and cover bands, DJs spinning hip-hop, and American Idol wannabes warbling into the karaoke mic. The schedule shifts with the sands—call ahead to find out what's on the agenda.

Events

In July, Oceanside's military pride swells for **Independence Day.** The town celebrates for five days in a festival it likes to call Ofest. Highlights include a patriotic parade and a booming fireworks display off the pier.

Many of Oceanside's events are centered around the pier and the nearby **Oceanside Pier Amphitheater,** a classic band shell with bleacher seating built into the cliff that leads from street level to the beach.

There are numerous surfing competitions held near the pier and the jetties, but perhaps one of the longest running is the **Oceanside Surfing Club competition** that happens in mid-August each year.

Another adrenaline-pumped event that uses the pier as its centerpiece is the **Oceanside Pier Swim,** a freestyle competition that has run continuously every September for almost 80 years. Racers swim a one-mile course set around the landmark pier.

September is also the season for **Harbor Days,** the most popular street fair in town. In addition to live entertainment, food, and crafts vendors, this event also holds an annual fishing derby and a nail-and-sail competition that tasks participants to build a seaworthy craft and navigate it around a short course in the harbor.

SPORTS AND RECREATION
Surfing

The bros and wahines out in Oceanside primarily paddle out to the man-made breaks created by Oceanside Pier and Oceanside's jetties.

Be careful not to get tangled up in angler's lines as you carve the waves near the pier. People cast to the shallow water off of this fishing structure and surfing closer than 100 feet is prohibited. The rules might be a let-down when the peaks are pumping around the pier, but they are there for your safety. Tempers are short between the two groups and it isn't unheard-of for a grumpy angler to "enforce" the rules by casting for surfers.

Surf Oceanside Harbor and you'll have a choice between the reeling lefts off of the **North Jetty** and the breaking rights off the **South Jetty.** The beach off South Jetty is a nice place to hang between sessions. Build up a crackling fire in one of the rings provided by the city to cook up your meat caveman-style or rest beneath the rustling palapa umbrellas that are perched on nearby picnic tables.

For supplies and board rentals, **Real Surf Shop** (1101 S. U.S. 101, 760/754-0670, www .realsurfshop.com, 10 A.M.–6 P.M. daily) is a good option.

Officially the maps say that San Diego County ends at the northernmost boundaries of the expansive Camp Pendleton Marine base, but most San Diego residents will tell ya that **San Onofre State Park** ("San O" in local speak) is still on their turf. This massive coastal park butts right up against Camp Pendleton and is heaven for the longboard enthusiast. Seriously, don't even think about bringing one of those potato-chip boards out here. These waves are gentle and lazy, but consistent and perfect for hanging a few toes from the nose. From south to north the three major breaks here are the **Point, Old Man's,** and **Dogpatch.**

Just north of San O is one of the most storied breaks in all of Southern California, **Lower Trestles.** Named for the railroad track that surfers once had to scamper over to get to this out-of-the-way spot, Lower Trestles is now accessible from a one-mile trail that starts at the San Mateo Campground. This break's renowned left peak has been praised by legends from Kelly Slater to Rob Machado and frequently is the site of the kind of professional surf invitationals that draw international rippers to this shore. If it is too crowded here, your consolation prize is not so bad, with the breaks **Upper Trestles, Cottons,** and **Churches** all to the immediate north.

Cycling
Coast Highway (U.S. 101) merges with I-5 at Oceanside, so the only way to continue on and connect with U.S. 101 in Orange County is to make nice with the marines. If you bring government identification and promise to follow all of the road rules—including wearing a buckled helmet—the Marine Corps will let you ride through Camp Pendleton until its road reaches the main access road in San Onofre State Park. From there it is a straight route back to 101.

Access via Camp Pendleton is not always guaranteed, however, so it pays to give the Marine Corps Community Services Information line (760/725-3400) a call to ask about closures due to training exercises or changes in the base security posture.

Another cycling route option when the base is closed is to do an out-and-back along the **San Luis Rey River Bike Path,** which runs more than seven miles from Coast Highway along the river.

Fishing
When you approach **Oceanside Pier** (250 N. Pacific St., 760/966-1406, 24 hrs. daily) from the beach in the right light it sometimes seems like a giant spider has woven a web of shimmering monofilament from the railings to the water. Under the moonlight anglers try for squid. Once the sun rises they'll ply the deeper railings for pelagic varieties like bonito or mackerel. Halfway down the pier the biting's best with nibbles from multiple types of croaker, halibut, and sand sharks. And inshore fishing yields corbina, croaker, guitarfish, and several kinds of rays.

Like all piers in Southern California there's no license requirement to fish here. But be sure to bone up on local limits and regulations because state fishing deputies are known to wander these planks looking to bust poachers. Bait, lures, hooks, and lines are for sale at the bait shack halfway down the pier. The facility also sells snacks and drinks and rents rods and reels on an hourly basis. There are also basic restroom facilities on the pier, but I'd recommend bringing hand sanitizer as there is no soap in sight.

ACCOMMODATIONS

Oceanside's lodging choices are extremely limited, with many "bargain" and chain motels that are dirty or threadbare still running above $110 per night in spite of the town's distance from metropolitan San Diego. Often the more decent options are ruined due to close proximity to the train lines that run through town. In a pinch it can make sense to stay in town, but unless you are camping I'd generally recommend driving south to Carlsbad, Encinitas, or Del Mar.

If you are desperate and tired after driving through L.A. and Orange County, **Oceanside Inn and Suites** (1820 S. U.S. 101, 760/433-5751, $89 d) can shelter you for an evening. Make no mistake about it, this is a motel—of the by a busy thoroughfare, carpet held together by duct tape, and ceiling panels flaking variety—but you might consider making a pit stop here if you are in need of a bed for a night, have under a hundred bucks in your pocket, and can't find a place to stay near the beach during high season. The two redeeming qualities about this place are that it doesn't seem to attract the skeezy characters that are usually drawn to a motel of this caliber, and the beds are actually reasonably comfortable. Just don't even think about paying extra for the suite. It isn't worth it.

Set on a private peninsula inside Oceanside Harbor, **Oceanside Marina Suites** (2008 Harbor Dr. N., 760/722-1561, www.omi hotel.com $260 d) is one of the big exceptions in Oceanside accommodations. The facility is clean, quiet, safe, and nicely decorated. It is a family-oriented hotel that rents one- and two-bedroom suites that are all equipped with full kitchens and fireplaces. On the grounds you'll find barbecue equipment, a volleyball court, heated pool, and a gazebo with a view of the harbor.

Camping

Some of North County's best campgrounds are in Oceanside or very close by. To the north, **San Onofre State Beach** has two of the best. The **San Onofre Bluffs Campground** (follow signs from Basilone Rd. exit off of

A rare crowd-free day at San Onofre Bluffs Campground.

© ERICKA CHICKOWSKI

I-5, 949/492-4872, $21 per site) sits above the beach. There are 176 tent and RV sites sitting on this long, rectangular campground. Sites are crammed together on gravel plots with no border shrubs or trees between most of them. But the crowd that comes here is generally respectful of your space if you want privacy and welcoming if you feel sociable. Dogs are allowed at the campground but not on the beach and there are restrooms with pedal-flush toilets and outdoor cold showers at regular intervals along the campground road. However, there are no hookups for RVs at this campground. It is also only open for camping between May and October.

On the northern border of the park **San Mateo Campground** (follow signs from Basilone Rd. exit off of I-5, 949/492-4872, $21 tent sites, $30 RV hookup sites) sits slightly inland and is a good back-up when the bluffs are booked or closed. A mile-long nature trail leads from the campsite to the famous Trestles surf break. The grounds have 67 sites with electrical and water hookups. The rest of the 90 sites are for tent campers. The outer-loop sites offer a little more privacy, but this is another somewhat cramped facility. Bathrooms have flush toilets and pay hot showers and there is an RV water and dump station on-site.

Also in Oceanside is the small and sometimes overlooked campground at **Guajome Regional Park** (3000 Guajome Lakes Rd., 760/724-4489) This beautiful park has a historic adobe home and numerous trails and is very close to Mission San Luis Rey. The grounds have full restroom facilities with sinks, hot showers, flush toilets, and water spigots outside to wash your dishes. It also has an RV dump station and partial hookups at each site. Cost is $20 per night, with an additional $1 fee per dog per day.

FOOD

There's no fancy nouveau cuisine in O'side, but the town really does shine when it comes to roadside diners and cafés. The most historic of the bunch is the ◖ **101 Café** (631 S. U.S. 101, 760/722-5220, 6:30 A.M.–midnight daily,

$6), a classic counter-and-booth diner along the Coast Highway that has been scooping out hand-dipped milkshakes since before I-5 was a gleam in some engineer's eye.

In downtown Oceanside **Mary's Family Restaurant** (307 N. U.S. 101, #B, 760/722-3052, 7 A.M.–8 P.M. Mon.–Sat., 10 A.M.–3 P.M. Sun., $8) whips up hearty breakfasts like biscuits and gravy, huge burgers and sandwiches for lunch, and comforting dinner entrées like meatloaf and country fried chicken. The friendly wait staff and the colorful murals depicting the pier, the city, and Camp Pendleton contribute to the homey atmosphere here.

If greasy food isn't your thing, skip on over to **Hill Street Café and Gallery** (524 S. U.S. 101, 760/966-0985, 7 A.M.–9 P.M. daily, $7) and choose between the organic and vegan options here. Tofu wraps, portobello steak with brown rice, and free-range chicken breasts are some of the culinary prospects at this arty café.

Finally, if all those fishing lines hanging off the pier have put ideas into your head, **Harbor Fish and Chips** (276A Harbor Dr. S., 760/722-4977, 11 A.M.–7 P.M. daily, $8) has got you covered. This salty seafood shack fries up fish hauled in fresh from a local fish market. Founded in 1969, the restaurant has accumulated a nostalgic collection of stuffed fish and photos of fishing trips long past.

INFORMATION AND SERVICES

The closest post office to the beach is at 517 Seagaze Drive. Only a few blocks away is the **Oceanside Library** (330 N. Coast Hwy., 760/435-5600, 9 A.M.–8 P.M. Mon.–Wed., 9 A.M.–5:30 P.M. Thurs.–Sat., closed Sun.), which resides along the Coast Highway corridor.

Oceanside police headquarters (3855 Mission Ave., 760/435-4900, www.oceanside police.com) are located east of I-5 closer to the town's residential district. This is also where you'll find emergency medical service from **Tri-City Medical Center** (4002 Vista Way, 760/724-8411).

NORTH COUNTY

GETTING THERE AND AROUND

The **Oceanside Transit Center** (195 S. Tremont S.) is the first Amtrak station stop in San Diego County. Amtrak's Surfliner train provides service to and from Oceanside all the way up to San Luis Obispo.

The center is also Oceanside's major hub for local transportation. This is the northernmost station on the Coaster commuter line that runs to downtown San Diego. As of December 2007 it is also be the easternmost station on the new **Sprinter** commuter line that runs 22 miles to Escondido. Some of the major bus routes that run through the center include #395 north to Camp Pendleton and San Clemente, #310 express south to University Town Center in La Jolla, and #320 express that goes east to Escondido.

Escondido and San Pasqual

Located in the heart of the county, Escondido is a key San Diego destination for fat-tire enthusiasts with its miles of mountain bike trails. Most trails are multi-use, so there are lots of opportunities to explore by foot as well. It is also home to the San Diego Wild Animal Park, San Diego Zoo's 1,800-acre wildlife preserve.

SIGHTS
Town Sights

North County visitors often overlook Escondido, which is a shame because this small inland town has a lot to offer families in search of a change of pace from normal seaside activities. The best places to see are centered around Escondido City Hall and the surrounding Escondido Art District, which is a hub of museums and galleries.

The centerpiece of the district is the **California Center for the Arts** (340 N. Escondido Blvd., 760/839-4138, www.artcenter .org, 10 A.M.–4 P.M. Tues.–Sat., noon–4 P.M. Sun.), a 12-acre campus for the arts that includes a 1,500-seat concert hall, a 400-seat theater, and a visual arts museum. The museum primarily celebrates the region by bringing in original art and traveling exhibits with work from American and Mexican artists who live and work in Southern California. Cost to get in is $5 for adults, $4 for seniors and military, and $3 for students. Kids 12 and under get in free.

Reward the little ones for suffering through the art gallery by marching them right next door to the **Escondido Children's Museum** (380 N. Escondido Blvd., 10 A.M.–2 P.M. Tues., Thurs., Fri., noon–4 P.M. Wed., 11 A.M.–3 P.M. Sat.). This hands-on museum teaches kids about art and science while making sure they always have fun. There's the "Wildlife Treehouse" exhibit, which features a climbing structure and learning exhibit about animals and plans; a toddler exhibit with games, toys, and obstacles designed to improve fine motor skills; and numerous other rotating exhibits. Outside there's a children's garden, play houses, and climbable sculptures by Niki de Saint Phalle. The cost is $4 for kids and adults. Because the fun is geared for toddler age and up, only babies under 12 months get in for free.

On the same block as the museums and city hall is also Escondido's most celebrated gathering place, **Grape Day Park** (321 N. Broadway, 760/839-4691, sunrise–sunset daily, free). This is the city's oldest park and since 1908 people from all over Southern California have come here to participate in the town's Grape Day Festival. After petering out in the 1950s, the festival was revived in 1996 and is held each year to celebrate the Escondido valley's agricultural heritage.

The three-acre park is centered around the grassy public green that is dotted by trees. There is a rose garden, a playground for kids, horseshoe pits, and picnic tables are scattered around the grounds.

What really makes Grape Day Park so

special, though, is Heritage Walk. This historic lineup of vintage buildings from all over Escondido was created as part of a bicentennial project in 1976. The buildings are owned by the city but they are maintained by the Escondido History Center, which is based out of the park and has furnished each of the buildings to act as a part of the **Heritage Walk Museum.** For $3 you can walk through an old Victorian house, a blacksmith shop, watch the breeze blow on two antique windmills, and clamber over the boarding platform of an old Santa Fe Train Depot, which has an authentic train car parked right outside. The museum is open Tuesday through Saturday from 1 P.M. to 4 P.M.

◖ San Diego Wild Animal Park

People who visit San Diego Zoo for the first time are often surprised to learn that the Zoological Society of San Diego runs not one, but two, mini-ecosystems for exotic and endangered wildlife.

The "other" zoo, San Diego Wild Animal Park (15500 San Pasqual Valley Rd., 760/747-8702, www.sandiegozoo.org), is actually far more expansive than its venerated counterpart. Set on 1,800 acres of rocky land in Escondido's San Pasqual Valley, this wildlife sanctuary tries to better approximate the natural landscapes that its largest beasts are used to roaming. The park's pride and joy is the "Journey to Africa" exhibit, a sprawling open-enclosure range that is grazed by rhinoceros, giraffes, onyx, and other roving animals used to coexisting peacefully in the wild. The park's decades-old monorail system was retired in 2007; now the way to check out open enclosures is through a special tram that costs a little extra above admission price. The best way to get the full park experience is to pick up the Best Value Ticket, which is $33 for adults and $22 for kids and includes the Journey into Africa tram ride.

The full cost of admission will also gain you access to the other walkable exhibits, including Condor Ridge's American desert habitat, Elephant Overlook, Lorikeet Landing's hands-on aviary, and my favorite, Lion Camp.

The exhibits at the San Diego Wild Animal Park make you feel like part of the environment.

© ZOOLOGICAL SOCIETY OF SAN DIEGO

NORTH COUNTY

Part of this lion enclosure is built to look like an abandoned research camp and these massive felines are deceptively cute when they decide to snooze in the stripped-out Land Rover that's been set up as a kitty house for them. "Meow," indeed.

Like the San Diego Zoo, the Wild Animal Park is open late between June and September. Hours then are 9 A.M. to 9 P.M. The rest of the year the park is open from 9 A.M. to 5 P.M.

San Pasqual Battlefield

History buffs headed to the Wild Animal Park on a weekend afternoon may want to make time to take a brief detour to San Pasqual Battlefield State Historic park (15808 San Pasqual Valley Rd., 760/737-2201, 10 A.M.–5 P.M. Sat.–Sun.), which is just east of the animal sanctuary.

This was the site of one of the most controversial battles in the Mexican-American War, an 1846 clash between U.S. and Californio troops that lasted no more than 15 minutes but has had military historians arguing over its outcome for 150 years. The park's visitors center features exhibits that provide context to the battle, the history of the valley prior to the war, and the events leading up to it.

ENTERTAINMENT AND EVENTS
Casinos
More than 1,600 slot machines jingle, jangle, and whir loudly on the floor of **Harrah's Rincon** (777 Harrah's Rincon Way, Valley Center, 760/751-3100, www.harrahs.com, 24 hrs. daily). Located northeast of Escondido along Highway S-6, this gaming establishment also features seven different kinds of table games and an active poker room that spreads a Texas Hold 'Em tourney every day of the week.

Wine Country
The history of Escondido has been intertwined with grape vines since the Franciscan padres first laid eyes on the wild grapes that grew naturally in the area's local soils. The neophytes of Mission San Luis Rey first cultivated the area with wine-producing varietals and the region has steeped in fermentation ever since.

As San Diego development has crept up to Escondido, though, many of the former vineyards have retreated north to the Temecula Valley in Riverside County. But there still remain a number of vineyards and wineries on San Diego turf that oenophiles swear by.

One of the best is **Orfila Vineyards and Winery** (13455 San Pasqual Rd., 760/738-6500, www.orfila.com) in the San Pasqual Valley. This 70-acre estate lies on the road that connects downtown Escondido with the Wild Animal Park. Travelers are invited to stop by at 2 P.M. each day for a 25-minute tour through the grounds and the cellar. The tasting room is open from 10 A.M. to 6 P.M. daily and when the weather's fine (and it usually is this far inland) wines can be savored underneath the adjacent grape arbor just outside the tasting room. You'll be able to pick 5 wines for $6 and they let you keep the glass as a souvenir.

About six miles away from downtown,

Belle Marie Winery (26312 Mesa Rock Rd., 760/796-7557, www.bellemarie.com) primarily uses grapes from Baja Mexico's Guadalupe Valley, but it does have a lovely demonstration vineyard on the property for those who insist on seeing grapes grow as they taste their wines. Tastings are held daily between 11 A.M. and 5 P.M. You'll get five sips for $5, along with a free wine glass.

Continue on about four miles farther north, near the Welk Resort, and you'll find **Deer Park Winery** (29013 Champagne Blvd., 760/749-1666, call for hours). Deer Park offers tastings, and the flights here are $5 for five tastes and a wine glass. If you stop here, be sure to check out the expansive auto museum on the premises. Housed within rustic barns on the property are dozens of old fantails and speedsters dating from 1886 all the way to the mid-1970s. The winery also operates a deli that serves sandwiches and accoutrements to go with the wine.

Events
Escondido's **Grape Day Festival** has deep roots. Started in 1915, the yearly event held the day after Labor Day each year began as a celebration of the abundant grape harvest that at one point was the main economic driver for the region. As grape production declined in the middle of the century, the event did as well. By 1950 the event became but a memory. That is, until civic leaders decided to revive it in 1996 to pay homage to Escondido's long-running love affair with the Muscat grape. The all-day festival now features a parade, live music, grape stomping, and wine tasting.

SHOPPING
The Escondido Art District is a vibrant mesh of art studios and galleries clustered around the California Center for the Arts in downtown Escondido. There are dozens of storefronts to wander that showcase fine art paintings, folk crafts, handmade beads, ancient sculpture, and other work that spans the spectrum of perceived beauty.

One of the most eclectic collections is held

at **Distinction** (317 E. Grand Ave., 760/781-5779, www.distinctionart.com, noon–5 P.M. Wed.–Fri., 10 A.M.–5 P.M. Sat.), a gallery which rents out 14 working studios to local artists. The contemporary work here is largely from emerging artists and exhibits change frequently, about once every two months. This is also the hub of activity on the second Saturday of each month when the gallery hosts the reception for **Escondido's Artwalk** between 5 and 8 P.M.

Also notable is the **Lillian Berkley Collection** (128 E. Grand Ave., 760/480-9434, www.lillianberkley.com, 11 A.M.–5 P.M. Tues.–Sat.), which was selected as one of the top 50 galleries in the United States by *Art & Antiques* magazine. This is the place to go for Russian art from the non-conformist art movement of the former Soviet Union.

The art at **Bill Kasper Studio and Gallery** (415 W. Grand Ave., 760/310-7379, www.billkasperglass.com, 11 A.M.–7 P.M. Mon.–Fri., 11 A.M.–5 P.M. Sat.) is hot. Really. It all reaches 2,300 degrees before Kasper blows it into flowing bulbous and vibrant glass displays that include bowls, vases, sculptures, and lighting fixtures. Visit the studio on Saturdays to watch the magic happen during the live glass-blowing demonstrations held on-site.

SPORTS AND RECREATION
Trapeze High
Ever want to run away and join the circus? Trapeze High (2470 Melru Ln., 760/740-2454, www.trapezehigh.com) can train you to make your escapist fantasies a reality without all the needless hassle. Ladies don't have to grow a beard, fellas needn't stick their head in a lion's maw.

The safe and supportive facility at Trapeze High is a fun way to learn the art of swinging from the rafters. Classes are held Tuesday and Thursday at 4 P.M. and on the weekend at 10 A.M., noon, 2 P.M., and 4 P.M. They last 90 minutes and cost $45 per person.

Mountain Biking
Escondido is the gateway to the North County backcountry. In fact, if you start at city hall and drive in just about any direction you're likely to stumble upon one or more classic San Diego trailheads. The beauty of this area for the fat-tire enthusiast is that the great majority of these trails are still open to mountain bikers, a rare phenomenon in the increasingly restrictive SoCal riding zone.

Best of all, these aren't just wide and planed fire roads or flat rails-to-trails gravel. There are a lot of windy, technical trails that have enough elevation change to satisfy the most sadistic bombers in your pack. And there is a lot of pretty single-track that leads through natural chaparral and coastal scrub that has been untouched except by the occasional forest fire.

Before heading out, consider stopping by **Hidden Valley Bike Shop** (1040 E. Valley Pky., Ste. B, 760/746-1509, 9 A.M.–6 P.M. Mon.–Fri., 9 A.M.–5 P.M. Sat., closed Sun.) in town to pick up spare tubes, water-bottle cages, and other essentials for the trail.

Some of the best riding in the county is right in town at **Daley Ranch** (3024 La Honda Dr., 760/839-4680, dawn–dusk daily, free), a 3,058-acre plot of land purchased by the city to open to the public and protect from the encroachment of tract homes. The ranch has 25 miles of interconnected single-track opened to hikers and bikers. The routes ramble by swaying meadows, seasonal ponds lined with cattails, irregularly shaped boulders, and shady stands of Engelmann oak.

For some real lung-burners, try the 7.6-mile round-trip up and down the hills of **Elfin Forest Recreational Reserve** or battle your way up the 3.6-mile trail to the top of Bernardo Mountain. Both have an elevation gain of about 1,000 feet and both offer unique views of nearby Lake Hodges. The reserve's trailhead parking lot is located between mile markers 6 and 6.5 on Harmony Grove Road in Escondido. Rangers can be contacted at 760/632-4212.

If you'd like to get a closer look at Lake Hodges there are also numerous trails along the shoreline. These are ideal for family bike rides, especially the **Piedras Pintadas** (Painted Rocks) interpretive trail. The ancient

Kumeyaay pictographs that lend this trail its name are restricted, but along the trail there are many signs that offer tidbits about the plants and animals native to the area and the culture of the natives that expressed themselves so long ago. To get there take the West Bernardo Road exit off of I-15 and head west along West Bernardo Road for about half a mile until you see the trailhead.

Hiking

All of the trails suitable for mountain biking are also great on foot. Hikers also have the added advantage of being granted access to even more trails in the immediate vicinity that don't allow mountain bikes.

If you're saddled with the wee ones, a fun and gentle spot is at **Kit Carson Park** in the southern part of Escondido. The park has a five-acre arboretum, a beautiful sculpture garden, and a network of nature trails that ramble past three little ponds.

Or hike down to the splishity-splash of the hidden **Hell Creek** at Hellhole Canyon Park, a deceptively named place that is actually quite pleasant to wander. Though a lot of the trails here traverse hot and dusty scrubland, the creek sluices through craggy boulders underneath the shade of oak and sycamore.

Between Escondido and Ramona you can also venture out to **Boden Canyon Ecological Reserve,** another oaky enclave that offers up to 5.5 miles of exploration through the canopy. The scrub and wild grapevines here provide cover for woodland creatures such as the endangered Arroyo toad, deer, mountain lion, and dozens of species of birds. To get to Hellhole Canyon park, take the Valley Parkway exit off of I-15 and go east to Lake Wohlford Road. Turn right there, go up the hill and continue past the lake for three miles until you reach Paradise Mountain road. Take a right on Paradise Mountain Road and then another right on Los Hermanos Ranch Road. Then take a left on Kiavo Road and continue to the end. Boden Canyon Ecological Reserve is in Ramona off of Highway 78, five miles east of the Highway 78 and Highway 67 intersection.

Golf

There are a number of very satisfying links within Escondido's borders. One of the best is **The Vineyard at Escondido** (925 San Pasqual Rd., 760/735-9545, www.vineyardatescondido .com, $65), a municipal golf course that embraces the local grape-grower heritage by weaving through area vineyards.

Built around the trickling brook of the same name, **Castle Creek Country Club** (8797 Circle R Dr., 760/749-2422, $64) has a 50-year legacy. The course here is now public and provides a good straightforward challenge to intermediate golfers.

Welk Resort (8860 Lawrence Welk Dr., 760/749-3225, www.welksandiego.com, $45) offers two different courses to accommodate varying skill levels. For the beginner, the Oaks Course is a welcoming par-3 rambler. This walking-only course is a good one to hoof it without worrying about crazy cart drivers. And the Fountains is a well-regarded executive course that hosts the Junior Golf Championships every July.

ACCOMMODATIONS
Under $100

Located right off of I-15, **Palms Inn** (2650 S. Escondido Blvd., 760/743-9733, $89 d) is a pretty standard motel that is convenient to the downtown arts district and only a short jaunt away from the Wild Animal Park. Considering the 45-minute drive back into San Diego, this can make an excellent place to crash for the night after over-indulging on the wines of the Temecula and San Pasqual Valleys. The property has a pool and spa and the room rate includes continental breakfast.

$100-200

For an intimate experience, **Castle Creek Inn Resort and Spa** (29850 Circle R Way, 760/751-8800, www.castlecreekinn.com, $189 d) is a small inn set along the fairways of Castle Creek Golf Course. Six queen suites and a three-bedroom villa open their French doors onto patios overlooking the course. The facility also has tennis courts, a modest swimming pool, hot soaking pools, and a garden path that winds through a whole palette of floral colors.

$200-300

The one- and two-bedroom villas of **Welk Resort** (8860 Lawrence Welk Dr., 760/749-3225, www.welksandiego.com, one bedroom suite $259, two bedroom suite $359) are set on a 600-acre complex that has two golf courses, tennis courts, a pool with a water park–type slide, a dinner theater, and even a little museum dedicated to the one-time virtuoso of the variety show, Lawrence Welk. This is no counterpart to the luxury of La Costa or Aviara in Carlsbad, but it is a nice, comfortable one-stop vacation for middle-class families and retirees without an extravagant annuity. All the villas come with separate bedrooms, kitchenettes, and private patios.

Camping

Set adjacent to Daley Ranch, **Dixon Lake** (1700 North La Honda Dr., 760/839-4680, $20 tent, $25 full hook up) has 45 sites lining the shoreside campground loop. All sites at this city-run campground have a fire ring, table, and a locker to secure your food. Some sites also have hookups for RVs. The cost is $20 for basic sites and $25 for RV sites. The grounds here make a great place to settle before boating Dixon Lake with fishing poles in tow or exploring the surrounding 500-acre recreational area. Exploration of the ranch also awaits campers. This is also a quiet spot for those with accessibility challenges to get close to nature—the campground operates a wheelchair-accessible cabin that rents for $30 per night.

Northeast of Dixon Lake is another lakeside retreat on the water of Lake Wohlford. On the north end of the lake, **Lake Wohlford Resort** (25484 Lake Wohlford Rd., 760/749-2755) is a private campground that offers sites with full RV hookups.

FOOD

Art lovers who have come to walk the galleries of Escondido can sup on a classy meal at nearby **Bistro 221** (221 E. Grand Ave., 760/737-7398, 11:30 A.M.–2:30 P.M. and 5 P.M.–9P.M. Tues.–Sat., closed Sun.–Mon., $15), which serves lunch and dinner indoors or on its foliage-ringed sidewalk patio. Lunchtime brings light salads, sandwiches, and pasta, while dinner leans on Continental favorites such as steak au poivre and chicken saltimbocca.

Who says you can't get good seafood farther inland? **Sandcrab Café** (2229 Micro Pl., 760/480-2722, www.sandcrabcafe.com, 11 A.M.–9 P.M. Mon.–Thurs., 11 A.M.–10 P.M. Fri., noon–10 P.M. Sat., noon–9 P.M. Sun., $22) proves all the naysayers wrong with its New England–style seafood feasts. Clams, crab, shrimp, and fish are boiled up with corn and potatoes and dumped on butcher-papered tables in front of eager diners waiting with mallets in hand. The only trick is finding the place—it is a bit out of the way on the east side of I-15 in a business park. The drive is only a couple of minutes from downtown, but be sure to consult a map before you strike out for those sweet, sweet crustaceans.

Lake Wohlford Café (25484 Lake Wohlford Rd., 760/749-6585, 5:30 A.M.–9 P.M. daily) also serves fish, but its specialties come from freshwater, not salt. The café is known for its all-you-can-eat catfish dinner on Friday night. This can be a tasty consolation prize if you've been skunked while out fishing Wohlford, or if you've just worked up a powerful hunger from scrambling the Escondido backcountry. If you can't make it on a Friday, the café still serves a full breakfast, lunch, and dinner menu with hearty omelets, patty melts, and fried chicken rounding out the bunch.

Best known for its highly popular Arrogant Bastard Ale, **Stone Brewing Company** (1999 Citracado Pkwy., 760/471-4999, www.stone worldbistro.com, 11 A.M.–11 P.M. Sun.–Thurs., 11 A.M.–2 A.M. Fri.–Sat., entrée $18) is a venerated institution among brewpub aficionados. The brewery runs a stylish restaurant to showcase Arrogant Bastard and its dozens of other sudsy concoctions. Sup and sip here amidst towering ceilings and chic

NORTH COUNTY

warehouse vibe that is accented by décor featuring lots of glass, metal, and—appropriately enough—stone.

INFORMATION AND SERVICES

Information about Escondido and North County can be gathered at **San Diego North Visitor Center** (360 North Escondido Blvd., 760/745-4741, 8:30 A.M.–5 P.M. Mon.–Fri.), which is located inside the California Center for Performing Arts. The post office is right across the street from the arts center. Also in the neighborhood is the public library (239 South Kalmia St., 760/839-4684, 10 A.M.– 9 P.M. Mon., Tues., Thurs., 10 A.M.–6 P.M. Wed., Fri.–Sat., closed Sun.), just two streets away. The library has Internet access and computers available for public use.

The Escondido **police station** is also located downtown, just off of the Valley Parkway exit from I-15. It is a straight shot from there along Grand Avenue to **Palomar Medical Center,** about nine blocks away. This full-service hospital has a 24-hour emergency room. Grand Avenue is also your best bet for banks and gas stations. Several of each are scattered along this stretch between the police station and the hospital.

GETTING THERE AND AROUND

Escondido is serviced by the North County Transit System's Breeze bus lines. Routes through the city include #302 to Oceanside, the #308 to Solana Beach, #386 to the Wild Animal Park. The #351 and #352 circular routes provide service within the city.

The Metropolitan Transit System of San Diego also provides service from downtown San Diego to Escondido on the #810 route, an hour-long express ride that leaves Escondido every 15 minutes on weekday mornings and returns every 15 minutes from downtown each afternoon.

Starting in late 2007, NCTS also commenced commuter train service to Oceanside aboard its light-rail Sprinter train.

JULIAN AND ANZA-BORREGO

Drive east from any point along the coast—doesn't matter which way, due east, northeast, southeast, on any old highway route—and within an hour you'll hit the yin to the ocean's yang. Here in the middle of the county are San Diego's mountains, a craggy and boulder-strewn collection of ten ragtag ranges that stretch all the way from the international border up into Riverside County.

The mountains are wrinkled with trails and scenic highways. Hidden in the valleys and meadows are quaint mountain communities that reveal the pioneer spirit that made San Diego what it is today. Visitors can relive the bygone era, taking a locomotive ride along a historic border railway in Campo or roaming through an abandoned mine built during the Julian gold rush. Outdoors enthu-

siasts will find peace in the shade of oak and pine forests on foot, by bike, or on horseback. And casual wanderers can rest their heels at the comforting bed-and-breakfasts scattered about the hillsides.

East of the green and granite-flecked peaks of the Lagunas, the Cuyamacas, and the Palomar Mountains lies the untamed beauty of the desert. About a quarter of the entire county is covered by one of the largest state parks in the United States, Anza-Borrego Desert State Park.

The amazing landscape here is made up of badlands, high and low desert, dry lakes, oases, and hidden waterfalls. Visitors can scramble up cactus-covered peaks, roam through groves of mesquite humming with bees, or jostle their way along dusty jeep roads. The park features

© ERICKA CHICKOWSKI

HIGHLIGHTS

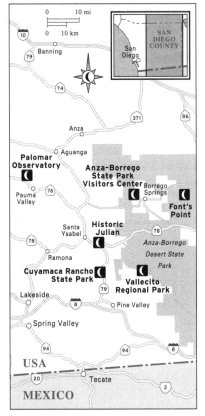

◖ **Cuyamaca Rancho State Park:**
Stands of statuesque oak, hills of golden grasses, and happily-splashing creeks shaded in green riparian vegetation can all be found at this serene recreational park (page 202).

◖ **Historic Julian:** This pioneer town crawled with gold prospectors in the 1870s. Now it is the premier mountain getaway in San Diego (page 209).

◖ **Palomar Observatory:** Built atop one of the region's highest peaks, this distinctive white observatory shelters the amazing 200-inch Hale Telescope (page 215).

◖ **Anza-Borrego State Park Visitors Center:** This award-winning interpretive center is an important stop for desert wanderers seeking historic and ecological perspectives about the surroundings (page 218).

◖ **Font's Point:** Easily accessible from Borrego Springs, this awe-inspiring outlook affords views of the forbidding Borrego Badlands (page 218).

◖ **Vallecito Regional Park:** Deep in the southern desert landscape is the Vallecito Stage Station, a reconstruction of one of the most-welcomed stops for wagon-bound travelers along the Butterfield Overland Stage (page 218).

LOOK FOR ◖ TO FIND RECOMMENDED SIGHTS, ACTIVITIES, DINING, AND LODGING.

© JOANNE DIBONA/SAN DIEGO CVB

Borrego Springs

smooth sandstone slot canyons and ancient pictographs. In the spring, the desert floor is awash in colors as the wildflowers give their annual show.

Those who want to witness the beauty needn't rough it, either: The resort town of Borrego Springs is centrally located.

PLANNING YOUR TIME

The wild country of San Diego will take some time to explore, if only just to allow time to get there. Northern outposts such as Palomar Mountain State Park and Warner Springs can take about an hour and a half to reach and the trip to some of the farthest points in Anza-Borrego Desert State Park can take longer than two hours.

If you plan on hitting any of the backcountry, you'll need to schedule it as a day trip at least. Some of the more accessible areas around Pine Valley, the Laguna Mountains, the Cuyamaca Mountains, and Julian are easily visited in one day if you only have a few specific spots you'd like to check out.

The desert is best explored as an overnight trip or longer. It is definitely doable to trek out there in a single day, but it will be a long day with a lot of driving. Spending the night in Borrego Springs, at a designated campground, or just simply camped out anywhere in the park is part of the experience, anyway.

Anywhere you roam in the forests, meadows, cactus fields, and mountains, the more time you have to devote the better. There are countless trails to tromp, vistas to enjoy, and solitude to find. It is something you simply can't rush.

JULIAN

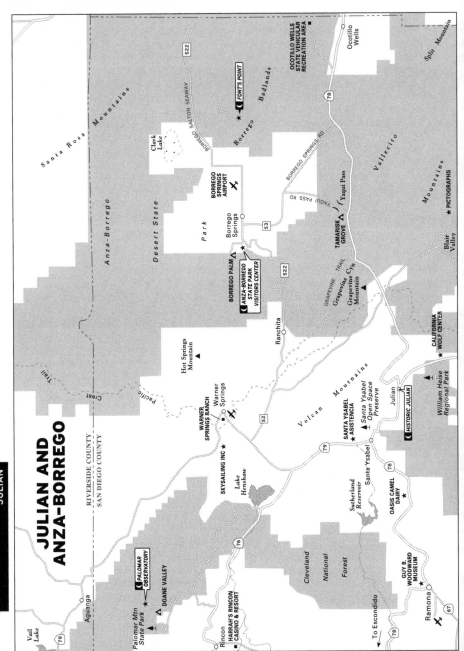

JULIAN

JULIAN AND ANZA-BORREGO

RIVERSIDE COUNTY
SAN DIEGO COUNTY

Vail
Lake

Aguanga

79

Palomar Mtn
State Park

DOANE VALLEY

PALOMAR OBSERVATORY

Rincon

HARRAH'S RINCON CASINO & RESORT

76

To Escondido

67

Ramona

GUY B. WOODWARD MUSEUM

78

OASIS CAMEL DAIRY

Santa Ysabel

Sutherland Reservoir

Lake Henshaw

SKYSAILING INC

WARNER SPRINGS RANCH

Warner Springs

Pacific   Crest   Trail

Santa Rosa Mountains

Anza-Borrego

Desert State

Park

Clark Lake

Hot Springs Mountain

Ranchita

S22

BORREGO PALM

ANZA-BORREGO STATE PARK VISITORS CENTER

Borrego Springs

S3

BORREGO SPRINGS AIRPORT

BORREGO SALTON SEAWAY

FONT'S POINT

Borrego   Badlands

S22

Split Mountain

OCOTILLO WELLS STATE VEHICULAR RECREATION AREA

Ocotillo Wells

78

BORREGO SPRINGS RD

YAQUI PASS RD

Yaqui Pass

TAMARISK GROVE

GRAPEVINE TRAIL

Grapevine Cyn

Grapevine Mountain

Vallecito   Mountains

PICTOGRAPHS

Blair Valley

CALIFORNIA WOLF CENTER

Julian

HISTORIC JULIAN

William Heise Regional Park

S2

Volcan   Mountains

SANTA YSABEL ASISTENCIA

Santa Ysabel Open Space Preserve

79

Cleveland

National

Forest

78

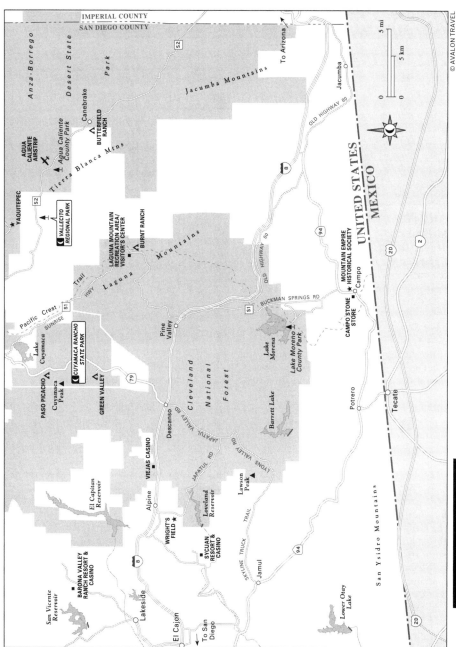

© AVALON TRAVEL

JULIAN

Campo to Julian

Home of the Laguna and Cuyamaca Mountains, this area is a fine place to stretch out the legs and explore a little. Recreation and scenic drives are the name of the game here, with dozens of trails just waiting to be discovered by bike or foot, and lakes that are meant to fished.

For those who don't want to try their luck against nature but still want to roll the dice, there are more than a few Indian casinos in the area also.

SIGHTS
Museums

Sequestered in the sleepy border town of Campo, there is a trio of museums that offers an interesting perspective on this region's position in San Diego's history. Located about sixty miles from the big city and only a mile from Mexico, Campo Valley is the crossroads of San Diego development. It lay on the alternate stage route to Yuma, Arizona, during the mid-1800s and when the San Diego and Arizona Railway laid its track to finish the last link of the transcontinental railway to San Diego, the trains chugged through Campo.

The **San Diego Railroad Museum** (Hwy. 94 and Forest Gate Rd., Campo, 619/478-9937, www.sdrm.org, 9 A.M.–5 P.M. weekends and major selected holidays) takes visitors on a trip through history over some of those same rails. For $10 visitors hop aboard the Golden State and rumble across the rugged landscape for a nostalgic ride. When the train returns to the Campo Depot, all are invited to wander through the museum's warehouse of engines and cars, some restored and some romantically rusting away outside.

Trains weren't the only transportation link to San Diego that ran through Campo. In 1914, Old Highway 80 (it was new then) curved its way around the mountains and toward the sea. Here, trucks of all shapes and sizes kept the region rolling with goods from the eastern

San Diego Railroad Museum in Campo
© ERICKA CHICKOWSKI

states. The **Motor Transport Museum** (31949 Hwy. 94, 619/478-2492, 10 A.M.–5 P.M. Sat.) pays tribute to those wheeled ferries of progress with its extensive collection of antique trucks, tractors, and trailers. Volunteers work on one or two restorations at a time, but there are hundreds of vehicles in various states of decay scattered across the yard outside of the museum's cavernous workshop. It is enough to make a gearhead's eyes widen to the size of dish platters.

It hasn't always been easy traveling in the borderlands, though. Campo has been on the front lines of frontier border disputes since the United States gained possession of this land after the Mexican-American War. One of the most famous incidents was the Campo Gunfight in 1875, when a group of Mexican bandits attacked the Gaskill Brothers Stone Store and Hotel. This historic building now houses the **Mountain Empire Historical**

JULIAN

Society museum, which recounts this incident and how it precipitated the establishment of the U.S. Customs Service station in Campo. The museum also covers the history of Camp Locket, which was built in Campo in 1941, remaining the last operational horse cavalry post in the country until its closure in 1946. Though the army was fully mechanized at that point, it believed that soldiers on horseback would be the most expedient way to guard the rough terrain at the border.

This base was also a notable prisoner-of-war camp during World War II, interring Italians and Germans captured during the North African campaign against Rommel.

Laguna Mountain Recreation Area

San Diego is known for fun, sun, surf, and... snow? Yes, that's right. The mountains in the heart of the county are known to get a dusting of snow each year, and none receive

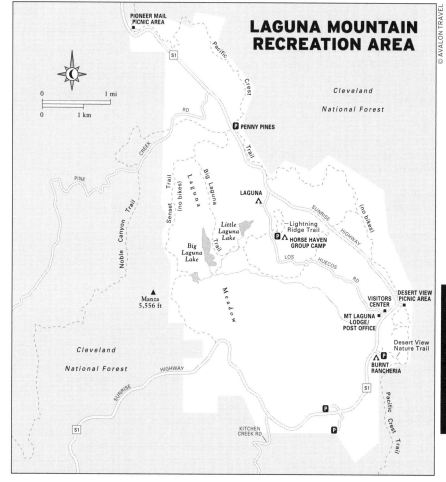

© AVALON TRAVEL

JULIAN

The trails in Cuyamaca Rancho State Park lead through mixed oak and pine forests.

more of the white stuff than Mount Laguna. The mountain is a part of the Cleveland National Forest's Laguna Mountain Recreation Area. Situated along the Sunrise Highway, this outdoor playground has lots of hills to sled down and terrain to traverse by cross-country ski when there's enough powder. Be sure to pack your hiking boots, too, because snow only hits a few days of the year and isn't very predictable.

You won't be disappointed either way. This mixed pine and oak forest area is home to hiking and mountain-biking trails galore, plus plenty of campgrounds and picnic areas. There's a serene mountain meadow here, and some amazing views of the desert floor to the east.

To learn about the flora and fauna, be sure to stop off at the **Laguna Mountain Visitor Information Center** (10 mi north of I-8 on Hwy. S-1, 619/473-8547, 9 A.M.– 5 P.M. Sat., 9 A.M.–3 P.M. Sun., 1–5 P.M. Fri.). Usually staffed by a kindly volunteer, the center has interpretive displays and a collection of books and maps to get you started

on your adventure. If you stop there, be sure to keep a lookout for the Desert View Picnic Area, just a quarter mile north. This offers one of the best lookouts to Anza-Borrego State Park along the entire length of Sunrise Highway.

◖ Cuyamaca Rancho State Park

The country south of Julian, filled with rising and falling peaks and meadows dotted with fluttering oak trees, was called "Ah-ha-Kwe-ah-mac" by the indigenous people here, translated roughly as "the place of rain." The name has stuck, albeit modified by the Europeans, and the area is now known as the Cuyamaca Mountains. Much of this beautiful area has been saved for posterity, set aside by the state within the 25,000-acre Cuyamaca Rancho State Park (12551 Hwy. 79, Descanso, 760/765-0755, www.parks.ca.gov, www.cuyamaca.us, dawn–dusk daily).

Indeed, it does rain here more than in the surrounding regions and the resulting woodland forest offers some of the greenest natural landscapes in the county. The

Cuyamacas are no stranger to drought, however, and the land here is subject to the natural cycle of growth, wildfire, then re-growth that is so common in Southern California. In 2003 these mountains were ravaged by one of the most devastating wildfires in decades, the Cedar Fire. Driving along Highway 79 through the heart of the state park, visitors will see the effects of this conflagration for at least a decade as the forest heals itself from the flames. The area is a power-ful testament to Mother Nature's power for destruction and rebirth. In the areas where the flames swooshed through, great stands of "ghost forest" remain like legions of burnt and spindly matchsticks. But it is far from a desolate sight. Saplings, lowland scrubs, and wildflowers cover the woodland floor and this greenery continues to grow taller and thicker each year.

With over a hundred miles of trails that roam through grasslands and boulder-specked

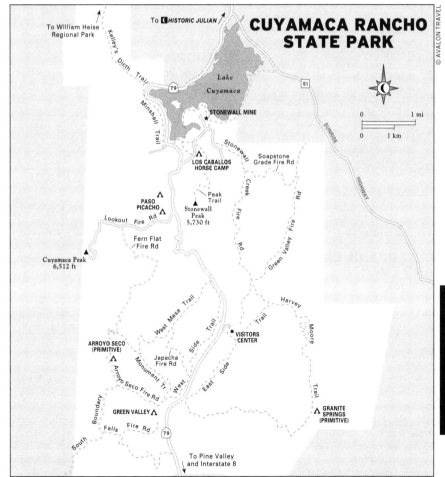

© AVALON TRAVEL

JULIAN

MOUNTAIN DRIVE

You don't need to huff and puff your way up the side of a cliff to enjoy San Diego's alpine scenery. Some of the best views unwind before you from the ribbon of pavement that winds through the county's mountains. My favorite drive takes you through the oak and pine forests of both the Laguna Mountains and the Cuyamacas.

From downtown San Diego, take I-8 past Pine Valley and exit onto Sunrise Highway. Take this windy road up through the chaparral, into the pine of the Lagunas. If you get a chance, be sure to stop off at the Desert View platform to get a look at the desert floor to the east. Then continue northeast until the junction with Highway 79.

Take a left to complete the loop. You'll curve south past Lake Cuyamaca and into Cuyamaca Rancho State Park. Here you'll be greeted by majestic oak and swaying grasslands. Keep following the road back down the mountainsides until you reach I-8 for the return trip back into town.

mountains, this state park offers a lifetime's worth of exploration.

ENTERTAINMENT AND EVENTS
Casinos

Stow some cash in those hiking boots and make a wager at any one of the numerous Indian casino based in the area. Most convenient to the city is **Sycuan Casino** (5459 Sycuan Rd., El Cajon, 800/279-2826, 24 hrs. daily) and **Viejas Casino** (5000 Willows Rd., Alpine, 800/847-6537, 24 hrs. daily), which are both located just off of I-8. Both are Vegas-style ventures with loads of slot machines, plus table games (except craps, which is not legal in the state of California) and dedicated poker rooms. Sycuan also has a full resort and golf course on its property, while Viejas features a concert venue and an outlet shopping center.

Halfway between I-8 and Ramona, **Barona Valley Ranch** (1932 Wildcat Canyon Rd., Lakeside, 888/722-7662, www.barona.com, 24 hrs. daily) is a slightly smaller casino that is lighter on the slot machines but has one of the largest collections of table and poker games of any of the casinos in the county.

Concerts

Also adjacent to the casino, Viejas hosts **Concerts in the Park** at its 1,500-seat outdoor concert arena. Shows here are all over the map, with frequent sets from country megastars, rock-band reunion tours, stand-up comedians, and emerging artists.

SHOPPING

Located adjacent to Viejas Casino, **Viejas Outlet Center** (5005 Willows Rd., #229, Alpine, 10 A.M.–9 P.M. Mon.–Sat., 10 A.M.–7 P.M. Sun.) is a popular spot to pick up brand-name items on the cheap. It has over 60 different outlet stores from shops like Borders, Eddie Bauer, Tommy Hilfiger, and Ralph Lauren.

SPORTS AND RECREATION
Hiking

Some of the most accessible San Diego backcountry trails lie between Alpine and Pine Valley, on the south side of I-8. Here Pine Valley Creek runs through Cleveland National Forest, which offers a number of easy-to-reach trails, such as the scramble to the top of **Lawson Peak** off of Lyons Valley Road. Take the Japatul Valley Road exit and head south on that road until you can take a left on Lyons Valley Road. Continue south on Lyons until you reach mile marker 13 and the unpaved Carveacre road. This road twists and winds its way to the granite-topped Lawson, where it is an easy enough scramble to the top. Or you can take on **Espinosa Trail** in Horsethief Canyon or **Secret Canyon Trail,** which both offer long exploration of chaparral-draped mountain sides. For both, take the Japatul Valley Road exit off I-8 and head in the same direction as Lawson Peak, but only go as far as the Japatul Fire Station. The trailhead is right at the fire station.

© ERICKA CHICKOWSKI

Big Laguna Meadow's mixed-use trail is a fun spot to bring your furry friends.

For an easier jaunt, Roberts Ranch is a short stroll through a meadow sprinkled with dignified oaks. Feel free to bring along your furry pal on any of these dog-friendly trails. This is also off of Japatul Valley Road, less than a mile from the freeway. Park at the Caltrans maintenance station to explore here.

The town of Campo maintains a special place in the heart of the endurance hikers who have tromped over hill and dale to make the 2,650-mile hike from the Mexican border to the Canadian border. Campo marks the **start of the Pacific Crest Trail** (PCT) one of the most famous long-distance trails in the Americas. You don't have to hike the whole thing, though.

There are numerous trailheads between Campo and Julian that are good places to set out on a day hike along the PCT. The trail runs right by **Lake Morena County Park** (2550 Lake Morena Dr.). Or you can start at the Boulder Oaks Campground just south of where the PCT crosses under I-8 and hike 2.25 miles north of the freeway to **Kitchen Creek Falls.** Here a spray of rivulets cascade 150 feet

down alternately smooth and blocky chunks of granite mountainside. To get to the trailhead, take the Buckman Springs Road exit of I-8 and take Old Highway 80 south for two miles.

Farther north, the PCT wanders along a pine-covered ridge that looks east to majestic desert vistas. Park at Burnt Rancheria Campground (9.4 mi north of I-8 on Sunrise Hwy.) and travel this stretch of the PCT that is alternately known as **Desert View Trail** at this point. The opportunities to make up your own route along this trail are nearly limitless, but be sure to leave your pup at home, since dogs are restricted on this route.

Cuyamaca Rancho State Park and the surrounding Cleveland National Forest land in the Cuyamacas is another prime region to trod in hiking boots. Just in the park alone there are over 100 miles of trails. Peak baggers will enjoy the ascent up **Stonewall Peak Trail,** reachable from Paso Picacho Campground (12551 Hwy. 79), or along **Monument Trail** to the top of Japacha Peak. Along the latter route, at about 4,700 feet elevation, there is an old biplane engine block mounted on a concrete monument in honor of a pioneering airman who crashed here in 1922. The trailhead is located on Highway 79 approximately 7.5 miles north of I-8.

Another notable trail on flatter terrain is the **California Riding and Hiking Trail** along the south shore of Lake Cuyamaca, which passes the site of an old gold mine, the Stonewall Mine. Park at the trailhead 10.7 miles north of I-8 along Highway 79 to hike here.

For an easy nature walk of less than a mile, try the **West Side Trail,** which is known for the Indian grinding holes that pock the granite here. These *mortreros* are some of the last signs of the Kumeyaay people who would spend the summers here collecting acorns to grind into meal. This trail is also reachable from Paso Picacho Campground.

Mountain Biking

Within an easy 30-minute drive from downtown San Diego, **Wright's Field** in Alpine makes for a quick taste of the country or a good warm-up before hitting the more remote trails in the county. This 230-acre nature preserve has a two-mile loop that rolls up and over meadowland that is speckled with boulders. The occasional oak dapples the route with shade. To get here, take the Tavern Road exit off I-8 and follow Tavern Road a little over a mile until you reach MacQueen Middle School. Park near the school; Wrights Field is adjacent to it.

Cuyamaca Rancho State Park doesn't allow any mountain biking on its trails, so the best single-track in this region is located south in the Laguna Mountains. The quintessential San Diego backcountry fat-tire route runs here through the tranquility of the **Big Laguna Meadow.** Here you can roll through the grassland of Big Laguna Trail, around Laguna Lake, and through the herds of cattle that graze here. The flat trail is perfect for recreational riders and families who are interested in a leisurely ride, and it is easily accessible from the Laguna Campground (12.6 mi north of I-8 on Sunrise Hwy., $17 per site). Those looking to get their fill of the picturesque and still get their heart rate pumping can use the Big Laguna route as a

link to the **Noble Canyon Trail,** which humps it way up and down the mountainsides for ten miles until it reaches Pine Valley. This trail is also accessible on its own from Penny Pines Trailhead, which is jabout 14 miles north of I-8 along Sunrise Highway.

Though there is no riding along trails within Cuyamaca Rancho, the fire roads here are open to exploration by wheel. The coup de grace of them all is the 2.8-mile road up to San Diego County's second-tallest mountaintop, **Cuyamaca Peak,** from Paso Picacho Campground. This is a real lung-buster, with 1,700 feet of elevation gain bunched together in a number of very steep ascents. The reward at the top is your view of the Pacific, the desert, and the mountain ranges that stretch between them.

Cycling

The backroads of the southern mountain ranges are very popular with endurance and touring cyclists. Some favorite routes include the out and back along **Old Highway 80** and the loop from Pine Valley through the Lagunas on **Sunrise Highway** (Hwy. S-2) and down through the Cuyamacas and back to Pine Valley on **Highway 79.**

World Cycles (9621 Campo Rd. Ste. A, Spring Valley, 619/337-2817, www.worldcycles .com, 11 A.M.–7 P.M. Mon.–Sat., closed Sun.) in Spring Valley, and **Big Ring Cyclery** (8691 La Mesa Blvd., La Mesa, 619/463-2453, 10 A.M.–7 P.M. Mon.–Sat., 11 A.M.–4 P.M. Sun.) are good sources for bike rentals.

Fishing

The mountainous corridor from the border up to Julian offers some of the most fruitful freshwater fishing in all of San Diego County, perhaps in all of Southern California. Close to the city along the I-8 corridor, **El Capitan Reservoir** is a 1,562-acre lake stocked with Florida-strain largemouth bass, crappie, bluegill, channel catfish, blue catfish, green sunfish, and carp. Though there is about four miles of accessible shoreline for fishing, the best access is by boat or float tube. There is a boat launch here, but no concession, so come prepared with a fishing license and all the bait you'll need. Also bring cash to pay the $5 lake-use fee.

Only ten miles from El Cap, **Lake Jennings** (10108 Bass Rd., Lakeside) is the centerpiece of a popular county park. In addition to a boat ramp there are picnic areas, campsites, and a concession stand here. You'll find largemouth bass and bluegill all year, blue and channel catfish in the summer, and rainbow trout in winter.

Lake Morena (2550 Lake Morena Dr., Campo, 858/694-3049, 8 A.M.–5 P.M. Mon.– Fri.) is another popular county holding. Located just outside of Campo, this lake stocks similar strains to Lake Jennings, with the addition of crappie in the summer and German brown trout in winter. There is a boat ramp and the county operates a boat rental facility here, letting out motorboats for $35 per day and rowboats for $15 per day. This includes a lake-use fee, which is $6 per day for private boats.

Just north of Cuyamaca Rancho State Park, **Lake Cuyamaca** is the only lake in the county that stocks trout all year long. Also in the lake are catfish, smallmouth and largemouth bass, bluegill, crappie, and sturgeon. This 110-acre lake is open to float tubes during the week and boats daily. There is a full tackle shop and a boat concession that rents motorboats for $40 per day, rowboats for $15 per day, and kayaks for $10 per hour. Also on the lake is a full-service restaurant and a campground open to RVs and tent campers.

ACCOMMODATIONS

Most of the best overnight options in this part of the county involve a stay under the starry skies. But there are a couple of places to take advantage of a soft bed and a warm shower.

Located on the border between the outskirts of town and the middle of nowhere, **Sycuan Resort & Casino** (3007 Dehesa Rd., El Cajon, 619/442-3425 or 800/457-5568, $240 d) offers the complete casino resort experience. The golf course here is perennially rated as one of the best in the county and there is also a spa, tennis courts, and 72-hole golf course on the property.

The rooms at **Ayres Inn** (1251 Tavern Rd., Alpine, 619/445-5800 $109 d) in Alpine are surprisingly plush for what looks like a gussied-up motel on the outside. The rooms have leather-upholstered chairs and dark mahogany furniture, with top-of-the-line linens. Rates come with an expanded continental breakfast and a free shuttle to the local casinos.

Pine Valley Inn (28940 Old Highway 80, Pine Valley, 619/473-8560, $80 d) is an ideal spot to stay when you are planning on hitting road at first light of day and would rather not pay city prices if you aren't going to be around to enjoy the stay. It is a simple motel with a refrigerator and microwave in each room, along with Internet access.

You can choose between modest motel rooms or rustic cabins at **Laguna Mountain Lodge** (10678 Sunrise Hwy., Mt. Laguna, 619/445-2342, www.lagunamountain.com, motel rooms $55–70 d, 1-br cabin $70–85 d, six-person 2-br cabin $105–150), which is within walking distance to the Laguna Mountain Visitor Information Center and the Pacific Crest Trail. The property is shaded by the pine and oak typical of the Laguna Mountains; each cabin comes with its own picnic table and barbecue. There are also pet-friendly cabins available here.

Camping

Camping in this region is plentiful, with a full range of camping experiences available, from primitive forest-service sites to full-hookup RV campgrounds.

Near the border, **Lake Morena County Park** (2550 Lake Morena Dr., Campo, 858/694-3049) has spots for tenters and RV sites with partial hookups. The sites here are situated in an oak grove near the lake, with views of the granite-studded hillsides that surround the park. There are numerous hiking trails nearby, including the Pacific Crest Trail.

The most popular campground in the Laguna Mountains is the aptly named **Laguna Campground** (12.6 mi north of I-8 on Sunrise Hwy., $17). Located along the very scenic Big Laguna Meadow, this facility has primitive bathrooms and cold-water faucets. These woodland sites are mostly designed for tent campers, equipped with picnic tables and fire

JULIAN

rings. There are no RV hookups, but there are a few sites with paved spurs.

Also nearby in the Laguna Mountain Recreation Area is the large **Burnt Rancheria** campground, which has direct access to the Pacific Crest Trail, and the primitive hike-in site **Aqua Dulce**. Prices are $17 per site per night for Burnt Rancheria and free for Aqua Dulce. Inquire at the Laguna Mountain Visitor Information Center for directions (10 mi north of I-8 on Hwy. S-1, 9 A.M.–5 P.M. Sat., 9 A.M.–3 P.M. Sun., 1–5 P.M. Fri.).

The two largest sites in Cuyamaca Rancho State Park are **Green Valley Campground** and **Paso Picacho.** Green Valley has a pretty little creek running right through the campground, a real treat for the kids in the summer. And Paso Picacho is only two miles south of Lake Cuyamaca. Both sites accept RVs, but there are no hookups. All campsites come with picnic tables and fire rings, and both sites have flush toilets and pay showers.

Just north of the state park, **Lake Cuyamaca** is one of the best places for RV travelers in the area. Here they have 23 RV sites with power and water hookups.The grounds are scenic, ringing the lake to provide good views of anglers plying the waters.

FOOD

It is catch as catch can in this region when it comes to food. Unless you've packed your own lunch, you'll be relying on a few roadside diners and markets sprinkled between the vast tracts of open land dominating the landscape. Fortunately, many of them are quite good.

As you head east along the I-8 corridor, Alpine is the last bastion of civilization easily accessible from the off-ramp until you hit the county line. If you'd like to fill your belly before heading to the hinterlands, this little hamlet is a reliable stop with a good selection of fast-food joints and a few cafés that will do the trick. Same goes for when you are speeding back into town on an empty stomach, just looking for the first place you can find.

If you don't feel like eating the same old fast food, **Fred's Old Fashioned Burgers** (2754 Alpine Blvd., Alpine, 619/445-1264, 10:30 A.M.–8 P.M. daily, $5) is a homey hamburger stand that cooks up fresh patties and crispy fries. Another quick and delicious alternative is the affordable Mexican fare at **Mi Ranchito** (1903a Alpine Blvd., 619/445-8907, 8 A.M.–9 P.M. Sun.–Thurs., 8 A.M.–10 P.M. Fri.–Sat., $7). Both restaurants are accessible from the Tavern Road exit in Alpine.

Hands down, my favorite roadside diner in all of San Diego County is **La Posta Diner** (32337 Old Highway 80, Pine Valley, 619/478-5600, 7 A.M.–8 P.M. daily, $10). It's got big, two-handed burgers that taste so fresh I wouldn't be surprised to hear mooing coming from the kitchen. The chicken-fried steak is tender and crisp, and served with real mashed potatoes and fresh veggies. Finish with one of their tempting slices of pie and you'll be unbuttoning your pants for the rest of the drive. La Posta is also open for breakfast and lunch.

Near the border, **Campo Diner** (1367 Dewey Pl., 619/478-2888, 8 A.M.–8 P.M. daily, $11) can really hit the spot after taking a ride on the San Diego Railroad Museum's Golden State. It might sound weird considering how far from the ocean this '50s-style diner is situated, but it has some of the best fish-and-chips in the whole county. Portions are huge, so don't be afraid to split a plate. Also on the menu are lumberjack-size breakfasts and lots of sandwiches.

Drivers headed up Highway 79 to Julian have two diner choices along the way. **Descanso Junction Restaurant** (8306 Hwy. 79, Descanso, 619/659-2199, www.descanso junction.netfirms.com, 7 A.M.–8 P.M. daily, $11) is in the blink-or-you'll-miss-it town of Descanso. Adorned in old-timey Coke ads and other frilly bits you'd see in grandma's house, this eatery has a selection of steaks, barbecue, burgers, and sandwiches, plus breakfast in the morning. Like grandma's house, the staff here is usually happy to whip you something off-menu if they have the ingredients for it.

Lake Cuyamaca Market and Restaurant (15027 Hwy. 79, Julian, 6 A.M.–8 P.M. daily,

$9) is a nice little café with a view of the lake. Sandwiches, salads, and burgers are all on the menu, as are a host of breakfast standards. The market has a decent selection of goodies and cold drinks for the rest of the ride.

INFORMATION AND SERVICES

The closest major medical center in this area is **Sharp Grossmont Hospital** (5555 Grossmont Center Dr., 619/740-6000) just west of Alpine in La Mesa.

The **San Diego County Sheriff** runs substations in Alpine (1347 Tavern Rd., #2, 619/659-2600), Campo (378 Sheridan Rd., 619/478-5378), and in Pine Valley (28848 Old Highway 80, 619/473-8774). This particular section of the San Diego backcountry has pretty decent cell phone coverage, especially near the I-8 corridor, so you may just be able to call 911 in the case of an emergency. Always play it safe by telling someone when you plan on exploring the wilderness, giving them details about where you'll be and for how long.

GETTING THERE AND AROUND

This far out of the city there aren't many good public transit options available. Your best bet is to travel by car. Most routes this way will head east along I-8 until you veer off north or south to your destination. To the south the major roadways are Old Highway 80, Buckman Springs Road, and Highway 94. Going south to Campo from San Diego it might make sense to take Highway 94 the whole way and completely bypass I-8. To the north, the major thoroughfares are Sunrise Highway, also known as S-1, and Highway 78.

If you plan on parking at any of the trailheads within Cleveland National Forest, you'll be required to display an Adventure Pass parking permit. These passes are available at a number of outdoor supply stores in the city, including Sport Chalet and REI. You can also pick one up at the **Laguna Mountain Visitor Information Center** (10 mi north of I-8 on Hwy S-1). Daily passes cost $5 and annual passes are $30.

Julian

Once upon a time this was San Diego's home to gold prospectors; now it plays host to dozens of bed-and-breakfasts, museums, and shops. Located more than 4,000 feet above sea level, the town is also a center for winter activity when the snow falls. San Diegans are awfully proud of this fact, as the area is one of the few in the United States where you can conceivably take a dip in the ocean and frolic in the snow within an hour. West of town is the "big city" of Ramona. This is the gateway to San Diego County's mountain and desert retreats, and a great place to stop for affordable lodging and convenient grub.

SIGHTS
◖ Historic Julian

The gold-mining operations that were once the lifeblood of Julian are long since shut down, but you can relive the fervor for that shiny stuff

at **Eagle & High Peak Mine Tours** (2320 C St., 760/765-0036, 10 A.M.–3 P.M., last tour 2:30 P.M. daily year-round, $8 adults, $4 children 5–15, free children 4 and under) right in the center of Julian. At one time these were two separate mine shafts, but they're connected now and open for a look-see. The affable and knowledgeable guides here will lead you through the timbered passageways, shedding light on how these dark caverns were worked. Once you reemerge and give your eyes some time to readjust, you'll have a chance to see the giant stamp press on property and try your hand at panning for gold.

A perfect complement to the mine tour is a visit to the **Julian Pioneer Museum** (2811 Washington St., 760/765-0227, 10 A.M.–4 P.M. Fri.–Sun. Apr.–Nov., 10 A.M.–4 P.M. Sat.–Sun. Dec.–Mar., $3) only a couple of blocks away.

JULIAN

THERE'S GOLD IN THEM THAR HILLS

Julian may have never been much more than a few shacks in the mountains if it weren't for a freed slave named A. E. "Fred" Coleman. In 1869 Coleman was watering his horse while herding cattle near Volcan Mountain when he saw a shimmery glint in the small creek they stood near. This was more than two decades after gold rush fever hit California at large with the discovery of the shiny stuff at Sutter's Mill, so Coleman knew right away what to start doing. He unpacked his skillet and started panning.

Though the gold near Julian was hardly the second coming of the Mother Lode, it was enough to draw prospectors and pioneers to build a town. The height of Julian's gold production only lasted a couple of decades and the gold mined here only totaled about $5 million. But San Diegans are still awfully proud of their one and only mining town out in the county's hillsides.

The museum has an interesting collection of mining equipment and rock samples on top of the other exhibits highlighting the establishment of this historic town. There's a restored stagecoach, household equipment, photos of the town's earliest residents, and a remarkable lace collection. Also on display are numerous artifacts from the Native Americans who predated the gold-seeking settlers.

Once you've learned about all those hardy town founders, you can pay your respects to many of them at the **Julian Pioneer Cemetery.** This small-town burial ground has graves marked back to 1870.

At the town's primary intersection at Main and Washington Streets, you can wave down a horse-drawn carriage from **Country Carriages** to get some more perspective on the town's history. You'll clip-clop around the town and some of the surrounding scenic roads while the driver regales you with Julian lore.

Woodward Museum

Julian doesn't have the lock on historic sights in this neck of the woods. Settled in an 1886 pioneer home, the Guy B. Woodward Museum (645 Main St., Ramona, 760/789-7644, www.woodwardmuseum.org, 1–4 P.M. Thurs.–Sun.) tells the unique stories of the Indians, farmers, cowboys, vaqueros, miners, and stagecoach drivers who once populated San Diego's mountains and deserts.

Santa Ysabel Asistencia

Situated between Julian and Ramona, Santa Ysabel Asistencia (Hwy. 79, Santa Ysabel, 760/765-0810, 8 A.M.–4 P.M., 8 A.M.–5:30 P.M. Memorial Day–Labor Day) was built as a "submission" of Mission San Diego de Alcalá in 1818. The original church fell to ruins after the secularization of the missions, but there is an adobe chapel that was erected in its place in 1924. There is a small museum on the property, as well as a cemetery.

Oasis Camel Dairy

Driving the back roads of Ramona goes a little something like this: horse, horse, cow, horse, cow, barn, camel…screech, What? Yep, right in the middle of the typical American rural landscape of Highway 78 is the first and only camel dairy in the United States, Oasis Camel Dairy (26757 Hwy. 78, 760/787 0983, www.cameldairy.com). The curious humpbacked creatures are milked here to create a line of smooth camel-milk soap. Tours are available, though infrequent. Check the website or give a call to see when the next scheduled tour occurs. Cost is $10 for adults, $7 for children, and $8 for seniors.

California Wolf Center

Dedicated to the preservation of the North American Gray Wolf, the California Wolf Center (449 KQ Ranch Rd., 760/765-0030, www.californiawolfcenter.org) shelters recovering wolf packs so that they can breed and be released into the wild. Every Saturday staff and volunteers here sponsor an hour-and-a-half program meant to educate the public about the

JULIAN

beauty of these mysterious canines. Watch a slide show, ask the program leaders questions, and encounter the wolf-ambassadors at this animal sanctuary. Open for program tours only on Saturdays at 2 P.M. sharp for $10. Reservations are required.

ENTERTAINMENT AND EVENTS

If you are in Julian on a Sunday afternoon, be sure to mosey over to Main Street to check out a performance by the **Julian Doves & Desperados.** These 1880s-era historic reenactors perform skits starring characters who very well could have roamed these same streets when the mines were flush with gold. Shows are north of Washington Street and are held at 1 P.M., 2 P.M., and 3 P.M.

In May, the R&B Bicycle Club holds its annual **Julian Bicycle Festival,** featuring a mountainous 58-mile road course and an equally hilly 22-mile mountain bike route.

July brings bunting and fanfare for the annual **Independence Parade** down Main Street, a homey event known by San Diego locals as a means to get away from the crazy crowds at the beach. Don't expect serenity here either, though. The crowds throng town on the Fourth.

The best-known event all year is the **Apple Days Festival** in October, a fall classic celebrating the crisp fruit that has kept Julian on the map since the gold ran out.

SHOPPING

Both Julian and Ramona are well known as repositories of vintage relics, western heirlooms, and general miscellany from bygone times. Ramona is preferred by serious antique hunters, while Julian's shops tend to wrap a big ribbon round their collections, surrounding their stock with candles, soaps, postcards, and newer knick-knacks to appeal to the typical tourist.

For creaky treasures in Ramona, try **The Original Old Town Ramona Antique Fair** (734 Main St., 760/789-0574, 10 A.M.–5 P.M. Mon.–Fri., 10 A.M.–5:30 P.M. Sat., 11 A.M.–5:30 P.M. Sun.) and **Country Town Antiques** (746 Main St., 760/788-0076, 10 A.M.–5 P.M.

Mon.–Sat.), which are two of the biggest and located close together.

Some favorites include **Antique Boutique**'s (2626 Main St., 760/765-0541,10 A.M.–5 P.M. daily) cottage packed full of old stuff from dozens of grannies' attics, the old jewelry at **Julian Yesteryears** (2116 Main St., Ste. D, 760/765-1020), and the old and not-so-old books at **The Julian Bookhouse** (2230 Main St., 760/765-1989).

There are many straight-up gift shops as well. One of my favorites is the **Old Julian Garage** (2126 Main St., 760/765-1836, 9:30 A.M.–5:30 P.M. daily), a one-time mechanic building and now a shop full of candles, jams, toys, and souvenirs. Another is **The Birdwatcher** (2775 B St., 760/765-1817, www.thebirdwatcher.net., 9 A.M.–5 P.M. daily), which holds bird feeders, books, wind chimes, CDs with bird calls, and anything else having to do with our winged friends.

SPORTS AND RECREATION

Hiking

A short drive northeast of Julian along Farmer Road leads you to **Volcan Mountain Wilderness Preserve.** Hike the three-mile round-trip trail that leads up, up, up to find a ridge with a whopper of a view of the town and the surrounding Pine Hills. On Saturdays and Sundays a five-mile loop up to the summit of the mountain is also open.

The lightly forested humps southeast of Julian are known as Pine Hills. Head here via Pine Hills Road off of Highway 79 to find trailheads to two of the county's best waterfall hikes. At the terminus of Eagle Peak Road's dirt section is the trailhead to the cataract of **Cedar Creek Falls,** a 4.5-mile round-trip. Or continue southwest where Cedar Creek Road intersects with Eagle Peak Road until you reach the trailhead to **Three Sisters Waterfalls,** an impressive three-tiered cascade.

Also in the Pine Hills vicinity is **William Heise County Park** (4945 Heise Park Rd., 760/765-0650), which has several miles of trails throughout the park. One of the most popular routes is along Kelly Ditch Trail, which synchs

© PAUL CHICKOWSKI

There are plenty of opportunities for riding horses in Julian.

up with the trails in Cuyamaca Rancho State Park south of town.

Mountain Biking

Santa Ysabel Open Space Preserve offers over eleven scenic miles of riding through grassy meadows, a splashing creek shaded by sycamore trees, and hillsides covered in pine trees. Don't be surprised to find yourself riding by a rafter of wild turkeys in dusk or dawn. These birds roam freely around the hills of Julian.

Another scenic ride follows the **Old Banner Toll Road,** east of town. Once a wagon road that linked Julian to the desert, this 1.5-mile trail rides through mine country. You'll see boarded up shafts along the route and at about the mile mark you can explore the ruins at the old Warlock Mine, one of the longest-running in Julian.

For mountain bike rentals and tours, **Julian Stables** (760/765-2200, www.julianactive .com) is the only gig in town. Open by reservation only. Call for directions.

Horseback Riding

There are several outfitters in the Julian area that can help you enjoy the scenery on top of an equine buddy. The longest-running in town is **Julian Stables** (760/765-1598, www.julian active.com, reservation only), which guides one- and two-hour tours on its private ranch trails near Volcan Mountain. Another option is **Kenner Ranch.** In addition to the standard one- or two-hour guided jaunts around its property, Kenner also offers advanced riders the option to take longer four-hour rides on local trails.

ACCOMMODATIONS

The bed-and-breakfast reigns supreme in Julian, which boasts over 20 bed-and-breakfasts of all stripes in the immediate vicinity. The following are just a few tried-and-true picks. For a survey of some of the other choices talk to the folks at the **Julian Bed and Breakfast Association** (760/765-1555, www.julianbnb.com) to see if they can hook you up with suitable digs.

◖ **Julian Gold Rush Hotel** (2032 Main St., 760/765-0201, www.julianhotel.com, $165

Julian Gold Rush Hotel

here also offers four-course meals on Tuesday, Thursday, Saturday, and Sunday.

Those who prefer a cozier bed-and-breakfast experience should book a night at the two-room **Mountain High Bed and Breakfast** (760/765-1083, www.mountainhighbnb.com, $150–170 d). Situated in the heights of Pine Hills, it has a country-style cottage with full kitchen, living room warmed by a wood-burning stove, and private deck. There's also a room off the main house with a private bathroom and separate entry and patio. The highlight of the inn is its Sky Shed observatory. The innkeeper knowledgeably hosts nightly sky tours for guests through his 14-inch Meade telescope.

If fancy bed-and-breakfasts aren't your thing, the **Julian Lodge** (2720 C St., 760/765-1420) offers straightforward and sensible motel rooms for about $100 per night. It is only a block away from Main Street and the standard room rate includes continental breakfast each morning.

Another affordable option are the motel accommodations at **Ramona Valley Inn** (416 Main St., Ramona, www.ramonavalleyinn.com, $68 d). Located on the northeast part of downtown Ramona, the property has the added benefit of a pool.

Camping

The campground at **William Heise County Park** (4945 Heise Park Rd.) is lightly wooded with oak and pine. About half of the 80 sites here are for tent camping only, the other half allows RVs but doesn't have hookups. All sites are $15 per night. There are flush toilets, hot showers, and outside spigots with potable water. Also available are rustic wilderness cabins for $45 per night.

FOOD

For a small village of only a couple of blocks, Julian offers a pretty decent dining selection. Most places are diners or cafés featuring their own spin on country cooking, such as the **Julian Café and Bakery** (2112 Main St., 760/765-2712, 8 A.M.–7:30 P.M. Mon.–Thurs., 8 A.M.–8:30 P.M. Fri., 7 A.M.–9 P.M.

d) is the longest continually operating hotel in Southern California. Built in 1897 by a freed slave, Albert Robinson, and his wife, Margaret, this well-kept two-story charmer is furnished with authentic Victorian antiques. Afternoon tea and a full-service breakfast, both of which are included in the room rate, are served in the library sitting room downstairs. As for Mr. Robinson, he's said to be close by even now: Guests have reported ghostly activity in the upstairs bedrooms.

The Craftsman-style lodge and cottages at **Orchard Hill Country Inn** (2502 Washington St., 800/716-7242, www.orchardhill.com) sit on a picturesque plot of land that rises gently above Julian. There's a gurgling crick that splashes down into a lily pond complete with fat koi. Antique farm equipment rusts gently into gardens full of native flowers. And trails on the property lead to views of town and to a nearby gold mine. Rooms are elegant but unpretentious. The room rates vary from $250 to $425 and include an evening cocktail hour and a full-service breakfast. The gourmet kitchen

© ERICKA CHICKOWSKI

JULIAN

JULIAN APPLE COUNTRY

After the mines dried up, Julian's gold was replaced by Golden Delicious. The soil and the weather near this mountain town make it well suited to grow apples, and the town has made a name for itself through the production of area orchards.

Ask any San Diegan from sea to desert what Julian is best known for and they won't skip a beat: It's the apple pie, of course! Just about every restaurant in this tiny town has its own variation of the flaky treat. Here's a primer on the best pies in town:

Best No-Sugar-Added Apple Pie: Julian Pie Company (2225 Main St., 760/765-2449)

Best Old-fashioned Pie: Mom's Bakery (2119 Main St., 760/765-2472)

Best Dutch Apple Pie: Julian Café (2112 Main St., 760/765-2712)

Best Apple-Berry Pie: Apple Alley Bakery (2122 Main St., 760/765-2532)

Pie isn't the only gig in town, of course. There are also lots of great cider and jams to be had as well. The best of the best in either department can be found at **Julian Cider Mill** (2103 Main St., 760/765-1430), right smack in the middle of town.

If you'd prefer to get your own bushel full to try your hand at your very own pies (or to just snap into a bite of fresh apple), seek out a couple of spots just outside of town. About halfway to Banner on Highway 78, **Meyer Orchards** (3962 Hwy. 78, 760/765-0233) operates a fruit stand with many varieties of apples when they're in season, along with veggies and other fresh fruits.

If you prefer the thrill of the pick, visit **Calico Ranch U-Pick Orchard** (4200 Hwy. 78, at Calico Ranch Rd., 760/765-3620), which lets visitors roam its trees in search of plump and juicy apples in harvest season in late September and October.

Harvest season is great for those who'd like to taste the fruit during its peak of flavor. But be warned – there are lots of like-minded folks in town who want the same thing as you. The bakeries have lines out the door in autumn and those who wait to pick up pies until the end of the day risk going home empty-handed.

Sat., 7 A.M.–8:30 P.M. Fri., $11). The lodge-like interior is decked out in Americana and the chicken pie is rich and scrumptious.

The long and skinny dining room at ◖ **Miner's Diner** (2143 Main St., 760/765-3753, 10:30 A.M.–5 P.M. Mon.–Thurs., 10:30 A.M.–6 P.M. Fri., 8 A.M.–6 P.M. Sat., 8 A.M.–5 P.M. Sun., $6) showcases the old-fashioned soda counter. Burgers and sodas abound, meant to be washed down with a root beer float served up by the soda jerk. Kids will want to wander to the pharmacy and gift store next door, which has a few stairs leading down to the **Mine Shaft** candy store.

The smoky aroma coming from **Bailey's Woodpit Barbecue** (2307 Main St., 760/765-3757, noon–7 P.M. Thurs.–Sun., $13) is intoxicating, albeit frustrating because of this place's sporadic hours. If you can catch while it is open you are in for very large, pioneer-size, portions of barbecue with coleslaw, cornbread, and other fixin's.

An intimate bungalow decorated in old photos and frilly fabrics, **Julian Grille** (2224 Main St., 760/765-0173, 11 A.M.–2 P.M. and 4:30 P.M.–8 P.M. Tues.–Sun., 4:30 P.M.–8 P.M. Mon., $21) prepares steak and seafood dinners for a sophisticated palate. Lunch is simpler fare like sandwiches and homemade soup, but equally delicious.

Romano's Dodge House (2718 B St., 760/765-1003, 11:30 A.M.–8:30 P.M. Wed.–Mon., closed Tues., $15) offers an alternative to homestyle cooking with its menu of Italian dishes such as halibut in Florentine sauce and chicken cacciatore, as well as its crispy pizzas.

Most places in Julian shutter the doors early. **Rongbranch Restaurant** (2722 Washington St., 760/765-2265, 11 A.M.–9 P.M. Sun.–Thurs., 11 A.M.–10 P.M. Fri.–Sat., $10) is the only place in town open during later evening hours. If you want some grub, you can either eat there or drive 22 miles to Ramona for a late dinner. If you eat at Rongbranch, do yourself a favor and order a burger. The restaurant likes to tout its barbecue, but I found the meat a little tough.

INFORMATION AND SERVICES

The **Julian police** (760/765-4718) have an office at 2907 Washington Street. Speaking from experience, obey the traffic laws in this area—they will pull you over if you break them. Just off of main street, the Julian **public library** (2133 Fourth St., 760/765-0370, Noon–8 P.M. Tues., 10 A.M.–6 P.M. Wed.–Thurs., 10 A.M.–5 P.M. Fri.–Sat.) is a quiet retreat that offers free wireless Internet.

The **town's doctor** (760/765-1223, 8 A.M.–5 P.M. Mon.–Fri.) is also nearby at 2721 Washington Street. For critical care you'll need to trek back to La Mesa or Encinitas.

Palomar Mountain and Vicinity

Palomar Mountain is home to the famous observatory and to a scenic state park. The area's undeveloped nature is what makes it such a good place for stargazing, so other than the nearby Warner Springs Ranch refined accommodations are limited. But camping abounds in this thickly forested zone of the county.

SIGHTS
Palomar Observatory

Palomar Observatory (35899 Canfield Rd., 760/742-2119, www.astro.caltech.edu/palomar) is a distinctive white bullet of a building that is home to one of the world's most powerful telescopes, the 200-inch Hale Telescope. First established in 1936, this famed astronomical outlook is still a major research installation for Caltechs storied astronomy department.

You can get a look at the Hale Telescope and the three other major telescopes when you come for a tour at the observatory's Visitor Center. Be sure to check out the collection of dark-sky photos here. Because the observatory is still a place of serious scientific research, it is only open in the daylight hours, 9 A.M.–4:30 P.M. daily. Tours of the Hale Telescope are only offered at 11:30 A.M. and 1:30 P.M. on Saturday from April through October.

Palomar Mountain State Park

San Diegans like to consider Palomar Mountain State Park their little slice of the Sierras. The high country here is densely wooded with the most diverse collection of evergreens in the region. There's ponderosa pine, Jeffrey pine, Coulter pine, white fir, big-cone Douglas fir, and incense cedar. The three-acre Doane Pond is a tranquil spot for bird-watching, fishing, picnicking, and camping.

Surrounding the park boundaries is the northern sector of **Cleveland National Park,** which has miles of trails and additional campgrounds and picnic areas to choose between.

SPORTS AND RECREATION
Hiking

In Palomar Mountain State Park, **Doane**

HALE TELESCOPE FACTS

- It took ten years of polishing the mirror to perfect it before being installed

- Over 10,000 pounds of glass was shaved away during the process

- Dedicated in 1948

- Mirror diameter is 200 inches

- Was world's largest telescope for nearly three decades

- Still acts as the cornerstone for the famed Caltech astronomy department

Valley Nature Trail offers an easy one-mile loop through the aromatic cedar and pine woodlands of the mountain. The loop is intersected with other longer treks along notable routes such as **Thunder Spring Trail, Chimney Flats Trail,** and **Weir Trail.**

Outside of the park's boundary, and therefore open to hikers with dogs, **Observatory Trail** winds a little over two miles up the mountain from Observatory Campground to the Palomar Observatory. There is a meadow view, a bubbling creek in the winter and spring, and a thick canopy of needles for much of the route.

The country north of Warner Springs is a good place to pick up the Pacific Crest Trail. The trail follows **Agua Caliente Creek** for about four miles, sometimes over the shady creek's shore, sometimes scrambling over baked hillsides covered in chaparral and cactus.

Golf

The subtly undulating golf course at **Warner Springs Ranch** (31652 Hwy. 79, Warner Springs, 760/782-4200, 6 A.M.–sunset) is open to public play Monday through Thursday. The course is fairly straightforward but scenic. On the horizon you can see Hot Springs Mountain, San Diego County's highest peak, plus views of Palomar Observatory and Lake Henshaw. The greens fee is $40 with a cart.

Sky Sailing

Soar the skies above Palomar Mountain, Hot Springs Mountain, and the meadows and foothills between them. **SkySailing Inc.** (31930 Hwy. 79, Warner Springs, 760/782-0404, www.skysailing.com, 9 A.M.–5 P.M. daily except Thanksgiving and Christmas) offers sailplane rides on their gliding and graceful motorless aircraft. You'll rumble along the tarmac connected by rope to a tow plane that pulls you up above 7,000 feet. Release the rope in midair and from there the sailplane harnesses the power of the strong geothermic thrust above this region to stay aloft. While doing so you'll have the opportunity to take over the controls of the plane from your professional copilot to test your hands at gliding.

Rides available from 9 A.M. to sunset, starting at $110 for 20 minutes in the air.

Fishing

It's shoreline-fishing-only at the postcard-perfect **Doane Pond.** Hunt trout by reel or fly all year long. Other than Lake Cuyamaca this is the only San Diego lake to stock trout in the summer.

Lake Henshaw is a large reservoir that's well-stocked with a variety of warm-water species, including largemouth bass, crappie, bluegill, and catfish. Day-use fees are $7.50, plus $5 to use the boat ramp. Boats are available for rent as well. The cost is $30/day for motorboats and $10/day for rowboats.

ACCOMMODATIONS

Accommodations are few and far between in this remote region of the county. However, there are a couple of real gems that are perfect for weekend getaways.

On top of the list for outdoorsy types and horse lovers is **◖ Warner Springs Ranch** (31652 Hwy. 79, Warner Springs, 760/782-4200, www.warnersprings.com). This 2,500-acre resort drapes over the foothills and meadows east of Palomar Mountain. Lodging is rustic, with no phones or TVs in the rooms, but you'll want to spend most of the time roaming the grounds anyway. There's hiking, biking, horseback riding, tennis, and golf here. But the real centerpiece of the ranch experience is the hot springs pool, fed from the historic springs that lend the resort its name. The property is member-owned, and advanced reservations are restricted because members have priority to make reservations. However, if you can make back-up plans and deal with only a month of lead time you will be well rewarded for the hassle.

Right on Palomar Mountain, **Bailey's Palomar Resort** (33691 Bailey Meadow , Palomar Mountain, 760/742-1859, www.baileys palomarresort.com, $125 per night for two people) rests on a picturesque property with shady walnut and apple trees and a private pond. Guests at this pet-friendly establishment are invited to stay in a circa-1888 pioneer home or to opt for private cabins.

Practically bordering the county line, **Pala Casino and Resort** (11154 Hwy. 76, 760/510-5100, 5 P.M.–10 P.M. Sun.–Thurs., 5 P.M.–11 P.M. Fri.–Sat., $170 d) is a respite from the rugged country up here. This classy retreat towers over ranch lands and scenic byways and the rooms play up the scenery with picture windows that lend great views of the surrounding landscape. The pool area is huge, with an inviting adults-only whirlpool tub to retreat from the kiddies when they're roughhousing in the pool. Also on-site is a relaxing spa and, of course, the excitement of the casino floor.

Camping

At Palomar Mountain State Park, **Doane Valley Campground** is in a shady glen near Doane Pond. Each of the 31 sites here comes with a picnic table and either a pedestal barbecue or a campfire circle with a grate. Bathrooms on-site have flush toilets and pay showers and there are water spigots sprinkled between the sites. There are no hookups, but small RVs can park here.

Slightly down the mountain from the actual observatory, **Observatory Campground** is a National Forest Service facility. Campsites are equipped similarly to the Doane Valley sites, but bathrooms only come with vault toilets.

In addition to its lodge rooms and cabins, **Bailey's Palomar Resort** also offers camping on its private grounds. There is a bathroom with flush toilets and cold showers and sites come with picnic tables and fire rings.

FOOD AND SERVICES

Come stocked with food, because there are precious few restaurants and no grocery stores around here. On top of the mountain your only choice is **Mother's Kitchen and Bakery** (junction of Hwys. S-6 and S-7, Palomar Mountain, 760/742-4233, 11 A.M.–5 P.M. Mon. and Thurs., 8:30 A.M.–5 P.M. Sat.–Sun.), which is only open five days a week. If you can catch Mother's while it is open you'll be able warm up with a bowl of the homemade chili, get your greens fix at the salad bar, and then overindulge on a slice of pie or fresh cookies. On weekend mornings breakfast is also an option here.

Farther east at Pala Casino and Resort (11154 Hwy. 76, 760/510-5100) you can fill up at one of eight different restaurants and cafés, including **Mama's Cucina Italiana.** You'll find huge portions of pastas, including spaghetti with softball-sized meatballs.

Gas is available at the Pala Station and the Warner Springs Station.

Anza-Borrego Desert State Park

As the highways twist and wend their way down the eastern slopes of San Diego's mountains, pine and chaparral transitions to teddy-bear cactus and ocotillo. The descent leads to Borrego Desert, a massive chunk of the Sonoran Desert that covers much of eastern San Diego. Wander here and you'll find badlands and dry lakes, lush palm oases and hot springs. Summer bakes the desert floor and at its end brings torrential rains that carve washes and rivulets into the land and activates the aroma of ancient creosote bushes. Winter and spring are best for exploring. If the rain comes down hard enough in the fall, the desert is washed in blooming wildflowers the following spring.

The largest state park in the 48 contiguous states, Anza-Borrego Desert State Park spans more than 900,000 acres across eastern San Diego County and covers almost all of the Borrego Desert. The compound name is a combination tribute. The first part comes from Spanish explorer Juan Bautista Anza, the first European to establish an overland route from Mexico through the Sonoran Desert and to the Pacific Coast. The second is the Spanish word for bighorn sheep, a hardy species that roams the park's territory.

BORREGO SPRINGS

An island of private land in the state park, the little town of Borrego Springs offers convenience

JULIAN

Photos hardly do justice to this Font's Point view of the Borrego Badlands.

ERICKA CHICKOWSKI

JULIAN

and accessibility to the untamed wilds of the desert. A handful of quaint shops and restaurants are collected here, as well as an assortment of resorts and golf courses. But the town is not overrun by glitz and fake greenery the way Palm Springs is. It is a desert community first and foremost, a place where it is still OK to go to dinner in hiking boots or with helmet hair.

(Anza-Borrego State Park Visitors Center

Conveniently located in Borrego Springs, the state park's visitors center (200 Palm Canyon Dr., 760/767-4205) is an award-winning information center and museum featuring exhibits on desert ecology and native peoples and a robust schedule of educational activities and events. The center is well staffed with friendly volunteers and stocked to the gills with maps and books to help you plan your adventure. The center is inside an attractive brick building settled into a hillside. Just outside the doors there is a gorgeous interpretive garden of native fauna to get you started on identifying plantlife. Be sure to check out the pond

featuring the rare desert pup-fish. Bet you never guessed there were fish in the desert!

(Font's Point

Only a few miles away from Borrego Springs, Font's Point affords one of the best (and most accessible) views of the Borrego Badlands. Come around during a winter sunset and you're likely to share the show with fellow travelers who often bring wine and hors d'oeuvres to help savor the moment. There is a short drive along a sandy road, but it is usually passable even in a passenger vehicle.

Agua Caliente Regional Park

This county park lies on land leased from the state park. It is known for its "warm waters." There are two popular hot spring–fed pools in the center of the park, a warmer indoor pool and a cooler pool set al fresco. Also nearby are a collection of nature trails. Day-use fee is $5.

(Vallecito Regional Park

Just four miles north of Agua Caliente, this is another sub-park run by the county. This historic valley has offered a patch of green refuge to people traveling this desert for over 150 years. The land was used as an army supply depot in the early 1850. By 1857 it had evolved briefly as a stop for the "Jackass Mail," a mounted mail service that traversed the county and rode to Arizona. Only a year later this service was made irrelevant by the establishment of the Butterfield Overland Stage, which at 2,800 miles long was the longest stage ride in the world. It closed the gap between Missouri and San Francisco and used Vallecito as a key resting point in the harsh desert clime. At the park, the **Vallecito Stage Station** is a rebuilt rendition of this circa-1859 stop along the Butterfield Stage. If you look out along the east side of Hwy. S-2 in this vicinity you can still see the wagon ruts between the cactus.

ENTERTAINMENT AND EVENTS

Without a doubt the best entertainment in the desert is presented by Mother Nature. Provided there was enough rain in the fall, the **wildflower bloom** in the spring is the highlight of the year. The spindly whips of ocotillo flare up in green and orange, the sand verbena washes the floor with fluorescent purple, and even the teddy-bear cholla and barrel cactus sprout petals. To find out whether the desert is blooming, call the state park's wildflower hotline (760/767-4684).

Try to plan your wildflower visit around the **Circle of Art.** Held in Borrego Springs each March, this family-friendly art fair attracts painters, sculptors, and musicians from all over the country.

In April the storytellers come out of the woodwork to spin yarns at the **Peg Leg Liar's Contest** in Borrego Springs. The contest of wits and prevarication is named for the greatest fabricating scalawag the town has ever known. In the 1850s the mountain man Peg Leg Smith would saunter into Borrego Springs and spout tales of gold he'd found out in the desert hinterlands. Problem was, he couldn't quite

DESERT TEMPERATURE EXTREMES

The Borrego Desert is formidable for its extreme temperatures. In the winter, evening temperatures frequently dip down below freezing. And in summer, daytime temperatures bump the mercury well over 100. The record high was set in June of 1997 at an incredible 121 degrees.

The following chart shows monthly averages for the last sixty years:

Annual Average Temp (F)	Jan	Feb	Mar	Apr	May	Jun	Jul	Aug	Sep	Oct	Nov	Dec
Annual Average High	69.2	72.5	77.8	84.4	93.2	102.8	107.3	105.9	100.7	89.8	77.8	69.0

Annual average maximum temperature: 87.5

Annual Average Low	44.0	46.7	50.1	53.8	60.7	68.4	75.6	75.3	70.0	60.5	50.4	43.4

Annual average minimum temperature: 58.2

JULIAN

remember where his strike was and never really could find his lost gold again. Travel about eight miles east of town on Hwy. S-22 and you'll see a plaque raised in his honor.

Summer is scorching and every moving thing either shutters its doors or scurries underground for respite. The desert comes alive again in October and Borrego Springs celebrates with the **Borrego Days Desert Festival.** There's a parade, live music, a carnival, and the annual Miss Borrego Pageant.

SHOPPING

Borrego Springs shopping is divided between two creatively named shopping centers, The Mall and The Center. At **The Center** (590 Palm Canyon Dr., 760/767-5164) you can check out the art at **Leisel Paris Art Studio** or **Matson Gallery,** pick up a souvenir at **The Desert Robin,** or bundle up against cold desert nights with a sweater from **Jane Eric Originals.**

At **The Mall** (590 Palm Canyon Dr., 760/767-5164), **Borrego Goldsmith Jewelers** not only has jewelry but also an interesting assortment of precious minerals and gemstones collected in the area. **Tumbleweed Trading Company** is a hodgepodge of expensive furniture and decor. And **Gourmet Outfitters** has a selection of culinary doodads and picnic-basket fillers.

If you are looking for more desert reference materials and maps, there are two great places to check out in Borrego Springs. The Anza-Borrego Foundation and Institute runs a store within the **park visitors center** (200 Palm Canyon Dr., 760/767-4205, 8 A.M.–4:30 P.M. Mon.–Fri.) with a selected collection of books, maps, and mementos commemorating the park. And inn the middle of town, the Anza-Borrego Desert Natural History Association's **Borrego Desert Nature Center** (652 Palm Canyon Dr., 760/767-3098, www.abdnha.org) has an interesting collection of books, maps, jewelry, and desert fine art.

SPORTS AND RECREATION
4x4 Driving Tours

One of the best ways to really explore the deep backcountry in Anza-Borrego is to turn off the pavement and four-wheel your way along the hundreds of miles of dirt roads that crisscross their way through this rugged terrain. Some roads are smooth enough to allow even a normal passenger car to traverse a short way, the majority require four-wheel-drive, and then there are a few rocky and treacherous routes that are only passable to the most sturdy of SUVs.

To find the perfect route, a visit to the park visitors center is highly recommended. In addition to a whole passel of books and detailed maps, the center is staffed by volunteers who are well versed in desert travel. They'll be able to point you to the best routes depending on what kind of terrain you'd like to see, how much time you have, and your means of travel.

Similarly, the Anza-Borrego Foundation and Institute is an excellent planning resource. It operates a book store and gift shop in Borrego Springs (587 Palm Canyon Dr., Ste. 220 & 224, 760/767-4063) that is well equipped with maps and books to set you on the right path.

Some of the most popular routes that you can ask about include the boulder-strewn mountain area traversed by Old Culp Valley Road, the rugged high country in Sheep Canyon, the mostly smooth but scenic Blair Valley loop, and the route along Canyon Sin Nombre that leads to the Old Carrizo Stage Station in the southwest sector of the park.

Road conditions are determined year to year by what Mother Nature has been doing. During the rainy season violent downpours will sculpt the landscape, shifting dirt and debris so that one route that was easy to navigate one year may be rocky and rutted the next. Even between periods of rain, strong desert winds can shift lose dirt and sand in a way that will alter the roads' passability.

Before you head out, it is a good idea to visit or call the park visitors center and inquire about the state of the route you hope to take.

Or you can just abandon your own vehicle altogether and rely on someone else to do the heavy-lifting for you. Headquartered in Borrego Springs, **California Overland** (1233 Palm Canyon Dr., 760/767-1232, www.california

Hiking

There are hundreds of miles of hiking in the 1,000 square miles of Anza-Borrego. Many isolated trails test the wits and physical endurance of some of the best-conditioned navigators. My intention here is not to give you any semblance of a complete hiking guide. Instead, I offer a few classics with the easiest access from the paved roads.

Should you need supplies before heading out, **Borrego Outfitters** (579-E Palm Canyon Dr., 760/767-3502, www.borrego outfitters.com, 10 a.m.–5p.m. Mon.–Thurs., 9 a.m.–5 p.m. Fri.–Sat., 10 a.m.–4p.m. Sun.) has an assortment of apparel, bags, and gear at its Borrego Springs location.

The quintessential hike in Anza-Borrego is an easy 1.5-mile scoot through a rocky gulch called **Borrego Palm Canyon.** The trailhead is one of the most accessible in the entire park, located only a half mile from the visitors center. The terminus of the trail was once home to the largest grove of naturally occurring palms in North America, but a violent flash flood in 2004 uprooted a good chunk of the palms and carried them down the canyon. Their trunks remain a striking reminder of the power of desert gully-washers. What remains of First Palm Grove is still an impressive stand of greenery and the splashing waterfall and pool at the grove is perhaps even more enjoyable now that some of the thick vegetation was cleared away.

If falls are your thing, then you might want to carve out some time for a hoof up to **Maidenhair Falls.** The trailhead is only three miles west of the visitors center off highway S-22. You'll tromp 2.4 miles into Lower Hellhole Canyon until you reach the thundering roar of the falls. Sycamores, palms, and cottonwoods all clamor for moisture near the pool and mosses and ferns cling to the rocks surrounding the spray. After a thorough cooldown here it is hard to remember you're still in the desert.

Formed by millennia of flood and wind erosion, the undulating slot canyons here are ripe for hiking and scrambling. One of the most popular slot canyon explorations in the park is

Hundreds of miles of Jeep roads await off-roaders in Anza-Borrego Desert State Park.

© ERICKA CHICKOWSKI

overland.com) offers a mix of group rides aboard its fleet of retrofitted military troop carriers and Jeeps.

All of the park's roads are meant to be enjoyed by any street-legal vehicle whose driver isn't scared of a little dirt. However, you must remember that off-road travel is strictly prohibited. Anza-Borrego Desert State Park is an environmental treasure and taking your car or truck off of designated roads threatens its beauty.

Besides, if you really want to cut loose in a four wheeler or motorcycle, there's a much better place to do it just east of the park. The Ocotillo Wells State Vehicular Recreation Area allows all forms of off-road travel. The whine of dune buggies and dirt bikes can be heard across the more than 40,000 acres of open desert here. **Sand and Sea Toyz** (5965 Highway 78, Ocotillo Wells, 760/767-5269, www.sandandseatoyz.com) in the tiny settlement of Ocotillo Wells offers quad ORV rentals starting at $50 per day, between 8 a.m. and 5 p.m. daily.

JULIAN

Anza-Borrego Desert State Park is the site of numerous ancient pictographs. This one is in Blair Valley.

© ERICKA CHICKOWSKI

the squeeze through **Palm Wash** and its tributaries. Located about 19 miles east of Borrego Springs along Highway S-22, the route here runs through smooth, sculpted sandstone walls with interesting strata and occasional rocky accretions. Even with little knowledge of geology, it is easy to admire the natural artwork of these canyons. Be aware that there are tight quarters here and it is not a hike for the claustrophobe. Also use common sense—don't come here if there's even a hint of rain. Desert storms can cause the slots to flood in an eye blink.

One of my favorite areas in the park is **Blair Valley,** south of Borrego Springs along the quiet ribbon of Highway S-2. Here between Granite Mountain and Whale Peak it is easy to fall in love with the calm serenity of the desert. The wind whooshes through the valley like a thousand whispers over the barren beds of two dry lakes. Jackrabbits scamper through the creosote and agave. The valley is crossed by two flat dirt roads, usually easy to drive in a passenger vehicle, which take to you the trailheads of several hikes that have real payoffs at the end. In the southeast corner of the valley there is a flat hike through a cut in the mountains called Smuggler Canyon. Less than a mile from the trailhead you'll find ancient rock paintings left by the Kumeyaay Indians, which lends this route its name, **Pictograph Trail.**

Just southwest from that trailhead is another starting point, this one up the side of Ghost Mountain. The short one-mile trek up the mountain leads you to the desolate and haunting site of **Yaquitepec.** In the 1930s and '40s this was home of the desert ascetic Marshal South, his wife, Tanya, and their three children. South gained renown for his dispatches to *Desert* magazine describing the primitive life his family eked out here, an experiment in simplicity. The Souths built an adobe hut and an intricate rain-catching system up here, hauling water up the mountain as necessary. The ruins of their crude buildings still remain, slowly being reclaimed by the desert.

Mountain Biking and Cycling

All 500 miles of the primitive jeep roads and

paved stretches in the park are open to exploration on bike. Most trails are closed, unless otherwise designated as bike trails. Some of the most popular mountain bike areas include **Grapevine Canyon** and **Split Mountain.** At Grapevine Canyon, take Old Culp Valley Road down to Jasper Trail, where you'll head south amid the creosote and cactus as many as 16 miles to Yaqui Well. Be sure to remember that the exhilarating downhill ride out means a punishing slope back up to the tent, so only go as far as your body will let you. And don't forget to pack more than enough water for your journey—a gallon at the very least.

Road cyclists often get their kicks by touring the blacktop along **Borrego Springs Road, Palm Canyon Drive,** and **Highway S-22** east of Borrego Springs. The really motivated will make the 60 mile out and back along S-22 from Borrego Springs all the way into Imperial County to the Salton Sea.

Unfortunately there are no bike shops in Borrego Springs, so repairs and rentals will need to be taken care of before you make the drive. **Ranchita Bike and Hike** (760/782-3900) does offer one option to those who don't have the means to haul their own bikes out to the desert: This tour operation supplies you with bikes and drives you up the steep and curving Montezuma's Grade on S-22 for an exhilarating plunge down the mountain and back into Borrego Springs. Call for pick-up and location information.

Golf

This is a good time to repeat the fact that this is not Palm Springs. There are no courses here designed by golf legends. But, the courses in town do provide enough entertainment to visiting duffers to keep them busy weeks at a time. Of the four public courses here, probably the nicest of the bunch are the three nine-hole

THE SOUTH FAMILY: AN EXPERIMENT IN DESERT LIVING

It takes at least a little bit of eccentricity to live through the heat and the cold, the lack of water or resources, and the loneliness of the desert. Still, the quiet solitude and the beauty tend to make up for the isolation in many people's minds.

This was the conviction of Marshal South, whose supreme belief in the spiritual nature of desert living led him to convince his wife Tanya to give up the trappings of normal life to raise their family in the high desert.

The Souths spent several years building an adobe home on the top of Ghost Mountain. Completed in 1932, they named it Yaquitepec. They built an elaborate rain-catching cistern and hauled any additional water or necessities up the mountain. This included the schoolbooks Tanya used to educate their three children.

Marshal wrote about their ascetic life from 1930 to 1946 in a monthly column for *Desert Magazine* with help from Tanya, who occasionally also wrote stories and poems for the publi-

cation. Their experience as nudists who raised their children in simple joys of primitive living captivated the magazine's readership.

It was a grand experiment in natural living that couldn't last, however. By the mid-1940s, Tanya was worried that the children might never have the chance to assimilate into normal society if they weren't introduced to it soon enough. She and Marshal fought bitterly about the subject, along with other endless squabbles that came as a product of isolation. Finally she and the kids hiked down the mountain one day in 1946, never to return to Yaquitepec again. Marshall soon followed. Some speculate the dissolution of his marriage took a toll on him physically. He died only two years later a victim of a heart condition.

The winds of Ghost Mountain have greatly eroded their home there, but remnants still remain. If you have the time, it is worth the steep hike up to the mountain just for the view alone.

JULIAN

courses at **Borrego Springs Resort** (1112 Tilting T Dr., 760/767-5700, 6 A.M.–sunset, $80). These rolling courses offer a decent challenge with a robust bunker system and five lakes shared between the 27 holes.

For beginners or those looking for a quick nine holes, **The Springs at Borrego RV Resort and Golf Course** (2255 Di Giorgio Rd., 760/767-5457, 7 A.M.–sunset, $25) has a well-kept course that has a fun island green, waterfalls, and abundant palm trees. Right next door, the **Road Runner Golf and Country Club** (1010 Palm Canyon Dr., 760/767-5373, 7 A.M.–sunset Mon., Wed., and Fri.–Sun., noon–sunset Tues. and Thurs., $25) is an executive three-par course open to those beginners or practicing golfers who'd like a slightly longer course.

Another no-fuss option is at **Club Circle Golf Course** (Club Circle W., 760/767-5944, 7 A.M.–sunset, $20) a three-par, nine-hole course that lets golfers play as much as they'd like for $20 a day.

ACCOMMODATIONS

There's no need to go without the conveniences of modern living while kicking up dust in the desert. Borrego Springs has a healthy mix of affordable lodging and swanky digs to suit most price ranges.

In the former category, **Oasis Inn** (366 Palm Canyon Dr., 760/767-5409, www.oasisinnborrego.com, $85 d) is a simple cinderblock motel with a pool, spa, and barbecue. **Palm Canyon Resort** (221 Palm Canyon Dr., 760/767-5341, www.palmcanyonresort.com, $109 d) offers a step up from that with its Western-themed hotel. The clapboard building is lined with verandas on the outside and river-rock accents inside the lobby. Also on the property is a popular RV park, as well as a pool and two restaurants.

The rooms at **Borrego Springs Resort** (1112 Tilting T Dr., 760/767-5700, www.borregospringsresort.com, $150 d) are comfortable, clean, and spacious, but don't come expecting a five-star resort experience. Fortunately, the rates are adjusted accordingly, so

you can head out for a golf vacation for under $150 per night.

Located near the park visitors center, **The Palms at Indian Head** (2220 Hoberg Rd., 760/767-7788, www.thepalmsatindianhead.com, $159 d, suites $229 d) is a quirky little inn housed in a 1950s-era hotel building that was once a part of a resort getaway for Hollywood hipsters. This restored mid-century beauty presides over a giant Olympic-size pool that is viewable from every room in the house.

Far and away the nicest resort in town, ◖ **La Casa del Zorro** (3845 Yaqui Pass Rd, 760/767-5323, www.lacasadelzorro.com, $385 d, casita with private spa $395) can tempt even the hardiest of hikers to forget about all of those amazing desert trails and just hang around the lush confines of the property all day long. This exclusive and intimate enclave has deluxe, but comfortable, Southwest-style rooms and casitas that are surrounded by a remarkable mix of native desert foliage and rich green grass. There are five main pools on the property, plus a couple of private pools adjoining some of the casitas, so a quiet dip in the water is never very far away. Also on the premises are championship tennis courts, table tennis, shuffleboard courts, bocce ball courts, and two championship croquet greens that are so perfectly maintained that the grass hardly looks real. There is also a fitness center that includes a lap pool. Guests who pay the full rate here (as in, no special packages) are treated to breakfast at the Butterfield Room at no additional cost.

Camping

Outdoor adventurers not already head-over-heels for Anza-Borrego are usually tipped over the scale when they learn that there is an open camping policy in the entire park. You can pull over and pound in stakes wherever you please, with no fee or pass required. Campfires are allowed as long as they are built in a contained metal receptacle of some sort.

The downside to this nomadic lifestyle is that there are no bathroom facilities and no water in sight when you're out in the backcountry. If squatting in the bushes and

JULIAN

hauling in your own water doesn't do it for you, then you're still in luck. There are a handful of public and private developed campsites scattered throughout the park.

The immediate vicinity around Borrego Springs affords the most options. The go-to site for most casual desert visitors is at the spacious **Borrego Palm Canyon Campground** (200 Palm Canyon Drive, 760/767-5311, www.reserveamerica.com, $20 tent, $29 full RV hook-up) on the east side of town. This is the larger of the two state campgrounds in the park, with 120 sites total. Be sure to book in advance during the cooler months, because it still fills up fast. There are numerous tent sites, as well as about 52 full hookup RV sites. There are restrooms with flush toilets, water spigots, wheelchair-accessible nature trails, and a host of ranger-led activities in the winter.

Also in town is **The Springs at Borrego,** an RV resort that hardly even qualifies as a campground. Guests are invited to pull their rigs into the full hookup sites that also include wireless Internet and cable TV connections. The lush grounds are lined with palms and include a nine-hole golf course, tennis courts, swimming pools, hot mineral baths, and a catch-and-release fishing hole.

For something a little simpler but still in town, **Oasis Inn** (366 Palm Canyon Dr., 760/767-5409, www.oasisinnborrego.com) has an RV park with water and power connections, picnic tables, and fire grates. Guests here are welcome to use the motel's small pool and whirlpool tub.

South of Yaqui Pass from Borrego Springs on Highway S-3, **Tamarisk Grove Campground** (junction of California Route 78 and County Road S-3, 760/767-5311, www.reserveamerica .com,$20 tent) is another statepark–run site with running water and bathrooms featuring flush toilets. All the sites here have the added benefit of ample shade from the tamarisk trees that cover the campground.

If you prefer to explore the southern reaches of the Anza-Borrego via Highway S-2, there are three convenient sites to seek shelter. Within four miles of one another, **Agua Caliente Regional Park** (39555 SR S-2, 760/765-1188, $15 tent, $25 full RV hook-up) and **Vallecito Regional Park** (37349 SR S-2, 760/765-1188, $15 per site) are county-run parks that both feature developed campgrounds. There are no hook-up sites available, but RVs are allowed there. Agua Caliente has the added benefit of two mineral pools on the grounds, but most of the campsites are exposed to the elements and the pools tend to attract more crowds. Vallecito is quieter, home of the Vallecito Stage Station. Many of the sites here are situated under mesquite and smoke trees.

Just a little north of these sites, **Butterfield Ranch** (14925 SR S-2, 760/765-1463, $20 camping, $25 full RV hook up, $95 cabins) is a private facility that offers RV and tent camping, primitive camping huts, and more comfortable cedar cabins. This very family-oriented property takes the rough out of roughing it. There are two swimming pools on-site, a clubhouse with games and books, and a small general store. Also on site is a comfortable lounge with a big-screen TV, fireplace, and wireless Internet access.

FOOD

Borrego Springs is pretty much the only place to find restaurants out in the desert. Most places here are informal, but there is one exception to that. La Casa del Zorro's **Butterfield Room** (3845 Yaqui Pass Rd, 760/767-5323, www.lacasadelzorro.com, 8 A.M.–11 A.M., 11:30 A.M.–2:30 P.M. and 6 P.M.–9:30 P.M. daily, $30) offers a fine-dining experience with Contemporary California cuisine and a wine selection that has won accolades from *Wine Spectator* magazine. The menu changes frequently, but look for the venison and the lamb if available; both are melt-in-your-mouth delicious. This is also a good spot for a nicely prepared breakfast.

On the opposite end of the spectrum, **Jilberto's Mexican Restaurant** (655 Palm Canyon Dr # F, 760/767-1008, 7 A.M.–10 P.M. daily, $4) is the kind of place where you order at the counter and pick up your food when

JULIAN

your number is called. This a favorite place for ravenous hikers and cyclists who come here to fill up on the absolutely huge portions for very cheap.

Across the street, **Carlee's** (660 W Palm Canyon Dr., 760/767-3262, 11 A.M.–9 P.M. daily, $10) is a sit-down bar and grill with a friendly vibe. The locals and snowbirds pack the place on winter weekends and most nights in the spring to select from pizza, steaks, burgers, and the like before crooning away on the karaoke machine. Call ahead to see if you can have them reserve a table.

On the east end of town at the Palms at Indian Head, **Krazy Koyote** (2220 Hoberg Rd., 800/434-6835, 5:30 P.M.–8 P.M. Wed.–Thurs., 5:30 P.M.–9 P.M. Fri.–Sun., $25) is a good place to sip on a martini and enjoy an appetizer like baked brie or pâté with crackers. Entrées include beef Wellington, prime cuts of steak, and pork chops. They are tasty, but a bit overpriced for what you get. If you're feeling naughty, just go for appetizers and dessert. The menu of prepared sweets here is one of the best in town.

To prepare for a long hike, I'd recommend **Red Ocotillo** (818 Palm Canyon Dr., 760/767-7400, 7 A.M.–9 P.M., $9) on the west end of town. Set in an old Quonset hut, this place offers huge breakfasts and lunches and even serves some to-go. The pet-friendly patio is a highlight of the place, with a lovely little garden and shaded seating.

Finally, if the mood strikes you for some ice cream, **The Fudge Factory** (590 Palm Canyon Dr., 760/767-5407, 8 A.M.–4 P.M. Tues.–Sun.) serves it up along with its tempting selection of fudge, locally cultivated honey, and other confectionaries.

If you are wandering around the southern section of the desert, there is a general store at Agua Caliente that serves cold beverages and has a limited supply of snacks and groceries.

INFORMATION AND SERVICES

Emergency services are available in Borrego Springs. The local county **sheriff's office**

is at 565 Palm Canyon Drive, and rangers can be reached at the **Anza-Borrego State Park Headquarters** (200 Palm Canyon Dr., 760/767-5311) on the same drive leading to the visitors center. The **Borrego Medical Center** (4343 Yaqui Pass Rd., Borrego Springs, 760/767-5051) offers a small emergency room and can facilitate airlifts in the event of major injuries.

GETTING THERE AND AROUND

Most people drive into the desert via car. There are three major routes from the west end of the county. You can take Montezuma's Grade along Highway S-22 from the Warner Springs area to Borrego Springs and beyond. Or you can head down Banner Grade along Highway 78 from Julian. Note: Montezuma's Grade is not accessible to RVs. If you drive an RV, you have to take Highway 78 from Julian to Yaqui Pass. This route will give you three choices along the way. You can either cut north through Yaqui Pass and to Borrego Springs via Highway S-3. This is the favored route for San Diegans to reach the town. Or you can continue along Highway 78 into the tiny hamlet of Ocotillo Wells and the Ocotillo Wells State Vehicular Recreation Area. Or you can head southwest on Highway S-2, which will send you to the southern sector of the park. Another option for the southern reaches is to head east on I-8 until you cross the county line and then take Highway S-2 back northeast through the small town of Ocotillo and into the state park. This is the easiest route to Agua Caliente and Vallecitos from San Diego.

Gas is not readily available in most of the park, so plan ahead. Borrego Springs has three fill-up stations, Ocotillo Wells has one, and so does Ocotillo, just off I-8.

If your car is acting funny and you can limp it into Borrego Springs, **Tito's Auto Repair** (1233-A Palm Canyon Dr., 760/767-3029, 8 A.M.–5:30 P.M. daily) can help get you up and running again.

GATEWAY TO BAJA

Drive a half hour south of downtown San Diego and you might think to yourself, "It's like a different country down here." Um, that's 'cause it is. The southern county line borders Mexico. Just seventeen miles south of downtown lies Baja California, a 1,000-mile peninsula full of natural beauty and inhabited by friendly and warm people.

But before you drive over the border, don't just zip by "the rest of the county" on your march south. Known as South Bay, the culture here is a synthesis of the laid-back San Diego lifestyle and Baja's fun-loving appreciation for family and community.

Walk down Seacoast Boulevard in the sleepy town of Imperial Beach and you'll see wet-suited dad and son, surfboards atop their heads, sharing the sidewalk with a family of anglers loaded with fish freshly caught from the pier. At Bayfront Park in Chula Vista, carne asada sizzles on the grill next to hot dogs as kids play tag, screeching out at each other in "Spanglish."

The welcoming fiesta into Mexico is right over the border in Tijuana, a vibrant city 1.3 million people strong. Known simply as TJ to most San Diegans, Tijuana has drawn free-wheeling Americans for decades. The allure started during prohibition, when boozehounds would drink and gamble the night away at Agua Caliente Casino. Prohibition ended and the casino was torn down when Mexico banned gambling in the 1930s, but the tourists kept coming to TJ.

Today the all-night dance clubs and the lower drinking age still attract the partiers.

© ERICKA CHICKOWSKI

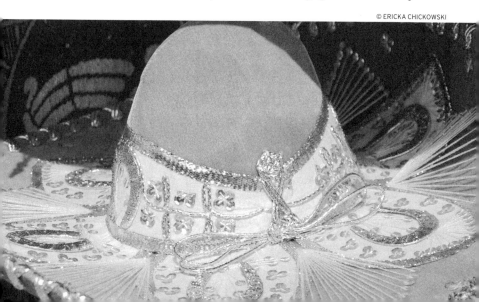

HIGHLIGHTS

◖ **Chula Vista Nature Center:** This wildlife zoo situated on the Sweetwater Marsh National Wildlife Refuge offers an interesting peek into the ecological diversity of the coastal wetland (page 230).

◖ **Avenida Revolución:** The cacophony of shopkeepers, night-club loudspeakers, and mariachi music is all part of the effervescent energy exuded on this most famous street in Tijuana (page 237).

◖ **Tijuana Cultural Center:** The distinctive sphere of the OmniMax theater greets visitors to one of the most important centers for art and history in Mexico (page 238).

◖ **Tecate:** This tranquil border town east of Tijuana offers a contrasting view of life along the *frontera*. Visitors tour the Tecate *cervecería*, sup on a lazy afternoon meal, stroll the plaza, and head home when the town shutters in the evening (page 247).

◖ **Riviera del Pacífico:** Built as a casino with mob money in the 1930s, this Mediterranean-style building is now home to a history museum, an art center, and some of the prettiest greenery in Ensenada (page 251).

◖ **La Bufadora:** This impressive marine sea spout sprays water more than 80 feet in the air above delightedly shrieking onlookers.

The walkway leading to this natural wonder is filled with a bustling flea market (page 252).

LOOK FOR ◖ TO FIND RECOMMENDED SIGHTS, ACTIVITIES, DINING, AND LODGING.

But the steady procession of adventure seekers also come to hunt for bargains in the city's mishmash of *mercados* (markets), to experience the thrill of a Mexican bullfight, and to eat their way through the city. Not only are the street tacos a big draw, but hidden away from the tourist clap-trap of Avenida Revolución there are a number of fine restaurants that rival some of San Diego's best.

There's plenty more of the Baja coast that is easily accessible in a couple hours' drive from San Diego. Just seventeen miles south of Tijuana, Rosarito is a carefree beach town that has a set of its own thumping discos.

Some of them are set right on the sand. Its collection of art galleries, furniture-makers, and craftspeople is one of the best in Baja.

Keep driving and you'll encounter the lobster village of Puerto Nuevo and its assortment of tasty seafood eateries, world-renowned surf spots, and incredible ocean vistas on the way to Ensenada.

This port town just 60 miles from the border is the last glimmer of civilization before the road south turns truly wild—bumpy roads, baked deserts, virgin beaches, and all. Some travelers down the coast choose Ensenada as a gateway to longer adventures,

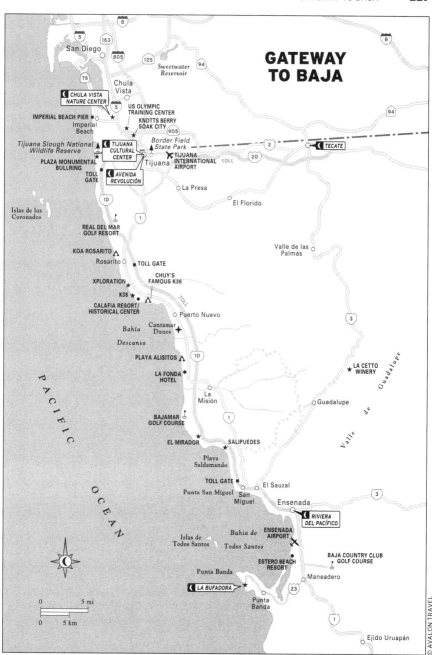

GATEWAY TO BAJA

San Diego

Chula Vista

Sweetwater Reservoir

CHULA VISTA NATURE CENTER

US OLYMPIC TRAINING CENTER

IMPERIAL BEACH PIER

Imperial Beach

KNOTTS BERRY SOAK CITY

TECATE

Tijuana Slough National Wildlife Reserve

TIJUANA CULTURAL CENTER

Border Field State Park

PLAZA MONUMENTAL BULLRING

TIJUANA INTERNATIONAL AIRPORT

Tijuana

AVENIDA REVOLUCIÓN

TOLL GATE

La Presa

El Florido

Islas de los Coronados

REAL DEL MAR GOLF RESORT

Valle de las Palmas

KOA ROSARITO

Rosarito

TOLL GATE

CHUY'S FAMOUS K36

XPLORATION

K38

CALAFIA RESORT/ HISTORICAL CENTER

Puerto Nuevo

Bahía Descanso

Cantamar Dunes

LA CETTO WINERY

PLAYA ALISITOS

LA FONDA HOTEL

La Misión

Guadalupe

BAJAMAR GOLF COURSE

EL MIRADOR

SALIPUEDES

Playa Saldamando

PACIFIC OCEAN

TOLL GATE

El Sauzal

Punta San Miguel

San Miguel

Ensenada

RIVIERA DEL PACÍFICO

Islas de Todos Santos

Bahía de Todos Santos

ENSENADA AIRPORT

BAJA COUNTRY CLUB GOLF COURSE

ESTERO BEACH RESORT

Maneadero

Punta Banda

LA BUFADORA

Punta Banda

Ejido Uruapán

0   5 mi

0   5 km

© AVALON TRAVEL

others pick it as a turnaround point back to San Diego. Either way they all stop for a walk along the waterfront *malecón*, a day of shopping, or a few margaritas at the centenarian bar, Hussong's Cantina.

PLANNING YOUR TIME

This chapter is meant to be a guide for those who have one to three extra days to add to their San Diego travels. The Baja destinations included here are all reachable in under two hours, most in under an hour. If you choose

judiciously, it is possible to tour all the way to Ensenada in a single day. However, in only one day I recommend limiting your travel to Tijuana or Rosarito Beach. This will give you more time for shopping, eating, and strolling the lively boulevards and *avenidas*.

Ensenada is best visited with two or more days on your hands. This way you'll have time to leisurely drive down the coast and to stop at roadside attractions along the way. It also ensures that you'll be around when local museums and parks are still open.

South Bay

San Diego's South Bay area is lined with bedroom communities leading southward to the border. Imperial Beach is the most southwesterly beach town in the States, and visitors there can check out the physical barrier that runs along the beach and into the water marking the international border. Chula Vista's parks and wildlife refuge are a pleasant stop for families. And the border crossing at San Ysidro is the busiest in the world.

SIGHTS
U.S. Olympic Training Center

You're bound to feel guilty about all those sumptuous vacation dinners when you watch the athletes sweat it out on the grounds of the U.S. Olympic Training Center (2800 Olympic Pkwy., 619/656-1500) in Chula Vista. Located next to Lower Otay Lake, this 155-acre complex is where athletes in field hockey, soccer, paddling, tennis, track, and cycling come to sharpen their skills and perfect their physiques in order to compete for medals in the summer games.

Visitors are invited to view the facilities from an elevated platform at the Copley Visitor Center between 10 A.M. and 5 P.M. Monday through Sunday; free guided tours of the grounds are conducted at 1:30 P.M. Tuesday through Saturday.

Knott's Berry Soak City

If the sand is rubbing you the wrong way, Knott's Berry Soak City (2052 Entertainment Cir., Chula Vista, 619/661-7373) offers a chlorinated alternative in the summer months. This 32-acre water park has a wave pool, a rafting river, and slides galore. There's the windy and twisted kind, the kind that'll push your stomach up to your eyeballs, and the itty-bitty ones for the tykes. The park is open every day from June through August and on the weekends in May and September. Hours are generally 10 A.M. through 6 P.M. or 7 P.M., but they vary so call ahead. Tickets are $27.95 for adults and $16.95 for kids and seniors.

◖ Chula Vista Nature Center

Located on the 316-acre Sweetwater Marsh National Wildlife Refuge, the Chula Vista Nature Center (1000 Gunpowder Point Dr., 619/409-5900, www.chulavistanaturecenter .org, 10 A.M.–5 P.M. Tues.–Sun., $6) is a regional zoo and aquarium that educates visitors about the fragile wetland ecosystem and its significance in light of the disappearing estuaries and marshes along the Southern California coastline.

Indoor and outdoor exhibits put the spotlight on the web of animals and plants that keep the San Diego Bay and Sweetwater Marsh in a healthy state of balance. Come one on one

© ERICKA CHICKOWSKI

Imperial Beach – the locals call it "IB"

with an American Kestrel or a Hooded Merganser at the raptor and shorebird aviaries. Or make fish faces at a spotfin croaker or a kelp bass at one of the many aquariums.

Outside there are a number of gardens onsite and a 1.5-mile nature trail winds through the marsh next to the center.

Beaches and Parks

After a morning or afternoon at the nature center, **Bayfront Park** (J St. and Marina Pkwy., 6 A.M.–10:30 P.M. daily) on Chula Vista Harbor is a nice place to relax with a picnic lunch or dinner. This peninsular park is situated across from Coronado Cays on the south end of San Diego Bay. The well-manicured greens here look over the fleet of sailboats moored at the Chula Vista Marina. In the breeze the trees that dot the lawns swish in time with the rhythmic pinging of rigging against mast. If you didn't bring anything to munch on there is a concession stand at the park, along with picnic tables, a gazebo, playground equipment, and fire rings.

There is also a small sandy beach, but if you crave the ocean you're better off driving a couple of miles south down to **Imperial Beach,** which is presided over by the 1,491-foot long **Imperial Beach Pier** (910 Seacoast Dr., 24 hours daily) at the Portwood Pier Plaza. The plaza is decked out with reminders of IB's pioneering watermen, sporting vintage surfboard benches and a giant board-inspired sculpture called **Surfhenge** that arcs over the entrance to the pier. In the summer visitors flock to the sand like seagulls to fast-food wrappers. They also gather at Dunes Park, a grassy beachfront area with picnic tables, a jungle gym, and horseshoe pits and volleyball courts.

There is respite from the crowds on the southwesternmost stretch of sand in the States at **Border Field State Park.** The beach here is always less crowded than Imperial Beach, as it is across the Tijuana Estuary from the more populous beach and requires a circuitous route from the town of Imperial Beach's main drags to reach it. Walk south down this shore and you'll eventually come across the rusty corrugated metal border fence that runs all the way out in the ocean to keep illegal immigrants from sneaking into the United States.

Border Field State Park is also home to the **Tijuana Slough National Wildlife Reserve,** a sensitive wetland that has in the past been plagued with toxic sewage and garbage dumped into the Tijuana River further upstream. This waterway mainly runs through Mexican soil until it takes a lazy turn north of the border to deposit itself into the ocean on the American side of the fence. Environmentalists on both sides of the border have been working hard to fix the pollution problem facing the Tijuana River and the U.S. Department of Fish and Wildlife has made incredible strides in rehabilitating the Tijuana Slough since the reserve was founded 25 years ago. Those who take a hike or ride horseback through the trails here will see evidence of that in the hundreds of species of birds that come here to hunt and nest.

The park has an award-winning visitors center (619/575-2704) that is open from Wednesday through Sunday between 10 A.M. and 5 P.M.

ENTERTAINMENT AND EVENTS
Beach Bars
Most of the hottest clubs and bars are just south of the border in Tijuana. But when the mood strikes for a midday pick-me-up by the beach, Imperial Beach does have a few establishments that can happily oblige.

If you're a sucker for bars that double as geographical novelties, **IB Forum Sports Bar & Grill** (1079 Seacoast Dr., 619/429-7507, 11 A.M.–11:30 P.M. Sun.–Thurs., 11 A.M.–12:30 P.M. Fri., 8 A.M.–12:30 P.M. Sat.) likes to trumpet its position as the most southwesterly bar and grill in the United States. It also happens to be a relaxing place to grab a long-neck and enjoy a ballgame on one of the numerous TV screens scattered about the bar.

On the other end of the beach strip is IB's iconic bar, **Ye Olde Plank Inn** (24 Palm Ave., 619/423-5976, 6 A.M.–2 A.M. daily). Built in the late 1880s, this is the oldest building in town. The bar is also the oldest watering hole in Impe-

rial Beach, first opening it doors in 1969 when this was still a seedy biker town by the sea. The place maintains a divey sensibility while drawing a much friendlier crowd these days.

Between Ye Olde Plank and IB Forum, **Woodies Waterfront Patio Bar** (710 Seacoast Dr., 619/628-0777, 11 A.M.–midnight daily) is within casting distance of the pier. The bar is part of the Beach Club Grille, so it's possible to sit in the ocean breeze while throwing down a couple of beers and eating your fill of pub grub.

Events
Summertime is events season in South Bay and Imperial kicks it off with a lick of spice and soulful music during the **IB Chili and Jazz Festival.** This weekend-long event in June would be the highlight of the year for most small towns, but is annually trumped by the even bigger to-do of the **U.S. Open Sand Castle Competition** held the last weekend in July. This is South Bay's biggest event, drawing 250,000 spectators and competitors over three days each year. During the competition revelers are entertained by a festive parade and a fireworks display from the pier.

You might not know it, but at one point Chula Vista used to be the lemon capital of the world. Suburbs and strip malls have mostly replaced the fragrant lemon groves, but the town likes to celebrate its heritage every August with the **Lemon Festival** street fair.

During the holiday season Chula Vista is also the best place in South Bay to find a good old-fashioned parade. Carolers, marching bands, floats, and Ol' Saint Nick stream by Third Avenue in procession during the **Starlight Parade** in early December.

SHOPPING
Shopping fans shouldn't be so quick to hurry through the Mexican border at San Ysidro. If you take the time to exit before crossing over you'll be rewarded with some pretty sweet deals at the outlet stores in this small border town. This is where many San Diego locals come to score brand-name clothes for cheap.

© ERICKA CHICKOWSKI

a quiet afternoon in Imperial Beach

The largest concentration is at **The Shops at Las Americas** (10 A.M.–9 P.M. Mon.–Fri., 10 A.M.–8 P.M. Sat., 10 A.M.–5 P.M. Sun.). This stylish plaza features over 100 stores, including bargain shops from Adidas, Guess, Calvin Klein, and American Eagle Outfitters.

Right across the street is the smaller **San Diego Factory Outlet Center** (10 A.M.–8 P.M. Mon.–Fri., 10 A.M.–7 P.M. Sat., 10 A.M.–6 P.M. Sun.) which also has a handful of shops. Here you can find outlets from OshKosh B'Gosh, Sunglass Hut, and Carter's Childrenswear.

SPORTS AND RECREATION

With both the pier and the jetties coming into play, Imperial Beach makes for a good spot to rip on the waves during a heavy swell. **The Surf Hut** (710 Seacoast Dr., Ste. D, Imperial Beach, tel. 619/575-7873, 11 A.M.–7 P.M. Mon.–Fri., 10 A.M.–6 P.M. Sat., 11 A.M.–5 P.M. Sun.) near the pier is a good place to rent gear and stock up on wax.

Imperial Beach's population of anglers can usually be found dangling their lines over the rails at Imperial Beach Pier. The bait shop of choice for many is **Cox Bait & Tackle** (996 Palm Ave., 619/429-8942, 9:30 A.M.–2 P.M. Sun., 9:30 A.M.–3 P.M. Mon., 8 A.M.–4 P.M. Tues.–Fri., 8 A.M.–5 P.M. Sat.), about a mile away from the pier.

ACCOMMODATIONS

Finding a place to rest one's head in Chula Vista can be a tricky proposition, as some areas are less safe than others. If you're interested in staying in the South Bay, try looking in downtown Chula Vista near Third Street. One of the best places to stay in this revitalized commercial district is **El Primero Boutique** (416 Third Avenue, 619/425-4486, $125 d). This Zig-Zag Modern building has a lot of art deco flair, both inside and out. The lobby is accented with diamond-pattern marble tiling, potted palms, and comfy modern furnishings that evoke the feeling of old Havana-style entrances in South Beach. Rooms are comfortable, bright, and clean. Each morning guests are treated to a healthy continental breakfast out in the center courtyard.

Those in town for the sandcastle competition in Imperial Beach can get a good view of the action from a beachfront room at **Seacoast Inn** (800 Seacoast Dr., 619/424-5183, $75 d). This motel is a little worse for wear and the rooms are basic, but it makes up the difference with its beachfront location and reasonable prices.

Camping

Those planning on rumbling their RV down I-5 toward Baja California should make plans to stop off at the **Chula Vista RV Resort** (460 Sandpiper Way, 619/422-0111, www.chula vistarv.com, $52). This well-cared-for property is as ritzy as an RV park gets. Backed up against the San Diego Bay, 237 full hookup sites are only about 50 yards from the Chula Vista Marina. Each one comes with a cozy shaded picnic table with cushioned benches. The property has two waterfront restaurants, a heated pool and spa, putting green, free Wi-Fi access, and a general store. Pets are also allowed.

Sweetwater Regional Park (3218 Summit Meadow Road, Bonita, 619/472-7572, $20 per site) on the Sweetwater Reservoir is one of the few natural spaces in South Bay appropriate for tent campers. All sites are also RV friendly and come with the standard fire grate and picnic table. The campground has a large picnic pavilion, making it an ideal spot for a trip with extended family. It also features a separate equestrian camping facility that can be a good headquarters for those bringing their horses to explore the Tijuana River Slough Wildlife Reserve.

FOOD
Beach Fare

The dining choices in Imperial Beach are limited, so don't go there expecting to nosh on much more than the traditional stock of burgers, hot dogs, and fried seafood. But what area beach shacks do make, they make well.

This is especially true at the much-loved ◖ **Stardust Donut Shop** (698 Hwy. 75, 619/424-6200, 8:30 A.M.–2 P.M. Tues.–Fri., 9:30 A.M.–2 P.M. Sat., closed Sun., $3), a stand on the road to Silver Strand whose house specialty is the cinnamon roll. This pastry glazed

with sticky icing is a secret that the late-waking regulars hope to keep under wraps for fear of stumbling up to the window after the shop has run out for the day. If you don't make it in time the donuts are still a fine consolation.

Over by the pier, **Cow-A-Bunga** (137 Elm Ave., 619/628-0508, 8:30 A.M.–sunset daily, $3) bills itself as a "Micro Ice Creamery" and in the style of a microbrewery it churns all of its ice cream fresh on the premises. There are usually at least ten flavors on display at any one time, including sugar- and fat-free options. It will mix in candies and fruits on the spot or scoop out a sundae to order.

For something more substantial, walk to the end of the pier for a seafood meal at **Tin Fish** (Pier End, 619/628-8414, 11 A.M.–7 P.M. Sun.–Thurs., 11 A.M.–8 P.M. Fri.–Sat., $11). Tin Fish doles out fried-fish platters in half a dozen ways. You can get fish-and-chips with waffle fries, a fish "dog" in a bun, and fish tacos. Plus there's clam chowder and several kinds of crunchy crustaceans. Take your wax paper–lined basket out on the pier deck and enjoy the sunset from beneath the patio umbrellas.

Mexican

This close to the border it is difficult to go wrong when searching for delicious Mexican eats. If you insist on finding the "best" Mexican *comida* in South Bay on your own you might just find yourself eating through a lifetime's worth of *chilaquiles,* tacos, tamales, and burritos.

I'll help with a little crib sheet. In Chula Vista, **Tacos El Gordo** (689 H St., 619/691-8848) serves up some of the most authentic Tijuana-style street tacos this side of the *frontera.* Simplicity is this street taco's key: a small round disc of corn tortilla topped with meat still sizzling from the grill and garnished with a little bit of cilantro, onion, and salsa. The attraction of this particular place is its dazzling array of meats, from carne asada to spicy *adobada* pork, and from chorizo to *tripas.* You'll be able to bone up on the Mexican ingredient dictionary right from the counter.

A block away from the waves of Imperial

Beach, **El Tapatio Mexican Food** (260 Palm Ave., Imperial Beach, 619/423-3443) is favored by surfers for its juicy carne asada burritos, but it also has other staples like fish tacos and *taquitos*. Those looking to score a tasty tamale after hanging at the beach should pull off at **Echale Mexican Restaurant** (1850 Coronado Ave., Imperial Beach, 619/429-1398) before hitting the I-5 on-ramp.

Also in this neck of the woods is a place suited for family members who can't agree exactly on the type of Mexican food they crave: **Victoria's Mexican Food** (1912 Coronado Ave., Ste. 107, Imperial Beach, 619/429-1109). The menu is huge, with *tortas,* tacos, burritos, and soups rounding out the list.

INFORMATION AND SERVICES

Palm Boulevard is the main drag in Imperial Beach, and is where you'll find an ample choice of banks and gas stations. Similarly, Third Av-

enue in Chula Vista will keep you in the gas and the cash. Emergency medical services are most conveniently provided at **Scripps Mercy Hospital Chula Vista** (435 H St., Chula Vista, 619/691-7000). The **Chula Vista police station** is at 315 4th Avenue (619/691-5137), while the **Imperial Beach police** can be found at 845 Imperial Beach Boulevard (619/498-2400).

GETTING THERE AND AROUND

South Bay is serviced by the **San Diego Trolley's Blue Line,** which makes seven stops in this region. To get to Imperial Beach via public transit you can take the #933 connector from the Palm Avenue trolley station.

Greyhound Bus stops right at the border at the **San Ysidro Greyhound Station** (799 E. San Ysidro Blvd., 619/428-1194). Visitors wishing to take a bus farther down the Baja peninsula can walk across the border to catch a bus located right on the other side.

Tijuana

Less than 30 minutes from San Diego, but a whole world away, Mexico is an often overlooked day trip for many U.S. travelers coming to the region. Which is a shame, because the northern Baja cities have a lot to offer to many types of travelers. Foodies will love the options—from street-cart tacos to world-class haute cuisine—shoppers will get a kick out of bargaining for Mexican pottery, silver, and handicrafts, surfers will be stoked to rip it up on the breaks that are scattered across the 70 miles between Tijuana and Ensenada, and adventurers will be absorbed by the vistas presented on the ribbon of road that leads down the Baja coast.

TJ, as the locals call it, is a must-visit for partiers and shoppers in town for a San Diego vacation. The town is home to dozens of open-air markets and a very thriving nightlife. Discos and bars are often open all night.

The rest of this chapter covers the highlights

of Baja that are easily reachable from San Diego. Prices given here are all in U.S. dollars.

SIGHTS
Tijuana Wax Sculptures Museum

Known as the Museo de Cera to the locals, the Tijuana Wax Museum is the first attraction that you'll stumble across after walking from the border and over the Rio Tijuana by way of the pedestrian footbridge. Located along the path leading east from the bridge, it is only about two and a half blocks away between Avenidas Negrete and Madero. Use the giant Tijuana Arch as your guide—the museum is in the same plaza as this towering landmark.

This small museum presents an immobile parade of both American and Mexican celebrities and icons. There's Arnold Schwarzenegger and Elvis, Frida Kahlo and Emiliano Zapata.

Madame Tussaud's this is not, but let's get real. You're allowed to stroll through here for

GATEWAY TO BAJA

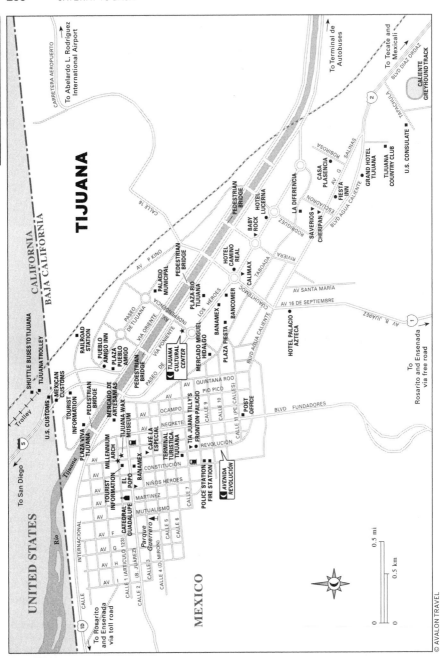

TIJUANA

UNITED STATES

CALIFORNIA
BAJA CALIFORNIA

MEXICO

To San Diego

To Terminal de
Autobuses

To Tecate and
Mexicali

CALIENTE
GREYHOUND TRACK

U.S. CONSULATE

To Abelardo L. Rodriguez
International Airport

CARRETERA AEROPUERTO

BLVD DIAZ ORDAZ

TECATE

GRAND HOTEL
TIJUANA

TIJUANA
COUNTRY CLUB

CASA
PLASENCIA

ROBINSOSA

AV. G

FIESTA
INN

SALINAS

SAVERIOS

CHERIPAN

LA DIFERENCIA

RODRIGUEZ

BLVD AGUA CALIENTE

BABY
ROCK

HOTEL
LUCERNA

PEDESTRIAN
BRIDGE

CALLE 18

AV. P KINO

PALACIO
MUNICIPAL

PEDESTRIAN
BRIDGE

PLAZA RIO
TIJUANA

HOTEL
CAMINO
REAL

RIVIERA

CALIMAX

TABOADA

AV SANTA MARÍA

CUAUHTEMOC

AV 16 DE SEPTIEMBRE

HOTEL PALACIO
AZTECA

AV B. JUAREZ

To
Rosarito and Ensenada
via free road

PASEO
DE TIJUANA

VIA ORIENTE

INDEPENDENCIA

LOS HEROES

MERCADO MIGUEL
HIDALGO

BANAMEX

BANCOMER

PLAZA FIESTA

TIJUANA
CULTURAL
CENTER

PASEO DE

VIA PONIENTE

RAILROAD
STATION

PUEBLO
AMIGO INN

PLAZA
PUEBLO
AMIGO

PEDESTRIAN
BRIDGE

QUINTANA ROO

PID PICO

AV

AV

CALLE 9

CALLE 10

CALLE 31 (PE. CALLES)

POST
OFFICE

BLVD   FUNDADORES

OCAMPO

NEGRETE

REVOLUCIÓN

CONSTITUCIÓN

NIÑOS HEROES

MARTINEZ

MUTUALISMO

TIA JUANA TILLY'S

FRONTON PALACIO

TERMINAL
TURISTICA
TIJUANA

CAFÉ LA
ESPECIAL

AVENIDA
REVOLUCION

POLICE STATION
FIRE STATION

SHUTTLE BUSES TO TIJUANA

TIJUANA TROLLEY

MEXICAN
CUSTOMS

TOURIST
INFORMATION

PEDESTRIAN
BRIDGE

MERCADO DE
ARTESANIAS

TIJUANA WAX
MUSEUM

MILLENNIUM
ARCH

PLAZA VIVA
TIJUANA

U.S. CUSTOMS

Trolley

BANAMEX

EL
POPO

TOURIST
INFORMATION

CATEDRAL
GUADALUPE

Parque
Guerrero

INTERNACIONAL

CALLE 1 (ARTICULO 123)

CALLE 2 (B. JUAREZ)

CALLE 3

CALLE 4 (O. MIRON)

CALLE 5

CALLE 6

CALLE 7

AV

AV

AV

AV

AV

AV

AV

AV

F

G

H

Rio

Tijuana

To San Diego

5

To Rosarito
and Ensenada
via toll road

1D

CALLE

0   0.5 mi

0   0.5 km

© AVALON TRAVEL

© ERICKA CHICKOWSKI

street musicians in Plaza Santa Cecilia

only about $1.50, so don't be a cheapskate whiner when you see the misshapen face of 1980s-era Sylvester Stallone. The artist did a better job with him than his plastic surgeon did in later years, after all.

◖ Avenida Revolución

Stepping out of the wax museum you'll now be in place to march toward the biggest tourism spectacle in town, Avenida Revolución—or just "La Revo" to those in the know. The square you are in at the moment is Plaza Santa Cecilia, named for the patron saint of musicians. The namesake becomes apparent as you walk this small plaza and encounter the nattily dressed mariachi and *norteño* musicians standing at the ready to entertain passersby and diners who have stopped at one of numerous cafés and small restaurants here. If you feel like listening, be sure to tip these hardworking artists, as that is their sole source of income.

Right in the thick of the plaza is the **Millenium Arch,** a 200-foot glimmering curve that is spoked with giant wires holding up a giant clock. This huge landmark straddles the corner of Calle 1 and La Revo, a giant beacon to the pandemonium to come. Take a left and head down to Calle 2, but before you overstimulate your senses take the time for a brief detour.

Head two blocks west on Calle 2 to take a look at Nuestra Señora de Guadalupe on the northeast corner of that street and Avenida Niños Heroes. Built in the 1940s this church is a beautiful Mexican cathedral that is worth a look no matter your faith. Diagonal from the church is a very authentic *mercado* called **El Popo** that is filled with trinkets, candies, and savories.

Now, take a deep breath and head back toward La Revo. Heading south you've got about eight or nine blocks to wander, all filled with nightclubs, jewelry stores, leather shops, curio stands, and restaurants. Street peddlers hawking glittering bracelets and knock-off sunglasses mingle between the tourists that throng the sidewalks. Shopkeepers stand guard at their doors, calling out to entice passersby for a look. Club promoters blow whistles and hand out flyers for drink specials and upcoming fiestas.

As you walk the sidewalk you'll also come across at least one of the ever-so-exotic "Tijuana zebras," donkeys painted in stripes to look like their equine cousins. Since the 1940s they have been fixtures in the city's tourist zones, enticing visitors to buy a photo opportunity with them in front of the colorful Mexican murals they stand near. I say that after about four decades or so, something so everlastingly tacky just morphs into a historical landmark, no?

Between Calles 7 and 8 stands **Frontón Palacio,** the arena that used to entertain spectators with fast-paced jai-alai matches. The athletes are gone now, but it is an impressive example of Spanish architecture with an ornate and colorful pediment over its three arched entryways.

This makes a good turnaround point to give yourself time for another detour off of La Revo. Head back to Calle 4 and veer left (west), walking five blocks until you reach a green square of tranquility they call **Parque Teniente Guerrero.** This little urban oasis is a pleasant daytime destination for Tijuana families to come for a stroll or a picnic or some fun time on the playground. Couples cuddle on benches, kids tug on their parents' sleeves to beg for popcorn or candy from street vendors. In the distance you can see the arch standing guard over the city.

Be sure to come here with plenty of daylight left, as this area leads a double life. When the sun is shining it is pleasant and safe, but at night the shady characters take over the park and it is not a nice place to be after dark.

C Tijuana Cultural Center

Even though it sits at the extreme northwestern point of the country, Tijuana is actually one of the largest axis points of art and culture in Mexico. At the epicenter of this scene is the Tijuana Cultural Center, called Centro Cultural Tijuana or just CECUT by the locals. This large-scale hub of art and history takes up an entire city block along Paseo de los Héroes between Calle Mina and Avenida Independencia. The complex is made up of two major buildings. The most distinctive is the giant brown snowcone of a structure that holds an OmniMax Theater. This dome dominates the central plaza, which leads up to the facility's main structure.

Inside there is a 1,000-seat performing arts hall, and numerous public corridors displaying a rotating crop of fine art. This is where the Museum of the Californias is located. This historical museum chronicles the history of Baja California and Tijuana with artifacts, reproductions, and scale models. Never mind if your Spanish isn't so good—most of the exhibits here are also described with English placards. CECUT and the museum are open Tuesday through Sunday, 10 a.m. through 6 p.m. Museum admission is $2. The IMAX usually shows a handful of movies daily. Tickets are $4.

ENTERTAINMENT AND EVENTS
Bullfights

Brought over by the Spanish colonials who first founded Mexico, the ancient sport of bullfighting is alive and well in Tijuana, where the matadors still don their flashy, sequined outfits and wave their capes at raging *toros* to get them close enough for the kill. As with most places that still practice this sport, its continued existence in Tijuana is a divisive one between certain circles. Some believe the sport is barbaric and inhumane. Others say that it is an important

BULLRING LIMBO

Tijuana once had two bullrings, but the historic Toreo de Tijuana currently faces an uncertain future and is indefinitely closed. This ring is owned by Hugo Hank, a powerful Tijuana figure who acted as mayor of the city and also owns the Agua Caliente racetrack and gambling empire in town. He had plans to tear the bullring down for other development but was stopped halfway through demolition by a grassroots organization intent on saving the historic building. Until the community figures out what to do with the facility it sits dormant.

cultural pastime, part of the fabric of Mexican life. Dating back all the way to Roman times, the ritualistic fight between man and bull is regarded by fans as a test between man and nature, a contest of courage between the matador and bull. Many Mexicans are passionate about the sport and bullfighting aficionados pick apart a fight like they would a work of art, discussing nuances and events in the bullring that are often missed by the uninitiated.

But the end of a successful fight is the death of an animal, so it is important to remember this before buying tickets. Those who do enjoy the fights don't take kindly to squeamish foreigners who might try to impose their opinions about the gory nature of bullfighting.

Bullfighting season runs from June through September, with fights held at the **Bullring by the Sea** (tel. 664/680-1808), also called Plaza Monumental. Tickets can be bought in advance from www.bullfights.org.

From downtown drive six miles west on Highway 1-D. It is the largest building in Playas de Tijuana and is located directly off the highway, so you can't miss it.

Lucha Libre

Vince McMahon and his WWE cronies have got nothin' on the masked marauders of Mexican wrestling. Translated loosely as "free fighting," *lucha libre* packs in twice the drama and adrenaline of its more staged American counterpart.

Donning colorful masks and flamboyant costumes, the *luchadores* are often seen flying from the ropes while on the quest to pin their opponents to the mats. Aside from soccer and bullfighting, *lucha libre* is one of Mexico's most heralded spectator sports. In Tijuana the locals pack **Auditorio Municipal** (Blvd. Agua Caliente 12421, tel. 664/681-64-74) to the rafters on Friday nights to cheer on their favorite wrestlers. Matches begin at 8:30 P.M. and tickets usually start at around $8.

Dog Racing

Wagering types will want to stake out a spot on the bleachers of the **Hipódromo de Agua Caliente** (Agua Caliente Racetrack, Blvd. Agua Caliente 12027, tel. 664/633-73-00). Every night the greyhounds run after the mechanized bunnies that shoot around this oval. Races start at 7:45 P.M., with an additional run at 2 P.M. on Saturday and Sunday. Admission is free, but parking will set you back $1. As for the bets, well, that's all up to you.

Wine and Brew Tours

There are two temples to fermentation in Tijuana to savor and sip your favorite alcoholic beverage. Located southeast of the Avenida Revolución neighborhood, **L.A. Cetto Winery** (Calle Canon Johnson #2108, tel. 664/685-30-31, 10 A.M.–5:30 P.M. Mon.–Fri., 10 A.M.–4 P.M. Sat., closed Sun., tours $2) is Mexico's most prolific producer of vino. The grapes are grown in the Guadalupe Valley, between here and Ensenada, and much of the fermentation is done at this Tijuana facility. Tour the winery and then stop at the very cozy tasting room to sample the reds and whites of Baja.

Take a cab even farther south to the **TJ Brewery** (Blvd. Fundadores #2951, tel. 664/684-24-06, 1 P.M.–2 A.M. Mon.–Sat., closed Sun., tours free with reservation), which is a little slice of the Czech Republic. This is the only brewery in the city and the proprietors are pretty proud of their small-batch pilsners. The bar is made up in wood paneling and the menu is an interesting blend of Mexican and Eastern European fare, in honor of the origin of the brews' recipes.

Nightlife

Tijuana has lured four generations of party-loving Americans to cross the border for hopping nightlife. It started during Prohibition, when booze flowed liberally down Mexico way. Today the crowds come for the thumping clubs and bars crammed into downtown and the **Zona Río.**

Most Tijuana clubs work without posted hours and even those that have them tend to be a little more open to interpretation than in the States. The rule of thumb for nightclubs down here is that the party usually doesn't start in earnest until about midnight (though most clubs are open by 10 P.M. or so) and it doesn't shut down until around 5 A.M.

The clubs along **Avenida Revolución** are a zoo come nightfall. The establishments here are teeming with under-21 college students and sailors who come down here from San Diego for the lowered legal drinking age (it's 18, incidentally). Like the shopping in the daytime, you don't come to La Revo for any one specific bar. The standard routine is to amble your way from club to club until dawn or so.

Most Tijuanans consider clubbing in La Revo a low-class experience. The locals much prefer the bars and clubs in the Zona Río, which tend to have nicer and more spacious facilities, and serve better-quality drinks. They do tend to be more spaced out, so you might need to utilize a taxi or two to jump between spots. One of the enduring classics here is **Baby Rock** (Calle Diego Rivera #1482, tel. 664/684-94-38), a pumping saturnalia of techno and dance music illuminated by strobe light. More sophisticated **Como Que No** (Blvd. Sanchez Taboada #9590) usually brings in live salsa bands on the weekends, and during the week plays a mix of recorded salsa and other dance music. Salsa dancers in the know like to

CASINO HISTORY

The American Prohibition was a key time for the development of northern Baja as a host for American entertainment. Mexicans knew there was big financial incentive to give those Americans what they wanted, namely a lot of booze, dancing, and gambling. Entrepreneurs and mobsters teamed up during this time period to open big casinos in Tijuana, Rosarito, and Ensenada. The repeal of Prohibition and the ban on casino operations by the Mexican government in 1935 made short work of these glitzy ventures, but during their short reign they managed to throw such a bacchanalia of entertainment that their legends still live on even today. So do some of their buildings, some of which are tourist attractions in their own right nowadays.

AGUA CALIENTE
Opened in 1926, this Tijuana nightspot was known for entertaining the likes of Charlie Chaplin and Al Capone. The performances here were a major draw and launched the Hollywood careers of such notables as Jimmy Durante, Rita Hayworth, and Fred Astaire.

Upon closure much of the complex was given to the Tijuana public for schools and the opulent decorations were auctioned off throughout the region. The only tourable building left is a minaret on Agua Caliente

Boulevard and the Agua Caliente racetrack, which has replaced ponies with dogs.

ROSARITO BEACH HOTEL
The town of Rosarito was built around this landmark hotel, which in 1925 was opened in the middle of *rancherias* and open land as a glamorous casino resort meant to attract the Hollywood set. When it was forced to shut down the casino, it kept the hotel up and running. Today visitors to the old casino floor are entertained with a nightly dinner and dance show.

RIVIERA DEL PACÍFICO
Ensenada was a late bloomer. It didn't inaugurate its very own gambling establishment until 1930. But when it did, it opened the doors to perhaps the best of the bunch: Riviera del Pacífico. Money was poured into the project publicly by Jack Dempsey, and rumor has it that even the likes of Al Capone had a piece of the pie.

Set on the then-undeveloped Ensenada Bay, this sprawling casino resort was left in ruins for decades after it closed its doors in 1935. In 1978 the government took over the remaining buildings and began restoring its Spanish Revival architecture to develop a cultural center. Today the old casino hall and the bar that once buzzed with starlets is refurbished and open to public tours, as is a beautiful garden outside the building that pays tribute to the opulence of a bygone era.

also branch off to **Antigua Bodega de Papel** (Calle 11, between Revolución and Madero, tel. 664/633-9174), a little café that pushes its tables back for salsa and merengue on Friday and Saturday night.

Club-hopping sans taxi cab in Zona Río isn't completely impossible. Many indecisive clubbers like to go to **Plaza Fiesta** (Paseo de Los Heroes and Ave. Independencia), where there are dozens of clubs, late-night cafés, and bars clustered together in a single edifice. Some of the more popular establishments include the modern digs at **Monte Picacho** (Paseo de Los Heroes and Ave. Independencia, tel. 664/634-16-40) and the Swiss-themed **Sotano Suizo** (Paseo de Los Heroes #9415, tel. 664/684-8834). Same goes for **Pueblo Amigo** (Via Oriente #9211, tel. 664/624-27-00), a plaza across the river from Plaza Fiesta that is home to the ever-present **Señor Frog's** (tel. 664/682-49-58) and to **Rodeo Santa Fe,** (tel. 664/682-49-67) a kitschy club that features a real-live rodeo in its indoor ring every evening at midnight.

SHOPPING

Going to Tijuana to shop for something specific is a bit like spooning through stew to pick out just the carrots or the meat. You'll find the right morsels eventually, but why not take a bite of the entire concoction to get an intact taste of its flavor?

The streets here are a simmering blend of jewelry dealers, leather shops, pottery barns, stained-glass stalls, and curio stands. They're set in open-air markets, underground dens, and shopping plazas that are often a jumbled mix of wares with no real rhyme or reason. But that is the fun of it all. The idea is to browse leisurely—you don't look for something to buy in Tijuana, you stumble upon it.

Plaza Viva Tijuana to Artisan Market

If you're walking across the border, your shopping warm-up routine will be at the Plaza Viva Tijuana, an open square that presents itself right as you pass through the clanking border gates. This is where you may have some of your more dismal expectations of Tijuana fulfilled. There is a roving band of sometimes-shady street vendors and beggars lined up here. Some of them will try to sell you bracelets and paintings. Others will hawk trinkets that you'll find carbon-copied all over the blatantly tourist-oriented shops in town.

My suggestion is to practice saying "No, gracias" and high-tail it farther into town to start your real shopping. Walk across the pedestrian bridge on the west side of the plaza and look for the **Artisan Market** (Mercado de Artesanías) along Calle 2 (also called Benito Juárez) between Avenidas Negrete and Ocampo. You'll see this labyrinthine market on your left just after you cross over the bridge. The maze of alleys and pathways is lined with vendors and artists selling all those things you never knew you needed so badly; carvings, metalwork, hand-painted ceramics, and blown-glass can all be found in this market.

El Popo

Follow Benito Juárez west four blocks from the Artisan Market to find one of the best open-air markets in downtown Tijuana, El Popo. You'll know you're there when you see the colorful piñatas strung from the rafters and tables full of honeycomb, cheese, meats, nuts, and candies. Wander under the canopy and in between booths to browse collections of sweets and savories, herbs and cooking utensils. Also sprinkled in are some unique handicrafts that you won't find in every other shop in town—a frustrating phenomenon at some of the more touristy *mercados.* There are religious icons, handwoven blankets, and trinkets for the kids.

Avenida Revolución

El Popo is often overlooked by tourists who are hypnotized by the spectacle of Avenida Revolución on the way from the border. To reach this shopping circus, double back a block east along Benito Juárez. From this point you are at the north end of La Revo. In front of you lies about eight blocks of mixed shopping where anything goes. You'll find Mexican blankets stacked up

GATEWAY TO BAJA

© ERICKA CHICKOWSKI

Let the arch guide you to Avenida Revolución.

next to handcrafted guitars and shot glasses that are emblazoned with the town's name along with sombreros or donkeys, or better yet, donkeys wearing sombreros. Some of the better finds are buried below street level, accessible by short unmarked corridors, so don't be afraid to explore a bit. You'll probably be coaxed down a few by the engaging curio salesmen that line the streets in front of their stores. They're not shy, enticing eager shoppers with deals, "Look, señorita. You like? Good price for you, almost free. Come see . . ."

Sometimes it really may be worth a look, as these areas are a good place to find silver jewelry and leather work. Incidentally, as you are wandering the streets here you are likely to encounter many street peddlers carrying trays full

of jewelry. Unless you are content with fake silver, pass these vendors up in favor of stationary jewelry stands. The established salespeople are much less likely to rip you off.

Mercado Miguel Hidalgo

If this strip is too touristy for your taste and you'd like to get a little more authentic, duck off La Avenida once you reach Calle 4, 5, or 6 and head east. These side streets are dotted with produce and meat vendors, along with the occasional taqueria. Zig-zag your way southeast, heading south on Avenidas Negrete, Ocampo, and Pio Pico in between your easterly march up the numbered Calles until you reach Calle 9 and Avenida General Rodolfo Sanchez. You're now in the Zona Río (River Zone) and in front of the most historic markets in the city.

A motley collection of around 80 open-air stalls and stands, Mercado Miguel Hidalgo has operated from this square for more than 50 years. The vendors' wares are a rainbow of food and trinkets. There are the warm-colored mounds of grains, separated and lined up in bright blue pails. Over them hang the multi-hued piñatas, flashy *lucha libre* masks, and soccer balls hanging from cellophane plastic bags. Brown and beige pottery is stacked here and there between tables covered with rows and rows of dried peppers, herbs, and candied fruits. Exotic delicacies like cactus and tamarind husks mingle with fresh fruit and vegetables. Also at hand is an assortment of Mexican cooking utensils, things like tortilla shapers and mortars and pestles for grinding up spices.

SPORTS AND RECREATION

You might not know it walking the concrete jungle of Avenida Revolución, but hidden away in the middle of a long Tijuana canyon there is a verdant oasis that is just prime for taking a stroll with a bag full of golf clubs. This course at the Tijuana Country Club, or **Club Campestre Tijuana** (Blvd. Agua Caliente 11311, in Tijuana tel. 664/104-75-45, from the U.S. tel. 888/217-1165), is a decent property, about on par with what you'd find at the nicer municipal courses in San Diego. On Monday, Tuesday,

Thursday, and Friday greens fees for an 18-hole round will cost about $21. The fee jumps to $42 on Wednesday, Saturday, and Sunday. The course is rolling and easily walkable, but if you insist on wheels carts are available for $21.

Drive just outside city limits south of Las Playas de Tijuana to find an even nicer set of fairways at **Real Del Mar Golf and Country Club** (Km 19.5 Tijuana–Ensenada Scenic Toll Road, from U.S. tel. 800/803-6038, in Tijuana tel. 664/631-36-70, www.realdelmar.com.mx). This oceanview course dips in and over the hillsides of the Real Del Mar Resort. Grounds are well maintained with no brown spots and lined with palm trees and manicured shrubs. There are a fair number of water hazards, some with cascading waterfalls. Greens fees are $69 Monday through Thursday and $89 Friday through Sunday.

Real Del Mar also has an **equestrian center** open to the public, as well as a full-service **spa** that performs massages, facials, and body treatments.

ACCOMMODATIONS

Don't let some of the seedier hotels along Avenida Revolución scare you off. Staying in Tijuana can actually be a pretty pleasurable experience if you know where to look.

Generally the nicest places are going to be away from downtown in the Zona Río or along the highway heading down to Rosarito. These places have 24-hour security, and rooms are furnished up to American specs with all the typical amenities like irons and ironing boards, televisions, and the ever-present Gideon bible (they're bilingual here).

Many in the Zona Río are on or very close to Paseo de los Héroes. This is where you'll find the boisterously painted **Camino Real Tijuana** (Paseo de los Héroes 10305, tel. 664/633-40-00, $220 s/d). A collage of hot pink, vivid yellow, and bright white enrobe this building as a testament to the Mexican love of loud colors. Just remember, in the U.S. bold colors might mean tacky interiors. Here it is a symbol of luxury—this hotel's penthouse is generally where musicians stay when they come to town.

Inside, the lobby is a huge marbled affair, a classy and cavernous entryway that echoes with the high heels and dress shoes of the business people who often frequent the hotel. The rooms are clean and spacious, including the large white marble bathrooms. The beds are a bit on the hard side, but that is a problem endemic to Tijuana and Baja hotels in general.

One of my favorites is **Hotel Lucerna** (Paseo de los Heroes #10902, tel. 800/582-37-62 or 664/633-39-00, $95 d), which is very quiet and intimate. A bubbling stone fountain greets you at the entrance and in the center courtyard the pool is flanked by palm trees and flowers. Over a narrow part of the pool stands a pretty pedestrian bridge adorned with balustrades. All in all it is a nice sanctuary after a day on La Revo or a night dancing at the clubs. The rooms are also well appointed, some with whirlpool tubs and all of them featuring the comfiest beds in TJ.

Also nearby is the **Grand Hotel Tijuana** (Blvd. Agua Caliente 4500, tel. 664/681-70-00, $178 s/d), which has two sleek towers that sit on the edge of the Tijuana Country Club. Many of the rooms here have a view of the surrounding greenery, as does the patio area which features a heated pool, whirlpool, tennis courts, and saunas in each of the locker rooms. If you can get a good deal, try to book a room on the executive level. This will also gain you access to a swanky lounge with a fantastic bird's-eye view of the golf course and the city, along with flat-screen TVs, computers with high-speed Internet, and a wet bar.

Bargain hunters looking for a room under $100 should try the **Hotel Hacienda del Río** (Blvd. Rodolfo Sanchez Taboada 10606, tel. 664/684-86-44, $84 s/d), a pleasant and clean motel not far from the Paseo. There is a small pool at the back of the property and a little café on-site.

Budget travelers might consider taking a look at the digs within Avenida Revolucion's trademark **Hotel Nelson** (Ave. Revolucion #926, tel. 664/685-43-02, $50 d), which sits in a distinctive pink building right in the heart of the La Revo hubbub. Rooms are somewhat shabby, but are some of the cleanest in the neighborhood. The building has security, and rooms come equipped with telephone and TV.

If you'd like to get away without driving all the way down to Rosarito, **Real del Mar** (Km 19.5 Carr Cuota, tel. 664/631-36-70, $129 s/d) is only about 12 miles south of the border along the Tijuana–Ensenada Scenic Toll Road. This Residence Inn by Marriott is staggered on a hillside that overlooks the ocean. Rooms are extremely comfortable, decked out in Mexican tiling and floral prints. All rooms come with kitchen efficiencies. The property has an adjacent golf course, tennis courts, basketball courts, and volleyball nets. There is also a heated pool and whirlpool, plus a fitness center equipped with saunas and steam rooms.

FOOD
Avenida Revolución

Most of the restaurants along Avenida Revolución are about what you'd expect from a Mexican tourist destination. Menus are filled with tacos and enchiladas. Dining rooms are serenaded by warbling mariachi singers. If this is what you're craving, two of the old standards are **La Placita** (Ave. Revolucion #951, tel. 664/688-27-04, $8) and **Tijuana Tilly's** (Calle 7 at Ave. Revolucion, tel. 664/685-60-24, noon–midnight Sun.–Thurs., noon–3 A.M. Fri.–Sat., $10). La Placita has a second-story rooftop patio that overlooks the parade of revelers below. And Tijuana Tilly's sits at the foot of the Frontón Palacio on the south end of La Revo.

If you would like a little fast food, Tijuana style, another option are the local street taco stands. Just be aware that not all street tacos are created equally. Above all else trust your sense of observation—if the food smells bad or the preparation area looks dirty, move on. If you want to stay safe, pass on any taco vendor that sells its wares from wheeled carts. Instead opt for established stalls and stands. One tried-and-true option that is right on the well-beaten path is the stand run by Tijuana's oldest-running restaurant, **Café La Especial** (Ave. Revolucion #718, tel. 664/685-66-54, $1 tacos). The restaurant is down the stairs under the entryway,

but the stand is right there at street level serving a variety of meats straight from pan to tortilla for only about $1 per serving.

Zona Gastronómica

Foodies will be happy to hear that Tijuana dining isn't just street tacos and burritos. The town is actually a chest of culinary treasures, with fine restaurants that serve many varieties of ethnic fare and contemporary cuisine. The hippest chefs in town have taken to fusing Mexican and Mediterranean flavors in a daring style they've dubbed Baja-Med.

Many of the city's best restaurants can be found in the Zona Gastronómica, east of the racetrack between Paseo de los Héroes and Boulevard Agua Caliente.

This is where you can dine on the light and flaky empanadas of **Cheripan** (Calle Escuadron 201 #3151, tel. 664/622-9730, 1 P.M.–11 P.M. Mon.–Thurs., 1 P.M.–1 A.M. Fri.–Sat., 1 P.M.–10 P.M. Sun., $15), a hip Argentinian restaurant that caters to a young and well-heeled crowd. The trendy interior is modern, with contemporary art and marble table tops. In back there is a terraced patio that can be a relaxing spot to savor a glass of wine from the extensive list. The house specialty here is the Parrillada Cheripan, a mixed grill of chorizo, chicken, beef, and pork that costs around $19 and can be split among two or three people if you order empanadas to go with it.

A particular favorite among the intrepid eaters is **La Diferencia** (Blvd. Sanchez Taboada #10611-A, tel. 664/634-33-46, www.ladiferencia.com.mx, $15), which specializes in unusual delicacies from around Mexico and the rest of the world. Entrées featuring ostrich, crocodile, and *camoles* (ant caviar) are among the highlights. The timid can dip their toe into the menu. I'd suggest ordering crepes with *cuitlacoche* (corn fungus—a staple of southern Mexico) or the cricket tostadas. If it helps, close your eyes. They're actually really tasty.

Also in the culinary district is **Villa Saverios** (Blvd. Sanchez Taboada and Escuadron 201, tel. 664/686-64-42, www.villasaverios.com, $22), an elegant restaurant that specializes in

Baja-Med cuisine with a particular emphasis on Italian dishes. If you go there, be sure to save room for desert. The fried plantain with caramel and ice cream is delicious.

Saverios's sister restaurant, **Casa Plasencia** (Carlos Rovirosa #250, tel. 664/686-36-04, www.casaplasencia.com, $22), is also close by. This romantic Mediterranean restaurant features an open kitchen and a dining room decorated with accents that echo Old World Spain. The specialty here is the paella. The dining room is usually pretty quiet, but tramp up the rickety steps leading to the restaurant's bar, Meson Burladero, and you'll encounter a lively scene. Decorated from floor to rafters in memorabilia, costumes and photos honoring the great tradition of bullfighting, this is where the sport's aficionados come after a match to debate the performance of the *toreador*.

Playas de Tijuana

Far away from the hubbub of downtown, **C Rincon San Román** (Km 19.5 Tijuana–Ensenada Scenic Toll Road, tel. 664/631-22-41, www.rinconsanroman.com, $23) is worth the 12-mile drive out to its location at the Real Del Mar resort. This restaurant is run by one of Baja's biggest celebrity chefs, Martin San Román, who was integral in first popularizing the Baja-Med movement. He received his training in the great schools of Paris and his menu here blends the best ingredients and methods of Mexican cooking with the French culinary tradition. The hilltop dining room is intimate and faces the resort's golf course and the ocean below.

INFORMATION AND SERVICES
Tourist Offices

The **Tijuana Tourism and Convention Bureau** runs several information offices and kiosks that are staffed with bilingual employees. Almost all of the literature handed out at these information booths is available in both Spanish and English. If you cross the border by foot you can't miss the **Plaza Viva Tijuana** (tel. 664/973-04-24, 8 A.M.–5 P.M. Mon.–

Fri., 9 A.M.–1 P.M. Sat.–Sun.) information office between the border and Avenida Revolución. There is also a booth directly on Avenida Revolución between Calles 3 and 4 (tel. 664/685-22-10, 10 A.M.–4 P.M. Mon.–Thurs., 10 A.M.–7 P.M. Fri.–Sun.).

Consulates

Americans in need of diplomatic assistance should visit the **United States Consulate** (Calle Tapachula 96, tel. 664/622-74-00, 8 A.M.–4:45 P.M. Mon.–Fri.), which is located near the Agua Caliente Racetrack. If the office is closed and you have an emergency situation, you can call the consulate in the States at 619/692-2154.

Similarly, Canadians can look for help at the **Canadian Consulate** (German Gedovious 10411-101, tel. 664/684-04-61, 9 A.M.–1 P.M. Mon.–Fri.) in the Zona Río.

Medical Emergencies and Police

Should a medical emergency arise, one of the best hospitals in Tijuana is **Hospital Angeles** (Paseo de los Héroes 10999, tel. 664/635-18-00), a modern medical center in the Zona Réo that is well regarded by medical professionals on both sides of the border.

The **central police station** (tel. 664/688-55-52) is located on the corner of Calle 8 and Avenida Constitución.

In general the police in Tijuana are helpful peacekeepers, but there is an undercurrent of corruption with a few bad seeds on the force. Some corrupt officers have been known to target tourists with threats of jail time unless they pay a "fine" directly to the officer. Tourism officials have worked to stamp out this kind of bribery corruption and these types of incidents occur less and less frequently—but they are still a reality. If you are harassed by a dishonest cop, the tourism officials urge you to immediately contact the Tourist Assistance Hotline by dialing 078 from any phone in the city.

GETTING THERE
By Air

Service by air into the city is provided at

Tijuana International Airport (Carretera Aeropuerto, tel. 664/607-82-01), which is located right by the Otay Mesa Border Crossing. Major airlines that fly here include Aeromexico (tel. 800/021-40-00, www.aeromexico.com), Aerolitoral (tel. 800/021-40-00, www.aero mexico.com), Mexicana (tel. 800/502-20-00, www.mexicana.com), and Aerocalifornia (tel. 800/685-55-00).

There are taxis waiting at stands in front of the International Arrivals gate, with fares varying from $17 to $40 to area hotels.

By Car

Only seventeen miles from downtown San Diego, Tijuana is an easy drive away. Head south on I-5 to get to the **San Ysidro Border.** This is the busiest border crossing in the world, but it is actually pretty easy to pass through going south. The wait is almost nonexistent on the way into Mexico because there are little to no authorities waiting to inspect inbound traffic. For additional information about driving across the border, see the *Border Crossing* section under *Getting Around* in the *Essentials* chapter.

Getting back home is another matter entirely. Depending on the homeland security stance and the time of day, it can take anywhere from 30 minutes to several hours to pass through the U.S. Border Patrol inspection gates. Be sure to have your passport ready for authorities when you hit the lineup and relax already! Everyone else in line is in the same boat as you and you aren't going to get across any sooner by riding up on someone's bumper or zipping from lane to lane. There are tons of enterprising vendors roving between the cars to keep you amused. They're peddling tchotchkes and churros and many would be happy to whet your whistle with an *agua fresca* or a cold soda from their wheeled coolers.

Avoid getting into any lanes marked "SEN-TRI." These are fast-track commuter lanes for drivers who have special SENTRI cards. If you pass through this gate without the card you'll be asked to circle back into Mexico and wait at the back of the line or pay a whopping $5,000 fine.

Another alternative to crossing at San Ysidro is traveling across the **Otay border,** five miles east near the Tijuana International Airport. To get there follow the signs from downtown to the Garita de Otay. To compare border waits, consider calling the San Ysidro border crossing information line at 619-690-8999 and the Otay Mesa line at 619/671-8999.

Rental Cars and Mexican Car Insurance

If you are planning on driving a U.S. car rental into Mexico, be sure to ask ahead of time because many American rental agencies prohibit driving out of the country. No matter what car you use, also be sure to purchase Mexican car insurance. Mexican law requires drivers to carry special liability insurance that your American policy doesn't have. If you are caught driving without it you could spend a long, cold night in a Tijuana jail.

There are numerous insurance shops in South Bay that can get you set up with a policy in a matter of minutes, including **Border Insurance Services** (2004 Dairy Mart Rd., #103, San Ysidro, 619/428-0095, www .mexborder.com), **Instant Mexico Auto Insurance** (223 Via de San Ysidro, San Ysidro, 619/428-3583), and **Baja 4 Less Mexican Insurance** (120 Willow Rd., San Ysidro, 619/428-4406). You can also buy insurance online through Border Insurance Services' website (www.mexborder.com). Policies usually range between $15 and $30 per day. Many American policies do cover damages to your own property while in Mexico, so make sure that you don't get up-sold to a policy that duplicates what you already have.

Finally, if you want to avoid the hassle of border crossing and insurance altogether consider driving down to San Ysidro, parking there, and walking across the border. There are a number of safe, well-lit border parking stations that surround the pedestrian border crossing there. One of the biggest, **Border Station Parking** (4570 Camino de la Plaza, San Ysidro, 619/428-1422, www.borderparking.com), also offers a bus shuttle to Avenida Revolución.

Trolley

The **San Diego Trolley Blue Line** runs all the way down San Ysidro, leaving you steps from the border. From the downtown Santa Fe Station this is a 45-minute ride that costs $2.50. The trolley shuttles over the line every 15 to 30 minutes morning through night. The last train to depart San Ysidro leaves at 12:59 A.M. on weekdays and 1:59 A.M. on weekends. If you get there at the stroke of one or two the train won't turn into a pumpkin, but you will end up having to pay a cabbie more than $50 to get back up to San Diego. Or you could just turn around and go back to the club until dawn, right around when that trolley starts running again.

By Bus

Shuttle service from San Diego is available on the cool and comfy red buses run by **Mexicoach** (619/428-9517, www.mexicoach .com). These private buses depart from Old Town Transit Center (4005 Taylor St.) at 8:30 A.M., 11:30 A.M., 4:30 P.M., and 7:30 P.M. each day. They deposit riders at the tourism terminal at Avenida Revolución 1025, between Calle 6 and 7. Return buses to Old Town depart from here daily at 6 A.M., 9 A.M., 2 P.M., and 5 P.M. The round-trip cost is $20.

Mexicoach also offers shuttles from Border Station Parking (4570 Camino de la Plaza, San Ysidro) to the tourism terminal for $5 one-way or $8 round-trip. These buses run every half hour each day between 8 A.M. and 9 P.M.

GETTING AROUND
By Taxi

If you are just in town for the day, taxis are a reliable and cheap way to ferry you between the various walking districts in town. At the border the first thing you will see is a giant taxi stand that is jammed with a pack of yellow chariots waiting to whisk you away.

The cabs here have no meters, so be sure to ask how much it will cost before you shut the door. From the border it will typically cost about $5 to $7 to Avenida Revolución and the Zona Río. Fares to the Bullring by the Sea are usually closer to $12.

There are plenty of cabs streaming by the major commercial areas as well, so you should have no problem hailing a cab for the return trip home. Should you come up empty the number for Yellow Cabs is tel. 664/682-98-92.

By Car

The rules of the road in Tijuana are very similar to American street laws. Stop at the big red "Alto" signs and red lights; go on green; signal before you turn.

Generally Tijuana drivers are a little more aggressive than those in San Diego, though, so be sure to drive defensively and don't always count on someone to let you in.

Most of the major shopping centers in town offer free parking, and streetside parking is available as well. Your car is generally pretty safe in the major commercial areas, but always make sure your doors are locked and store any and all expensive-looking items out of view.

EAST OF TIJUANA
◖ Tecate

Thirty-four miles away from the frenetic chaos of Tijuana is Tecate, a cozy Mexican village that actually goes to sleep at night. Tecate's plazas and squares are a good spot to stroll. The main park, **Parque Hidalgo,** has a shady walkway and an attractive gazebo topped in barrel tiles.

Brewery buffs will be happy to find this is indeed the hometown of the Mexican beer of the same name. Stop in at the **Cuauhtemoc Brewery** for a tour and get one cerveza on the house.

The town is also known for its bread. The pan de Tecate comes in various forms, generally sweet and light, and is a must-taste item while in town. Several shops line Avenida Juarez near Parque Hidalgo, including the most-humble **El Mejor Pan de Tecate,** between Portes Gil and Rodriguez.

If you plan to stay the night (especially if you've been sampling a lot of those Tecate beers at the brewery), consider a stay at **Hotel Tecate** (tel. 665/654-11-16, $30 d), which has rooms overlooking the main plaza. There are just a handful of rooms at this small hotel, which is set above a restaurant. These digs are somewhat humble, but can do in a pinch.

If it is luxury you are looking for, you'll need to travel out of town for that. About 30 kilometers (19 miles) east of Tecate is **Hacienda Santa Veronica** (tel. 665/681-7428), which features rooms with fireplaces and private patios. Here you can enjoy tennis courts, a swimming pool, basketball court, volleyball court, equestrian trails and trails for off-road vehicles. The hacienda is located near kilometer 106 on the free road or kilometer 94 on the toll road.

Should you need information or assistance while in Tecate, there is a state tourism office (9 A.M.–7 P.M. Mon.–Fri., 9 A.M.–3 P.M. Sat., 10 A.M.–2 P.M. Sun.) on the south side of Parque Hidalgo.

Tecate is reachable by either taking Highway 94 from downtown San Diego and crossing at the Tecate border or taking one of two major roads from Tijuana: the toll road (Mex. Hwy. 2-D) or the free road (Mex. Hwy. 2). While the toll road is safer and quicker, visitors should be mindful that once they get on the road and head east out of Tijuana there are no turnarounds until they get to Tecate.

Guadalupe Valley

El Ruto del Vino—the wine route of Baja—runs from Tecate to just north of Ensenada along Mexico Highway 3. This scenic drive cuts through the Guadalupe Valley, the most prolific wine-producing region in all of Mexico. Several vineyards along the way offer tours and tastings, including **L.A. Cetto** (Km 73.5 Hwy. 3, tel. 646/155-22-64, 10 A.M.–5 P.M. daily), **Adobe Guadalupe** (tel. 646/155-20-94, call for directions) and **Mogor Badán** (Km 86.5 Hwy. 3, tel. 646/177-6769, 9 A.M.–dusk daily).

Rosarito to Ensenada

Farther south, the coastal towns of Rosarito and Ensenada are away from the hustle and flow of border activity.

Closest to Tijuana, Rosarito is a beach town built for revelers since its inception in 1925 when the Rosarito Beach Hotel was first built in the middle of what were then remote ranch lands. These days it is a little city in its own right, which primarily caters to partiers at night and shoppers by day. Clubgoers come here to hop between beachside establishments all night long. If that isn't your bag, but you are a fan of artwork and crafts, then the town is still worth a stop—there are dozens of vendors large and small who sell one-of-a-kind pieces here that you could never find in Tijuana.

As a cruise port of call, Ensenada is a bit more family-friendly than Rosarito. There are still plenty of places to unwind with a margarita, but the tourist district is cleaner and much better organized. There is more daytime sightseeing to be had, with attractions such as the Malecón and La Bufadora at hand. While there aren't as many artisans as in Rosarito, there are still plenty of shopping options for those seeking souvenirs, jewelry, and clothes.

The destinations in this section are organized to help you enjoy your road trip down from San Diego. In each section sites are listed from south to north, with those places closest to San Diego coming first. The listings small and large are meant to provide a few good pit stops along the way. As you travel down, your main routes will be either the Tijuana–Ensenada Scenic Toll Road or the Free Road (Mex 1) closer to the water. In Rosarito the Free Road is referred to as Boulevard Benito Juarez.

SIGHTS
Rosarito Beach

Like its San Diego counterparts, this sandy stretch of shoreline is a nice place to stake down an umbrella, craft a master castle from the sand, or ride the waves on your boogie board. Still, though, Rosarito Beach has its own unique personality that you can't get up north. The beach is lined with clubs that unfold right onto the sand. Peddlers wander between towel clusters to sell jewelry and sunglasses. Fruit carts spread themselves out among the more populated areas of the beach.

On some sections of the beach freewheeling tourists zip around on 4x4s. On others they clomp around on horseback.

The most prominent structure along the waterfront is the **Rosarito Beach Pier.** It costs $1 to walk to the end, payable to the person at the entry booth. Honestly, though, there's usually no one there to collect the fee so you might skate by for free. You'll see young men and old plying the water for fish, some with very interesting contraptions. I saw one guy working the water with monofilament wrapped around a 7-Up bottle. Can't say that I saw a pile of fish at his feet, though.

Once you stroll down the pier, be sure to stop off at the **Rosarito Beach Hotel.** The pier is owned by the hotel and adjoins the property. This historic resort was erected in 1925 when the surrounding area was nothing but virgin beaches and open ranch land. The lobby is covered in beautiful murals and the arcade that sits between the lobby and the restaurants has an impressive collection of paintings depicting Old Mexico prior to the 1920s. On Saturdays at 11 A.M. the concierge holds a tour here that covers the history of the property and the artwork held within.

Roadside Attractions

The most notable attraction on the drive between Rosarito and Ensenada is really the road itself. The **Tijuana-Ensenada Scenic Toll Road** curves and undulates with the rocky coast, mostly overlooking the water, sometimes zooming by it at eye level along a few interspersed beach areas. The closer to Ensenada you get, the more magnificent the views. There are a few glimpses of blue water against craggy cliffs that are so arresting you really need to be careful not to drive off the side of the road.

Along this stretch of 50 miles or so there are a number of notable roadside curiosities that are worth a stop if you are in no particular hurry to make it down to Ensenada. On their own they are hardly must-sees, but taken in together as part of a lazy drive south they make up an entertaining patchwork of amusement.

The first one you'll come across is **Xploration,** called Foxploration before it was purchased from Fox studios in 2007. This movie studio complex was built by James Cameron and his crew to film major portions of the 1997 blockbuster *Titanic.* After the movie, the studio built up a small theme park in response to so many looky-loos stopping by for a peek behind the curtain. This is not Universal Studios or any approximation thereof. But it can make for a fun hour or two, strolling through the *Titanic* memorabilia and sets and taking a look through its exhibit on prop-making and make-up. There's also a foam ball-house for the kids to bounce off the walls a bit before being cooped up in the car again.

The **Calafia Historical and Cultural Center** has a pretty grand name for its modest collection of historic odds and ends. But that is not why you stop there anyway. The center is part of a cliffside hotel complex that has a jaw-dropping view of the Pacific. Ask to be seated on the terraced patio and while away the time nursing a cool beverage and munching on appetizers. Then, when you are good and sated, wander into the center to take a look at its collection of antiques from the famous Agua Caliente Casino in Tijuana, memorabilia from the filming of *Titanic* and replicas of the Spanish missions.

Even though the rest stop and restaurant here is abandoned, you'll still want to take the exit for **El Mirador.** This stop off is built on the high bluffs of Punta Salsipuedes and provides a tremendous vantage point of the ocean and the last stretch of road to Ensenada. Once you're done marveling at the vista, peer down at the water in the large bay created by this point. See those giant rings that look like hula hoops floating in the ocean? Those are actually floating fish farms, incubators for some of the finest sashimi-grade tuna in the world. Ensenada makes a bundle exporting its crop of fish to seafood-loving Japan.

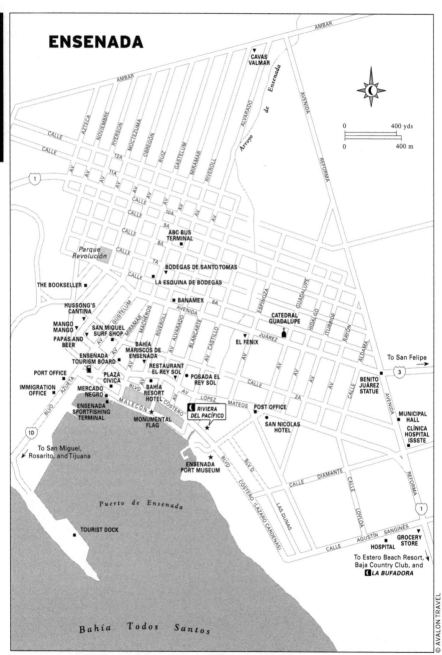

ENSENADA

CAVAS VALMAR

AMBAR

AMBAR

CALLE

CALLE

Parque Revolución

THE BOOKSELLER ■

HUSSONG'S CANTINA

MANGO MANGO

PAPAS AND BEER

ENSENADA TOURISM BOARD

PORT OFFICE

IMMIGRATION OFFICE ■

MERCADO NEGRO

ENSENADA SPORTFISHING TERMINAL

To San Miguel, Rosarito, and Tijuana

ABC BUS TERMINAL

BODEGAS DE SANTO TOMAS

LA ESQUINA DE BODEGAS

BANAMEX

SAN MIGUEL SURF SHOP

BAHÍA MARISCOS DE ENSENADA

RESTAURANT EL REY SOL

PLAZA CIVICA

BAHÍA RESORT HOTEL

MONUMENTAL FLAG

RIVIERA DEL PACÍFICO

ENSENADA PORT MUSEUM

POSADA EL REY SOL

POST OFFICE

SAN NICOLAS HOTEL

CATEDRAL GUADALUPE

EL FÉNIX

To San Felipe

BENITO JUÁREZ STATUE

MUNICIPAL HALL

CLÍNICA HOSPITAL ISSSTE

CALLE DIAMANTE

Puerto de Ensenada

TOURIST DOCK ■

To Estero Beach Resort, Baja Country Club, and LA BUFADORA

GROCERY STORE

HOSPITAL

AGUSTÍN SANGINÉS

Bahía   Todos   Santos

0   400 yds

0   400 m

© AVALON TRAVEL

© ERICKA CHICKOWSKI

Riviera del Pacífico in Ensenada

Malecón

When you drive into Ensenada along the bay, probably the first thing you'll notice is the enormous Mexican flag billowing atop the 338-foot flagpole. This giant swath of red, white, and green marks the center of the Malecón, Ensenada's own embarcadero. The half-mile boardwalk skirts the bay and its smattering of fishing boats, pleasure craft, and one absolutely massive cruise ship, if it is in port. There is a lot of activity at the west end of the strip, where the **Mercado Negro** fish market holds court from dawn to dusk.

◖ Riviera del Pacífico

About a block away from the eastern end of the Malecón is the splendid Riviera del Pacífico, a sweeping Mediterranean-style complex that was originally built in 1930 as a luxurious casino and resort that attracted Hollywood celebrities and a few high-profile mobsters. The city has restored the casino building and installed an attractive street-facing landscape. Grounds are open 8 A.M.–7 P.M. daily.

The Riviera is also home to the **Museo de Histórica,** which contains artifacts and reproductions that detail the life of indigenous Baja California natives and early European settlers to the area. The museum is open 9 A.M.–5 P.M. daily. Admission is $1.50

Ensenada Parks and Beaches

I didn't think city parks like **Parque Revolución** existed outside of the movies. This idyllic square in the northern outskirts of the tourist district is lined with deciduous trees and has a historic gazebo at its center. Here old couples stroll the sidewalks hand-in-hand, while their younger counterparts sit on the benches and share a laugh. Children chase each other round the playground or rumble along the pathways on their bikes. You don't hear much English spoken here—this park is slightly off the beaten path and not many tourists have the good fortune of finding it.

Not true for **Plaza Cívica,** the main square along the Boulevard Costero. Overlooking the smooth bricks of the plaza are giant bronze

© ERICKA CHICKOWSKI

The flea market at La Bufadora is a classic open-air shopping venue.

sculptures portraying the heads of three of Mexico's greatest heroes, Benito Juárez, Miguel Hidalgo, and Venustiano Carranza.

Long ago the waterfront where the Port of Ensenada sits used to be made up of a long sandy beach; then it was eaten up by the jaws of "progress." Politicos had the bottom dredged to make way for giant freighters and cruise ships, so now the closest traditional beach is six miles south at **Estero Beach Resort,** a private property that allows day-use entrance for $6.

Other Ensenada Sights

Bodegas de Santo Tomás is a must-see for wine lovers. This complex just north of Avenida Juárez is home to Santo Tomás, one of Mexico's oldest wineries. The ivy-covered brick facility offers tours in English of its fermentation vats and of antique equipment once used in the wine-making process. Free tours are held every 30 minutes between 9 A.M. and 5 P.M. daily. You can cap it off with one of the tastings for $5.

Those who appreciate religious architecture will want to stop by **Nuestra Señora de Guadalupe,** Ensenada's largest church. The building is Spanish Colonial, with two spires rising to the heavens.

Hidden away from almost all of the major tourist areas, the **Ensenada Port Museum** (Calle Todos Santos #115 Fracc., tel. 646/176-47-16, free) is a wonderful museum full of fossils and relics that tell the story of Ensenada and Baja from prehistoric years all the way through modern times. It helps if you know a little bit of Spanish, but most of the exhibits in this creaky three-story building have placards appended with English explanations. Call ahead to ask for an English-speaking guide to give you a tour. The museum is open Monday through Friday 9 A.M.–6 P.M., Saturday and Sunday noon to 6 P.M.

◖ La Bufadora

Set near the tip of Punta Banda more than thirty miles away from downtown Ensenada, La Bufadora is one of Baja's greatest natural wonders. Under the right conditions, this marine blowhole shoots a spray of water up to 80 feet high, spraying oohing and ahhing onlookers. The geyser is the product of a deep underwater canyon by the cliffside that sucks in water as the swells pound the cliffside and then expels the water sharply through a narrow cave on the surface.

The geyser is easily viewed on the multi-tiered decks overlooking the blowhole entrance. This sight is free, but you should bring cash anyway because it is surrounded by a bustling flea market filled with trinkets, blankets, and goodies. There are several established restaurants here, as well as an assortment of vendors hawking *aguas frescas,* churros, and tacos.

ENTERTAINMENT AND EVENTS
Rosarito Nightlife

Rosarito's nightlife easily rivals Tijuana to the north. Americans mingle with the locals for a nightly bacchanalia that on the weekend will rage until dawn. The downtown core has dozens of night clubs that spin hip-hop, rap, Latin dance and rock, and techno beats for the masses.

The behemoth of Baja clubbing is here on the sand. **Papas and Beer** (located directly on the beach just south of the pier, tel. 661/612-04-44, www.papasandbeer.com, 11 A.M.–3 A.M. daily) is a decades-old juggernaut that has built its reputation on the enormous open-air party zone that includes an enclosed private "beach," volleyball nets, picnic benches, and a mechanical bull. Inside the dance floor is always packed with attractive singles.

Competition keeps Papas and Beer sharp and also gives bar-hoppers lots of choices to skip around. Just off the beach only a couple of blocks away, **Club Maya** (tel. 661/100-22-55, 10 P.M.–5 A.M. daily) vies for the attention—and dollars—of discriminating clubgoers with its luxury tri-level building that has splashing waterfalls, a whirlpool tub, and heated pool on its VIP roof.

Set on Rosarito's main strip, Boulevard Juarez, **Festival Plaza** is the most distinctive building in town. The huge hotel and entertainment complex is designed to look like a big roller coaster and is painted in circus colors to

match. There are 10 clubs in this frenetic plaza, including **Rock & Roll Taco,** a club set in the spot where Wolfman Jack would broadcast his rock 'n' roll collection in the 1950s to evade U.S. censors. Those same stick-in-the-muds would probably have a heart attack if they visited the club today, which spins dance music in between live rock bands.

Those who want to socialize without splitting an eardrum will often head north of downtown to **Rene's Sports Bar.** This is a favorite hangout for the gringos who live in town, along with some of their Spanish-speaking neighbors and a good smattering of *turistas* too. On the weekends you might have the pleasure of watching a band sing Spanish covers of old rock classics from the '60s and '70s. There's pool and darts, plus the requisite bank of TV screens with a wide selection of sports tuned in.

Roadside Watering Holes

Along the way from Rosarito to Ensenada there are several serene spots to sit and watch the

Stop for a beverage along the road to Ensenada.

© ERICKA CHICKOWSKI

waves tumble into shore. Only a couple miles south of Rosarito, **Calafia** (Km 35.5 Tijuana–Ensenada Scenic Toll Road, tel. 661/612-15-80, www.hotel-calafia.com, 10 A.M.–midnight daily) is one of them. This is a bluff-top bar where you can embrace your inner tourist. Sit under the sun and proudly order a fruity drink like a frozen daiquiri or piña colada. The friendly waitstaff will happily oblige, carting over curvy glasses of these fruity concoctions, maraschino cherry, drink umbrella, and all.

If you don't mind driving the windy toll road at night, the **bar at Hotel La Fonda** (Km 59.5 Tijuana–Ensenada Scenic Toll Road, tel. 646/155-03-07, 11 A.M.–midnight) is one of the best places between Rosarito and Ensenada to watch the fireworks of sunset go off over the ocean horizon. There's a terrace that sits right above La Fonda's sandy beach that puts you front and center for the show. The restaurant here has been praised by a lot of people, but I honestly didn't find the entrées all that great. The appetizers, however, are pretty tasty.

Ensenada Nightlife

The booze also flows freely in Ensenada, but this seaside resort town is definitely more mellow than the raucous club zones of Rosarito or Tijuana.

If you choose only one bar to throw back a couple of cervezas or sip a margarita, make it **Hussong's Cantina** (Ave. Ruiz 113, tel. 646/178-32-10, 10 A.M.–1 A.M. Sun.–Thurs., 10 A.M.–2 A.M. Fri.–Sat.). This is the second-oldest bar in all of Mexico, established way back in 1892. The friendly regulars are fond of telling stories about when their fathers used to be regulars, when you could hitch your horse to the post outside. The easy atmosphere their forefathers were attracted to still remains pretty much unchanged in this saloon-like bar whose floor is covered in peanut shells and is packed with happy drinkers ready to sing along with the mariachis that perform here each night. The best time to come soak up the flavor with the locals is during the day—at night, especially on the weekends, it can often be a standing-room-only scene.

Right across the street Ensenada has its own **Papas and Beer** (Ave. Ruiz #102, tel. 646/174-

Ensenada's nightlife is a little less rowdy than Rosarito's, but it is still a blast.

© ERICKA CHICKOWSKI

01-45, www.papasandbeer.com, 11 A.M.–3 A.M. daily), a scaled-down version of that Rosarito favorite that still manages to maintain the beach vibe in spite of the inland location. Also close by is **Mango Mango** (Blvd. Lopez Mateos #335, tel. 646/178-16-68), a club owned by the same proprietors who made Papas and Beer a hit. This dance club specializes in salsa and merengue and has a patio that by daylight is a nice place to people-watch.

For a quiet evening over a bottle of wine, hit the secluded patio of **Capricho's Restaurant** (Av. Ruiz 138, tel. 646/178-34-33, 1 P.M.–midnight Mon.–Thurs., 1 P.M.–1 A.M. Fri.–Sat., 1–8 P.M. Sun.). This classy restaurant doubles as a wine bar, with an incredible collection of Baja regional wines and a very knowledgeable staff.

Events

The 50-mile **Rosarito-to-Ensenada Cycle** has grown into such a popular event that promoters had to split it up to make it biannual. This party on wheels rolls through the streets of both towns and the road in between in May and November. Weary but jubilant finishers will usually boogie the rest of the weekend in Ensenada.

The other spectacle on wheels to hit Ensenada is the **SCORE Baja 1000.** This 1,000-mile off-road race is known as the toughest rally on the planet and many contestants drive their 4x4s, motorcycles, and dune buggies out to the Ensenada start line each November to test their mettle on the course. Each year the course is a little different, with some years featuring a loop course that starts and ends in Ensenada and others using a point-to-point course that ends in La Paz. Either way, when the racers are in town there's bound to be some wild parties that crop up.

SHOPPING
Rosarito

The majority of Rosarito's shopping is art-related. Fine art paintings, sculptures, hand-painted ceramics, hand-carved furniture, tile, and even pink lawn flamingos. There are a number of stores and shops that line the main drag throughout town, but the best concentration is on the southern outskirts along the **Arts & Crafts Corridor** (tel. 661/613-18-40, www.afamaro.com). The corridor is along Boulevard Popotla, south of where Boulevard Juárez forks into this road. The selection of hand-crafted woods, ironworks, earthenware, and ceramics is probably the most diverse in all of the northern Baja cities. Many of the shops are open-air stalls facing the east side of the road, with free-standing shops interspersed. My suggestion is to drive south to the outskirts of town and make your way north up these shops, which include finer galleries such as the ivy-covered **Polos Gallery** (Km 40 Tijuana–Ensenada Scenic Toll Road, tel. 661/612-92-34, www.polosgallery.com), which features a variety of work from artists all over Baja, and the large upscale furniture store **Fausto Polanco** (Blvd. Benito Juarez #2400, tel. 661/612-22-71, 10 A.M.–6 P.M.).

In town, the **Rosarito Beach Hotel Shopping Arcade** (Blvd. Benito Juarez #31, tel. 661/612-01-44, 10 A.M.–6 P.M. daily) is also a good spot to root out fine art at galleries such as **Mission Gallery** and a **Galeria del Mar.** It is also a center for folksy interior decorations and dishes, with one of the town's most impressive collections of Día de los Muertos dolls and Talavera pottery. Some of the best items are at **Curios Maria** and **Plaza del Sol** (both at Rosarito Beach Hotel Shopping Center at Blvd. Benito Juarez #31, tel. 661/612-01-44, 10 A.M.–6 P.M. daily, 10 A.M.–6 P.M. daily).

North of that, in the heart of the club district, **Plaza Pueblo Shopping Center** (Blvd Benito Juarez and Ave. Eucalipto, 10 A.M.–6 P.M. daily) is another must-stop for shoppers. Located along Boulevard Juárez between Calle del Nogal and Eucalipto, this little plaza is set in a recessed nook away from the craziness of the main strip. There's a little waterfall that welcomes visitors into the green courtyard and inside you'll find shops carrying hand-crafted leather products, a rustic furniture shop, and a cigar shop.

© ERICKA CHICKOWSKI

© ERICKA CHICKOWSKI

Avenida Lopez Mateos in Ensenada

Ensenada

Of the three northern Baja cities, Ensenada's main tourist district has the most sane shopping scene. Almost all stores are in freestanding buildings, all marked with store names and with well-organized merchandise that is relatively free of dust. Likely this has to do with the fact that this port town is where the cruise ships dump off their American passengers for day trips, and shopkeepers have tried to keep up with the average tourist's tastes.

The bulk of these stores is clustered around **Avenida Lopez Mateos,** from Avenida Ryerson on the west to Avenida Espinoza on the east. Two of the store types you'll find in great abundance here are leather shops and silver jewelers. For the leather, especially boots and jackets, make a beeline toward **Iguanas Internacional** (Av. Lopez Mateos 529, tel. 646/178-26-32). Two of the nicest silver shops are **Mario's Silver** (Av. Lopez Mateos 1090) and **Los Castillo** (Av. Lopez Mateos 1076, tel. 646/178-23-35). If you insist on bringing home your weight in tourist tchotchkes like T-shirts and shot glasses, there

is no shortage of these items on Lopez Mateos. Like the Starbucks of Ensenada, **Habana Banana** has a store on practically every block of this avenue. These brightly colored stores are filled with cute stuffed animals, key chains, brightly colored pencils, and all of the other trinkets that say, "I was there. Prove it? I bought this stuff!"

Running parallel to Lopez Mateos just a block south, Boulevard Costero also has its share of stores to browse. Browse through the indigenous-style designs of the Mata Ortiz pottery at **Galleria de Perez Meillon** (Blvd. Costero 1094). Or just take a walk through jewelry and trinket stalls in front of the fish market.

For deals on clothes, take a walk away from the main tourist drags and blend with the locals. North of Lopez Mateos along Gastelum, Ruiz, and Obregon are the blocks where the locals go to shop. This area is less Americanized and you are more likely to find a deal on some nice threads or a cute pair of shoes. There are boutiques, such as **mistiK** (Ruiz 735), shoe stores like **Estilos** (Av. Obregon

438, tel. 646/178-16-71) and **Estrella** (Av. Gastelum 430, tel. 646/174-07-38), and jewelry shops such as **Diana Joyería** (Sexta 349, tel. 646/178-14-75).

It is also possible to immerse yourself in the authentic *mercado* experience as well. The **La Bufadora market** is at the end of Punta Banda, a spontaneous jumble of stalls that thrives on the tourist traffic that passes through to see La Bufadora blowhole. It is a spectacle of open-air shopping that has become an attraction all of its own. This is the place to go if you'd like to haggle a little bit over a woven poncho, some unique earrings, or a plate decorated by finger-painting artists who deftly conjure palm-tree beaches with the stroke of a pinky.

SPORTS AND RECREATION
Surfing
The coastal highway south of Tijuana is like

BARGAINING BASICS

Shopping south of the border is usually a unique experience for Americans who are used to a fixed price for most things they buy. In Mexico there is usually a fair amount of wiggle room for negotiation about items sold in most venues, and bargaining is common and expected. This is especially true for *mercados*, street stalls, and other open-air venues.

Bargaining is a game that many of the vendors down here are very well-versed in, so don't be afraid to participate in a bit of gamesmanship yourself to get the price down. The following are a few critical tips for improving your haggling.

- Don't show up in fancy duds or jewelry. Wearing "tells" of wealth like that puts you in a crummy bargaining position, one that a vendor will always silently note and sometimes may even harp on during a heated round of negotiation.

- Never seem too interested. One of my least favorite shopping partners in Tijuana is my grandmother, who can never seem to stop herself from exclaiming, "Look at this! How beautiful!" to every bauble that strikes her fancy. She doesn't seem to get it that we'll never be able to get a fair price if the vendor knows she's hell-bent on buying something.

- Be prepared to walk away. This is a corollary of the above rule. Some of the best offers you'll receive from vendors will be shouted at you just after you've shrugged your shoulders and started to meander away. If a vendor feels that they're losing you, he or she will usually start slashing the price.

- Never enter into bargaining negotiations if you have no intention to buy something. It's not fair to waste the seller's time.

- Spread your cash around — on your body, that is. A good way to get a deal is to make an offer that ends with, "This is my last twenty dollars." Sure it's a white lie but don't kid yourself, this is a game of fibbing. Just be careful not to carry too much cash in areas that are accessible to pickpockets.

- Don't be a jerk. Bargaining for the purchase of something is like reverse sales. The sweeter you are, the more likely you'll get your way. Its OK to be firm, but don't insult the poor salesperson.

- Bargain with a sense of humor. Bargaining can be a fun way to interact with the locals.

- Some things aren't negotiable. Certain stores do have fixed prices — you can usually tell because the mark-up isn't 40 percent more than the products are worth. If a shopkeeper tells you that there's no haggling, be sure to respect that. Similarly, food from restaurants and street vendors are not meant to be bargained for.

- Above all, bargain fairly. Remember the economic realities of the people you're bargaining with. Bargain with respect to the seller and decide on a mutually beneficial price. Doing so contributes to the local economy.

a bread-crumb trail to surfers hungry for new and interesting breaks. Many of the old spots north of Rosarito have been cordoned off by high-rise condo development, but go south and you can still drop in on waves that have been the stuff of legends for decades.

When you are trolling for a good break, it makes sense to depart Rosarito from the free road, Carreterra Libre Tijuana-Ensenada, which hugs closer to the coast than the toll road does until it curves inland at La Fonda. From there you can hop on the toll road the rest of the way to Ensenada.

If you were too worried about bringing an expensive quiver down to Mexico, board and wetsuit rentals are available at **Inner Reef Surf Shop** (Km 34.5 Tijuana–Ensenada Scenic Toll Road, tel. 661/615/08-41). This is a good place to stock up on wax, rash guards, and other accessories.

Just about five minutes south of that is where the hunt for waves begins. At kilometer markers 36 and 38, **K36** and **K38** are both well-known breaks with camping spots close at hand. K38 is best known for its right-breaking reef curls. Like many of the breaks on the road to Ensenada it is rocky here, so be sure to pack protective booties.

Twelve miles farther and you'll reach the resort of La Fonda, which overlooks a pretty consistent beach break. There is a popular campground and a motel on the cliff next to the resort, so you don't have to pay for expensive digs.

Translated to "leave if you can," **Salsipuedes** (Km 87, $5 per car) is a classic point break that many surfers have a heck of a hard time happily departing when the waves are firing. The undeveloped coast and the pretty little campground at Salsi may not remain a classic for long. Rumor has it that a big-city developer purchased the land and plans on assaulting the landscape with a big condo project. Stop here while you can, before this place disappears.

As you approach Ensenada's Bahia Todos Santos, **San Miguel** is a fun point break but it can be really crowded on the weekends. Best bet is to hit this in the middle of the week. Other nearby alternatives include **California Trailer Park, 3 Ms,** and **Stacks.**

The real kamikazes don't reach their favorite Ensenada spot by car. Located twelve miles off the shore of Ensenada at the mouth of Bahia Todos Santos, the Islas Todos Santos are positioned in front of one of the most extreme breaks off the North American coast. Dubbed **Killer's** for a reason, this break is created by a deep-water trench that harnesses the power of winter swells to create behemoth waves that can regularly reach thirty feet. This spot is not a joke, and you can easily be seriously injured or killed if you don't have the skills—and sometimes even if you do. Those who wish to test their mettle can get there by chartering a boat from **Juanito's Boats** (Ensenada Sportfishing Terminal at Blvd Costero and Ave. Macheros, tel. 646/174-09-53, dawn–dusk daily) in the port of Ensenada.

Fishing

If you've already got your rods, reels, and tackle at hand, **Rosarito Pier** can be a fun place to throw out a few casts. But really, the best fishing in this region is based in Ensenada. There the Malecón is a hub of fishing boats, and several outfitters will board from here to motor out of the bay to hunt deep ocean waters. The largest outfit in town is **Sergio's Sportfishing** (Ensenada Sportfishing Terminal at Blvd Costero and Ave. Macheros, tel. 646/178-21-85 or 800/336-5454 (from U.S.), www.sergio -sportfishing.com, day trips $50 and up).

Also an option is **Gordo's Sport Fishing Fleet** (Ensenada Sportfishing Terminal at Blvd Costero and Ave. Macheros, tel. 646/178-35-15). If you only need a boat, rentals are available from Juanito's Boats.

Golf

On the road to Ensenada, **Bajamar Golf Resort** (Km 77 Tijuana–Ensenada Scenic Toll Road, from U.S. tel. 619/425-0081, www .bajamar.com/golf, $99 weekends, $75 weekdays) likes to tout itself as the "Pebble Beach of Mexico." The key here is that last prepositional phrase. The course is one of the nicest in northern Baja, but don't come expecting the same level of landscaping or clubhouse amenities as you would from Pebble. Do expect great views, though. They come on the middle holes of the Oceano course, with fairways and greens set amid craggy cliffs wet with ocean spray.

Within Ensenada city limits, the **Baja Country Club** (Fancisco I Modero Cañon San Carlos, tel. 646/177-55-23, www.bajacountry club.com, $46.75) has a sun-dappled 18-hole course that runs in a wide valley. Beginners can have a good round on this course, which is mostly flat and has only a smattering of difficult hazards.

ACCOMMODATIONS
Rosarito

You can find **Los Pelicanos** (Calle Cedros 115 at Calle Ebano, tel. 661/612-04-45, $85 d) on the north end of Rosarito as you drive through town along the free road. This little inn is one of the best deals in town. The bilingual staff is friendly and accommodating, and most of the rooms come with an ocean view from the patio. The hotel exterior is evocative of a building you'd find in a town square in old Mexico, with irregular stonework and a wooden turret accenting the roof. Guest rooms are a bit dated with dark woods and out-of-fashion furniture, but they are clean.

Erected smack dab in the middle of the hooting and hollering entertainment district, **Festival Plaza Hotel** (Blvd. Benito Juarez #127-1, tel. 888/295-9669, www.festival plazahotel.com, 24 hrs., $150 d) is party central in Rosarito. The hotel is part of a giant complex with clubs, restaurants, a pool, volleyball courts, and a Ferris wheel. It is a great home base for groups of young singles who plan on carousing until all hours of the night. Not so much for anyone who plans on getting a little sleep. Rooms are extremely basic with no phone, no TV, not even a painting on the wall. Which is convenient, because the frames would probably rattle to the beat of the pounding bass anyway.

Situated on the south end of town right on the beach, **Rosarito Beach Hotel** (Blvd. Benito Juarez #31, tel. 661/612-01-44, www .rosaritobeachhotel.com, $129 d) is geared toward families and couples who are tired of the clubbing scene. This historic resort was founded in 1925 as a club and casino for rich Americans who had money burning a hole in their pockets and a powerful thirst for Mexican liquor. The casino's long since shut down, but the hotel still remains the "it" hotel in town. It has two pools, an oceanview bar, an art gallery, and an area to play billiards and foosball. The hotel frequently leads arts and crafts activities for the kiddies and at night it runs a dinner show on the former casino-room floor.

Also on the property is a cozy spa, which is set in the former guesthouse of the hotel's founder. The lavishly decorated interior was where he'd invite his celebrity guests to stay. Their former guestrooms are now the spa's treatment rooms.

Roadside Accommodations

There are a number of notable hotels on the road to Ensenada that can either make a convenient place to spend an evening along the way or a comfortable spot to settle in for the whole getaway.

Just south of Rosarito, **Hotel Calafia** (Km 35.5 Tijuana–Ensenada Scenic Toll Road, tel. 661/612-15-80, www.hotel-calafia.com, $115 d) rests on a rocky ledge above a little bay. Guestrooms are sprinkled throughout a property that has a small Japanese garden and several reproductions of Spanish missions in Baja and San Diego. Each room does come with an ocean view, but rooms are small and the finishing work in the bathrooms has something left to be desired. If you can get a good deal in the shoulder season it can make a suitable evening rest stop, but avoid this place when rates are above $100 in the summertime.

A better choice in the same area is **Grand Baja** (Km 44.5 Tijuana–Ensenada Scenic Toll Road, tel. 661/614-14-88 or 877/315-1002 (from U.S.), $79 d, one bedroom villa $159) just outside of Puerto Nuevo. This is a complete resort along the waterfront with a pool, tennis courts, and spa. Furnishings are modest, but the rooms are clean and spacious.

About halfway between Rosarito and Ensenada, **Hotel La Fonda** Km 59.5 Tijuana–Ensenada Scenic Toll Road, tel. 646/155-03-07,

$100 s, $165 d) has cozy oceanfront rooms along a quiet, sandy beach. The property overlooks a popular surf break and the restaurant here has a stunning view from its *palapa*-shaded tables. Rooms are modest and they don't come with a TV or a phone. This hotel has a lot of loyal followers who come every summer, which tends to make rates at that time overpriced for what the hotel is worth.

Ensenada

Without a doubt, Ensenada has some of the nicest hotels in northern Baja. Two of the best American-style resorts are on the north end of the city as you approach the port. ◖ **Hotel Coral Resort and Marina** (Km 103 Tijuana–Ensenada Scenic Toll Road, tel. 646/175-00-05, $125 d) is a large facility that has immaculate rooms equipped with new furnishings, mini-fridge, and bathrooms with marble countertops and floors. The building is designed so that all rooms come with a view of the full-service marina. The property has an outdoor heated pool surrounded by beautiful landscaping, an additional indoor pool, and a fitness center. Tennis courts are free for guests, as are racquet rentals.

Only a few doors down, **Las Rosas Resort and Spa** (Km 105.5 Tijuana–Ensenada Scenic Toll Road, tel. 646/174-43-10, $132 d) is a more intimate option. Its rooms also feature marbled bathrooms, comfortable beds, and tasteful decor. The highlight here is the infinity pool that looks out to the ocean.

San Nicolas Resort (Guadalupe 1530, tel. 646/176-19-01, www.sannicolashotel.com, $65 d) is closer to downtown but it isn't as nice. The furniture and decor is dated—the whirlpool-tub suite looked like it was done up by the set designer from *Scarface*. Still, though, it is a good value for families who don't need trendy digs. The pool here is huge and the beds are the most comfortable in all of Baja. I have it on good authority that the mattresses are handmade by a local craftsman.

The rooms are also dated at **Posada el Rey Sol** (Ave. Blancarte #132, tel. 646/178-16-01 or 888/311-6871 (from U.S.), www.posada elreysol.com, $85 d), but who cares? This is the nicest motel downtown and it is within stumbling distance of Hussong's. There's a modest breakfast included in the room rate and the neighborhood is safe.

◖ **Estero Beach Resort** (Ave. Jose Moreles and Lupita Novelo O., tel. 646/176-6230, www.hotelesterobeach.com, $125 d) is kind of a trek from downtown, but it is well worth the travel time. This family-oriented resort has enough to keep you busy without ever leaving the premises. There's a heated pool with swim-up bar shaded by palms, a waterfront boardwalk with bike rentals available, and a beachfront café. The large property also has basketball, volleyball, and tennis courts, plus a children's playground. It is also home to one of the few sandy beaches in Ensenada.

Camping

Camping the Tijuana–Ensenada Scenic Road is a rite of passage for many American surfers and adventure seekers, who are drawn to the simplicity and the beauty of the oceanside digs along the way. Many sites here are nothing more than empty lots where you're free to pitch a tent, with very little in the way of bathroom facilities or picnic tables.

There are a few exceptions, however, including **KOA Rosarito** (7.5 miles south of the Tijuana Toll Gate, San Antonio exit, tel. 661/613-3305, $25 per site). This RV campsite sits on a bluff looking out over the ocean and features hot showers, laundry facilities, a grocery store, dump station, and night security.

Not far south from there, **Chuy's Famous K36 Camping** (Km 36.5 Carr. Libre Tijuana–Ensenada, tel. 664/613-20-53, $13 per site) is a popular site with surfers who come to paddle out in the water just below the campground. It is also only two clicks north of one of the most well-known surf breaks on this stretch, K38.

Halfway between Rosarito and Ensenada, **Playa Alisitos** near La Fonda allows campers to pitch a tent on bluff overlooking the ocean. This a popular choice with penny-pinching surfers. Day use is $5 per car and overnight is $7.

It is a rocky and bumpy route down a dirt road from the toll road, but drivers with four-wheel drive are well rewarded when they reach **Salsipuedes** (Km 87) campground. The grounds are shaded by eucalyptus and pepper trees and it is just a short walk down the low-lying bluff to the waves crashing onto a rocky beach. The cost is $8 per night.

Just a couple miles north of Ensenada, the beach at **San Miguel** is open to tent camping for only $10 per night. There are also RV hookups nearby, also for $10 per night.

Facilities are bare-bones, but there are hot showers available.

FOOD
Rosarito

The *carnitas machaca* at **La Flor de Michoacán** (Blvd Juarez 291, tel. 661/612-18-58, 8 A.M.–10 P.M. daily $5) can be an instant hangover cure in the morning when paired with this little eatery's fresh-squeezed orange juice. The restaurant specializes in roasting pork, serving up piles of juicy and crisp *carnitas* any which

---

MEXICAN GRUB GUIDE FOR GRINGOS

Many of us have the basic Spanish food terms down pat: *cerveza* for beer, *arroz con frijoles* for rice and beans, *pollo* for chicken, and so on. But this is only the tip of the iceberg in the Spanish-speaking lexicon for foodies in search of gastronomic adventure while down in Mexico and San Diego at large.

If you're interested in trying new flavors but would like to know what you are in for before ordering, the following list is a good cheat sheet for understanding Mexican food terminology.

- *Adobada:* spicy pork, also referred to as *al pastor*
- *Agua Fresca:* lightly mashed fruit in sugar water
- *Barbacoa:* barbecue
- *Birria:* spicy stew, often made with goat, lamb, or mutton
- *Buches:* pork belly
- *Cabeza:* literally cow head, but usually just the cheek
- *Caldo:* soup
- *Carnitas:* shredded pork
- *Cesos:* brains
- *Chilaquiles:* fried tortillas in mole or ranchero sauce, typically served for breakfast
- *Chorizo:* Mexican sausage
- *Churro:* fried pastry stick, similar in taste to a sugar donut
- *Elote:* fresh corn

- *Empanada:* pastry turnovers, usually stuffed with meat
- *Langosta:* lobster
- *Lengua:* cow tongue
- *Mariscos:* seafood
- *Menudo:* a traditional spicy soup made with tripe and hominy
- *Molcajete:* a bowl made from lava rock designed for grinding food mortar-and-pestle style; on a menu it is usually filled with grilled meats
- *Mole:* a rich sauce traditionally using chocolate and ground chiles, typically served over meats
- *Nopalito:* cactus
- *Parrilla:* grill
- *Telera:* a tasty roll used to make *tortas*
- *Torta:* a Mexican sandwich
- *Tripas:* tripe

© ERICKA CHICKOWSKI

Some tourists head to the source for dinner. Ensenada is a great place to seek out fresh fish if you have the means to cook.

way you want it during each meal of the day. The food here is a great deal for families, who can split about of pound of *carnitas* with tortillas, beans, and rice for about $15.

Hidden away from the craziness of Boulevard Juárez in the Plaza Pueblo shopping center, **Suzanne's** (Blvd. Benito Juarez 4356, tel. 661/613-11-87, 1 P.M.–9:30 P.M. Sun.–Mon. and Wed.–Thurs., 1 P.M.–10:30 P.M. Fri.–Sat., $12) offers a healthy and elegant alternative to the taquerias and *birrias* that checker this main strip. The menu features a good variety of fresh salads and unique dishes such as jalapeño-cream-cheese empanadas and chicken enchiladas in a white sauce with jalapeño-infused strawberries. The quiet dining room is decorated with wine bottles and grape leaves, a tranquil refuge from the party scene outside of the plaza.

Save room for dessert and head across the street to **La Michoacana** (Blvd. Benito Juarez across street from Fiesta Plaza Hotel, 10 A.M.–8 P.M. daily, $3), an ice cream shop that churns all of its

flavors in-house. There are a ton to choose from, such as rum-raisin, mango, burnt cream, and coconut. There are other sweets on the menu, as well as a variety of fresh fruit shakes.

Puerto Nuevo

Once nothing more than a couple of fishermen's shacks along the highway, Puerto Nuevo village has grown up around the appetites of passing travelers who stopped for lobster, tortillas, and beans, washed down with a few cervezas. Nostalgic Baja travelers usually wax on about the good old days in the 1970s when the "restaurants" were just a simple kitchen table in local families' dining rooms.

Now the small village is more commercialized, with half a dozen restaurants lining the street. They all serve the same thing here, Puerto Nuevo–style lobster that is flash fried and served with Mexican accoutrements. **Lobster House** is one of the best known in town, owned by the family that first started feeding hungry travelers all those years ago.

Ensenada

By far the most famous restaurant in Ensenada, **(((El Rey Sol** has prepared fantastic French cuisine since it opened in 1947. The white-tablecloth tables are attended by a knowledgeable staff that can capably pair a fine wine with dishes such as chicken in prune and port wine sauce or duck aux Beaux Arts with a mélange of fresh fruits.

For a real authentic Ensenada seafood feast on the cheap, try the numerous **taco stands** that are adjacent to the Mercado Negro fish market. Usually open between 9 A.M. and 6 P.M., these stalls serve up seafood cocktails and street tacos any way you'd like them. You can usually fill up on $5 or less here.

If you'd rather sit down, **Bahía Mariscos de Ensenada** (Calle Riverol # 207, tel. 646/178-10-15, $11) also serves up fresh Ensenada seafood. There's a whole page of *ceviche* on the menu, including shrimp and octopus, served with fresh guacamole, salsa, limes, and tostadas. Also on the menu are broiled and fried seafood platters, seafood chowders, and seafood cocktails.

There's plenty of places to grab a fast and tasty fish taco in the tourist district, but you'll need to take a bit of a hike uptown to the secret spot the locals prefer. Called **(((El Fenix** (corner of Juárez and Espinoza, $3), this taco stand on the serves some of the most perfectly seasoned and crisp fish tacos I've ever tasted. There are about four people crammed behind the counter: one to prepare the seafood, another to make the batter, the other to dip and fry, and a fourth to take the hot fish out of the oil, place it on to a soft tortilla, and place it in your hands. All along the counter there are bowls of garnish—radishes, pickled carrots, salsas, and onions—and a throng of people chowing down. Best of all, a fish taco only sets you back about a buck. Eat three and you should be set.

INFORMATION AND SERVICES

Rosarito visitors can contact the **Rosarito Convention and Visitor Bureau** (Km 28 Carr. Libre Tijuana–Ensenada 13-B, tel.

661/612-30-78, 9 A.M.–5 P.M. Mon.–Fri.) for brochures and more information about the city. ATMs can be easily found along the entire stretch of Boulevard Juárez in Rosarito. There are also several Pemex gas stations on this road as well. Situated in the Rosarito Beach Hotel shopping complex, **Cyber Café** (Blvd. Benito Juárez #23, 10 A.M.–6 P.M. daily) offers access to a wireless Internet connection.

The **Ensenada Visitors Info Center** (tel. 646/178-24-11, call for hours) is located at the entrance of town on the far eastern corner of Boulevard Costero. Ensenada visitors are also welcome to visit the **Ensenada Tourism Board** (Blvd. Lazaro Cardenas 609, #5, tel. 646/178-85-78, www.enjoyensenada.com, 9 A.M.–5 P.M. Mon.–Fri.) for information and advice about the area.

In Ensenada there is a Pemex station right across Boulevard Costero from the Visitors Info Center and the Mercado Negro. An ATM machine is located nearby inside of Sanborns along Boulevard Costero.

The state tourism office can be reached at 078 while in Baja. If you are harassed by dishonest police, tourism officials urge you to call this number and report the incident.

Emergencies and Police

During an emergency while in Rosarito or Ensenada you can dial 060 to reach the police and 066 to reach the Red Cross for an ambulance. In Rosarito medical treatment is available at the **Baja Medix** medical clinic (Calle Mar del Norte 488, tel. 661/612-12-66). In Ensenada, **Velmar Hospital** (Arenas 151, tel. 646/177-31-63) is a private and modern hospital that has a bilingual staff and accepts most major American insurance policies.

GETTING THERE AND AROUND
By Air

The **Ensenada Military Airport** (tel. 646/176-19-02) is also open to civilian aircraft and international entry. **Ensenada Concierge** (800/418-4613, www.ensenadaconcierge.com) arranges seats aboard private air charters from Southern California. Rides on these planes start at $399. Visitors flying into the airport can call ahead to arrange a free shuttle to downtown from the air strip.

By Car

Be sure to read *Getting There* in the *Tijuana* section of this chapter to understand the vagaries of border crossing and Mexican auto insurance before you make the drive south of Tijuana.

There are two highways to Rosarito and Ensenada. The free road, or Carretera Libre Tijuana–Ensenada, is also known as Old Highway 1. This is the slower route. It follows a more inland route to Rosarito, where it shoots out to hug the coast until La Fonda. From there it cuts back inland as the more easterly route until Ensenada.

The **Tijuana-Ensenada Scenic Toll Road** is Highway 1-D. This four-lane highway is smoother, drives more quickly, and is shorter, too. There are three toll stations between Tijuana and Ensenada that cost $2.70 to pass through. The roundtrip drive costs $16.20. If you are pinching pennies you can still drive the toll road and avoid the Rosarito toll station by exiting to the free road just before town and driving this route through the city. This is the main drag through Rosarito and you will encounter traffic and stoplights along the way. If you aren't in a hurry it is a colorful route that gives a flavor of the long and skinny town from this north to south drive.

The government subsidizes a group of roadside assistants called the **Green Angels** (tel. 646/176-46-75), or Ángeles Verdes, who patrol the roads in search of stranded motorists. The angels are recognizable by their green trucks with overhead light bars. They patrol the major highways and usually pass most points at least twice a day, with mechanics armed with gas and a few spare parts. To report an accident on the toll road, call 800/990-39-00.

By Bus

Mexicoach offers buses from Old Town San Diego and San Yisidro down to Rosarito. The cost is $36 and this ride usually takes about an hour and a half.

To Ensenada, a coach line called **ABC** runs routes from the Tijuana border. Round-trip cost is approximately $20. These modern coach buses have cushioned seats and air-conditioning. The ABC station is located right across the pedestrian crossing near the big yellow taxi stand and buses leave the terminal on the half hour 6 A.M.–9 P.M.

On your way to the bus station you may encounter employees from other bus companies or shady taxi drivers who will claim that they can offer you a better deal south. Avoid these shysters, as many of them are running scam jobs. Some cabbies may tell you that it is a short drive to Ensenada and they can ferry you there. Others might tell you that you need to go to the downtown station to catch the ABC and will try to give you a ride there. Ignore them; none of this is true.

By Taxi

It is possible to arrange a taxi ride to Rosarito from Tijuana, but it will cost anywhere from $35 to $40. This may be an option if you are with several people willing to split the fare. Otherwise, the Mexicoach is your best option. Once you are in Rosarito, taxis are easy to find on just about any city street, any time night and day. The city is pretty compact and most rides in town will only cost about $5.

In Ensenada there are two main taxi companies, **Blue and White Taxis** (tel. 646/178-32-06) and **Yellow Cab** (tel. 646/176-34-75). You can usually hail a cab from the street at most points on Avenida Lopez Mateos or Boulevard Costero. Most fares in town will cost between $5 and $10. The long drive to La Bufadora will usually cost $40, but can be a reasonable fair when split four ways. Even if you are traveling by yourself or with one companion you may be able to find fellow tourists headed that way in the mornings by hanging around the taxi stand at the corner of Lopez Mateos and Miramar.

Remember that no taxis in northern Baja have meters, so always ask for a price before the cabbie shifts into drive. If you are a good haggler it is an accepted practice to negotiate a better fare.

TIPS FOR TRAVELERS
Visas and Immigration
In 2008 the U.S. government began asking that all tourists, even Americans, present a valid passport to enter the country. This is a big deal for those Americans walking or driving across the Mexican border, who may have been used to simply using their license to re-enter the country. This is no longer an acceptable practice, so be sure to bring your passport if you plan to visit Baja.

Mexico requires visitors to carry a special **tourist visa card** that is waived for those who stay less than 72 hours and who visit Ensenada and parts north. If you plan to stay longer or drive south of Punta Banda you will need to get a validated card. They are available at the **Immigration Office,** which is located on Boulevard Azueleta in Ensenada less than a mile east of Costero. It is located along the east side of the port near the Harbormaster's office. You can also get a stamp at the immigration office located at the border in Tijuana. You will have to pay $20 and will need a valid passport or a birth certificate and valid photo ID. The cards are valid for six months.

Telephone
To call Baja telephone numbers from the United States, dial 011-52 and then the ten-digit number.

To call the United States from Baja, dial 00-1 and then the ten-digit number.

Money
In Baja, the currency is the Mexican peso but most places in Tijuana, Rosarito, and Ensenada typically accept U.S. dollars. Travelers who are going outside of these cities may want to exchange money before heading out. Money exchange is available at the border on either side and at the nationalized Banamex and Bancomer branches. Banking hours are typically 9 A.M.–5 P.M. Monday through Saturday. Tipping practices down in Mexico are also standard, though taxi drivers are not customarily tipped there.

HEALTH AND SAFETY
Crime
Don't let scary crime reports from Tijuana or Rosarito keep you away. I'm not going to sugar-coat things. Mexico is a developing country and Tijuana is a big city not without its foibles. The drug trade is rampant in TJ and along with it comes the all-too-real brutality of warring drug kingpins. But even though violent crime is a factor down there, it rarely affects U.S. tourists.

As one business owner told me over a glass of wine, "It's social pruning. The bad guys, they kill each other. And sometimes the politicians."

The fact of the matter is that if you follow the same level of precaution you would in, say, Los Angeles or New York City, you're probably going to be fine. Be aware of your surroundings. Watch what kind of neighborhood you park your car in, being sure to lock the doors and move valuables out of sight. Keep a firm hold of your purses and wallets to protect from pickpockets. Don't go walking alone at night, whether you're male or female. Even in a group, avoid dark alleys or parks at night. It is all the basic self-preservation stuff that your parents taught you when you were a kid.

Tourists should be especially wary of visiting the infamous red-light district in Zona Norte. Known as La Coahilla, the name of the main street here, this neighborhood is full of the criminal element. Even the cops are not so nice here—of all the places you risk a "shake-down" from a corrupt TJ officer, this is the most likely spot.

One final note of warning: Guns are outlawed in Mexico. Don't even think about bringing weapons into the country. If you are caught with one you could face serious legal troubles.

Sexually Transmitted Diseases
Prostitution is illegal in Mexico, but that doesn't stop the bustling sex trade in Tijuana's La Coahilla. City officials and peace officers frequently look the other way when it comes to this ugly side of the city as long as the money keeps streaming in from across the border.

AIRLIFTING TO U.S. HOSPITALS

Air transport to the United States is available through several companies, but these emergency lifts are expensive – sometimes upwards of $25,000. You'll need to work with the company to make sure your insurance will cover this cost before take-off and that can shave valuable minutes from emergency treatment time. Because of these challenges, it sometimes makes sense to receive treatment in a Mexican facility if the emergency is not too dire.

The following companies provide medical air transport between Baja California and San Diego:

Air Ambulance Specialists, Inc.
800/424-7060
720/875-9182
www.airaasi.com

AirLink
From Mexico: 800/024-8600
From U.S.: 888/673-7427
From Canada: 866/826-1177
www.airlinkambulance.com

Air Medical
866/945-8959
830/625-3500
www.air-medical.com

Air Trek Inc.
800/633-5387
800/247-8735
941/639-7855
www.medjets.com

Skyservice Air Ambulance
800/463-3482
514/497-7000
www.skyservice.com

If you decide to travel to Baja frequently, another noteworthy group to consider working with is the **Binational Emergency Medical Care Committee** (www.binationalemergency.org). U.S. citizens who join this group as a member have the right to call 619/425-5080 at any time for immediate transport out of Mexico.

If you're considering a visit to the ladies of the night (or, ahem, gents dressed like ladies) keep the following in mind. Though the government does try to regulate sex workers in the city and operates a health registry, inspections are sporadic and government workers are notorious for being easily bought out. A 2006 report published in *The Journal of Urban Health* conducted by researchers from the University of California–San Diego School of Medicine found that only half of the female sex workers in Tijuana have ever been tested for HIV. The same report also found that as many as one percent of Tijuana's inhabitants may be infected with the disease.

Illegal Substances

Though they might be readily available south of the border, marijuana and other street drugs are illegal in Baja Norte. Bringing drugs across the border or carrying them on your person or in your car puts you at risk of being thrown in jail. And that is something you want to avoid. Mexican jails make the county lock-up look like Disneyland. There are no cots, not even a mealtime. Prisoners must rely on family or friends to bring them food. The bureaucracy of the Mexican legal system is notoriously complex and the U.S. Consulate can only do so much for American citizens who've actually committed a crime in Mexico.

Dealing with the Authorities

Some corrupt officers in Baja have made it their mission to collect some almighty tourist dollars for themselves by preying on vacationing visitors. Knowledge is power in a shakedown situation, though. Many of these crooked cops will back down if you let them know you are aware of the laws. Ask them to politely write you a ticket in English or let you go. They are not allowed to detain you needlessly. Tell them that you are not willing to pay them personally, but will mail your ticket and fine to the address on the ticket. If you are the victim of any kind of misconduct, be sure to call the Tourist Assistance Hotline at 078 from anywhere in Baja.

BACKGROUND

The Land

GEOGRAPHY

San Diego County is the most southwesterly county in the United States. Sitting against the Pacific Ocean, this 4,255-square-mile trapezoid of land is cushioned between Orange County and Riverside County to the north, Imperial County to the east, and Baja California in Mexico to the south.

The region is made up of a mix of terrain whose diversity is unmatched in just about any other part of the country. Along the coast there are sandstone cliffs, brackish marshes, and sandy beaches. Venture inland and encounter verdant mountainsides, grassy valleys, and rivers hidden in secret canyons. Trek even farther east and those mountains slope down to the desert floor and even more hillsides, these ones baked and covered in agave, cactus, and other succulents.

GEOLOGY

Experts break the county up roughly into thirds when explaining the geological makeup of the region. First comes the Coastal Plain, which is largely defined by the layers of sedimentary rock that tell the story of over 140 million years of life by sea and river here. Visitors can view the "layer cake" themselves by visiting the cliff areas of La Jolla Cove or Sunset Cliffs Natural Park in Ocean Beach. Next

© ERICKA CHICKOWSKI

SAN DIEGO QUICK FACTS

Nickname: America's Finest City
Incorporated: 1850
Population: 1,311,162
Land area: 342.5 square miles
Time zone: Pacific Time
Second largest city in California
Eighth most populous city in the United States
County: San Diego
Ethnicity: 46 percent white, 27 percent Hispanic, 15 percent Asian, 7 percent black
Sunshine: 300 days per year
High/low temperature averages: 66°F/54°F in winter, 74°F/62°F in summer
Average rainfall: 9.32 inches annually
Major employers: Federal government, state and municipal government, Qualcomm, Sharp Medical Center
Area colleges and universities: University of California-San Diego, San Diego State University, University of San Diego, Point Loma Nazarene University, Thomas Jefferson School of Law, Mesa College, California Western School of Law, San Diego City College, San Diego Community College
Median income in 2006: $61,043
Sales tax: 7.75 percent
Hotel tax: 10.5 percent

are the Peninsular Ranges, mountains forged through the combination of volcanic activity and tectonic plate shifts. At their base, these mountains are made up of granitic rocks formed from cooling magma produced from the force of an ocean plate being subducted, or pushed under, the North American Plate. During the process the sediment surrounding the plates and the magma were also heated up and metamorphosed, or changed, into amazing minerals and gems such as marble, quartzites, schists, and tourmaline.

A lot of this metamorphic sedimentation can also be found in the third geological zone, the Salton Trough. Here in the Anza-Borrego Desert the sedimentation formed in the Peninsular and surrounding mountains, along with that carried by the ancient Colorado River, have filled a giant cavity in the earth's crust up to five miles deep. The cleft in the base rock is a tectonic extension of the Sea of Cortes, which separates Baja California from mainland Mexico.

The sediment filling the Salton Trough has left behind a treasure trove of rare gemstones and minerals, ancient marine deposits, and fossils.

Visiting rock hounds who are interested in more information should consider contacting the San Diego Mineral & Gem Society, which runs classes and field trips to local areas in search of various rare gems and minerals. Within Anza-Borrego State Park there is a strict "look, but don't touch" policy regarding fossils or geological specimens. If you are interested in learning more about rock formations in the desert, your best source of information will be the Anza-Borrego Visitors Center. The center has an 18-mile self-guided tour along the "Erosion Road" that can provide a good introduction to the Santa Rosa Mountains, the Borrego Badlands, and the Salton Sea without ever leaving the pavement.

CLIMATE

San Diego's legendary Mediterranean climate is about as perfectly sunny and fair as it gets. But meteorologists here don't have it as easy as you'd think. The region is actually broken up into four distinct "microclimates" that can swing the weather significantly in as few as two or three miles.

Coastal

This is the pleasantly sunny microclimate that defines San Diego. Summer highs typically only poke the temperature up into the high 70s and winter lows rarely dip below the mid 40s.

The only break in the sunshiny days is when the marine layer, a high-level fog, rolls in from the ocean some evenings. It usually burns off in mid-morning, except for some days in June where the sun's rays can't quite push through. San Diegans call this phenomenon June Gloom.

Inland Valleys

Just a couple miles inland from the coast, temperature highs and lows are more extreme. These areas also tend to catch the brunt of rain and thunder showers that pass over the coast. In the summer the temperatures are regularly ten to fifteen degrees hotter than along the shoreline and in the winter they can drop below the coastal norms.

Mountains

Once in the mountains, you can encounter quickly fluctuating weather patterns. The mountains here are the cause of a natural effect called a "rain shadow." When stormy clouds blow over the county the mountains trap them from passing and generally get soaked as a result. Winter brings more rain here than at the coast, along with an occasional dusting of snow. Summer brings intermittent thundershowers. Weather can get hot in the summer, but once the sun goes down even tank-top days can turn to sweater evenings. Winter months are chilly, so be sure to pack a fleece.

REGIONAL WILDFIRES

San Diego is a land of water and fire. Just as the ocean is an environmental constant in the region, so too are wildfires. The chaparral landscape that is so persistent in San Diego and Southern California in general is one that thrives on the natural cycle of fire and regrowth that runs in the region. In fact, many plants in this ecosystem will only germinate after being exposed to the extreme temperatures found in a wildfire.

Typically, wildfire season is in October when the warm Santa Ana winds sweep in from the north and eastern deserts. Vegetation is already dry from so little precipitation during the spring and summer months, so all it takes is one spark from human or natural sources to get a blaze started. Once the flames begin, the winds can potentially whip them up to monumental proportions.

One of the worst San Diego fire seasons on record occurred in 2007, when more than 325,000 acres burned across the county with multiple simultaneous fires blazing at once. Fires licked the pine trees of Palomar Mountain, barreled through Rancho Bernardo and Poway, swept through Campo, and came dangerously close to Chula Vista.

Although many residents claim to have seen an increase in wildfire frequency and intensity in the region over the past few decades, most scientists beg to differ. According to the Cen-ter for Biological diversity, cycles of wildfires in the San Diego area have been occurring for eons. Experts point to historical evidence of a massive 1889 fire in what is now Orange and San Diego Counties that burned more than 100 miles in length and 10 miles in width as proof that there have always been big fires in San Diego.

The only difference now is that the region's ever-expanding population is now pushing into fire-prone terrain that was once desolate. Nowadays tract homes and McMansions lie directly within the fire path – in 2007 more than 500,000 people were evacuated in the wake of the fire.

Fortunately, San Diego's firefighting force continues to improve its techniques to keep residents and visitors safe from impending fires. They are prepared with high-tech equipment, trained to find and predict the path of fires, and they communicate freely with the media to keep people from danger.

If you are ever in town during fire season and you smell smoke, be sure to check the radio or television to find out if there are any blazes in your vicinity. And if you go camping in the back country, be conscientious and adhere to burn bans when the forest rangers enforce them. You don't want to be responsible for a potentially catastrophic fire if you can help it.

© ERICKA CHICKOWSKI

The yucca plant is a member of the agave family.

Desert

There are two parts to every rain shadow. The desert microclimate is the mountains' foil. All of those storms trapped off of the mountains make for little cloud cover or rainfall in this microclimate. Average summer temperatures in the desert are up to 30 degrees hotter than in the mountains. Borrego Valley's average high in July is 110 degrees and many times the mercury hovers up at 120 degrees. Winter nights are cold, sometimes plummeting into the low teens.

ENVIRONMENTAL ISSUES

San Diego's perfect climate and beautiful environment is, unfortunately, causing its own undoing. So many people come to live here and visit that urban development has created serious problems that threaten the region's whole appeal.

Some of the biggest conflicts between environmental protection and development meant to accommodate tourist traffic and new residents to the area occurs around the coast. So many people want to live and stay around the beach, but more development cuts off access to the coastline and also threatens delicate beach and estuary habitats that can never be replaced once a development mars the landscape.

And the water itself is also a hot-button issue. Runoff from the streets and sewers frequently pollutes local waters, particularly after a bad storm. Area residents and environmental groups are working hard with municipal leaders to mitigate these problems, as this pollution causes long-term damage to fish populations, water vegetation, and reefs.

Flora and Fauna

It follows that an area with such a wide range of geological and climatic variations would also have a pretty broad scope in habitat. The breadth of plant and wildlife that flourishes here has a direct relationship with the wildly divergent geographic zones.

OCEAN

Sometimes the barren and choppy surface of the water can belie the teeming depths below. But look closely from shore or by boat and you will see what beckons from beneath San Diego seas. Strands of kelp wash in with the tides, dolphins frolic in the waves, fish skitter on the surface away from bigger predators below.

In terms of undersea flora, San Diego is best known for the Point Loma giant kelp beds just offshore. This is one of the largest kelp forests in the state. Other underwater plants include stands of eelgrass and other sea weeds, as well as a variety of algae.

Sea Mammals

San Diego is particularly blessed with a remarkable collection of sea mammals. Dolphins and porpoises are frequent sights in the water here. Sometimes they'll breach and spy hop just beyond the breakers, other times they'll snake a wave from resident surfers. You'll sometimes even see them in the shallow waters of Mission Bay.

As in many parts of the state, the charismatic California sea lion is a common sight near the marinas, piers, and rocky shores of San Diego. Their characteristic barks and honks are a portent of frustration for fishermen. These thieving mammals are well-known for poaching lunkers from right off the hook. They also like to bask on docks and rocks to soak up the sunshine.

Seals are also known to scoot up some of the sandy shores here. Children's Pool in La Jolla is a well-known hang-out of these hefty pinnipeds.

Grab a pair of binoculars and look out in the distance during the winter months and you're eventually going to spot a spout or two from migrating gray whales. These mammoth mammals shuttle down south every year to give birth to calves in the warm shallows of the Sea of Cortez.

Other Sealife

In the dark of the San Diego deep there are many pelagic species such as tuna, bonito, and mackerel. All swish away from several shark varieties: blue, mako, and thresher. In the kelp beds, barracuda and angel shark hunt while sheephead, calico bass, and whitefish hide.

Closer into the tidal zones and you'll see corbina, croaker, and guitarfish splashing against the breakers. Sand sharks, halibut, and stingray all take cover in sandy bottoms and lobster and abalone sequester themselves in the rocky crags. In calmer coves the most colorful and notable Garibaldi floats about in orange resplendence. This territorial sunfish is like a giant goldfish, a protected species that California has tagged as its state saltwater fish.

BEACHES AND MARSHES

Where the ocean meets the land is a very special habitat, one that has been greatly altered by the encroachment of developers hell-bent on building homes and businesses as close to the water as possible. What remains of San Diego's lagoons and marshes is only 10 percent of what was there before we made our mark upon the environment.

Fortunately there are still some remaining to appreciate. In and near the wetlands you'll encounter plants like goldenbush, saltgrass, cordgrass, and Southwestern spiny rush.

The water greatly varies in salinity in the lagoons, attracting an array of fresh and saltwater fish. In some saltier areas there are species like topsmelt and killifish, in other brackish and freshwater zones those like goby and striped mullet swish about.

Either way, the abundance of fish and invertebrates such as crab and clams attract hundreds of species. Bird-watchers can spot Great Blue Heron, egrets, terns, gulls, and pelicans circling and pecking at the water's buffet.

RIPARIAN

Closely associated with the marshy wetlands of the county are the region's river, or riparian, habitats. Many of these areas have been wiped out by development and damming of local rivers, but what remain are distinct ecological sectors consisting of plants that rely on a close and constant source of water. Some of the best-known riparian habitats include areas around the San Dieguito, San Luis Rey, and Santa Margarita Rivers. Cottonwood, willow, sycamore, and alder trees are all common in these areas. Water-loving animals that thrive here include California newt, Pacific tree frog, and belted kingfisher. You'll also see red-shouldered hawk floating in to feast on the frogs and fish in the river.

CHAPARRAL AND COASTAL SCRUB

The two most common habitats in the region are chaparral and coastal scrub, which share similarities but are actually distinct biospheres. Both are brushfields dominated by drought-resistant shrubs adapted to the Mediterranean climate. Animals common to both include gopher snakes, squirrels, brush rabbits, and coyotes.

Coastal scrub is sometimes nicknamed "soft

© ERICKA CHICKOWSKI

San Diego's mountains are primarily covered in chaparral.

withstand many months of dry weather. Other low-lying plants include ceanothus, also known as wild lilac, and deerweed. Larger shrubs and trees include toyon, Mexican elderberry, California scrub oak, and at higher elevations, manzanita. Here you might encounter grey fox, bobcat, scrub jays, or California thrashers.

Chaparral is especially susceptible to wildfire—in fact, this habitat depends on the cyclical nature of these blazes. The moisture-saving oils covering many chaparral leaves act as a fire accelerant in many cases. Wildfire here sweeps away a dense canopy of mature shrubs and trees and makes way for a new layer of young foliage. Roots and seeds belowground survive the wildfires to spring anew. Some chaparral seeds don't germinate until after a fire. The heat cracks their thick shells and chemicals released by smoke and flames spur on the new growth.

WOODLANDS AND GRASSES

The statuesque coastal live oak and Engelmann oak are at the foundation of the oak woodland scattered over the inland foothills in San Diego. These open forests are often spread between patchy grassland made up of native grasses such as purple needlegrass and non-native varieties such as cheatgrass, wild oats, mustard, and clover. Sometimes chaparral blends with these woodlands. Other times the understory and open spots will be filled with elderberry, coffee berry, and manzanita. Poison oak is also common here, especially in canyons and near streambeds.

Ground squirrels and acorn woodpeckers root for the oak's fruit in and around the trees. Other common sightings here include mule deer, California king snake, and woodrat.

Climb above 4,500 feet and oak woodland starts to be overtaken by coniferous forest. Oak might continue to grow here, but the landscape is more dominated by coulter pine, Jeffrey pine, incense cedar, and white fir. The occasional mountain lion stalks here, along with the great horned owl, and the high-flying golden eagle.

The canopy of these mountainous firs, cedars, and pines is occasionally interrupted by mountain meadows. One of the most

chaparral" because the leaves and twigs of the plants in these zones are more supple than the traditional chaparral vegetation. The sight and smell of sage dominates coastal scrub, with several variations such as California sagebrush and black sage popping up. Other plant varieties include lemonadeberry, bush monkeyflower, buckwheat, and laurel sumac. The rare Torrey pine is a tree that only grows in the coastal scrub of San Diego County. If you are lucky you might spot Audubon cottontail hopping along, soaring redtail hawks, or the occasional rosy boa or horned lizard rustling the bushes in these areas.

Coastal scrub typically thrives from sea level up to 1,500 feet. As the altitude rises and as you go farther inland, chaparral takes over. The plants here grow taller and thicker than coastal shrub, with bushes and trees so tightly set together that they sometimes seem all part of one giant plant spreading over a mountainside. The most common vegetation here is the chamise, a scratchy and needly bush that is well adapted to well-known in San Diego is Big Laguna Meadow. These moisture-rich habitats are highlighted with lupines, evening primrose, and goldenrod among other grassy varieties. Here you might spot blackbirds, mallards, meadowlark, and meadow mouse.

DESERT

Over the Peninsular Mountains the habitat changes drastically. At first blush the desert might seem a desiccated expanse of nothingness, but it is really animated with the hardiest stock of flora and fauna found in the entire region. Rocky slopes and desert floor are covered in cholla cacti of several varieties, barrel cactus, agave, and creosote. Desert willow and smoke tree billow in the wind and mesquite buzzes with bees collecting nectar for their hives. In the spring wildflowers like primrose and verbena burst into bloom and spindly ocotillo puts on its bright green jammies and orange nightcaps.

Keep still and quiet to catch sight of bighorn sheep, coyote, kit fox, and blacktailed jackrabbit. Roadrunner, kangaroo rat, chuckwalla, and spiny lizard skitter along the ground.

History

ANCIENT CIVILIZATION

San Diego's beaches have been popular for quite a while. It's estimated that the first inhabitants of the county arrived some 20,000 years ago, following herds of migrating animals across the Bering Strait. These original residents became the San Dieguito people, but it wasn't long before the Yuman and Shoshonian peoples made the foray West, occupying much of San Diego County, as well as an estimated one third of California. Not yet aware of fish tacos, many of these groups lived off of a mush made by meticulously grinding acorns and mixing the flour with

© ERICKA CHICKOWSKI

Signs of San Diego's indigenous people still linger in the hillside. Pictured here are ancient Native American grinding holes, called *morteros*.

water. From these groups emerged the Cupeño, Cahuilla, Ipai or Northern Diegueño, the Ipai or Kumeyaay, and the Luiseños, the descendants of whom still live in Southern California today.

SPANISH COLONIALISM
Early Exploration

The thunder before the storm for these indigenous peoples came on September 28th, 1542, when Portuguese-born explorer Juan Rodriguez Cabrillo, flying under the flag of Spain, landed in San Diego bay and claimed the area for the Spanish king. Even though Cabrillo left no permanent settlement, failed to find any cities of gold, died on his voyage, and even the name he gave the area (San Miguel) didn't stick, the expedition was still successful in proving that Alta California was not an island and cementing it into Spanish consciousness.

First European Settlements

Although Sebastian Vizcaíno was to visit briefly on behalf of Spain in 1602, the Spanish crown did much to lay the foundation for the leisureliness now common in San Diego by completely ignoring the area for over a hundred years. Not until Russia began establishing fur colonies in Northern California did Spain decide to assert their property claim in a more permanent way. Thus, in 1769, an expedition made up of Franciscan friars and Spanish soldiers set off for SoCal, some by ship and some by foot. Fraught with illness, bad weather, and maybe not the best of planning, the two groups of foot travelers finally met up with their shipborne companions and built a fortified camp at the top of today's Presidio Hill overlooking what is now Old Town. The original Catholic Mission was hastily built on the site by legendary priest Father Junípero Serra, only to be moved five years later to be closer to reliable water supplies and the Indians they hoped to convert to Christianity. The mission system in California had begun its march northward, colonists arrived from Spain and Mexico, and the first

of many transformations that would rock the area had commenced.

The Missions

The Spanish would go on to establish 21 missions in California, bringing the native people Catholicism, backbreaking labor, and European diseases. The ultimate goal of the missions in Southern California was to convert the Indians, teach them the basics of living in "civilized" society, and then to divest the mission land to the converted Indians (or neophytes) so they could live without the supervision of the clergy. Certainly, the system was heavily flawed, and to this day, controversy rages as to the degree to which the Missions benefited those they hoped to help. The padres ranged from highly compassionate to nearly despotic, but shared a disdain for the native people's pagan and uncivilized ways. That their help was not always appreciated is attested to by an uprising on the site of the present-day mission in 1775, in which angry Dieguenos surrounded the grounds and killed two Spaniards and one Father Louis Jaime, making him California's first official Christian martyr.

MEXICAN RULE

In 1821, Mexico won its independence from Spain and just one year later, California swore allegiance to Mexico. Despite the first homes having been built at the foot of Presidio Hill, San Diego was still essentially a Mexican backwater, and it made little difference to the local citizenry which flag flew atop the Presidio. The activities of the Mexican government would soon have a major impact on the area, however. In 1833, the Secularization Act was passed, effectively closing the missions and handing control over to the Indians they had been built to serve. Over the objections of mission leadership, each head of a household of neophytes was given a homestead, some cattle, and grazing land in common. Although provisions were put in place to prohibit this land and cattle from being sold, it was not long before the neophytes were bullied, cajoled, and downright swindled into parting with their property, and forced back into the wilderness from which they came. Many disreputable locals became wealthy landowners very quickly at the expense of the church and the long-suffering native population.

For many years following Secularization, the story of San Diego is one of decline. Populations fell and soldiers abandoned the venerable Presidio, allowing it to fall into ruin. The Mission buildings themselves were plundered for their tiling and other building materials. The once-promising city became little more than a handful of ranchos and farms, and again, slipped into obscurity. Residents of the province re-branded themselves as "Californios," drawing a distinction between themselves and newer settlers as well as residents of the rest of Mexico. If not for a gradual yet steady stream of Americans trickling across the deserts to the east, and the sudden hostility of the Mexican-American War in 1846, the story of America's finest city may well have become a footnote in the history of Tijuana.

MEXICAN-AMERICAN WAR

On July 29, 1846, U.S. Marines from the warship USS *Cyane* seized the virtually undefended city of San Diego without firing a shot, consummating their victory by raising the American flag in the plaza in Old Town. A few months later, the legendary Admiral Robert F. Stockton arrived by ship and set up his base in the ruins of the old Presidio, creatively renaming the fortress Fort Stockton. From here, he organized the defense of the city, which became violent on only a few occasions. One of these was the Battle of San Pasqual, near present-day Escondido, where the Californios handed heavy casualties to the Americans led by General Stephen Kearney. Despite the embarrassing loss, the United States was eventually victorious, with the Treaty of Guadalupe Hidalgo ceding to the United States all of California, Utah, and Nevada, and big chunks of Colorado, Arizona, New Mexico, and Wyoming to boot. American rule commenced in

earnest, and big changes were on the horizon yet again.

AMERICAN RULE

In the early days of American rule, life progressed much as it did in any growing western town, complete with its share of ranching, gambling, and minor controversy, albeit with more of a latin flair than many other western locales. In 1855, the first lighthouse in San Diego was built at the tip of Point Loma, a miserable affair that was obscured by fog and clouds far too often to be useful. The famous Butterfield Stage cut a path through the eastern portion of San Diego County, breathing life into the dust surrounding present-day Borrego Springs. And in 1857, the colorfully and descriptively named Jackass Mail Line, originating in San Antonio, delivered the first overland mail to the area.

Echoes of the American Civil War

The outbreak of the American Civil War had little immediate impact on San Diego, but left a significant legacy. After the end of hostilities in 1865, a virtual flood of broken men seeking to escape the scenes of savagery struck out for the West and all the myths and hope associated with it. In 1870, A. E. "Fred" Coleman, a former slave turned rancher, discovered gold in the Cuyamaca Mountains. For the next six years, gold fever would sweep through like a firestorm, leaving the towns of Julian, Ramona, and Banner in their wake. Former slaves worked hand in hand with former Confederate soldiers, not only digging ore but also building profitable inns, stores, and restaurants in these out-of-the-way places.

New Town San Diego

Back in the western part of the county, controversy was brewing. In 1850, businessman William Heath Davis valiantly tried and failed to relocate the center of San Diego from the traditional Old Town location to a more sensible place closer to the harbor, to the profound satisfaction of Old Town supporters such as Thomas Whaley. Things were to change, however, when merchant Alonzo Horton turned his considerable fortune and business acumen toward making this move permanent. Horton himself was financially crushed when land prices took a nosedive in the late 1880s, but the lasting success of the Horton Addition has assured his legacy as the "Second Father" of San Diego.

For the next 40 years, San Diego shared in the growth, maturation, and technological advances that transformed the country as a whole. The county of roughly 30,000 souls got telephones, a public library, an opera house, and access to the transcontinental railroad. In 1885, San Diego's heroine horticulturist Kate Sessions moved to town and began beautifying everything she touched, her work still being evident in Balboa Park and many other city areas today. The city's infrastructure also took a huge leap forward during this period, with the arrival of electric street lights, cable cars, and numerous water flumes, dams, reservoirs, and aqueducts. In 1888, the fabulous and iconic Hotel del Coronado opened its doors, later to play host to 15 American presidents and luminaries such as Thomas Edison and Charlie Chaplin. And curiously enough, the city founded by Franciscan missionaries became home to Katherine Tingley and Madame Blavatsky's Theosophical Society as well as the site for the Villa Montezuma, showplace home of famed spiritualist and musical medium Jesse Shepherd, still standing today in all of its eclectic Victorian splendor.

© ERICKA CHICKOWSKI

Kate Sessions was one of the civic leaders responsible for Balboa Park's ascendency during the Panama-California Exposition.

Panama-California Exposes a Park

In 1915, San Diego got a tremendous boost with the opening of the Panama-California Exposition in today's Balboa Park. Built to celebrate the start of traffic on the new Panama Canal, the ornate Spanish Colonial Revival–style buildings and international exhibits served to promote San Diego as a stopping point for ships headed west through the canal. Not only did the Exposition give San Diego some needed exposure, it also began the transformation of Balboa Park from largely open space into the cultural centerpiece it has

become. Many of the stunningly ornate original buildings have been heavily restored and now house museums. The exposition is also said to have planted the seeds for the world-famous San Diego Zoo when several animals that had been on display were quarantined by federal officials and not allowed to leave the site.

NAVY TOWN

It's no secret that San Diego owes much of its success to the United States Navy. The careful and concerted efforts of city boosters brought the mighty USN to San Diego in a gradual way. After making the world's first successful seaplane flight in the waters just off Coronado, Glenn Curtiss invited army and navy officers to the city for complimentary pilot training. This led to the 1911 establishment of North Island Aviation Camp, an area still used for naval aviation. Just eight years later, San Diego was selected as the headquarters for the entire

Pacific Fleet. Since that point, the military has played a huge role in the development of San Diego. From the submarine base at Ballast Point all the way to the Marine Corps' Camp Pendleton, the people and materials of the armed forces have been a vital component of the city's growth and well-being.

SAN DIEGO OF TODAY

A varied economy, based on tourism, defense, agriculture, and, lately, biotechnology, has seen the city through many of the ups and downs that have thrown other cities into serious decline. Despite budget mismanagement and pockets of corruption in city government, San Diego continues to chug right along. The Gaslamp Quarter, once a comfortable home for prostitutes and drug dealers, has been completely transformed into a chic destination for night-clubbers and fans of haute cuisine. Through careful management, San Diego's beach areas have (so far, at least) been spared the plague of being walled off by condos, as has been the fate of many other beach communities nationwide.

Government and Economy

As the home to the U.S. Navy's Pacific Fleet Headquarters and numerous military installations, San Diego's political and economic landscapes are deeply affected by the whims and wishes of Uncle Sam and those who work for him.

Military and defense is one of the top four economic industries in the region, along with tourism, manufacturing, and agriculture. It is only behind manufacturing in terms of financial impact to the area, bringing more than $13 billion into the local economy. In addition to the four biggest industries, the city also has a strong concentration of biotechnology companies, likely pulled in due to the heavy concentration of research colleges, clinics, and institutions in the area, including Scripps Institution of Oceanography, the Salk Institute, and the University of California–San Diego Medical Center.

Telecommunications is also an important niche in the city. In fact, the largest nongovernmental employer in the city is Qualcomm, which has more than 10,000 employees.

In addition to the economic importance of the military to San Diego, it also has a political impact on the area. With so many military families living in town, the city skews conservative, especially compared to other major California cities such as Los Angeles and San Francisco. However, the city is far from the Republican stronghold it once was in past decades. Currently registered Democratic voters edge out Republicans by about seven to six within the county.

Because the federal government has such a large stake of land in the region, it often has a bigger say in municipal politics than it does in many regions. For example, the region is currently in the process of planning a new international airport but it is currently embroiled in debate with military leaders over the preferred spot because its flight patterns could potentially be in conflict with the operations of Marine Air Station Miramar.

The city of San Diego is governed by a city council with a council president, but it has a strong mayor system, so the mayor has a larger say than in many cities who rely on a council executive. Currently the city is embroiled in an economic scandal that dates back to the early 2000s when city leaders voted to enact an overly ambitious—and some argue, illegal—pension system for the more than 11,000 workers employed by the city. The problem was exacerbated by political maneuvering that resulted in a delay of audits done by Wall Street financiers that ended up resulting in municipal bonds being downgraded to junk bond status. This particular problem has caused financial issues for the city that will likely linger for many years.

People and Culture

The people of San Diego are a living contradiction. Founded by priests and funded by the military, the region is full of independent and anti-establishment thinkers. At the same time these folk who rail against "the man" are hard-working family types, many of whom attend mass each Sunday or design advanced systems for the navy during the work week. The latest generation of San Diegans has a growing sense of stewardship over the oceans and beaches, mountains, and deserts that give them so much pleasure. They take advantage of the weather out on their surfboards or bikes, or out for runs and hikes, and they're reminded daily why they pay such a high cost of living and put up with expensive housing. They'd rather be throwing away rent money to live on the beach than be comfortably cooped up in a house on the prairie somewhere.

COMPAÑEROS DE MEXICO

Here's a real-life exchange I once had with an aging Caucasian lady from Seattle.

Me: So, I'm moving to San Diego soon.

Addled Old Lady: Oh, that's nice, that's a beautiful city.

Me: Indeed.

Addled Old Lady: Too bad all of those Mexicans are starting to invade the place.

Me: . . .

Addled Old Lady: They're really taking over. You can't go anywhere in San Diego without seeing one of them.

I try to keep my eyes from rolling to the back of my head when I hear something like this, because no matter what your stance on immigration is it is difficult to deny the fact that San Diego's population and culture is inexorably intertwined with Mexican and Hispanic heritage. You see it in the sights, the street names, the language, and the family-loving atmosphere.

When the Americans won Alta California from Mexico in the Mexican-American War, many of the "Mexicans" that settled here so long ago stuck around. They called themselves "Californios," many were tied to this beautiful region for generations, and they weren't about to let a new government push them away. In fact, some of these Californios embraced American rule, rejecting Mexico City's distant and disorderly oversight. These people aren't taking over San Diego. They've always been a part of the region.

MILITARY INFLUENCE

As the navy's Pacific Fleet headquarters, San Diego is home base for the largest naval fleet in the world. At Naval Station San Diego alone, more than 35,000 sailors and civilians staff the grounds. Thousands more are stationed at the county's nine other navy and marine installations, including the massive Camp Pendleton.

Beyond the economic impact of such a strong military showing, the presence is also felt within San Diego culture. The city leans to the right politically. Single soldiers and sailors kick loose in certain pockets of the city, and they've probably done a lot over the decades to keep beach-area bars and tattoo parlors in business. But they're largely reigned in and outnumbered by their family-oriented compatriots.

Probably the biggest cultural effect of this large population is its diversity. Enlisted people come from all over the country to serve here and many stay or come back once their time in is up. They bring with them new ideas, philosophies, and ways of life that are constantly freshening the San Diego scene.

SURFING CULTURE

Introduced to the region by Hawaiian legend Duke Kahanamoku in 1916, surfing is the sport that defines San Diego. It's soulful and it's aggressive. It's ragingly anti-establishment and relaxed to the point of indifference. Some surfers here spend their whole life in search of that perfect wave, happily renouncing steady employment and physical possessions in favor of their obsession. Others sneak into the ocean to steal a few mushy breaks, if only to have a moment of peace from their kids and jobs. It is blissful escapism in whatever dose they're willing to take.

Out of the water these athletes have been known as iconoclasts and as bums, nihilists and druggies, ever since the sport really started taking off here in the late 1930s. This was a frivolous pastime in a serious world and yet here were these kids throwing everything away to hang out at the beach. Or so said the elders. As time passed into the '50s and '60s the non-conformists who practiced the art of wave-riding embraced their bad reputation. They grew out their hair. They took drugs and partied. They invented skateboards so they could keep riding all hours of the day. And even as society's curmudgeons were wagging their fingers, these surfing bums were building a movement that would spring forth whole communities of like-minded individuals who understood the serenity of paddling out, the cosmic connection with the ocean when dropping into a tube. Communities like Ocean Beach, Encinitas, and Oceanside were all built on a culture tied to the sea and the stoke of surfing.

Today these places are inhabited with a new generation of surfers. There's still a wild streak ingrained in the surfing psyche, but the population has grown more mainstream. There will always be those surfing rebels living out of their vans, hopping beach to beach. But they're joined in the lineup by doctors and lawyers, students and teachers. And, every once in a

MAKING FRIENDS IN SAN DIEGO

San Diego is a transient town. Waves of residents are washed in and out with the tide. That high quality of life draws 'em in and the reality of expenses spits 'em out. Because of this the population is used to making friends quickly, opening themselves up like blooming flowers in the ever-present sunshine.

One sunny day in August, I was walking home from the beach when an unknown neighbor hailed me over and offered me a free beer from his keg. He and his girlfriend and a couple of people were sitting around on kitchen stools and folding chairs on the front lawn, sipping out of red plastic cups. The keg was left over from a charity event the day before and they were inviting every single person that walked, jogged or biked by to stop for a pour or three to help them kill it. By the time I left this "stranger party," there were at least fifteen people huddled around the keg laughing and talking as if they'd known each other for ages. There was the German ex-pat in town to do research with Scripps Hospital, the hotel marketing director just cruising by on her bike to the grocery store, tatted up surfers and primped out beach babes. This was the truest embodiment of the San Diego community I've ever experienced.

while, by one of the old guard who remembers what it means to be a real surf bum.

ESSENTIALS

Getting There

BY AIR
San Diego International Airport

San Diego International Airport is the largest in the region, with over 20 airlines routing domestic and international flights over its tarmac. Major airline carriers include:

- AirTran Airways (800/247-8726, www.airtran.com)
- Alaska Airlines (800/252-7522, www.alaskaair.com)
- American Airlines (800/433-7300, www.aa.com)
- America West Airlines (800/235-9292, www.americawest.com)
- Continental Airlines (800/525-0280, www.continental.com)
- Delta (800/221-1212, www.delta.com)
- Frontier Airlines (800/432-1359, www.frontierairlines.com)
- Hawaiian Airlines (800/367-5320, www.hawaiianair.com)
- JetBlue Airways (800/538-2583, www.jetblue.com)

© ERICKA CHICKOWSKI

- Midwest Airlines (800/452-2022, www.midwestairlines.com)

- Northwest Airlines (800/225-2525, www.nwa.com)

- Southwest Airlines (800/435-9792, www.iflyswa.com)

- United Airlines (800/864-8331, www.ual.com)

- US Airways (800/428-4322, www.usairways.com)

Los Angeles International Airport

One of the nation's largest airports, Los Angeles International (LAX), is also within striking distance. Depending on the fare, it might make sense for some international travelers to book a trip directly into LAX and drive the rest of the way down the coast.

If you are simply a domestic traveler looking to save a couple of bucks by choosing an LAX arrival, be forewarned that you'll still pay. Oh, yes, you will pay. It'll either come in the form of a ridiculous shuttle fare, up to $300 in some cases, or through the depletion of your precious vacation time.

Though Amtrak runs from downtown San Diego to L.A., it does not go directly to LAX. You'll have to make a transfer on the Los Angeles World Airport FlyAway Bus from Union Station to the airport. And the 124-mile driving distance is beguiling. That "easy two-hour drive" can potentially double if you're ensnared in L.A. rush hour (which, in my estimation, is between the hours of 6 A.M. and 5:30 A.M. the following day). Plus, rental cars are more expensive out of this airport than San Diego International.

Other Regional Airports

McClellan-Palomar Airport is the only other airport in the county that offers daily flights from any of the major commercial airline services. United Express flies to and from LAX about seven times each day and US Airways operates a daily shuttle between McClellan-Palomar and Phoenix.

Other municipal airports include **Gillespie**

Field (1960 Joe Crosson Dr., El Cajon, 619/956-4800), **Brown Field** (1424 Continental St., San Diego, 619/424-0455), **Borrego Valley Airport** (1820 Palm Canyon Dr., Borrego Springs, 760/767-7415), and **Montgomery Field Airport** (3750 John J. Montgomery Dr., San Diego, 858/573-1440).

Only a half hour away from San Diego, **Tijuana International Airport** (Carretera Aeropuerto, Tijuana, tel. 664/607-82-01) is often an economical alternative for those flying between San Diego and Mexico. Major airlines include: Aeromexico (tel. 800/021-40-00, www.aeromexico.com), Aerolitoral (tel. 800/021-40-00, www.aeromexico.com), Mexicana (tel. 800/502-20-00, www.mexicana.com), and Aerocalifornia (tel. 800/685-55-00).

BY BUS

San Diego County is serviced by Greyhound Bus Lines at six stations in the region. Three of the most convenient stops are Oceanside (205 S. Tremont St., 760/722-1587), downtown San Diego (120 W. Broadway, 619/239-3266), and at the border in San Ysidro (799 E. San Ysidro Blvd., 619/428-1194).

You can reach Tijuana and Rosarito in the plush shuttle buses run by Mexicoach. These red buses depart San Diego from Old Town and San Ysidro.

Once you cross the border, you can step aboard the private buses run by ABC to reach Ensenada to the south.

BY TRAIN

Amtrak's Surfliner runs through Southern California's coastal cities all the way down to the Santa Fe Depot in downtown San Diego. This train makes several other stops in the county, including Oceanside and Solana Beach.

For easy travel from Los Angeles and Orange County, MetroLink might also be an option. This network of trains north of San Diego County makes forays down to Oceanside Station.

BY CAR
Into San Diego

There are three major routes into San Diego.

From the north, I-5 and I-15 run roughly parallel to one another until they start to converge and come to a point in San Diego's city center. I-5 is the easiest route along the coast from Los Angeles and Orange County. I-15 is best for those headed down from Riverside and the rest of the Inland Empire. This is also the preferred route from Las Vegas. From the east, I-8 is the major route. In the summer this is the annual escape hatch used by Arizonans to flee the blazing temperatures in Phoenix, Scottsdale, Tucson, and Yuma.

Getting Around

BY CAR

Like most of SoCal, San Diego has more than its fair share of concrete cloverleaves. In addition to the major routes mentioned in the *Getting There* section of this chapter, there are also a number of other convenient freeways and highways that connect the county's sites.

In the center of the city both I-805 and Highway 163 are good north to south alternatives to I-15 and I-5.

In North County, Highways 52 and 56 are major east–west connectors between I-5 and I-15. Running parallel to these along the county line, Highway 76 is a two-lane highway that runs through the most remote stretches of the county's northern reaches. Similarly, Highway 78 runs across the middle of the entire county, from I-5 through Ramona, Julian, and the desert. In the central mountains Highway 79 is the main north to south route, running through Cuyamaca Rancho State Park, Julian, and up through Warner Springs. In Anza-Borrego Desert State Park, Highway S-22 runs through the northern part of the park and Highway S-2 curves through the southwest corner.

From downtown, Highway 94 runs southeast into the county's border mountain ranges. Also south of downtown is Highway 904, a spur off of I-5 that leads down to the Otay Mesa border crossing.

Car Rental

San Diego has plenty of rental car agencies. Contact the following to compare rates: **Alamo** (2942 Kettner Blvd., 619/297-0311), **Avis** (3180 N. Harbor Dr., 619/231-7171), **Dollar** (2499 Pacific Hwy., 619/234-3389), **Enterprise** (1691 Hancock St., 619/225-8881), **Hertz** (3202 N. Harbor Dr., 619/220-5222), and **National** (3280 N. Harbor Dr., 619/497-6777).

BY BUS

In the city of San Diego, Metropolitan Transit System runs a fairly robust bus system that covers most of the main tourist areas including downtown, the beaches, Uptown, and more. Some areas are serviced more sporadically than others. The MTS website (www.sdcommute.com)

© ERICKA CHICKOWSKI

San Diego's trolley system travels all the way to the border.

offers a good interactive planning tool to map out your travels in advance.

In North County the North County Transit District runs a more limited line of buses throughout the area communities. There are buses that run between North County and downtown, but they are mostly designed for commuters in these bedroom communities so many routes are set up for work-hour traveling.

BY RAIL

The San Diego Trolley System is one of the most efficient means of public transport to reach your destination—as long as the tracks go there. You'll find the trolley rumbling through downtown, by Old Town, into Mission Valley, and down to the border. This rail system is run by Metropolitan Transit System. Visit the website (www.sdcommute.com) for route and schedule information.

Those traveling between downtown and North County should consider taking the Coaster. This commuter train runs from downtown all the way to Oceanside with six stops along the way.

BY FERRY

Skip the Coronado Bay Bridge and head across the bay by boat. The Coronado Ferry leaves downtown at the Broadway Pier (1050 N. Harbor Dr.) every hour on the hour starting at 9 A.M. and arrives at Coronado's Ferry Landing Marketplace (1st St. and B Ave.) about a half hour later. Similarly, the ferry departs from Coronado at the half hour every hour starting at 9:30 A.M. During the week, the last ferry departs from downtown at 9 P.M. and from Coronado at 9:30 P.M. Operation is extended by one hour on Fridays and Saturdays.

BORDER CROSSING

By car, most San Diegans head south on I-5 in order to venture into Baja. This freeway ends at the San Ysidro border, the busiest border crossing in the world. Crossing into Mexico is simple. Drive through the border stalls and keep your eyes peeled for the traffic light. If the green bulb that says Pase lights up, then

you are free to zip through. This will happen most of the time. If the red Alto light goes off you will be asked to veer right toward the inspection area. No worries—these inspections are picked randomly by a computer and are usually quite brief.

Getting back up to San Diego can take quite a bit longer, anywhere between 30 minutes to several hours. You can call the San Ysidro border crossing information line at 619/690-8999 to ask for approximate wait times. An alternative to San Ysidro is five miles east at the Otay border, near the Tijuana International Airport. To get there, follow the signs from downtown Tijuana to the "Garita de Otay." The wait here is sometimes significantly shorter than at San Ysidro, but usually it only wins out by a hair. Call the Otay information line at 619/671-8999 for wait times.

No matter which border you chose, don't try to hop into the faster lanes marked SENTRI. They are for commuters holding special SENTRI cards and illegal use of these lanes results in a $5,000 fine unless you are willing to circle back into Mexico and wait in the real line.

Those travelers only headed to Tecate can bypass Tijuana altogether and cross directly over the Tecate border crossing. This quiet crossing is only open between 6 A.M. and midnight. To reach it from San Diego take Highway 94 for 35 miles until you reach Highway 88, which will take you right to the border.

If you do drive down, be sure to pick up special Mexican insurance for your car. Your normal insurance does not cover liability in Mexico and if police pull you over without it they can take you straight to jail. It is usually less than $25 per day and can be purchased in about five minutes from a number of vendors that are set up near the border. One of the most popular is **Border Insurance Services** (2004 Dairy Mart Rd., #103, San Ysidro, 619/428-0095, www.mexborder.com).

If you'd like to avoid the hassle of driving and are just going to Tijuana, consider simply walking over the border. There are several parking lots on the U.S. side of the border that cater to walkers. The biggest is **Border Station**

Parking (4570 Camino de la Plaza, San Ysidro, 619/428-1422), which also offers a bus shuttle straight to Avenida Revolución.

If you don't feel like parking down there, consider hopping on the trolley from downtown. The Blue Line runs from downtown San Diego to San Ysidro all day long—the trip usually takes about 45 minutes and costs $2.50.

If you are heading down to either Tijuana or Rosarito, you can also consider taking **Mexicoach** (619/428-9517, www.mexicoach .com) buses, which have a handful of departures from the Old Town Transit Center each day. To get all the way down to Ensenada by bus you will first need to cross the border into Tijuana

and then catch the bus from **ABC** coach line. The ABC station is located right across the pedestrian crossing near the big yellow taxi stand and buses leave the terminal on the half hour from 6 A.M.–9 P.M.; the fare is around $20.

Once you are in Tijuana, Rosarito, or Ensenada, you'll be able to easily get around via taxi. Hail a cab off of the street just as you would in any American city, but remember that these taxis don't run off of meters. You need to negotiate a rate before you start toward your destination.

For information on visa and immigration requirements crossing the border in and out of Mexico, please see *Tips for Travelers* in the *Gateway to Baja* chapter.

Tips for Travelers

TRAVELING WITH PETS

With its plethora of dog-friendly parks, restaurants, hotels, and ample animal critical-care facilities, it is no wonder that *Dog Fancy* magazine named San Diego DogTown USA 2007.

San Diego is a great town for traveling with pets. With a bit of careful planning you should be able to spend a maximum amount of time with your furry best friend while on vacation here. Throughout the book I've tried to include pet-friendly establishments, parks, and trails. In addition to those I've detailed there are a number of other notable off-leash parks in town, including Nate's Point and Morley Field in Balboa Park, Capehart Park in Pacific Beach, and Dusty Rhodes Neighborhood Park in Ocean Beach.

Unfortunately, pets are restricted from all trails in state parks. You'll also be barred from many of the larger attractions unless yours is a service dog. Should you like to bring your dog with you on vacation but still have the freedom to visit these pet-free areas, kenneling and day-care services are readily available throughout the county. My favorite place in the city to take my little Sandy is **Camp Diego** (2926 Garnet Ave., 858/490-6440) in Pacific Beach. Cages are only used in the evening; this boarding and

day-care facility lets its dogs loose all day in its indoor/outdoor play yard. When I'm able to make the drive out to Alpine, my absolute favorite place to put Sandy up is **Alpine Dog Ranch** (619/659-5034, www.alpinedogranch .com). Set on a four-acre property, the ranch also adheres to the play-all-day philosophy. The owner, Thomas, has a very special connection with the dogs he tends to.

Finally, if an after-hour health issue arises there are several emergency vets in town, including **A Animal ER of San Diego** (5610 Kearny Mesa Rd., 858/569-0600) and **VCA Emergency Hospital** (2317 Hotel Circle S., 619/299-9068).

TRAVELING WITH CHILDREN

San Diego falls over itself to cater to vacationing families, which makes it pretty easy on parents to find a restaurant or hotel with staff that won't bat an eye when the kids are fussy.

One great trick for Mom and Dad to buy themselves some time alone together is to send the kids to a surf day camp. Many of the surf schools mentioned in this book run half-day or all-day camps, allowing just enough time to visit a museum or just get a little peace and quiet. Most kids love learning to surf and parents will be returned a happy and tired brood at the end of the session.

A big challenge many families face while visiting San Diego is the expense. Hotels and food add up quickly, and that's not even including the cost of tickets to attractions. It is possible to do your San Diego touring on the cheap and still have fun, though. There are many very nice camping facilities in and around the city. And there are tons of free sights to visit. Here are five free family-friendly places, right off the top of my head:

Beaches: Most of the city's municipal beaches are free to use and provide days of family enjoyment. Stay frugal by bringing plastic cups to craft sand castles instead of buying beach toys. Don't waste your money on a boogie board you'll need to throw away at the end of the trip. Instead, try your hand at bodysurfing. Catch the wave like you would on a boogie board and extend one of your arms out straight forward to increase your planing surface.

Trails: There are tons of easily accessible hikes that are kid-friendly. Trot along the trails at Torrey Pines, scramble up Cowles Mountain, or take a scenic walk along the sandstone at Sunset Cliffs. Other fun—and flat!—alternatives are the lagoon trails up in North County around Batiquitos Lagoon and Buena Vista Lagoon.

Tidepools: Get your hands on a tide chart and cart the kids out to one of San Diego's many tidepools when the water is low. These natural wonderlands are teeming with sealife that'll likely have toddlers squealing with delight and will fascinate older kids. The top tidepools with free access include Tourmaline Surfing Park and Shell Beach at the foot of Ellen Browning Scripps Park. If you're willing to pay a small entry fee, some of the very best pools are at Cabrillo National Monument and Cardiff State Beach.

Balboa Park: Sure the museums cost money, but your kids don't want to go inside anyway. You can easily spend a whole day exploring the gardens and looking at the pretty buildings at the park. On Sunday the family can rest a bit listening to the free concerts at the Spreckels Organ Pavilion.

Pepper Grove Playground: This is a very comfortable area where youngsters could easily spend a whole afternoon scampering around. There's a ton of playground equipment, swings, a tot lot, picnic tables, barbecues, and restrooms all at hand here.

MAKING THE MOST OF LEAVE: MILITARY VISITS

San Diego is one of the best places in the country for military personnel to catch a little R&R. The weather is perfect and this navy town is inviting and supportive of the troops and their families. The high percentage of sailors and marines in the county works to your advantage, as almost every sight in town and many of the hotels and restaurants offer discounts to active-duty military members.

The city is also home to two USO Centers. At Lindbergh Field's Terminal Two, **Airport USO Center** (San Diego Lindbergh Field Terminal 2, 619/296-3192, 8 A.M.–11 P.M. daily) is the largest airport center in the entire world. There's free coffee, pastries, and Internet access, as well as plenty of couches for sitting back and watching a little bit of television.

The **Downtown USO Center** (303 A Street Suite 100, 619/235-6503, 11 A.M.–9 P.M. daily) also offers free Internet access, plus two big-screen televisions, pool tables, and a very robust list of activities and holiday events. Every Tuesday night this center cooks up a complimentary dinner for active-duty military and their families.

Both active-duty and retired military members can also take advantage of the local area Navy Lodges and Marine Inns to save on accommodations. These military-run hotels offer up to a 40 percent savings over San Diego's expensive hotels. Some of the most popular include **Navy Lodge San Diego** (619/234-6142) at Navy Base San Diego, **Navy Lodge North Island** (619/435-0191) at North Island Naval Air Station, and the **Marine Inn Ward Lodge** (760/725-5304 or 760/725-5194) at Camp Pendleton.

Similarly, active and retired military members can take advantage of some of the very well-respected navy golf courses in town. Two of the best are **Admiral Baker Golf Course** (Admiral Baker Way, 619/556-5520, 6 A.M.–dusk daily) in Mission Gorge and **Sea 'n' Air Golf Course** (Naval Air Station North Island Building 800, 619/545-9659, 6 A.M.–dusk daily) on Coronado.

Navy Federal Bank has numerous ATMs in the San Diego area, as well as a large Mission Valley branch (8660 Rio San Diego Dr., 866/454-3135, 8:30 A.M.–6 P.M. Mon.–Fri., 8 A.M.–2 P.M. Sat.) in the Rio Vista Shopping Center.

TRAVELERS WITH DISABILITIES

San Diego is an extremely accessible town and most of the major tourist attractions, hotels, and restaurants provide means for those with disabilities to enjoy their vacation as much as the next person.

Before a trip to San Diego consider getting in contact with **Accessible San Diego** (858/279-0704, www.accessandiego.org). This is one of San Diego's oldest travel service organizations and an excellent planning resource. The group has published an annual Accessible Travel Guide to the city for over fourteen years.

San Diego is a beach town and the city has made every effort to ensure that those with disabilities aren't left out of the fun. The following beaches offer accessibility via roll-out mats: Silver Strand State Beach (619/435-0126), Ocean Beach (619/522-7346), Mission Beach (619/221-8899), and La Jolla Shores. The latter three beaches also provide free motorized sand chairs. Call the lifeguard numbers provided to ask about reservations.

If you're the active type, get wet at Mission Bay. The Mission Bay Aquatic Center (1001 Santa Clara Point, 858/488-1036) rents adapted equipment for those with disabilities to enjoy activities such as water-skiing, sailing, canoeing, and riding personal watercraft.

All of San Diego's public transit systems are designed for maximum accessibility. In addition, **USA Cab** (619/231-1144) offers taxi rides in accessible vehicles. If you prefer the freedom of your own ride, **Wheelchair Getaways** (877/388-4883) rents vehicles with wheelchair ramps or lifts, hand controls, power doors, and outside entry controls.

Those travelers with disabilities who wish to visit Baja should be aware that Mexico is decades behind the United States and European nations when it comes to accessibility regulations. This can make it difficult to travel south of the border, but definitely not impossible. Many of the expensive resorts do make an effort to accommodate those with disabilities, so don't be afraid to call ahead and ask what kind of accessibility options are offered. A good resource for information about sights, hotels, and tours while in Mexico is the **Society for Accessible Travel & Hospitality** (212/447-7284, www.sath.org).

GAY AND LESBIAN TRAVELERS

San Diego might be one of the most politically conservative cities in all of California, but don't let this fool you. The people here are an accepting lot.

Maybe it's the happy weather or the devil-may-care Southern California attitude, but most folks don't give a hoot about sexual orientation in this town. In a July 2007 story about the many gay and lesbian political officials in the city, Eric Wolff of *San Diego CityBeat* put it most succinctly: "Forget 'Don't ask, don't tell.' In millennial San Diego, the motto these days is, 'Who knows, who cares?'"

As a result, there's no real "lavender line" here. However, there is a thriving gay and lesbian community focused around the neighborhood of Hillcrest, a sanctuary of tolerance since the 1960s when San Diego's residents weren't nearly so open-minded. Hillcrest is a nerve center for the community at large, with many gay-friendly bars, hotels, and businesses. It is also the main gathering place during Pride Week festivities in July.

At Hillcrest's core is The Center, a gay, lesbian, bisexual, and transgender community center that is extremely active and hosts events throughout the year. This is a good resource to get the scoop on current happenings within the community.

And what of the military influence? Does it spur on any homophobia around here? Not really. In fact, you're likely to see plenty of fresh flattops interspersed in the crowds at Hillcrest's craziest watering holes. Guess even Uncle Sam doesn't know or care around here.

When traveling to Mexico, gay and lesbian travelers should remember that Mexico is a very conservative Catholic country whose residents will not be nearly as welcoming to gays and lesbians as San Diegans are. Nevertheless, Baja is known to be one of the most open-minded parts of the country and Tijuana is especially known for its acceptance of gays and lesbians. In fact, the Zona Norte is well known to have a number of gay bars that cater to both Americans and locals.

ON THE ROAD

San Diegans are one of the friendliest groups of people I've ever met. But there is a dark side to all the graciousness. Put those same affable people behind the wheel of a car and they become, well, a wee bit obnoxious. Granted, not all of it is intentional. Some of them are absentminded. Some are just bad drivers, period. But the net effect is all about the same. Accidents are frequent and near-misses happen every day. Don't believe me? Ask an insurance adjuster. When I moved here from Seattle my insurance doubled!

So be forewarned. Drive defensively and keep an eye out for loony-toon drivers. If it looks like they're about to do something crazy, they probably will. Give 'em a wide berth.

Freeway Driving

The driving style here is fast and sudden. Be prepared to be cut off. You'll frequently encounter a lot of zippy seamsters and seamstresses—they like to weave in and out of lanes to get that extra millisecond lead in congested traffic. And you'll often need to make way for people moving over quickly to make an exit. Part of the reason this happens is because folks around here just don't like to let

people into their lanes. It is also likely a result of tourists who don't know their exit has come up until the last minute. Avoid contributing to the problem by planning your route in advance and knowing approximate mileage to your exit.

Intersections

I came up in a town where people were courteous to a fault at intersections. They'd fall over themselves to let you go first if you even appeared to hit the intersection before them. Here, not so much. Be ready to go when it's your turn or wait until everyone else has gone, because if you blink for a second people will take that as their cue to cut ahead of you.

In the same vein, be wary of inattentive drivers flying through stop signs. This is particularly a problem in the wild-and-woolly beach areas, so watch out.

Pedestrians

Another problem that is particularly bad in the beach party zones is careless pedestrians. Jaywalking in San Diego is an Olympic sport. Many people like to train by walking out in front of speeding cars from every point in the road. Even though these people don't really have the right of way, that won't matter one bit to your conscience if you accidentally hit one of them.

Driving Under the Influence

Contrary to what you may have read or heard about Lindsay Lohan or Nicole Richie's drunk driving "punishments," the DUI laws in California are some of the strictest in the country. So if you're going to selfishly put other people at risk by driving intoxicated, think of that before you do.

Do everybody a favor and call a cab, ride the trolley, or use a designated driver. Another option is to call the **Designated Drivers Association of San Diego** at 866/373-SAFE (866/373-7233). This organization offers a free, safe ride home for you and your car, no questions asked.

Health and Safety

CRIME

If you don't count every time SeaWorld charges $5 for a drink, San Diego's crime statistics are quite low. According to the FBI, the city ranks below the national average in almost every violent and property crime category that is tracked. The only exception is car theft, which is 1.65 times the national average. So, be sure to use common sense when parking your car. Keep the doors locked and bring valuables with you or stow them in the trunk in order to take away any temptations. Also, be sure to keep tabs on your keys at the beach. Surfers especially have been known to suffer at the hands of plotting thieves who watch them exit their cars and place the keys in a "safe spot." Once the car owner is out in the water the thief strikes. Find a way to fasten a key around yourself or consider wearing a wetsuit with a place to put a car key.

Beyond that, exercise the same caution you would in any midsize to large city. Keep an eye on your kids, don't leave your valuables unmonitored, and don't go walking alone in dark alleys at night.

To read more about crime in Baja, Mexico, see *Health and Safety* in the *Gateway to Baja* chapter.

WATER SAFETY
Water Pollution

Rain is a welcome phenomenon to this region in all respects but one: water pollution. Because rain is so infrequent here, all of the nasty street runoff in the cities concentrates on the asphalt and storm drains until the heavens open up. A good rain will send this pollution right into ocean drainages. On top of this, San Diego County's sewage system is notoriously rickety. A heavy rain is sometimes all it needs to push the system into overflow mode,

The rule of thumb is to avoid contact with the water for 72 hours after it rains. And take heed of signs like these.

sometimes sending thousands of gallons of raw sewage into Mother Ocean. It is a disgusting trend and environmental groups like **Surfrider Foundation** (www.surfrider.com) have been working to improve the way that we care for our oceans and beaches. But for now the reality remains, and for this reason the rule of thumb around here is to avoid any ocean contact for 72 hours after a rain.

Rip Currents

According to the United States Lifesaving Association, 80 percent of the rescues that ocean lifeguards make involve saving swimmers caught in rip currents. These seaward-moving currents are responsible for about 100 deaths a year in the United States. Sometimes misunderstood as "undertow" or "rip tide," a rip current is actually neither.

It only moves horizontally, never pulling someone under water. People drown not from any kind of sucking motion in the water, but instead from tiring after trying to beat the rip by swimming directly into the current towards shore.

As for the tide, it isn't directly linked with tidal phenomenon. Instead a rip current is usually formed when strong waves break around areas where there is a depression in the ocean floor, perhaps where there is a break in a sand bar. As the water gets pulled back to sea it tends to follow the path of least resistance, where the waves coming in are the least strong. Since the onshore depressions can diminish wave size, this is the route the water takes. Other natural and man-made features that can weaken wave size and facilitate the formation of a rip are rock jetties, piers, natural reefs, and even large groups of people. Either way, the result is effectively a river of ocean water heading out to sea. The phenomenon is sometimes so pronounced that you can spot a rip current from shore by looking for a strip of discolored or churning water where the break is less pronounced.

Depending on the size of the waves and the beach conditions, rip currents vary in speed. Some of the fastest move at a rate that even world-class swimmers can't overcome.

Fortunately they are isolated channels of water, usually only a couple of yards across. For this reason lifeguards advise swimmers caught in a rip to swim parallel to shore until they are out of the current. At that point they can try swimming toward shore. Above all else, don't panic while you're in a rip current. Conserve your energy as best as possible—exhaustion is the only real killer in the situation.

Jellyfish

When the ocean water warms up in the summertime, Arizonans aren't the only ones that come for a swim at the local beaches. The higher temperatures tend to attract purple-striped jellyfish. More of an irritant than a danger, these gelatinous sea creatures do sting when you come into contact with them.

No matter how badly your buddy wants to pee on you, don't let him. That popular saw about urine being the best relief for a jellyfish sting is a bunch of bunk. In fact, it may activate some of the remaining nematocysts on your skin, making the sting worse.

Here's what to do if you're stung. First, rinse the affected area with salt water or vinegar if it is handy. Salt water is key, because fresh water changes the pH on your skin and releases more venom from the nematocysts. The only exception is an eye sting, for which you should irrigate the eye with about a gallon of fresh water. Mouth stings can be treated with a quarter-strength solution of vinegar.

For particularly bad stings, you'll next need to remove any remaining tentacles. Then you should apply either shaving cream or a baking soda paste to the sting area and either shave it or scrape it with a credit card. The shaving cream counteracts the toxin and the scraping gets rid of the last invisible jelly bits from the skin.

If for some odd reason, you don't go to the beach armed with vinegar, shaving cream, and razors (a beach list that sounds like the set-up for a dirty joke), ice will keep the venom from spreading until you can get the necessary supplies. San Diego lifeguards are also very handy in these kinds of situations, so feel free to ask for help if you are near a lifeguard shack.

Stingrays

Ever done the "stingray shuffle"? No, it isn't that dance you did with your gram-gram at the retirement home. It's a way of scuffing the sand as you enter the surf to avoid the painful barbs of lurking stingrays.

These oddly shaped fishes enjoy shallow and warm water, sandy bottoms, and the tasty little invertebrates that live there. Their number one dislike? Being stamped on the head by tourists. They don't usually voice their displeasure with a complaint letter, instead opting for an unceremonious jabbing to the feet with a venomous barb. It usually gets the point across pretty quickly.

The best way to treat a sting is to avoid it altogether, hence the shuffle. Kicking up sand in front of you will let the stingrays know you're a-comin' and will usually make them skedaddle before they have to resort to blows. It's usually how you tell the locals from the tourists. One slowly slogs into the water, the other happily high-steps and splashes in.

Sometimes a barb is unavoidable, though. I once came down off of my surfboard straight onto a poor ol' ray.

In this instance, pee is still not the answer. For some reason old wives just really like urinating on each other at the beach, because this is their erroneous relief from stingrays as well. But it doesn't work.

First of all, if you are allergic to bee stings you need to get immediate medical attention. Stingray venom has the same chemical makeup as bee venom and a sting can send an allergic person into anaphylactic shock.

Most stingray stings can be relieved by putting your foot into a bucket of fresh water that is as hot as you can possibly tolerate for about a half hour. This will relieve the pain and flush the wound. Once that is out of the way, give it a good washing with soap and water and apply topical antibiotic as needed.

Sometimes, though, the stingers or even the whole barb will remain in your foot. You'll need to remove this with tweezers. Particularly large rays can also gash the skin, causing bleeding. As much as it hurts, be sure to get in there once the stingers are removed and really clean the wound well. The larger the wound, the more important an antibiotic is. In fact, if it looks pretty bad don't be afraid to go to a clinic and ask for an oral antibiotic. This is the best way to prevent a stinger-induced infection. If you do that, don't forget the sunscreen. Antibiotics tend to make your skin more sensitive to sun.

BACKCOUNTRY TIPS
Rattlesnakes

Outdoor enthusiasts will need to keep their eyes and ears alert on the trail for signs of rattlesnakes. Four species of this venomous reptile live in the county, but you're most likely to encounter western rattlesnakes. They live throughout the county, from coastal scrublands into the mountains and parts of the desert.

Experts advise that most rattlers can strike about half their body length. Give these suckers a wide berth when you see or hear them and you'll likely be fine. Most of the rattlesnake bites that county hospitals treat are struck in defense when the "victim" goes all Jeff Corwin on the snake. They might be dangerous, but rattlesnakes are an important part of the ecosystem and they don't need to be killed when you come across them. So don't try, OK?

Most rattlers like rocky outcroppings. Be sure to look under that nice-looking boulder before you sit on it and never stick your hands or feet into areas you can't see. Also avoid tall grass without heavy boots and mostly try to stick to the trail.

If you are bitten, seek medical attention as soon as possible. Rattlesnake bites are rarely fatal but are still serious enough to warrant professional care. Area clinics and hospitals usually have antivenin at the ready. In the interim don't apply ice or tourniquets, and don't make incisions on the wound. All of these methods can cause further injury. The best first aid is to wash the bite with soap, immobilize the wound, and keep it above the heart. Suction cups that come with snake-bite kits can also be used to help draw the venom from the wound. Again, don't make an incision. Finally, if you think it will be longer than thirty minutes before you can get to a hospital you can wrap a pressure bandage above the bite wound to slow the venom as long as it doesn't completely restrict blood flow.

Rattlesnake bites are deadly to pets, so take care to keep your dog on a leash in the backcountry. The venom works very quickly, especially on smaller breeds, so act as swiftly as possible to get your buddy straight to a critical-care vet center. Similar to humans, incisions, ice, and tourniquets do more harm than good. Try to keep the dog quiet and immobilized to slow the venom's spread and hurry! Time is of the essence.

Cougars

Cougar sightings are fairly rare in San Diego County compared to northern regions of California. Nevertheless, these big cats do roam the mountainous areas, especially near Julian and the Cuyamacas. One of the best ways to protect yourself is to hike with a companion and be sure to keep your dog on a leash so that it won't attract a mountain lion toward you. If you encounter a cougar, don't run. This can trigger its predator instinct and might elicit an avoidable attack. Don't play dead, either. The best way to scare one off is to make yourself look big—spread out your coat, wave your arms, and make a lot of noise. Maintain eye contact and even throw rocks or sticks at the animal. If it does attack, keep fighting back. You want to convince it that you are not dinner.

Plants to Avoid

Other than a trip to the naughty parts of Tijuana, the most likely places to find yourself the recipient of an unbearable itch are in the backcountry canyons east of the desert. These areas are so full of poison oak I wonder if San Diego's dermatologists are planting the stuff.

Probably not, though. Poison oak just really thrives in the partial shade of oak trees and the moist soil near streambeds. Remember: "Leaves of three, let them be!" The best way to avoid a rash is to wear long-sleeve shirts and pants. If your clothes do come into contact with poison oak be sure to take them off and give them a good washing. The irritating oil in this plant can remain on clothing and still cause a rash if you come into contact with it later.

In the desert, you're more likely to curse the existence of teddy-bear cholla, also known as "jumping cholla" because its spines manage to jump right off the plant and onto passersby. Desert rats like to carry around combs to help pull the cactus clusters from their skin and clothes. Tweezers and pliers also come in handy. Especially be sure to have them around if you're hiking with kids or dogs, both of whom have a knack for attracting owies out in the desert where almost everything has thorns or spines. Other desert plants to avoid include cat claw, a thorny shrub that you'll often see along washes, and agave, which has a rosette of broadsword-shaped leaves that have a thorn at the tip laced with a natural irritant.

Desert Survival

Exploring remote desert areas is an exhilarating experience that can quickly turn deadly without taking the proper precautions. Dehydration, heat stroke, losing one's way, and even drowning are all dangers that you might face without appropriate safety measures.

First and foremost, be sure to pack in plenty of water. The rule of thumb is about a gallon a day, more as the thermometer gauge or your activity level rises.

Most desert experts tell you that the best way to store water in the desert is inside your body, not in a water bottle. Keep drinking, even if the situation seems dire. Instead of conserving water in the bottle, try to conserve your sweat. Travel during the cooler hours of the day, seek shelter during the hot hours if you can. If not, rest off the ground—it is usually much cooler that way. Wear a broad brimmed hat for shade and light-colored long-sleeve and loose clothes to keep your sweat from evaporating. In that same vein, keep your mouth closed as much as possible. Water evaporates quickly from the mucous membranes in your mouth. Some people suggest sucking on a pebble or a button to keep saliva from drying out inside the mouth.

Finally, don't eat if you are running low on water. The digestive process uses up your system's water stores and you can survive much longer without food than you can without water.

If you do lose your way, remember this little tip. In all Anza-Borrego regions except for the Carrizo Badlands, all of the desert washes flow east toward some highway or settlement. Follow the washes east and you'll have a better chance of flagging down help. In Carrizo, follow the washes west.

Speaking of washes, be aware that it isn't always dry in the desert. When the rain comes, it comes hard. Flash floods are a common occurrence during these downpours. If it looks like it might rain, don't camp or hang around the slot canyons or gullies.

One last concern to think about is the temperature extremes you'll encounter in the desert. Even on some of the hottest days in Anza-Borrego, the temperature can dip quite low in the evening. In the winter months the nightly averages are in the low 40s. Come prepared with a warmer layer to snuggle up in once the sun drops below the horizon.

Road Kit

If you plan on exploring the backcountry by car you should prepare yourself for a breakdown. Finding yourself stranded on a remote byway is a major inconvenience at best, dangerous at worst.

Packing some necessities in the trunk will help you get yourself back on your way or at least keep you safe until help arrives. The following road kit is a loose guide to get you started:

- An inflated spare tire, preferably full-size
- A jack
- Basic tools, especially wrenches and screwdrivers
- Duct tape or electrical tape
- Extra car fluids, including water, washer fluid, antifreeze, and oil
- Signal flares
- A cell phone
- Extra food and water for you
- A warm change of clothes

This is by no means a comprehensive list if you plan on traveling very rugged roads, especially in the desert. In that case I'd recommend finding a specialized book about desert off-roading for a better list. And, most importantly, be sure to have your car inspected before leaving the pavement.

Loose-fitting clothes and hats will keep you cool and retain moisture on your body.

© ERICKA CHICKOWSKI

Information and Services

MAPS AND TOURIST INFORMATION

The **San Diego Convention and Visitors Bureau** (619/232-3101, www.sandiego.org) is an excellent resource of information about the region at large while you are planning your trip. Contact the organization to ask for a free mailing that includes a booklet about activities and events in town, a comprehensive list of lodging and food, and informative maps.

If you'd prefer, you can also get information once you are in town at the bureau's **International Visitor Information Center** (1040⅓ W. Broadway, at Harbor Dr., 619/236-1212 or 619/230-7084, 9 A.M.– 5 P.M. daily June–Sept., 9 A.M.–4 P.M. daily Oct.–May) on the Embarcadero or at the **La Jolla Visitor Center** (7966 Herschel Ave., 619/236-1212) in La Jolla Village.

If you require maps of anywhere in the region, including Baja, the best source in the entire city is **Map Center** (7576 Clairemont Mesa Blvd., 858/278-7887 or 888/849-6277, www.mapworld.com) in Clairemont. In addition to local, regional, and international maps, it also has a full spate of nautical maps and GPS units.

MONEY

San Diego's currency is the U.S. dollar. Sales tax throughout the region is 7.75 percent and hotel tax within the city is 10.5 percent. Tipping practices are similar to those throughout the states, with the customary gratuity coming out to between 15 and 20 percent of the total bill. The exception to this is when the tip has already been added to the bill.

In Baja, the currency is the Mexican peso but most places in Tijuana, Rosarito, and Ensenada typically accept U.S. dollars.

COMMUNICATIONS AND MEDIA

Telephone

There are three major area codes in San Diego. Within the city center, downtown, and south, the code is 619. Some city beach neighborhoods and northern parts of the city use 858. Everywhere else in the county is 760. Cell-phone reception is good throughout the city and North County coastal areas, but can be spotty in the mountains and desert.

In Baja there are two major area codes, 646 and 661, but to call Baja telephone numbers from the U.S. you will need to start by dialing (011-52) and then the ten-digit number.

Throughout the book I have written all seven-digit numbers as they'll usually appear in Mexico, with two hyphens, in order to distinguish them from domestic calls.

Internet Access

San Diego is a very connected city and there are numerous hot spots throughout. However, if you are having a difficult time finding free access quickly, don't worry about wandering around looking for an Internet café. Instead, make a beeline to one of the many branches of the San Diego library (www.sandiego.gov/public-library), all of which offer free access. Almost every branch has computers available to use.

If you need Wi-Fi access during your travels, the San Diego International Airport also offers free access within its terminals.

WEIGHTS AND MEASURES

San Diego uses the Imperial system of measurements, but Baja is on the metric system. While in Mexico, you'll notice that gas is sold by the liter and distance is measured in kilometers.

The entire San Diego region is in the Pacific Time Zone and also practices Daylight Savings Time. Between the second Sunday in March and the first Sunday in November, clocks are pushed one hour ahead.

RESOURCES

Spanish Phrasebook

Your Baja Mexico adventure will be more fun if you use a little Spanish. Mexican people, although they may smile at your funny accent, will appreciate your halting efforts to break the ice and transform yourself from a foreigner to a potential friend.

Spanish commonly uses 30 letters – the familiar English 26, plus four straightforward additions: ch, ll, ñ, and rr.

PRONUNCIATION

Once you learn them, Spanish pronunciation rules – in contrast to English – don't change. Spanish vowels generally sound softer than in English. (Note: The capitalized syllables below receive stronger accents.)

Vowels

a like ah, as in "hah": *agua* AH-gooah (water), *pan* PAHN (bread), and *casa* CAH-sah (house)

e like ay, as in "may:" *mesa* MAY-sah (table), *tela* TAY-lah (cloth), and *de* DAY (of, from)

i like ee, as in "need": *diez* dee-AYZ (ten), *comida* ko-MEE-dah (meal), and *fin* FEEN (end)

o like oh, as in "go": *peso* PAY-soh (weight), *ocho* OH-choh (eight), and *poco* POH-koh (a bit)

u like oo, as in "cool": *uno* OO-noh (one), *cuarto* KOOAHR-toh (room), and *usted* oos-TAYD (you); when it follows a "q" the **u** is silent, as in *qué* kay (what), or *quiero* kee-AY-roh (I want).

Consonants

b, d, f, k, l, m, n, p, q, s, t, v, w, x, y, z, ch
pronounced almost as in English

c like k as in "keep": *cuarto* KOOAR-toh (room), Tepic tay-PEEK (capital of Nayarit state); when it precedes "e" or "i," pronounce **c** like s, as in "sit": *cerveza* sayr-VAY-sah (beer), *encima* ayn-SEE-mah (atop).

g pronounce hard, like g as in "gift" when it precedes "a," "o," "u," or a consonant: *gato* GAH-toh (cat), *hago* AH-goh (I do, make); otherwise, pronounce **g** soft, like h as in "hat": *giro* HEE-roh (money order), *gente* HAYN-tay (people).

h sometimes occurs, but is silent – not pronounced at all.

j like h, as in "has": *Jueves* HOOAY-vays (Thursday), *mejor* may-HOR (better)

ll like y, as in "yes": *toalla* toh-AH-yah (towel), *ellos* AY-yohs (they, them)

ñ like ny, as in "canyon": *año* AH-nyo (year), *señor* SAY-nyor (Mr., sir)

r is lightly trilled, with tongue at the roof of your mouth like a very light English d, as in "ready": *pero* PAY-doh (but), *tres* TDAYS (three), *cuatro* KOOAH-tdoh (four).

rr like a Spanish r, but with much more emphasis and trill. Let your tongue flap. Practice with *burro* (donkey), *carretera* (highway), and Carrillo (proper name), then really let go with *ferrocarril* (railroad).

Note: The single small but common exception to all of the above is the pronunciation of Spanish **y** when it's being used as the Spanish word for "and," as in "Ron y Kathy." In such a case, pronounce it like the English ee, as in "keep": Ron "ee" Kathy (Ron and Kathy).

Accent

The rule for accent, the relative stress given to syllables within a given word, is straightforward. If a word ends in a vowel, an n, or an s, accent the next-to-last syllable; if not, accent the last syllable.

Pronounce *gracias* GRAH-seeahs (thank you), *orden* OHR-dayn (order), and *carretera* kah-ray-TAY-rah (highway) with stress on the next-to-last syllable.

Otherwise, accent the last syllable: *venir* vay-NEER (to come), *ferrocarril* fay-roh-cah-REEL (railroad), and *edad* ay-DAHD (age).

Exceptions to the accent rule are always marked with an accent sign: (á, é, í, ó, or ú), such as *teléfono* tay-LAY-foh-noh (telephone), *jabón* hah-BON (soap), and *rápido* RAH-pee-doh (rapid).

BASIC AND COURTEOUS EXPRESSIONS

Most Spanish-speaking people consider formalities important. Whenever approaching anyone for information or some other reason, do not forget the appropriate salutation – good morning, good evening, etc. Standing alone, the greeting *hola* (hello) can sound brusque.

Hello. Hola.
Good morning. Buenos días.
Good afternoon. Buenas tardes.
Good evening. Buenas noches.
How are you? ¿Cómo está usted?
Very well, thank you. Muy bien, gracias.
Okay; good. Bien.
Not okay; bad. Mal or feo.
So-so. Más o menos.
And you? ¿Y usted?
Thank you. Gracias.
Thank you very much. Muchas gracias.
You're very kind. Muy amable.
You're welcome. De nada.
Goodbye. Adios.
See you later. Hasta luego.
please por favor
yes sí
no no
I don't know. No sé.
Just a moment, please. Momentito, por favor.

Excuse me, please (when you're trying to get attention). Disculpe or Con permiso.
Excuse me (when you've made a boo-boo). Lo siento.
Pleased to meet you. Mucho gusto.
My name is . . . Me llamo . . .
What is your name? ¿Cómo se llama usted?
Do you speak English? ¿Habla usted inglés?
Is English spoken here? (Does anyone here speak English?) ¿Se habla inglés?
I don't speak Spanish well. No hablo bien el español.
I don't understand. No entiendo.
How do you say...in Spanish? ¿Cómo se dice...en español?
Would you like . . . ¿Quisiera usted . . .
Let's go to . . . Vamos a . . .

TERMS OF ADDRESS

When in doubt, use the formal *cena* (you) as a form of address.

I yo
you (formal) usted
you (familiar) tu
he/him él
she/her ella
we/us nosotros
you (plural) ustedes
they/them ellos (all males or mixed gender); ellas (all females)
Mr., sir señor
Mrs., madam señora
miss, young lady señorita
wife esposa
husband esposo
friend amigo (male); amiga (female)
sweetheart novio (male); novia (female)
son; daughter hijo; hija
brother; sister hermano; hermana
father; mother padre; madre
grandfather; grandmother abuelo; abuela

TRANSPORTATION

Where is . . . ? ¿Dónde está . . . ?
How far is it to . . . ? ¿A cuánto está . . . ?
from...to . . . de...a . . .
How many blocks? ¿Cuántas cuadras?

Where (Which) is the way to . . . ? ¿Dónde está el camino a . . . ?
the bus station la terminal de autobuses
the bus stop la parada de autobuses
Where is this bus going? ¿Adónde va este autobús?
the taxi stand la parada de taxis
the train station la estación de ferrocarril
the boat, ferry el barco, el transbordador
the airport el aeropuerto
I'd like a ticket to . . . Quisiera un boleto a . . .
first (second) class primera (segunda) clase
roundtrip ida y vuelta
reservation reservación
baggage equipaje
Stop here, please. Pare aquí, por favor.
the entrance la entrada
the exit la salida
the ticket office la oficina de boletos
(very) near; far (muy) cerca; lejos
to; toward a
by; through por
from de
the right la derecha
the left la izquierda
straight ahead derecho; directo
in front en frente
beside al lado
behind atrás
the corner la esquina
the stoplight la semáforo
a turn una vuelta
right here aquí
somewhere around here por acá
right there allí
somewhere around there por allá
street; boulevard calle; bulevar
highway carretera
bridge; toll puente; cuota
address dirección
north; south norte; sur
east; west oriente (este); poniente (oeste)

ACCOMMODATIONS

hotel hotel
Is there a room? ¿Hay cuarto?
May I (may we) see it? ¿Puedo (podemos) verlo?

What is the price? (rate) ¿Cuál es el precio? (tipo)
Is that your best rate? ¿Es su mejor precio? (tipo)
Is there something cheaper? ¿Hay algo más económico?
a single room un cuarto sencillo
a double room un cuarto doble
double bed cama matrimonial
king-size bed cama king-size
twin beds camas gemelas
with private bath con baño
hot water agua caliente
shower ducha
towels toallas
soap jabón
toilet paper papel higiénico
blanket frazada; manta
sheets sábanas
air-conditioned aire acondicionado
fan abanico; ventilador
key llave
manager gerente

FOOD

I'm hungry Tengo hambre.
I'm thirsty. Tengo sed.
menu lista; menú
order orden
glass vaso
fork tenedor
knife cuchillo
spoon cuchara
napkin servilleta
soft drink refresco
coffee café
tea té
drinking water agua pura; agua potable
bottled carbonated water agua mineral
bottled uncarbonated water agua sin gas
beer cerveza
wine vino
milk leche
juice jugo
cream crema
sugar azúcar
cheese queso
snack antojo; botana

breakfast desayuno
lunch almuerzo
daily lunch special comida corrida (or el
  menú del día, depending on region)
dinner comida (often eaten in late afternoon);
  cena (a late-night snack)
the check la cuenta
eggs huevos
bread pan
salad ensalada
fruit fruta
mango mango
watermelon sandía
papaya papaya
banana plátano
apple manzana
orange naranja
lime limón
fish pescado
shellfish mariscos
shrimp camarones
meat (without) (sin) carne
chicken pollo
pork puerco
beef; steak res; bistec
bacon; ham tocino; jamón
fried frito
roasted asada
barbecue; barbecued barbacoa; al carbón

SHOPPING

money dinero
money-exchange bureau casa de cambio
**I would like to exchange travelers
  checks.** Quisiera cambiar cheques de
  viajero.
What is the exchange rate? ¿Cuál es el tipo
  de cambio?
How much is the commission? ¿Cuánto
  cuesta la comisión?
Do you accept credit cards? ¿Aceptan
  tarjetas de crédito?
money order giro
How much does it cost? ¿Cuánto cuesta?
What is your final price? ¿Cuál es su último
  precio?
expensive caro
cheap barato; económico

more más
less menos
a little un poco
too much demasiado

HEALTH

Help me please. Ayúdeme por favor.
I am ill. Estoy enfermo.
Call a doctor. Llame un doctor.
Take me to . . . Lléveme a . . .
hospital hospital; sanatorio
drugstore farmacia
pain dolor
fever fiebre
headache dolor de cabeza
stomachache dolor de estómago
burn quemadura
cramp calambre
nausea náusea
vomiting vomitar
medicine medicina
antibiotic antibiótico
pill; tablet pastilla
aspirin aspirina
ointment; cream pomada; crema
bandage venda
cotton algodón
sanitary napkins use brand name, e.g.,
  Kotex
birth-control pills pastillas anticonceptivas
contraceptive foam espuma
  anticonceptiva
condoms preservativos; condones
toothbrush cepilla dental
dental floss hilo dental
toothpaste crema dental
dentist dentista
toothache dolor de muelas

POST OFFICE AND COMMUNICATIONS

long-distance telephone teléfono larga
  distancia
I would like to call . . . Quisiera llamar a . . .
collect por cobrar
station to station a quien contesta
person to person persona a persona
credit card tarjeta de crédito

post office correo
general delivery lista de correo
letter carta
stamp estampilla; timbre
postcard tarjeta
aerogram aerograma
air mail correo aereo
registered registrado
money order giro
package; box paquete; caja
string; tape cuerda; cinta

AT THE BORDER

border frontera
customs aduana
immigration migración
tourist card tarjeta de turista
inspection inspección; revisión
passport pasaporte
profession profesión
marital status estado civil
single soltero
married; divorced casado; divorciado
widowed viudado
insurance seguros
title título
driver's license licencia de manejar

AT THE GAS STATION

gas station gasolinera
gasoline gasolina
unleaded sin plomo
full, please lleno, por favor
tire llanta
tire repair shop vulcanizadora
air aire
water agua
oil (change) aceite (cambio)
grease grasa
My...doesn't work. Mi...no sirve.
battery batería
radiator radiador
alternator alternador
generator generador
tow truck grúa
repair shop taller mecánico
tune-up afinación
auto-parts store refaccionería

VERBS

Verbs are the key to getting along in Spanish. They employ mostly predictable forms and come in three classes, which end in *ar, er,* and *ir,* respectively:
to buy comprar
I buy, you (he, she, it) buys compro, compra
we buy, you (they) buy compramos, compran
to eat comer
I eat, you (he, she, it) eats como, come
we eat, you (they) eat comemos, comen
to climb subir
I climb, you (he, she, it) climbs subo, sube
we climb, you (they) climb subimos, suben
Got the idea? Here are more (with irregularities indicated).
to do or make hacer (regular except for *hago,* I do or make)
to go ir (very irregular: *voy, va, vamos, van*)
to go (walk) andar
to love amar
to work trabajar
to want desear, querer
to need necesitar
to read leer
to write escribir
to repair reparar
to stop parar
to get off (the bus) bajar
to arrive llegar
to stay (remain) quedar
to stay (lodge) hospedar
to leave salir (regular except for *salgo,* I leave)
to look at mirar
to look for buscar
to give dar (regular except for *doy,* I give)
to carry llevar
to have tener (irregular but important: *tengo, tiene, tenemos, tienen*)
to come venir (similarly irregular: *vengo, viene, venimos, vienen*)
Spanish has two forms of "to be." Use *estar* when speaking of location or a temporary state of being: "I am at home." "*Estoy en casa.*" "I'm sick." "*Estoy enfermo.*" Use *ser* for

a permanent state of being: "I am a doctor."
"*Soy doctora.*"
   Estar is regular except for *estoy*, I am. *Ser* is
very irregular:
to be ser
I am, you (he, she, it) is *soy, es*
we are, you (they) are *somos, son*

NUMBERS
zero cero
one uno
two dos
three tres
four cuatro
five cinco
six seis
seven siete
eight ocho
nine nueve
10 diez
11 once
12 doce
13 trece
14 catorce
15 quince
16 dieciseis
17 diecisiete
18 dieciocho
19 diecinueve
20 veinte
21 veinte y uno or veintiuno
30 treinta
40 cuarenta
50 cincuenta
60 sesenta
70 setenta
80 ochenta
90 noventa
100 ciento
101 ciento y uno or cientiuno
200 doscientos
500 quinientos
1,000 mil
10,000 diez mil
100,000 cien mil
1,000,000 millón

one half medio
one third un tercio
one fourth un cuarto

TIME
What time is it? ¿Qué hora es?
It's one o'clock. Es la una.
It's three in the afternoon. Son las tres de
   la tarde.
It's 4 A.M. Son las cuatro de la mañana.
six-thirty seis y media
a quarter till eleven un cuarto para las
   once
a quarter past five las cinco y cuarto
an hour una hora

DAYS AND MONTHS
Monday lunes
Tuesday martes
Wednesday miércoles
Thursday jueves
Friday viernes
Saturday sábado
Sunday domingo
today hoy
tomorrow mañana
yesterday ayer
January enero
February febrero
March marzo
April abril
May mayo
June junio
July julio
August agosto
September septiembre
October octubre
November noviembre
December diciembre
a week una semana
a month un mes
after después
before antes

(Courtesy of Bruce Whipperman, author of
Moon Pacific Mexico)

Suggested Reading

Davis, Mike, Kelly Mayhew and Jim Miller. *Under the Perfect Sun: The San Diego Tourists Never See.* New York, NY: New Press, 2003. Gets inside the scandals and the gritty reality behind San Diego politics.

Innis, Jack S. *San Diego Legends: Events, People, and Places That Made History.* El Cajon, CA: Sunbelt, 2004. A collection of stories, both historical and mythical, that make up the region's lore.

Jackson, Helen H. *Ramona.* Charleston, SC: BiblioBazaar, 2007. Often compared to *Uncle Tom's Cabin,* this social commentary wrapped within a fictional novel turned the nation on to the troubles facing Native Americans when it was published in 1884.

Kohner, Frederick. *Gidget.* Berkeley, CA: Berkeley Trade, 2001. This reprint of the 1957 myopic on the adventures of a teenaged girl growing up in the early days of SoCal surfer scene offers a glimpse into the birth of the beach-shack subculture that still defines San Diego today.

Lindsay, Diana. *Anza-Borrego A to Z: People, Places, and Things.* Osceola, WI: Voyageur Press, 2000. The comprehensive guide to the nature and history of San Diego's expansive desert.

MacPhail, Elizabeth C. *Kate Sessions: Pioneer Horticulturist.* San Diego, CA: San Diego Historical Society, 1976. This is the definitive biography of Kate Sessions, the city's first gardener and the "Mother of Balboa Park."

McLaughlin, David J. *Soldiers Scoundrels, Poets & Priests Stories of the Men and Women Behind the Missions of California.* Scottsdale, AZ: Pentacle Press, 2006. The founding of the California mission system played an integral part in the establishment of San Diego. This book details the religion, politics, and scandals that drove the development of the missions.

Saldivar, Jose D. *Border Matters: Remapping American Cultural Studies.* Berkeley, CA: University of California Press, 1997. A textured and well-rounded look at the collision of cultures that occurs within the nation's border towns.

Schad, Jerry. *Afoot and Afield in San Diego.* 3rd edition. Berkeley, CA: Wilderness Press, 1998. Known as the adventure bible for most outdoors enthusiasts in San Diego, this tome offers the most comprehensive collection of regional trail descriptions.

Schaelchlin, Patricia. *The Newspaper Barons: A Biography of the Scripps Family.* Carlsbad, CA: Kales Press, 2001. After the family made a fortune in the news business, the Scripps clan made a difference in San Diego with a legacy of philanthropy that still extends into the city's art, science, and nature preservation even today.

Smythe, William. *History of San Diego 1542–1908.* San Diego, CA: The History Company, 1908. This is one of the classic books on early history in San Diego. The original is long out of print, but readers can find the entire book online at the San Diego History Society's website, www.sandiegohistory.org.

Wolfe, Tom. *The Pump House Gang.* New York, NY: Farrar, Straus and Giroux, 1965. The namesake story in this collection is based on the surfers and rebels who hung out at the pumphouse set near Windansea Beach in La Jolla during the mid 1960s.

Internet Resources

Balboa Park
www.balboapark.org

Comprehensive site about America's second-largest municipal park. It contains background information, hours, and detailed information about the numerous attractions and gardens at Balboa Park.

Cleveland National Forest
www.fs.fed.us/r5/cleveland

Learn about the open space that dominate's San Diego County's Backcountry at this official site for Cleveland National Forest.

Discover Baja California
www.discoverbajacalifornia.com

Information and tips about Baja travel are offered here by the State Tourism Secretariat of Baja California.

Gaslamp.org
www.gaslamp.org

The official site of the Gaslamp Quarter Association, with historical background and information about this historic district.

San Diego Association of Governments
www.sandag.org

Demographic and geographical information about the entire county can be found at this site, the official website of the San Diego Association of Governments.

San Diego Convention and Visitor's Bureau
www.sandiego.org

The official site of the San Diego Convention and Visitor's Bureau. Includes comprehensive information about sightseeing, dining, lodging, and events.

San Diego Golf
www.sandiegogolf.com

One of the most comprehensive regional golf sites, this one offers local course descriptions, information on green fees, and online tee time reservations.

San Diego History
www.sandiegohistory.org

Run by the San Diego Historical Society, this site has hundreds of articles and photos that chronicle the city's extensive history.

San Diego Reader
www.sdreader.com

Run by the San Diego Reader, this site is a good resource to find out about local shows and events through its online entertainment calendar.

Sign On San Diego
www.signonsandiego.com

The online portal for San Diego's major daily newspaper, the *San Diego Union Tribune.*

Index

Acknowledgments

I'd like to thank my husband, Paul, for all of his love and support during the countless hectic hours put into writing this book. His patience during the crazy times, his thoughtful proofreading and advice, and his consistent encouragement throughout this process really were critical to making the book a possibility.

I'd also like to give special thanks to my editor, Elizabeth McCue, who helped shepherd the manuscript (and its wayward author) through the editorial cycle. Her keen eye and thoughtful comments polished my material into something I'm proud to see on the shelves. Her patience also lessened the trauma of writing as a first-time book author!

Also, thank you to Nicole Shultz in production and the guys in the cartography department for all of their efforts to make my words look pretty.

Eric Lucas also deserves many thanks for his mentoring and support over the years. His encouragement and good advice gave me an extra boost of confidence when I wondered whether I could tackle a project like this one.

Other thanks go out to Carole Griggs, my trusty dog-sitter during countless weekends away, and Kathy Collins, my knowledgeable tour-guide south of the border. Additionally I'd like to thank the numerous CVB and public relations representatives who helped me along the way, including: Junvi Ola with the San Diego CVB, Juan Saldaña with the Tijuana CVB, Luis Alberto López with the Ensenada Tourism Board, Lauren Clapperton with Bailey Gardiner, Jeff Brown with Warner Springs Ranch, John Brice with Brice & Associates and Judith Adams.

www.moon.com

For helpful advice on planning a trip, visit www.moon.com for the **TRAVEL PLANNER** and get access to useful travel strategies and valuable information about great places to visit. When you travel with Moon, expect an experience that is uncommon and truly unique.

HANDBOOKS | METRO | OUTDOORS | LIVING ABROAD